Interactions of Degree and Quantification

Syntax & Semantics

Series Editor

Keir Moulton (*University of Toronto, Canada*)

Editorial Board

Judith Aissen (*University of California, Santa Cruz*) – Peter Culicover (*The Ohio State University*) – Elisabet Engdahl (*University of Gothenburg*) – Janet Fodor (*City University of New York*) – Erhard Hinrichs (*University of Tubingen*) – Paul M. Postal (*Scarsdale, New York*) – Barbara H. Partee (*University of Massachusetts*) William A. Ladusaw (*University of California, Santa Cruz*) – Manfred Krifka (*University of Texas*) – Pauline Jacobson (*Brown University*)

VOLUME 42

The titles published in this series are listed at *brill.com/sas*

Interactions of Degree and Quantification

Edited by

Peter Hallman

BRILL

LEIDEN | BOSTON

The preparation of this volume was supported by the Austrian Science Fund (FWF) grant P30409 to Peter Hallman.

Library of Congress Cataloging-in-Publication Data

Names: Hallman, Peter, editor.
Title: Interactions of degree and quantification / edited by Peter Hallman.
Description: Leiden ; Boston : Brill, 2020. | Series: Syntax & semantics, 0092-4563 ;
    volume 42 | Includes bibliographical references and index.
Identifiers: LCCN 2020020263 (print) | LCCN 2020020264 (ebook) |
    ISBN 9789004431119 (hardback) | ISBN 9789004431515 (ebook)
Subjects: LCSH: Grammar, Comparative and general–Quantifiers. | Semantics.
Classification: LCC P299.Q3 I58 2020 (print) | LCC P299.Q3 ebook) |
    DDC 415/.5–dc23
LC record available at https://lccn.loc.gov/2020020263
LC ebook record available at https://lccn.loc.gov/2020020264

Typeface for the Latin, Greek, and Cyrillic scripts: "Brill". See and download: brill.com/brill-typeface.

ISSN 0092-4563
ISBN 978-90-04-43111-9 (hardback)
ISBN 978-90-04-43151-5 (e-book)

Copyright 2020 by Koninklijke Brill NV, Leiden, The Netherlands, except where stated otherwise.
Koninklijke Brill NV incorporates the imprints Brill, Brill Hes & De Graaf, Brill Nijhoff, Brill Rodopi,
Brill Sense, Hotei Publishing, mentis Verlag, Verlag Ferdinand Schöningh and Wilhelm Fink Verlag.
All rights reserved. No part of this publication may be reproduced, translated, stored in a retrieval system,
or transmitted in any form or by any means, electronic, mechanical, photocopying, recording or otherwise,
without prior written permission from the publisher. For parts of this publication that are designated Open
Access, additional rights are granted in the accompanying CC license.
Authorization to photocopy items for internal or personal use is granted by Koninklijke Brill NV provided
that the appropriate fees are paid directly to The Copyright Clearance Center, 222 Rosewood Drive,
Suite 910, Danvers, MA 01923, USA. Fees are subject to change.

This book is printed on acid-free paper and produced in a sustainable manner.

Contents

List of Figures and Tables　VII
Notes on Contributors　VIII

1　Introduction　1
　　Peter Hallman

2　Indeterminate Numerals and Their Alternatives　44
　　Curt Anderson

3　The Semantics of the Superlative Quantifier *-Est*　79
　　Barbara Tomaszewicz-Özakın

4　Quantification, Degrees and *Beyond* in Navajo　121
　　Elizabeth Bogal-Allbritten and Elizabeth Coppock

5　Separate but Equal: A Typology of Equative Constructions　163
　　Jessica Rett

6　Compounded Scales　205
　　Alan Bale

7　From Possible Individuals to Scalar Segments　231
　　Roger Schwarzschild

8　Measuring Cardinalities: Evidence from Differential Comparatives in French　271
　　Vincent Homer and Rajesh Bhatt

9　Quantifying Events and Activities　304
　　Haley Farkas and Alexis Wellwood

10　Split Semantics for Non-monotonic Quantifiers in *Than*-Clauses　332
　　Linmin Zhang

11　Nominal Quantifiers in *Than* Clauses and Degree Questions　364
　　Nicholas Fleisher

Index　383

Figures and Tables

Figures

- 5.1 A typology of equatives (to be revised)   183
- 5.2 A typology of equatives (final)   189
- 9.1 Screenshot of trial display for horizontal split and vertical split   318
- 9.2 Trial structure from Experiment 1   320
- 9.3 Consistency with number and height for test and control conditions for verbs *jump* (Experiment 1) and *move* (Experiment 2)   322
- 9.4 Consistency with number for trials that are unambiguous between number and height for Experiments 2, 3, and 4 with *move* for control condition and test condition   323
- 9.5 Experiment 1 responses coded for consistency with number, height, and duration   324
- 9.6 Experiment 2 responses coded for consistency with number, height, and duration   326
- 10.1 The rabbit in the hat   336
- 10.2 The subtraction of two intervals   343

Tables

- 3.1 Cross-linguistic comparison   89
- 3.2 Cross-linguistic variation (extended version of Table 1)   115
- 5.1 Subtypes of explicit equatives   188
- 9.1 Hypothesized links between phrasal form, meaning, and dimensions for comparison   311
- 9.2 Participant information for all experiments   316
- 9.3 Parameter sets for dimensions of movement   319
- 9.4 Display and animation differences between experiments   319
- 9.5 Generalized linear mixed effects model output for factors COMPARATIVE and SIMULTANEITY (Experiment 1)   325
- 9.6 Generalized linear mixed effects model output for factors COMPARATIVE and SIMULTANEITY (Experiment 2)   327

Notes on Contributors

Curt Anderson
received his PhD in 2016 from Michigan State University, and his research focuses on issues related to scalarity, modification, and the syntax-semantics interface. He is currently a visiting assistant professor in the Centre for French and Linguistics at the University of Toronto Scarborough, and previously was a postdoctoral researcher with Collaborative Research Center 991 at Heinrich Heine University Düsseldorf.

Alan Bale
is an Associate Professor in the Linguistics Program at Concordia University, Montreal, Canada. His work concentrates on the grammar of measurement, comparison, and number, especially as it relates to the mass-count distinction and language acquisition.

Rajesh Bhatt
is Professor of Linguistics, University of Massachusetts, Amherst. He is interested in the comparative syntax of the Modern Indo-Aryan languages and the syntax-semantic interface.

Elizabeth Bogal-Allbritten
received her PhD in linguistics from the University of Massachusetts Amherst in 2016. Her research considers issues in semantics from the perspective of understudied languages—in particular Navajo (*Diné Bizaad*)—and includes work on adjectival meaning, comparative and superlative constructions, attitude verbs, modality, and relative clauses.

Elizabeth Coppock
is an Assistant Professor of Linguistics at Boston University and a researcher at the University of Gothenburg. Her work deals with the semantics of phenomena such as reference, gradability, and quantification in diverse languages using a variety of methodologies.

Haley Farkas
holds MAs in linguistics from Northwestern University and the University of Southern California. Her research interests lie in formal semantics, psycholinguistics, and language acquisition, primarily focused on topics in event semantics and theories of quantification.

Nicholas Fleisher

is Associate Professor of linguistics at the University of Wisconsin–Milwaukee. His research is focused on the syntax–semantics interface, particularly issues involving gradability and comparison, scope and quantification, and binding and ellipsis.

Peter Hallman

is a researcher at the Austrian Research Institute for Artificial Intelligence. He has published in the areas of morphology, syntax and semantics and currently leads a research project on degree semantics in Arabic and other Semitic languages.

Vincent Homer

is Assistant Professor of Linguistics, University of Massachusetts, Amherst. His research investigates various phenomena at the syntax-semantics interface in English and Romance.

Jessica Rett

is Professor of Linguistics at the University of California, Los Angeles. Her research focuses on degree semantics as well as the semantics-pragmatics interface, including the study of exclamatives, evaluativity, evidentials, and equatives.

Roger Schwarzschild

is a Professor of Linguistics at the Massachusetts Institute of Technology. His specialty is natural language semantics. He has published work on plurals, intonation, degree constructions and expressions of measurement.

Barbara Tomaszewicz-Özakın

received a PhD in linguistics from the University of Southern California in 2015. She is currently a post-doctoral researcher at the University of Cologne. Her main interests are the syntax-semantics interface and psycholinguistics. To test theoretical predictions she uses experimental methods such as rating questionnaires, self-paced reading, eye-tracking and ERPs.

Alexis Wellwood

is an Associate Professor of Philosophy and Linguistics at the University of Southern California, where she directs the USC Dornsife Meaning Lab. Her research in semantics and psycholinguistics emphasizes interdisciplinary connections between linguistics, philosophy of language and mind, and cognitive psychology. Topically, she focuses on issues related to degrees, events, and pluralities.

Linmin Zhang
received her PhD in linguistics from New York University in 2016. She is now a post-doctoral fellow at New York University Shanghai. Her research focuses on theoretical and experimental semantics. Among her research topics are degree semantics, dynamic semantics, numerals, functional adjectives, counterfactuals, attitude reports, discourse particles, and the neural basis of semantic representation and compositionality.

CHAPTER 1

Introduction

Peter Hallman

1   Introduction

This book is a collection of studies on quantification over individuals and over degrees and the ways in which quantifiers in these domains interact. Such interactions are diverse, ranging from intervention effects to cross-domain parallels in composition and meaning. 'Individual quantifiers' are the traditional 'generalized quantifiers' that relate sets of individuals (Barwise & Cooper 1981). An individual quantifier like *every* holds of two sets of individuals when the first is a subset of the second (that the Canadians are a subset of the intrepid things in *Every Canadian is intrepid*). 'Degree quantifiers' relate sets of degrees. A degree quantifier like the comparative *-er* holds of two sets of degrees when the first is a subset of the second (that the degrees to which John is tall are a subset of the degrees to which Mary is tall in *Mary is taller than John*). The set of individuals and of degrees differ only in sort—they are both collections of semantically basic entities with no argument structure of their own. Further, both types of quantifiers are used to talk about quantity; both may be used to answer questions about how much or how many, suggesting that some notion of quantificationality characterizes meanings in both sortal domains. The parallels run so deep that for some quantifiers, parallel degree and individual quantificational analyses have been postulated, for example for the cardinal numerals *two, three*, etc., which may be taken to specify the cardinality of a set of individuals (Barwise & Cooper 1981) or to specify the maximal degree in the degree set corresponding to that cardinality (Krifka 1989, Landman 2004 and many others). Likewise, *many* and its comparative and superlative counterparts *more* and *most* have been analyzed as both individual quantifiers (Barwise & Cooper 1981, Westerståhl 1985b) and degree modifiers (Bresnan 1973, Hackl 2009). In the other direction, the comparative and superlative have been analyzed as relations between individuals rather than sets of degrees (Heim 1985, Bhatt & Takahashi 2011), bearing a stronger resemblance to individual quantifiers on this approach. Accordingly, individual and degree quantifiers are not blind to one another when found in the same syntactic environment: the Heim-Kennedy constraint (Kennedy 1999, Heim 2001) prohibits an individual quantifier from intervening between a degree quantifier and the variable it binds. The contributions to this volume venture into the shifting frontier between individual and degree quantification and dissect its nuances, and generally reflect the steady encroachment of degree semantics into the territory of generalized quantifier theory that the past 20 years have witnessed. In the following two sections, I describe the theoretical background to this pursuit, first in relation to individual quantification in section 2, then in relation to degree quantification in section 3. Section 4 describes the contributions to this volume individually against this background.

2 Individual Quantifiers

Building on work by Lindenbaum & Tarski (1936) and Mautner (1946), Mostowski (1957) defines a 'generalization' of the standard universal ($\forall$) and existential ($\exists$) quantifiers of predicate logic. Such 'generalized quantifiers' are functions that map propositional functions to truth values subject to a 'permutation invariance' requirement, which I describe in more detail below. Propositional functions are predicates, such as *Canadian, intrepid*, etc., that map individuals to truth values. In these terms, the existential quantifier maps a propositional function F to 'true' if $F(x)$ is true for at least one value of x; the universal quantifier maps F to 'true' if $F(x)$ is true for all values of x. But this system also accommodates quantificational notions like 'there are three' or 'there are finitely many', which maps F to 'true' if $F(x)$ holds for three or finitely many values of x respectively.

Mostowski discusses only quantifiers that denote properties of propositional functions, but Lindström (1966) observes that the features Mostowski attributes to generalized quantifiers extend fruitfully to relations between propositional functions. Mostowski and Lindström treat only formal logical calculi, but the significance of the notion of generalized quantifier for natural language was recognized by Montague (1973), Barwise & Cooper (1981), Keenan & Stavi (1986) and many others. Barwise and Cooper point out, in particular, that certain natural language determiners, such as *most*, cannot be defined at all as first-order quantifiers along the lines of $\forall$ and $\exists$. But as a generalized quantifer, *most* is characterizable as mapping a pair of propositional functions F and G to 'true' if G holds of more than half of the things F holds of. Barwise and Cooper define quantifiers as properties of sets rather than operators on propositional functions, taking first order predicates like *Canadian, intrepid*, etc., to denote sets (of Canadians, intrepid things, etc.). A few quantifier definitions along these lines are listed below.

INTRODUCTION

(1) For any sets A and B:
  a. $[\![\text{every}(A)(B)]\!]$ = true iff $A \subseteq B$
  b. $[\![\text{some}(A)(B)]\!]$ = true iff $A \cap B \neq \emptyset$
  c. $[\![\text{most}(A)(B)]\!]$ = true iff $|A \cap B| > |A - B|$
  d. $[\![\text{four}(A)(B)]\!]$ = true iff $|A \cap B| = 4$

A sentence like (2a) translates into the logical form in (2b), where **C** is the set of Canadians and **I** the set of intrepid things. (2b) dictates that this sentence is true if and only if the set of Canadians is a subset of or equal to the set of the intrepid things ('or equal to' because the sentence does not require there to be any intrepid things other than Canadians).

(2) a. Every Canadian is intrepid.
    b. $[\![\text{every}(\mathbf{C})(\mathbf{I})]\!]$ = true iff $C \subseteq I$

The mapping from the surface syntax to the logical form is not always trivial. In the simple cases above, the quantifier combines first with its syntactic sister, the nominal representing what is often called its 'restriction' (the set A in the definitions in (1)), then the result combines with the main predicate, often called the quantifier's 'nuclear scope' (the set B in (1)) (Heim 1983).

(3)

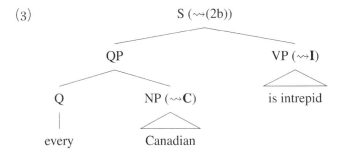

In other cases, though, the quantifier must be displaced from its surface position in order to derive a coherent semantic composition. In the sentence in (4a), for example, the verb *return* selects an individual-denoting object, yet the object position is filled by the quantifier *every book*, which denotes a function from sets to truth values. This combinatorial mismatch is rectified by displacement of the quantifier to a higher position, as illustrated in (4b). There, the sister to the quantifier contains a variable bound by an abstraction operator. The job of the abstraction operator is to derive a set of entities that make the underlying proposition true when substituted for the variable, in this case the set of things that Mary returned to the library.

(4) a. Mary returned every book to the library.
   b.

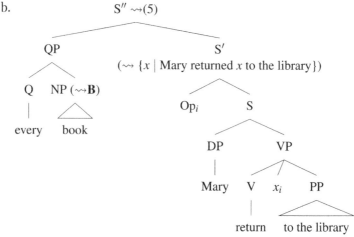

The definition in (1a) specifies the truth conditions in (5) for the structure in (4b), namely that the set of books is a subset of the things Mary returned to the library.[1] Here, the sentence in (4a) is mapped to the format with which truth conditions are associated by displacement of the quantifier, a syntactic process referred to as 'quantifier raising' (May 1977, 1981, 1985, Beghelli & Stowell 1997, Heim & Kratzer 1998, Bruening 2001).

(5) 〚every(**B**, {x | Mary returned x to the library})〛 =
     true iff **B**⊆{x | Mary returned x to the library}

Quantifiers display a number of logical properties relevant to the discussion of degree modifiers below. One is the permutation invariance property mentioned above. Following Mostowski, a permutation (more generally 'transformation') is a mapping of the entities that build the set-relata of quantifiers (the model's 'universe') to another, not necessarily different set with the same cardinality. Linguistic applications are usually limited to automorphisms—a mapping from a set onto itself. This guarantees sameness of cardinality. If ϕ is such a mapping, then for any n-ary relation R (denoting a set of n-ary tuples), R_ϕ is defined as in (6a) as the 'corresponding' set in the image of the permutation. A quantifier Q is permutation invariant if $Q(A)$ has the same truth value $Q(A_\phi)$

---

[1] Of course, the set **B** here is not naturally construed as the set of all books in the universe, but a set of relevant books, perhaps previously mentioned in the discourse context. See Westerståhl (1985a), von Fintel (1994), Cooper (1996), Stanley & Szabó (2000) and Stanley (2000, 2002), on context-dependent quantifier domain restrictions.

for any set A, extended in (6b) to n-ary quantifers (Mostowski 1957, Lindström 1966, van Benthem 1983, 1984, 2002, Peters & Westerståhl 2006).

(6) a. $[\![R_\phi]\!] = \{\langle\phi(x_1),...\phi(x_n)\rangle \mid \langle x_1,...x_n\rangle \in R\}$
b. $Q(A_1,...A_n) \equiv Q(A_{1\phi},...A_{n\phi})$

By virtue of the definition in (6a), if, for example, the subset of the universe that I ('intrepid') denotes has four individuals in it, so does I_ϕ, but not necessarily the same individuals. Suppose *Mary* denotes the quantifier $\lambda P \, . \, P(\text{Mary})$ (per Montague 1973, the set of properties that Mary has). Then *Mary* is not permutation invariant, since the truth of *Mary*(I) ('Mary is intrepid') does not guarantee the truth of *Mary*(I_ϕ) (Mary might be in the set I but not the set I_ϕ). But the truth of *four*(C)(I) ('Four Canadians are intrepid', with *four* defined as in (1d)) guarantees the truth of *four*(C_ϕ)(I_ϕ) and vice versa: If C and I share four things, then again by virtue of (6a), the images of those four things under ϕ will be in both C_ϕ and I_ϕ, validating *four*(C_ϕ)(I_ϕ). If C and I do not overlap in four things, then neither will C_ϕ and I_ϕ. Intuitively, a quantifier that is permutation invariant does not care about the identities of things in the sets it relates; replacing those things with other things in a way that preserves the overall structure of the universe does not effect the interpretation of the quantifier.

Another property relevant to the comparison between individual and degree quantifiers in section 3 is monotonicity. Different quantifiers display different entailment patterns on their arguments (Ladusaw 1979, Barwise & Cooper 1981, van Benthem 1983, 1984, Peters & Westerståhl 2006). For example, the first argument of *every* may be replaced with a subset of that argument's denotation preserving truth. Since the French Canadians are a subset of the Canadians, the truth of (2a) guarantees the truth of (7a). But if we restrict the second argument similarly to a subset of the intrepid things, for example the things that are both intrepid and thrifty, there is no guarantee of preservation of truth; (2a) does not entail (7b).

(7) a. Every French Canadian is intrepid.
b. Every Canadian is intrepid and thrifty.

This means that *every* is downward (from superset to subset) entailing (i.e. 'downward monotone') in its first argument, but not in its second. Rather, it is upward entailing ('upward monotone') in its second argument, since (2a) entails (8) on the assumption that all intrepid things are mortal.

(8) Every Canadian is mortal.

Not all quantifiers display the same entailment patterns; the quantifier *no*, for example, is downward entailing in its first argument ((9a) entails (9b)) but, unlike *every*, also downward entailing in its second argument ((9a) entails (9c) and not (9d)).

(9) a. No Canadian is intrepid.
    b. No French Canadian is intrepid.
    c. No Canadian is intrepid and thrifty.
    d. No Canadian is mortal.

Other quantifiers are neither upward or downward entailing on one or more of their arguments. Such quantifiers are 'non-monotone'. For example, *exactly three* entails neither downward nor upward on its first argument ((10a) entails neither (10b) nor (10c)), nor either downward or upward on its second argument ((10a) entails neither (10d) nor (10e)). *Exactly three* is non-monotone on both arguments.

(10) a. Exactly three Canadians are intrepid.
     b. Exactly three French Canadians are intrepid.
     c. Exactly three North Americans are intrepid.
     d. Exactly three Canadians are intrepid and thrifty.
     e. Exactly three Canadians are mortal.

As Fauconnier (1975) and Ladusaw (1979) point out, downward entailing contexts license negative polarity items like *any* or *ever*. As predicted, these terms occur the argument positions of quantifiers shown to be downward entailing above, and not elsewhere.

(11) a. Every Canadian I've ever met was (*ever) intrepid.
     b. No Canadian I've ever met was ever intrepid.
     c. Exactly three Canadians I've (*ever) met were (*ever) intrepid.

A final characteristic of quantifiers relevant to the comparison with degree modifiers below is the 'conservativity' property. Barwise & Cooper (1981), Higginbotham & May (1981), van Benthem (1983, 1984), Westerståhl (1985b), Keenan & Stavi (1986), Peters & Westerståhl (2006) and others describe a restriction on the interpretation of natural language determiners that excludes many logically possible determiner denotations. The conservativity restriction dictates that a natural language quantifier Q holds of sets A and B if and only if it also holds of A and $A \cap B$.

(12) For any sets A and B and any determiner Q:
$Q(A)(B) \equiv Q(A)(A \cap B)$

Every is conservative because *Every Canadian is intrepid* is true if and only if *Every Canadian is an intrepid Canadian* is true (to be an intrepid Canadian is to be in the intersection of the sets that *intrepid* and *Canadian* denote). Westerståhl (1985b) mentions that the 'Rescher' quantifer defined as R in (13a) is not conservative, and consequently cannot function as the denotation of any natural language determiner. If, for example *more* denoted the Rescher quantifier, (13b) would mean what (13c) means. But it cannot; (13b) is ungrammatical without a (potentially implicit) *than*-clause, in which case it expresses something very different from (13c).

(13) a. $[\![R(A)(B)]\!]$ = true iff $|A| > |B|$
 b. *More Canadians are linguists.
 c. There are more Canadians than linguists.

With this broad overview of natural language quantifiers and some of their more salient syntactic and logical properties in mind, I turn below to a discussion of degree quantifiers and parallels to individual quantifiers.

3 Degree Quantifiers

Seuren (1973), Cresswell (1976), Klein (1980), and others point out that natural language predicates that encode a gradable quality can be characterized as descriptions of an extent, or degree, of that quality. On one view, this degree functions as an argument of the gradable predicate, so that e.g. *tall* is a relation between an individual (*x* in (14a)) and a degree of height (*d* in (14a)) (Seuren 1973, Cresswell 1976). The definition in (14a) models this denotation as a set of individual-degree pairs meeting the condition that *x* has height *d*. On another view, the gradable predicate is not a relation but a function that maps an individual argument to a degree, so that *tall*, as illustrated in (14b), combines with an individual *x* and returns *x*'s height, a degree (Bartsch & Vennemann 1973, Kennedy 1999). I speak here primarily in terms of the relational view spelled out in (14a) below.

(14) a. $[\![tall]\!] = \{\langle x, d\rangle \mid tall(x, d)\}$
 b. $[\![tall]\!] = \lambda x . x$'s height

A primary difference between degrees and other entities, that has certain ramifications for the analysis of degree quantifiers, is that degrees are inherently ordered. Every degree carries information about how it is related to other degrees. Concretely, Cresswell (1976) defines 'degree' as a pair consisting of a coordinate u and an ordering relation $>$.[2] $\mathscr{F}(>)$ denotes the 'field' of $>$, the set of things that either stand in the $>$ relation to something, or that something stands in the $>$ relation to.

(15) A DEGREE (of comparison) is a pair $\langle u, > \rangle$, where $>$ is a relation and $u \in \mathscr{F}(>)$. (Cresswell 1976, p. 266)

A set of such pairs is a 'scale'. The particular relation $>$ at hand is determined by the gradable predicate itself. *Tall* determines a scale of height, *intrepid* of intrepidness, etc. Note that Cresswell's definition leaves some leeway for interpreting u. While u is commonly treated as an abstract coordinate, Cresswell himself mentions the possibility that u stands for an individual, which is then ranked with other individuals directly by the gradable relation, rather than through a relation to a degree. Contributions to the present volume by Alan Bale and Roger Schwarzschild pursue versions of this approach. Whether u represents a coordinate or an individual, the pairs that (15) defines are semantically basic elements with no argument structure of their own, like individuals, meaning that this definition of 'degree' does not impact the parallels in semantic type described below between individual quantifiers and degree quantifiers. In fact, it may go some way toward explaining the sortal difference between individuals and degrees. Individuals are singleton entities, degrees tuples. It seems reasonable that languages use a different vocabulary for quantification over the two sorts. I continue to use the variable symbol d to stand for the pairs illustrated in (15).

When the individual argument of a degree relation is saturated, we are left with a set of degrees. That is, *Mary is tall* is interpreted as the set of degrees to which Mary is tall. This set is typically, but not universally, treated in degree semantic studies as downward monotone, meaning that if Mary is tall to some degree, she is tall to every lesser degree as well. To put it another way, the formula 'tall(x, d)' is read 'x is at least d-tall'. Not all analyses of degree quantifiers proceed from the premise that degree scales are downward monotone

---

[2] For more on the ontology of degrees, see Landman & Morzycki (2003), Anderson & Morzycki (2015) and Snyder (2017), who analyse degrees as 'kinds' in the sense of Carlson (1977a) and Chierchia (1998).

(Schwarzschild & Wilkinson 2002, Zhang & Ling 2015). Those that do typically exploit the fact that if Mary is taller than John, the set of degrees to which Mary is tall properly contains the set of degrees to which John is tall. This fact plays an important role in the analysis of the comparative and superlative, to which I now turn.

Heim (1985) describes an approach to the comparative that makes it a relation between two individuals and a gradable predicate. This is referred to as the 'phrasal comparative' because it relates nominal phrases (DPs), as opposed to the 'clausal comparative' discussed below. I define the phrasal comparative as in (16), departing from Heim's definition somewhat to highlight parallels to individual quantifiers discussed in section 2 (see footnote 4 to follow). It holds when the set of degrees to which the first individual bears the scalar relation is a proper subset of the set of degrees to which the other individual bears the relation.

(16) $[\![\text{-er}(x_e)(P_{\langle e,\langle d,t\rangle\rangle})(y_e)]\!]$ = true iff $\{d \mid P(x, d)\} \subset \{d \mid P(y, d)\}$

This definition captures the meaning of a comparative sentence like *Mary is taller than John* directly as a relation between the two individual arguments *Mary* and *John* (on this view, the 'standard marker' *than* is vacuous). Bhatt & Takahashi (2011) claim that only this use is attested in Hindi-Urdu and Japanese, whereas English displays the 'clausal comparative' (following Lechner 2001, 2004). The argument structure illustrated in (16) is unexpected for a quantificational expression. At first glance, *-er* looks more like a transitive verb than a quantifier; the individual quantifiers discussed in section 2 never relate actual individuals, only sets.[3] However, although the phrasal comparative relates individuals, it qualifies as permutation invariant by the following line of reasoning. On the basis of the definitions in (6), when we ask whether *-er* in (16) is permutation invariant, we are asking whether an equivalence holds between $\text{-er}(x)(R)(y)$ and $\text{-er}(\phi(x))(R_\phi)(\phi(y))$. Suppose x bears R to the degrees 1 and 2, and y bears R to 1, 2 and 3 (for the sake of explication; whether it is reasonable to equate degrees with numbers is another matter I discuss below). By the definition of R_ϕ, $\phi(x)$ bears the R_ϕ relation to $\phi(1)$ and $\phi(2)$, while $\phi(y)$ bears it to $\phi(1)$, $\phi(2)$ and $\phi(3)$. Since the set of things that $\phi(x)$ bear R_ϕ to (namely $\{\phi(1), \phi(2)\}$) is a subset of the set of things that $\phi(y)$ bears R_ϕ to (namely $\{\phi(1), \phi(2),$

---

[3] Bhatt & Takahashi (2011) make this point in footnote 19, p. 606, where they attribute it to the syntactic type of individual quantifiers as determiners.

$\phi(3)\}$), the truth of *-er* is preserved across the permutation, and the phrasal comparative qualifies as quantificational in this sense.[4]

Another option for the analysis of the comparative characterizes it as a relation between degree set descriptions that are constructed in the syntax. This view seems to be required for sentences like (17), where the *than*-clause contains a sentence fragment. On the 'clausal' analysis of the comparative, (17) is syntactically analysed as containing an elided predicate in the *than*-clause identical with the main clause predicate (Bresnan 1973, Seuren 1973, Cresswell 1976, Lechner 2001, 2004).

(17) Mary is taller than John is.

In Seuren (1973), Cresswell (1976) and elsewhere, both the main clause and the *than*-clause are construed as sets of degrees related by the comparative morpheme *-er*. The comparative morpheme *-er* functions as the quantifier (qua relation between sets) and the *than*-clause as its restriction (Bresnan 1973, 1975, Carlson 1977b). Much of Heim's paper cited above concerns the question of whether the phrasal analysis can be reduced to the clausal analysis. Hankamer (1973), Hoeksema (1983) and others detail syntactic differences between the phrasal and clausal comparative, while Bhatt & Takahashi (2011) show that some languages dispose only of a syntactically phrasal comparative construction. The extent to which the syntactic distinction aligns with a semantic one remains under debate. Contributions to the present volume by Barbara Tomaszewicz-Özakın and by Bogal-Allbritten and Coppock discuss this issue, as I describe in more detail in section 4. In the clausal comparative, the mapping from the surface structure, in which *-er* is a suffix of the main clause degree predicate, to the logical form is, as in the case of non-subject individual quantifiers illustrated in (4b), not trivial. Quantifier raising analogous to what we see with individual quantifiers in (4b) displaces the degree quantifier *-er* and its restriction (the *than*-clause), to a position adjoined to the main clause (Seuren

---

4 Heim and others define the comparative in terms of the 'greater than' relation between maximal degrees in the relevant degree sets, along the lines of (i):

(i) $[\![\text{-er}(x_e)(P_{\langle e,\langle d,t\rangle\rangle})(y_e)]\!]$ = true iff $\max\{d \mid P(x,d)\} > \max\{d \mid P(y,d)\}$

For this definition to qualify as permutation invariant, we must ensure that the images of the degrees under ϕ are ranked with respect to > in the same order as the respective degrees. That is, we must carry some of the structure of the original model into the permutation model. Van Benthem (1982) discusses this issue in connection with both gradable adjectives and temporal modifiers, both of which make reference to linear orders (of degrees and times) which are preserved under permutation. See van Benthem (1983, 1986) and Peters & Westerståhl (2006) on restrictions on the transformations relevant to the notion of logicality.

1973, Postal 1974, Cresswell 1976, Williams 1977, von Stechow 1984, Heim 1985, 2001).[5] This derives the structure in (18b), where as in the case of the individual quantifier in (4b), displacement of the quantifier (with its restriction) goes hand in hand with abstraction of a degree predicate over the main clause (arguably *than* plays this role in the restriction). Quantifier raising creates an antecedent for ellipsis in the *than*-clause.

(18) a. Mary is taller than John is.
b.

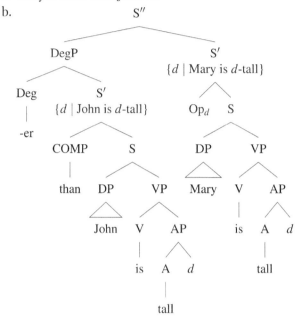

The two S′ constituents denote the set of degrees to which John is tall (call it A) and the set of degrees to which Mary is tall (call it B). The comparative morpheme *-er* takes these sets as arguments and is true when B contains degrees not included in A, or, put another way, A is a proper subset of B, schematized in (19) Heim (2006a).

---

5 The works cited here have in common that they attribute scopal flexibility to *-er*, though the mechanism takes a variety of shapes. Postal and Seuren attribute the ambiguity to different base structures, not different logical derivatives. von Stechow (1984) points out that the earlier works incorrectly leave the *than*-clause in situ. Bhatt & Pancheva (2004) claim that the degree quantifier *-er* moves but the *than*-clause is merged with *-er* in its derived position. Bresnan (1975) and Chomsky (1977) present syntactic evidence for A′ movement of a covert operator in the *than*-clause, which they associate with degree abstraction there.

(19) ⟦-er(A)(B)⟧ = true iff $A \subset B$

As spelled out in (20), the truth conditions for (18a) bear a certain resemblance to the truth conditions for the universal individual quantifier example in (4a) *Mary returned every book to the library* (recall **B** designates the set of books in that example).

(20) a. $\{d \mid \text{tall}(\text{John}, d)\} \subset \{d \mid \text{tall}(\text{Mary}, d)\}$
      b. $\mathbf{B} \subseteq \{x \mid \text{return}(\text{Mary}, x, \text{the-library})\}$

Both the phrasal comparative as defined in (16) and the clausal comparative as defined in (19) put two degree sets in the proper subset relation (the clausal comparative directly and the phrasal comparative indirectly). In spite of the similarity, the comparative *-er* and the individual quantifier *every* differ in both the kind of subset relation they invoke (proper in (20a) and non-proper in (20b)), and in the things they quantify over. The morpheme *-er* relates sets of degrees, while *every* relates sets of individuals. Again, degrees and individuals are both semantically atomic entities. They differ in 'sort'. Both quantifiers potentially involve quantifier raising in the derivation of a coherent logical form.

The degree quantifier *-er* as defined in (19) straightforwardly displays the permutation invariance property typical of natural language quantifiers, for reasons described above. Suppose for some sets of degrees A and B that A is a subset of B, so *-er(A)(B)* holds. And suppose some permutation ϕ maps the all the degrees in the universe to other things in a universe with the same cardinality. Since B_ϕ consists by definition of the images under ϕ of all the things in B, and B contains all the things in A, inevitably B_ϕ contains the images under ϕ of all the things in A, which is just A_ϕ. By the same reasoning, if $A \not\subset B$ then $A_\phi \not\subset B_\phi$. So *-er(A)(B)* ≡ *-er(A_\phi)(B_\phi)*.

As expected in light of the similarity in meaning between *-er* and *every*, the degree-set relata of *-er* display the same entailment pattern as the individual-set relata of *every* (Seuren 1973, Hoeksema 1983). Suppose John is taller than Jane. By virtue of the downward monotonicity of degree predicates discussed above, the set of degrees to which Jane is tall is a subset of the set of degrees to which John is tall. On this assumption, (21a) entails (21b), where we replace the set of degrees to which John is tall with a subset—the set of degrees to which Jane is tall. The degree quantifier *-er*, then, is downward entailing in its restrictor argument (the *than*-clause). Since John is taller than Jane, Mary being taller than John guarantees she is taller than Jane.

(21) a. Mary is taller than John is.
b. Mary is taller than Jane is.

Also like *every*, *-er* is upward entailing in its nuclear scope argument. Replacing *Mary* in (22a) by someone taller than her (Julie in (22b)) preserves truth.

(22) a. Mary is taller than John is.
b. Julie is taller than John is.

Accordingly, *-er* licenses negative polarity items in its restrictor argument but not its nuclear scope argument.

(23) Mary will (*ever) be taller than John will ever be.

Recent developments that bear on these monotonicity patterns deal with a perennially troublesome interaction between degree and quantification involving the interpretation of individual quantifiers in *than*-clauses. The monotonicity of degree predication (the fact that if $R(x,d)$ holds, then it holds for every $d' < d$ as well) predicts an unattested interpretation for sentences like *Mary is taller than every boy is*. If *than every boy is* [*tall*] denotes the set of degrees to which every boy is tall, then this set should include only the degrees to which the shortest boy is tall, since these are the only degrees that are common to the heights of all the boys. Consequently, the sentence should mean that Mary is taller than the shortest boy, but in fact it requires her to be taller than the tallest (von Stechow 1984). In principle, giving ultra wide scope to *every boy* solves the problem (then it means that for each boy, Mary is taller than him), but independent syntactic factors militate against this approach. Among other issues, *than*-clauses are typically barriers for extraction, as (24) demonstrates, from Larson (1988).

(24) *Who$_i$ is Felix taller than Moe persuaded t_i that Max is?

One type of solution to this problem involves various devices that give the quantifier internal to the *than*-clause wide scope without actually removing it from the *than*-clause (Larson 1988, Fleisher 2016, Nouwen & Dotlačil 2017). Nicholas Fleisher's contribution to the present volume, which analyses the effect as a kind of pair list reading (and *than*-clauses as a kind of question) is an example of this approach. This approach does not involve drastic revisions to the standard degree-semantic view of what the degree quantifier *-er* means nor the monotonicity of degree scales. Another type of solution to this conundrum is 'interval semantic'. Schwarzschild & Wilkinson (2002) present an analysis of the comparative along the following lines, developed in Heim (2006b), Gajewski (2008), van Rooij (2008), Schwarzschild (2008), Beck (2010), Abrusán & Spector (2010), Dotlačil & Nouwen (2016) and elsewhere.[6] Rather than denoting the set of degrees that all the boys have in common, the *than*-clause in *Mary is taller than every boy is* denotes a set containing the maximal heights of the individual boys in question. In turn, the main clause denotes a set containing the height of Mary. These are degree 'intervals' (or 'segments', as Schwarzschild calls them in this volume). The comparative says that the main clause interval is separated from the *than* clause interval by a positive difference, so the first contains only degrees higher than all the degrees in the second. On this view, the *than*-clause is no longer predicted to entail downward, and indeed, Schwarzschild and Wilkinson argue that the conclusion that *than*-clauses are downward monotone is premature, on the basis of facts like those in (25). The entailment from *exactly 7* to *at least four* that in (25a) illustrates, for example, is not reversed in the *than*-clauses in (25b).

(25) a. Exactly 7 of my relatives are rich → At least 4 of my relatives are rich.
    b. John is richer than at least 4 of my relatives were ↛
                    John is richer than exactly 7 of my relatives were.

In this volume, Linmin Zhang spells out an interval theoretic solution to the particular problem of non-monotone quantifiers (such as *exactly two*) in *than*-clauses, while Roger Schwarzschild presents an interval theoretic approach to the analysis of differentials in intensional contexts.

When we turn to the conservativity property, *-er* does not behave entirely parallel to individual quantifiers. The meanings of the two quantifiers *-er* and *every*, though similar, differ in the kind of subset relation they denote, proper in (20a) and non-proper in (20b). If Mary and John are exactly the same height, we cannot assert that Mary is taller than John. That sentence requires that the set of degrees to which Mary is tall contains some degrees not in the set of degrees to which John is tall, i.e., that the latter is a proper subset of the former. But if Mary and John are the same height, we can say (26a), an 'equative' degree construction discussed at length by Jessica Rett in the present volume. Example (26a) is true when Mary is tall to all the degrees to which John is tall. Although it implies that she is no taller than him, this implicature can be defeated, as in (26b). Consequently, it appears that we can give equative *as* the denotation in

---

6 Alrenga & Kennedy (2014) import certain elements of the interval semantic approach into a traditional monotone degree semantics.

(26c), which attributes the truth conditions in (26d) to (26a). These truth conditions are exactly parallel to *every*, albeit in the degree domain.[7]

(26) a. Mary is as tall as John.
   b. Mary is as tall as John is, in fact she's even taller.
   c. ⟦as(A)(B)⟧ = true iff $A \subseteq B$
   d. $\{d \mid \text{tall}(\text{John}, d)\} \subseteq \{d \mid \text{tall}(\text{Mary}, d)\}$

While equative constructions may represent a better parallel to the meaning of *every* than comparatives, there does not seem to be a counterpart to *every* that, in parallel to comparative *-er*, denotes proper subsethood. Such a counterpart in place of *every* in (20b) would entail that Mary returned something to the library other than and in addition to the books in question. An explanation for this missing counterpart to *every* presents itself in the form of the conservativity constraint. As discussed in section 2, conservativity prohibits a quantifier from saying anything about the members of B that are not also members of A in the schemas in (1). But this is precisely what the proper subset relation does: it holds precisely when there are members of B that are not also members of A. The proper subset relation is an impossible determiner meaning because it violates conservativity.

But then the fact that *-er* denotes the proper subset relation means that degree quantifiers (insofar as *-er* is representative) are not subject to conservativity. On one hand, this might be taken to represent a difference between individual and degree quantifiers. On the other hand, it has been pointed out that conservativity is a restriction that holds only of determiners, not of quantifiers in general. A clear case of a non-conservative quantifier is *only*. The sentence *Only Canadians are intrepid* is not equivalent to *Only Canadians are intrepid Canadians*. Von Fintel (1997) reasons that *only* is not a determiner, but an adverb, and therefore exempt from the conservativity requirement. This explanation of course carries over to *-er* and other degree quantifiers, as these are not determiners. But on the other hand, it supports the idea that conservativity is not foremost a restriction on quantifier meanings, but rather a restriction on the meanings of determiners (as a syntactic category) with no fundamental connection to quantification, other than the fact that determin-

---

7 Equative constructions are usually understood by default to mean *exactly as much as*. While a pragmatic account of this strengthening suggests itself (if the speaker knew Mary was taller than John she would say so), a reviewer of this chapter points out that *taller than* emerges as an alternative to *as tall as* when focus falls on *as*, as when we say *Mary is not AS tall as John, she's TALLER than him*. This is probably made possible by fact that the equative and comparative are duals, as Rett (this volume) points out.

ers often have quantificational meanings, as do adverbs and 'degree modifiers' (to put it in syntactic terms). If that is so, then the fact that degree quantifiers are not subject to conservativity does not represent a difference between them and individual quantifiers.

Another approach to the conservativity puzzle that *-er* presents is spelled out in Bhatt & Pancheva (2004). Following the suggestion of Fox (2002) and Sportiche (2005), they claim that conservativity is an epiphenomenon of the copy theory of movement. When a quantifier moves, it leaves a copy of its restriction in its θ-position that restricts the value for the variable in that position. Consequently, *Every Canadian is intrepid* is interpreted as *Every Canadian is Canadian and intrepid*, mimicking the conservativity equivalence in (12) simply as a result of quantifier raising. What is special about degree quantifiers such as *-er*, they claim, is that their restriction (the *than*-clause), can be inserted into the derivation after movement of the quantifier, so that it is not present in the base position. This makes non-conservative semantic relations available as denotations for degree quantifiers.

We have seen that degree relations are typically assumed to be downward monotone, in the sense that $R(x, d)$ implies $R(x, d')$ for all d' lower than d, and that this plays a role in the interpretation of degree quantifiers but not individual quantifiers, which do not have ordered domains. Another aspect of degree scales responsible for differences between degree and individual quantifiers is the fact that degree scales may be 'dense', meaning that for any two degrees on the scale, there is a third between them. By some accounts, all degree constructions involve dense scales (Fox & Hackl 2006), even those that measure out the cardinality of collections individuals, which I discuss in more detail below. The density of degree scales means that as soon as two scales overlap in two degrees, they overlap in infinitely many. For this reason, if cardinal quantifiers like *four* count the elements in the intersection of the two sets they relate (or compare their cardinalities like *most*), then they make little sense when applied to degree sets. Two scales that intersect in four points also intersect in the infinitely many points between them, so *exactly four* as a description of the cardinality of the intersection of two sets of degrees will never be true, and *at least four* is indistinguishable from the infinitely many other cardinal quantifiers above 'one'. Likewise, the claim that most of the degrees in set A are also in set B is not useful if both A and B contain infinitely many degrees. Such degree quantifiers are not logically impossible, but their communicative usefulness is so limited that it comes as no surprise that they are unattested.

These remarks suggest that hypothetical quantifiers that specify the cardinality of degree sets (i.e., that 'count' degrees) are not useful because of the density of degree scales. But this does not mean that degree semantics is entirely uninvolved in counting. A variety of evidence in fact indicates that cardinality is merely one kind of degree scale, and numbers, rather than being degree quantifiers like the comparative, are names for degrees.

Consider the fact that the comparative has 'quality' and 'quantity' variants (Gawron 1995) that correspond to comparisons of what I have called degree and cardinality above.

(27) a. Mary read a more interesting book than John. [quality]
b. Mary read more books than John. [quantity]

In parallel to (20a), (27a) denotes the proper subset relation between the set of degrees to which the book that John read is interesting and the set of degrees to which the book that Mary read is interesting. If *more* is a quantifier in (27b) corresponding to *-er* in (27a), then the two relata in (27b) are sets of degrees that correspond in some way to the number of books John and Mary read. That is, it is possible to make comparisons of cardinality using the same morphosyntactic machinery that languages use to make comparisons of degree. The same parallel can be seen in the superlative (28) and other degree modifiers like *very*, which implies a high degree of cardinality (29), as well as in the equative construction (not shown).

(28) a. Mary read the most interesting book. [quality]
b. Mary read the most books. [quantity]

(29) a. Mary read a very interesting book. [quality]
b. Mary read very many books. [quantity]

The quantity use of these degree quantifiers involves a plural (or mass) noun, whose cardinality (or 'amount') is being assessed. Plural nouns describe plural individuals—sums of atoms (Link 1983, Lønning 1987). Standard accounts of quantity constructions (the b-examples above) claim that, like gradable predicates, plural nouns also have a degree argument that corresponds to the cardinality of the plural individual—the number of atoms it has. Cresti (1995), Heycock (1995), Hackl (2000, 2009), Landman (2004), Wellwood (2015) and others claim that the degree argument is introduced by the modifier *many* (before count nouns) or *much* (elsewhere), which is subsequently deleted in some contexts. Others postulate a covert measure function for this purpose (Landman 2004, Kayne 2005, Rett 2006, Schwarzschild 2006, Scontras 2014, Snyder 2017). Cresswell (1976), Krifka (1989), Corver (1997), Solt (2015) and others claim that the degree argument is introduced directly by the plural noun, and that *many/much* merely morphosyntactically hosts the degree quantifier morphology when necessary.

On any account, a phrase like *(many) books* denotes a relation between a plural individual and a degree, which holds when the plural individual has the property *books* and the degree is its cardinality, as illustrated in (30). Compare the definition of *(many) books* in (30) with that in (14a) for *tall*.

(30) ⟦(many) books⟧ = {⟨x, d⟩ | books(x) & |x| = d}

Just as the quality comparative in (27a) says that the set of degrees corresponding to how interesting the book was that John read is a subset of the set of degrees corresponding to how interesting the book was that Mary read, spelled out in (31a), the quantity comparative in (27b) says that the set of degrees corresponding to the number of books that John read is a subset of the set of degrees corresponding to the number of books Mary read, spelled out in (31b). It appears that the language itself does not draw any sharp boundary between 'quality' and 'quantity' comparisons. Both involve abstraction over a degree argument.

(31) a. {d | ∃x [John read x & book(x) & interesting(x, d)]} ⊂
  {d | ∃x [Mary read x & book(x) & interesting(x, d)]}
  b. {d | ∃x [John read x & books(x) & |x| ≥ d]} ⊂
  {d | ∃x [Mary read x & books(x) & |x| ≥ d]}

The quantity constructions above compare the cardinality of sets of entities using the morphosyntactic components of degree comparison seen in the quality counterparts, again suggesting that cardinality and degree are not unrelated syntactically or semantically. It is particularly revealing that the term *most* occurs in both quality and quantity degree constructions, since *most* has always been held to be a paradigmatic case of an individual quantifier with set relata, since its meaning cannot be formulated in first order logic. The observations above might be taken to show that there is no determiner *most*. Rather, *most* is none other than the superlative morpheme *-est* in combination with a morphological host *much* (contracted to *mo-*) which may or may not play a semantic role in the composition of *most*, as mentioned above.

This is just what Hackl (2009) claims. He attributes to *-est* the meaning in (32), following Heim (1999) and others. Superlative *-est* combines with a set of entities C, a degree relation R, and an individual x. C represents a 'comparison' class of individuals we are comparing x to (we presuppose that C is not empty). R is a relation like *tall* or *interesting* that relates an individual to a degree. The

INTRODUCTION

morpheme *-est* holds of these relata when for each member *y* of *C* (other than *x* itself), *x* bears *R* to a greater degree than *y* does. The function *max* applies to a set of degrees and returns the greatest degree in that set (the degree that entails all the others on the relevant scale).

(32) $[\![\text{-est}(C_{\langle e,t \rangle})(R_{\langle d,\langle e,t \rangle \rangle})(x_e)]\!]$ = true iff
$\forall y \in C[y \neq x \rightarrow \max\{d \mid R(d)(x)\} > \max\{d \mid R(d)(y)\}]$

Consider now the quality superlative example in (28a). If we parse *-est* as adjoined to the NP *interesting book* as illustrated in (33), then that NP identifies *R* in (32). Mary identifies *x* and *C* is interpreted as a set of some salient books. As in other examples of degree constructions above, an operator derives a degree predicate over a constituent containing a degree argument, here the NP *interesting book*. The superlative morpheme *-est* applies to this NP to derive a set of individuals *x* that have the degree property *interesting book* to a greater degree than any alternative *y* in *C* does. The definite article *the* picks out the unique item in this set, which is a singleton set by virtue of the meaning of *-est*, which in turn functions as object of the verb *read*. This is referred to as the 'absolute' reading of the superlative; it picks out the absolute most interesting book (from the alternatives in *C*).

(33)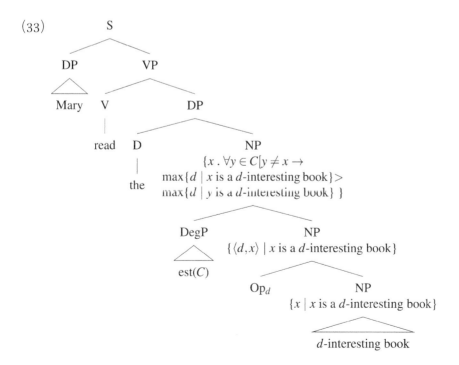

As is well known, another reading is available for (28a), often referred to as a 'relative' reading. Here, we compare not books but rather Mary to others in terms of how interesting the books were that they read. Szabolcsi (1986), Heim (1999) and others claim that this reading is derived by movement of the superlative morpheme *-est* to a higher position, just as *-er* moves in the comparative (but see Farkas & Kiss 2000, Sharvit & Stateva 2002 and Coppock & Beaver 2015 for analyses that do not involve movement). In this case, we abstract a degree relation over the entire VP, rather than just the NP, and we understand C as a set of people who read interesting books. This analysis is illustrated in (34). Note that it requires us to interpret the definite article as indefinite or altogether vacuous, since the different values of y in the end formula below read different books. I assume an existential quantifier over z is introduced at the level of VP (Heim 1983, Diesing 1992, Chung & Ladusaw 2004).

(34)
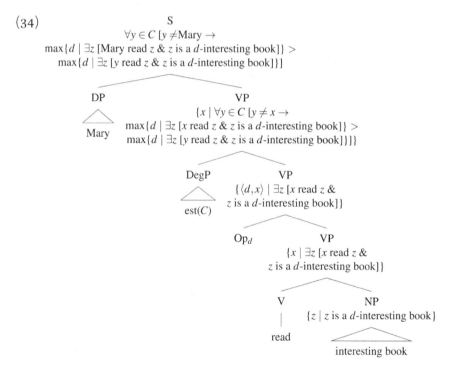

The interpretation of the quantity superlative in (28b) is just that found in the 'relative' quality superlative reading of (28a) diagrammed in (34). Here, the gradable property R is abstracted over the degree argument that the plural noun *books* introduces (on some accounts via the modifier *many*, as mentioned above), and the other argument of *books* is a plural individual—an algebraic sum of books. That is, *most* is functioning as a superlative here, not as an individual quantifier, as illustrated in (35).

(35)

$$
\begin{array}{c}
S \\
\forall y \in C\ [y \neq \text{Mary} \rightarrow \\
\max\{d \mid \exists z\ [\text{Mary read } z\ \&\ \text{books}(z)\ \&\ |z| \geq d]\} > \\
\max\{d \mid \exists z\ [y \text{ read } z\ \&\ \text{books}(z)\ \&\ |z| \geq d]\}]
\end{array}
$$

- DP: Mary
- VP: $\{x \mid \forall y \in C\ [y \neq x \rightarrow \max\{d \mid \exists z\ [x \text{ read } z\ \&\ \text{books}(z)\ \&\ |z| \geq d]\} > \max\{d \mid \exists z\ [y \text{ read } z\ \&\ \text{books}(z)\ \&\ |z| \geq d]\}]\}$
  - DegP: est(C)
  - VP: $\{\langle d, x\rangle \mid \exists z\ [x \text{ read } z\ \&\ \text{books}(z)\ \&\ |z| \geq d]\}$
    - Op$_d$
    - VP: $\{x \mid \exists z\ [x \text{ read } z\ \&\ \text{books}(z)\ \&\ |z| \geq d]\}$
      - V: read
      - NP: $\{z \mid \text{books}(z)\ \&\ |z| \geq d\}$ — (many) books

Now, Hackl (2009) points out that the reading of *most* corresponding to the generalized quantifier meaning in (1c) can be characterized as the 'absolute' superlative counterpart to the relative construction in (28b), which his analysis identifies with a certain scope for -*est* (see also Szabolcsi 2012). A sentence like (36a) has the structure in (36b) on this view.[8] As in the absolute quality superlative in (33), *est* has scope over just the NP object in (36b). It in turn derives an NP that compares a quantity of books *z* with all other non-equal quantities in the contrast set *C*. Hackl points out that if we take 'non-equal' to mean 'non-overlapping', the plurality *z* must have a cardinality that is more than half of

---

8 The phrase *most books* has a generic flavor that makes it somewhat awkward in object position in existential contexts. The addition of *of the* resolves this clash. See Schwarzschild (2006), Scontras (2014), Solt (2015), and Wellwood (2015), among others, on a more articulated internal structure for partitive constructions that addresses these issues.

the total number of books in C. The reason is that if it didn't, there would be an alternative plurality of books y comprising the rest of the books, that has a greater cardinality than z. The plurality z then must comprise more than half of the relevant books, as *most* does on the meaning the generalized quantifier analysis in (1c) attributes to it.

(36) a. Mary read most books.

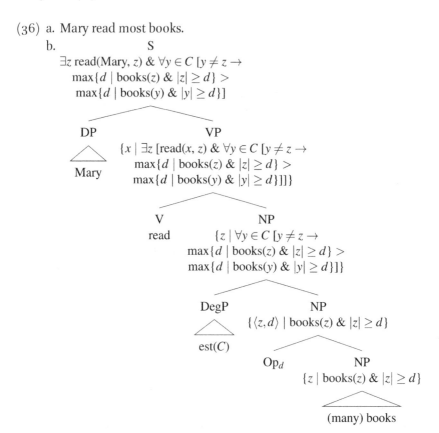

Hackl's analysis removes *most* from the pantheon of generalized quantifiers as relations between sets of individuals. Solt (2011) and Szabolcsi (2012) develop this analysis of *most*. Dobrovie-Sorin (2013, 2015) and Dobrovie-Sorin & Giurgea (to appear), on the other hand, claim that superlative *most* only has a relative reading, but that a bona fide generalized quantifier *most* exists alongside superlative *most*. The generalized quantifier *most*, they claim, only occurs with count nouns, explaining the pattern in (37). It is unclear why Hackl's absolute reading for superlative *most* would be incompatible with a mass noun as in (37b) (or, to the extent it is compatible, why this context requires the support of *of the*; see footnote 8).

(37) a. I am sure most men will arrive late.
     b. *I am sure most wine will be delivered late.

Whether or not a generalized quantifier *most* exists alongside the superlative, the superlative *-est* defined in (32), that underlies *most* on Hackl's analysis, is quantificational in the logical sense, since it is permutation invariant insofar as the 'greater than' relation among degrees is preserved in the permutation, as discussed in footnote 4. A permutation of the universe that respects the condition that $\phi(d) > \phi(d')$ whenever $d > d'$ ensures that the superlative relation between an individual and a property is preserved under the permutation.[9] Like the phrasal comparative, then, *-est* has the primary logical property of quantifiers, even though it has an individual argument.

Further, the notion of cardinality-as-degree represents another potential vehicle for the analysis of numeral modifiers like *four*, analyzed as intersective quantifiers in generalized quantifier theory. If *books* has (perhaps in combination with a covert *many*) a degree argument that tracks its cardinality (the number of atoms in the plurality), then a numeral modifier like *four* might be analyzed as a name for that degree. That is, in the expression *four books*, *four* saturates the degree argument slot of *books*. On this view, rather than denoting relations between sets, numbers denote degrees.

The issue of whether natural languages have degree-referring expressions is a contentious one. One strand of this debate goes back to Frege's (1884) claim, popularized by Dummett (1973, 1991), that the word *four* in (38) names a number. Frege maintains that this fact represents evidence for the existence of numbers external to language. If (38) is true, then *four* has a referent, which is equated there with the referent of *the number of Jupiter's moons*.[10]

(38) The number of Jupiter's moons is four.

A number of philosophers find fault with this argument's background assumptions about what (38) means (Higgins 1979, Moltmann 2013, Snyder 2017). Further, Bach (1986) expresses reservations about the validity of drawing metaphysical conclusions from linguistic evidence, but reaffirms the need for what Montague (1969) calls 'certain metaphysical entities' in a framework for natu-

---

9   As mentioned in footnote 4, this equivalence is easier to see if we define the superlative using the subset relation rather than using the > relation with maximalization, as in (32).
    (i) $[\![\text{-est}(C_{\langle e,t\rangle})(R_{\langle d,\langle e,t\rangle\rangle})(x_e)]\!]$ = true iff $\forall y \in C[y \neq x \rightarrow \{d \mid R(y,d)\} \subset \{d \mid R(x,d)\}]$
10 Jupiter turns out to have dozens more moons than the four largest observed originally by Galileo.

ral language interpretation. That is, *four* may name something in the model of the world that linguistic structures are interpreted with respect to, but whether the things that populate that model have counterparts in reality is not resolved by the linguistic facts. See Wellwood (this volume) on experimental evidence concerning the question of the primacy of metaphysics or conceptual models in linguistic cognition. I expand on the the notion of numbers as degree names below.

Other analyses treat bare numerals as predicate modifiers or as predicates that are composed by a rule of predicate modification with a noun to restrict its range.[11] That is, they restrict the argument of the noun to pluralities with the specified cardinality (Partee 1987, Kamp & Reyle 1993, Kadmon 1993, Krifka 1999, Winter 2001, Ionin & Matushansky 2006, Geurts & Nouwen 2007). This approach raises the question of what the proper analysis of specificational sentences like (38) should be, to which I also return below.

Another possible candidate for a degree name is found in 'measure phrases' such as *six feet* in examples like (39a) (Cresswell 1976, von Stechow 1984, Gawron 1995, Heim 2001, Matushansky 2002). If *tall* has a degree argument, a natural semantic role for *six feet* is that of name for that degree argument, so that *tall* as defined in (14a) composes with the two arguments in (39a) to yield the predicate logical formula in (39b).

(39) a. Mary is six feet tall.
    b. tall(Mary, six feet)

Other analyses cast measure phrases as predicate modifiers (Klein 1980, Hackl 2000, Landman 2004, Schwarzschild 2005, Kennedy 2013, 2015, Scontras 2014, Snyder 2017). The analyses of Klein and Kennedy explicitly make them degree quantifiers, a point I return to below. The body of research cited above—collectively and to a greater or lesser extent individually—connects the form and meaning of measure phrases like *six feet* or *six pounds* (*of rice*) with that of bare numerals like *six* in *six cookies*, by virtue of the premise that the latter contains a covert measure function measuring out cardinality (again covert *many* in some analyses). All these accounts seek to decompose measure phrases into their component parts, which compose semantically in lockstep with their syn-

---

11   Ionin & Matushansky (2006) point out that these two modes of combination (function application vs. predicate modification) are not equivalent when it comes to the composition of complex numerals like 200, since *200 years* does not describe a plurality of years that has both cardinality two and cardinality 100. They analyze numerals explicitly as predicate modifiers, i.e., functions of type $\langle\langle e, t\rangle, \langle e, t\rangle\rangle$.

tactic composition (though these accounts do not necessary agree on what the syntactic composition is). Landman (2004) explicitly pursues the goal of a unified theory of the semantics of measure phrases and bare and modified numerals. A numeral may be combined with what Landman calls a 'numerical relation' in both of its uses in (38) and (39a), as illustrated in (40) (as well as with a 'measure term' described below).

(40) a. The number of Jupiter's moons is exactly / more than / less than four.
b. Mary is exactly / more than / less than six feet tall.

Hackl (2000), Landman (2004), Snyder (2017) and others claim, essentially following Frege, that the meaning of the numeral is the corresponding number, as shown in (41a), but that that numeral may be combined with a numerical relation which, when null, is interpreted as 'exactly', and with a 'measure term' like *feet* or *pounds* which, when null, is interpreted as cardinality. Consequently, *four* has the basic use in (41a) but, combined with a null numerical relation and a null measure term, the derived use in (41b). An overt numerical relation like *less than* and an overt measure term like *pounds* (which denotes a function μ_{lbs} that maps an individual to its measure on a scale of pounds) yields the meaning specified in (41c).

(41) a. $[\![\text{four}]\!] = 4$
b. $[\![\emptyset \text{ four } \emptyset]\!] = \{x \mid |x| = 4\}$
c. $[\![\text{less than four pounds}]\!] = \{x \mid \mu_{lbs}(x) < 4\}$

The numeral in (38), then, functions as a number, or degree specification in (41a), while the numeral in e.g. *four moons* functions syntactically as an adjective with the meaning of the measure phrase in (41b), and is interpreted intersectively with the modified noun (*four moons* describes a plurality of moons with cardinality 'four'). The meaning of the measure phrase is derived by special composition rules for Landman, which Snyder reformulates as type lifts.

Kennedy (2013, 2015) pursues a quantificational analysis of the meaning of both bare and modified numerals, where they denote properties of sets of degrees, giving them the same logical degree order as degree quantifiers like *-er*. *Four* and *more than four* hold when the maximal degree in their degree set argument is equal to or above four respectively, as spelled out in (42).

(42) a. $[\![\text{four}]\!] = \lambda P_{\langle d,t \rangle} . \max\{n \mid P(n)\} = 4$
b. $[\![\text{more than four}]\!] = \lambda P_{\langle d,t \rangle} . \max\{n \mid P(n)\} > 4$

Kennedy (2015) suggests that the singular term use of numerals is derived from the degree quantifier in (42a), rather than representing the basic use (see also Hofweber 2005 and Ionin & Matushansky 2006, among others, for variations on this theme). He points out that feeding *four* as defined in (42a) a value for *P* meaning 'be equal to *d*' and abstracting over *d* derives the degree-property of being equal to four. This is accomplished by the applying Partee's (1987) BE operator, defined in (43a), to the meaning in (42a). Applying the IOTA operator defined in (43b) to the result derives a singular term meaning 'the number which is equal to four' (in this case). So we are 'back' at four.

(43) a. $\text{BE} = \lambda Q_{\langle\langle \alpha,t\rangle,t\rangle} \lambda x_\alpha . Q(\lambda y_\alpha . y = x)$
 b. $\text{IOTA} = \lambda P_{\langle \alpha,t\rangle} . \iota x_\alpha [P(x)]$

Hence, the meaning of the numeral is considered basic in Landman, Snyder, and Scontras' accounts (as well as Kennedy's earlier 2013 account) and the predicative use derived, while in Kennedy's (2015) account the degree-quantifier use is basic and the singular term use is derived.

Both of these approaches to the meaning of numerals (and measure phrases in general) remove numerals from the pantheon of generalized quantifiers understood as relations between sets of individuals, just as Hackl's analysis undermines the view of *most* as a relation between sets of individuals. The issue of whether Landman and Kennedy's meanings for numerals are permutation invariant, and therefore qualify as quantifiers in a logical sense, is not completely transparent. Landman mentions that numerals as adjectival modifiers obey a notion of 'quantitativity' he describes informally. The idea is, if a plural individual meets the description *four Canadians*, and we replace one of the atoms in that plurality with another, the result might no longer meet the description *Canadians*, but it will still meet the description *four*. This makes *four* 'quantitative' and *Canadians* not, as desired. One way of ensuring this result is to restrict the permutations we use to those that preserve the part structure of plural individuals (or mass nouns), as van Benthem (1984, 1986) suggests. A part-structure preserving permutation ϕ is a mapping from a universe to a universe of equal cardinality that respects the condition in (44).

(44) $\forall x, y, z \in U[x = y \oplus z \leftrightarrow \phi(x) = \phi(y) \oplus \phi(z)]$

With respect to such a condition, the truth of $Canadian(x)$ does not guarantee the truth of $Canadian(\phi(x))$ but the truth of $two(x)$ still guarantees the truth of $two(\phi(x))$, since if x consists of two elements y and z, $\phi(x)$ must consist of the images of those two elements and no others.

Recall that we concluded above that the comparative is permutation invariant (the same reasoning applies to equatives). If the degree set A is a subset of the degree set B, then any mapping of these degrees to other elements will ensure that A_ϕ is a subset of B_ϕ because the set B_ϕ is by definition just the set $\{\phi(x_1), \phi(x_2), \ldots \phi(x_n)\}$ for each x_i member of B. If all the members of A are in B then they all have images in B_ϕ. But Kennedy's definition for his numeral degree set modifiers does not involve any quantitative relation like 'subset of'. Rather, it attributes a name (a particular numeral) to the maximal degree in a degree set. The sentence *Jupiter has four moons* denotes the formula in (45) on Kennedy's analysis.

(45) $\max\{n \mid \exists x \text{ have}(\text{Jupiter}, x) \,\&\, \text{moons}(x) \,\&\, |x|=n\} = 4$

Suppose our permutation maps all the values for n, to, say, turtles. Then, even if we superimpose the degree order inherent in the number scale onto the turtles, so that each turtle bears a scalar relation to the other turtles reflecting the original ordering of degrees, the maximal element in this set is a turtle, not a number like *four*. But the quantifier *four* equates the maximal element in its degree set argument to the number *four*. If its argument A is a set of degrees but A_ϕ is set of turtles, then the truth of the degree quantifier *four* is not preserved across the the permutation. This situation is similar to lifts of proper names discussed by Montague (1973) mentioned in section 2. It is possible to construe a name like *Mary* as a generalized quantifier—a property of sets that is true of all the sets that contain Mary, i.e. all the properties Mary has. But this quantifier is not permutation invariant because Mary's being in a set A does not guarantee that she is in A_ϕ. Likewise for the definition of *four* in (42a) because it makes reference to a particular individual (in this case the number 'four'), like names do.

One response to this dilemma is to separate the equivalence schema from the specification of number, as Landman (2004), Scontras (2014) and Snyder (2017) do. Staying with Kennedy's nomenclature, the modifier *four* defined in (42a) actually consists of the two components in (46): the degree-denoting number four itself, and a quantificational relation MAX that combines with a number and a degree set and equates the maximal member of the degree set with the number. The number in (46a) is not permutation invariant because it names a thing, nor is the quantificational derivative in (42a) because it makes reference to the number. But the quantificational schema in (46b) that derives the degree quantifier in (42a) from the number in (46a) is itself permutation invariant. If a set A contains numbers, and these numbers are mapped to turtles preserving the scalar order between them, then the maximal turtle in A_ϕ is the image of the maximal number in A. The relation in (46b) therefore holds across permutations of the universe, even if the number in (46a) and its quantificational derivative in (42a) do not.

(46) a. ⟦four⟧ = 4
b. ⟦MAX(n)($A_{\langle d,t \rangle}$)⟧ = max{n' | $n' \in A$} = n

Van Benthem (1986: chapter 3) points out that the relations Partee (1987) observes between individuals, sets and quantifiers are preserved under permutation. To return to the example of Montague's lift of individuals to quantifiers, although neither the name *Mary* nor the set of properites $\lambda P.P$(Mary) are permutation invariant, the schema that maps the first to the second, namely $\lambda x \lambda P$. $P(x)$ is permutation invariant. This mapping bears a resemblance to the relation defined in (46b). This is significant because Landman's (2004), Kennedy's (2015) and Snyder's (2017) systems relating the various uses of numerals to one another (on which (46b) is based and which are more numerous than I have discussed here) are based on Partee's system of type changing rules. This approach, one might say, identifies the logical core of the way names for quantities are put to use in natural language, and identifies extensive similarities with rules that operate in the domain of individuals.

Just as the analyses above undermine the view of *most* and numerals as relations between sets of individuals, there is evidence that *some* has a use parallel to that of numerals. *Some* may be used as what Anderson (this volume) refers to as an 'indeterminate numeral' in expressions like *twenty-some people*. He claims that *some* in this use functions as an object language variable over numerals, which in combination with focus generates a set of alternative expressions in which *some* is replaced by a numeral. With the assertion *twenty-some people arrived*, the speaker expresses his or her ignorance about the value of *some*, but, accordingly, their certainty that the number of people who came lies between twenty and thirty. It is unclear how directly this use of *some* relates to its use as a determiner, but it implicates that *some* might not be safe from the encroachment of degree semantic analyses on the territory of generalized quantifiers as described here.

This leaves *every* as a clear case of a generalized quantifier in Mostowski's sense, and its status as a relation between sets of individuals is supported by the fact that it combines with a singular noun, as one would expect given that singular nouns denote sets of atomic individuals, as opposed to plurals, which denote sets of pluralities. Arguably *every*'s discourse-linked counterpart *each* and their complement *no* (when it combines with a singular noun as in *No Canadian is intrepid*) are also a relations between sets. It is somewhat anticlimactic that *every* and *no* can be expressed as first order predicate logical operators, the latter in the form of negation of existence. Though other generalized quantifiers in the traditional sense may exist, it is clear that much of the work for which generalized quantifier theory was originally envisioned is in fact done by degree quantifiers (or measure phrases as Landman and others formulate them). Where exactly the boundary lies between generalized quantifier theory and degree semantics remains the subject matter of current developments in semantics. As the discussion above shows, this enterprise is intimately related to the question of how quantificational terms are composed from their morphological component parts, both synchronically and diachronically. See Szabolcsi (2010) for a recent overview of advances in this area.

The contributions to this volume address this subject matter in diverse ways. I have hinted above at the kinds of contributions that some of them make. Below, I discuss each of them in turn and clarify how they relate to the issues in individual and degree quantification discussed above.

4 Contributions

As mentioned above, Curt Anderson's "Indeterminate Numerals and their Alternatives" deals with the use of English *some* as a numeral. Strawson (1974) points out that after hearing an utterance like *Some cabinet minister has been shot!*, it would be inappropriate to ask *Who?*, since the statement implies the speaker does not know who the cabinet minister in question is. Anderson points out that this ignorance implicature carries over to the use of *some* in numeral expressions like *twenty-some*, where *some* stands in for a number. This suggests that the same *some* is being used in both cases, in the latter case clearly in the syntactic distribution of a number. Anderson proposes a compositional analysis of numerals along the lines of Landman's analysis described above, in which the numeral itself is inserted into a quantificational schema that in turn has the noun as argument. The fact that complex numerals can be manipulated by compositional processes (replacement of a number by *some* in complex numerals like *twenty-some*) supports the view that complex numerals are compositionally derived. The ignorance implicature is modeled as competition between possible values for the position held by *some*.

Barbara Tomaszewicz-Özakın's "The Semantics of Superlative *Est*" discusses the semantic type of the superlative morpheme, and presents evidence for some flexibility in its argument structure. Just as the meaning of the comparative is compatible with different argument structures (the 3-place phrasal comparative in (16) and the 2-place clausal comparative in (19)), she shows that the denotation for superlative -*est* in (32) is in complementary distribution with another denotation that relates two degree set properties, i.e., that is missing the 'external' individual argument (x in (32)). Heim (1999) explored the idea that the "3-place" (because it has three arguments) denotation for -*est* described in foonote 4 above could be reduced to a two-place denotation that relates two degree sets. On the two-place definition, which bears a strong resemblance to the comparative defined in (19), the external individual argument is abstracted over an element in the scope of -*est* through association with focus. Romero (2012) claims modal superlative constructions (e.g. *the most candy possible*) implicate the existence of 2-place -*est*. In the present volume, Tomaszewicz-Özakın presents a series of new facts from Polish and Turkish that illustrate readings of the superlative not available in English, and shows that these readings are only derivable with 2-place -*est*. But she also shows that, contra Heim (1999), 2-place -*est* does not associate with focus, and certain constructions only admit 3-place -*est*. Consequently, the two semantic types for the superlative exist side by side, and their distribution is governed by the requirements of the particular context they occur in.

In similar vein, Elizabeth Bogal-Allbritten and Elizabeth Coppock describe the relation between the comparative and superlative in Navajo in "Quantification, Degrees and *Beyond* in Navajo". First they point out that syntactically speaking, Navajo is like Hindi as described by Bhatt & Takahashi (2011) in only admitting phrasal comparatives, signalled in Navajo by the presence of the standard marker *lááh*, which functions otherwise as the preposition meaning *beyond*. Superlatives are derived by attaching the 'unspecified object' prefix *'a-* to the standard marker *lááh*, which Bogal-Allbritten and Coppock analyze as an operator that introduces existential quantification over an argument position. They then show that combining the standard semantic analysis for the phrasal comparative with existential quantification fails in and of itself to derive the meaning of the superlative. But the combination of the degree quantifier analysis of the comparative usually associated with clausal comparatives with existential quantification introduced by *'a-* correctly generates the meaning of the superlative. This means that the semantic type of the comparative (whether it relates degree sets or individuals) is not strictly determined by its syntactic combinatorial status (phrasal or clausal). The account also represents a concrete analysis of a case where the superlative is morphosyntactically derived from the comparative, lending support to the idea that superlative meaning is derived from comparative meaning, a notion that cross-linguistic morphological evidence also lends some credence to (Bobaljik 2012). Bogal-Allbritten and Coppock also point out the significance of their results in light of the fact that Navajo lacks quantificational determiners. While one explanation for this fact might be that Navajo is a 'first order language', the existence of second order degree quantifiers in the comparative construction militates against this possibility.

In "Separate but Equal: A Typology of Equative Constructions", Jessica Rett discusses parallels between comparative and equative constructions in crosslinguistic perspective, and finds that just as some languages have comparative constructions that are not quantificational, non-quantificational equative constructions are also attested. She develops semantic tests for determining whether an equative construction involves degree quantification or not independently of its morphosyntactic form, and finds that all those equative constructions that do not display an overt marker associated with the degree predicate (corresponding to the first *as* in English *as tall as*) are non-quantificational. These are referred to as 'implict' equatives. But moreover, a bifurcation is found among 'explicit' equatives, that display an overt equative marker, between those whose marker functions otherwise as resultative or sufficientive morpheme (analogous to English *so*, related historically to *as*) and those whose marker functions otherwise as a degree demonstrative (analogous to English *that much*). The former is compatible with a factor modifier (*twice as much as*). The latter is not, but is otherwise similar to the former; in contrast to equatives without an overt marker, both classes of marked equative are non-evaluative (they do not entail that the degree property holds to a high degree; i.e., *Mary is as tall as John* does not mean that she is tall) and both classes have an 'at least' reading (*Mary is as tall as John* is compatible with her being taller than him). Rett develops a semantic analysis of both the non-quantificational implicit equatives, which involve a covert similarity relation, as well as for the equatives with a degree demonstrative marker, which involve direct reference to a particular degree. Specifically, the standard clause is type lowered to denote the maximum degree in the underlying degree set the standard clause denotes, which is then identified with the degree the demonstrative denotes in the main clause. Equative constructions, then, can be constructed through reference to degrees, rather than quantification over degrees.

In "Compounded Scales", Alan Bale takes up the issue of what exactly degrees are, and develops an approach to the comparative that bears a stronger resemblance to individual quantification than degree quantification. This approach pursues a possibility described by Cresswell (1976) that the values for u in the pairing $\langle u, > \rangle$ that in his system constitute a degree (see (15)) are not abstract coordinates but actual individuals. A scale of degrees of height determines a scale of individuals having those (maximal) degrees of height and vice versa. But Bale shows the two notions of scalarity (as rankings of individuals or of degrees) are not equally linguistically useful. Taking *-er* to relate individuals rather than degree sets presents a simple solution to the otherwise recalcitrant problem of why gradable predicates can be coordinated. On the degree quantifier view, *Seymour is more handsome and talented than Patrick is* is predicted to mean that Seymour has exactly the same degree of handsomeness and talentedness, and that this exceeds Patrick's degree of handsomeness and talentedness. But the sentence does not in fact require Seymour to have the same degree of handsomeness as talentedness, nor would this normally even be possible; handsomeness and talentedness correspond to different degree scales and do not intersect at all. But if, as Bale recommends, we understand *handsome* and *talented* to denote relations between individuals, so that Seymour bears the *handsome* relation to everyone he is more handsome than, then he can very well bear the conjunctive predicate *handsome and talented* to some other individual under the standard notion of what *and* means. In Bale's system, a 'degree' of some gradable relation is the set of individuals that bear that relation to all the same individuals, e.g., those that are identically handsome in the case of the gradable relation *handsome*. The comparative morpheme *-er* has a denotation similar to the phrasal comparative defined in (16) on this view (where in Bale's system the compared-to degree is derived from the *than*-clause by maximalization). Since each of the individuals in such an equivalence class can be replaced with any of the others preserving truth, this definition of *-er* (as relations between equivalence classes of individuals) is permutation invariant as long as the permutation respects these equivalence classes. Here as in the case of the (3-place) superlative discussed above, which also has an individual argument, the permutations we take into account in testing for invariance must preserve the various gradable relations in the model in order for the comparative to qualify as quantificational in this sense.

In a similar vein, Roger Schwarzschild develops an analysis in "From Possible Individuals to Scalar Segments" in which comparative constructions rank individuals rather than relating them to points on a scale. Developing Cresswell's suggestion mentioned above, he defines a degree as a set of pairs of individuals and possible worlds—'possible individuals'. Gradable predicates denote relations between individuals and degrees in this sense. Specifically, a gradable predicate relates an individual x to the set of possible individuals that x is greater than or equal to on the dimension in question. The central concept at work in comparative constructions is that of a 'segment'—a triple consisting of a starting degree, an ending degree, and a measure function μ_σ (where σ indexes the segment in question) that maps individuals to degrees, where degrees, again, are sets of possible individuals. A sentence like *Anu is taller than Raj* describes a segment whose measure is height, whose starting degree is $\mu_\sigma(\text{Raj})$ and whose ending degree is $\mu_\sigma(\text{Anu})$. Differentials are descriptions of such segments that specify the difference between the start and end points. The chapter explores various ways of morphologically dividing up the work of specifying the properties of segments. Ultimately, the English morpheme *-er* is argued to set the endpoint of a segment, and *-er* and the differential (when present) are argued to be present in both the matrix clause and the standard (*than*) clause in comparatives. The main work of comparison is done by *than*, which combines with the matrix and standard clauses to derive a description of a segment whose endpoint is specified by the matrix clause and whose starting point is specified by the standard clause. Because it puts a copy of the differential phrase (when one occurs) in both the main and standard clauses, this analysis accommodates cases in which a differential occurs in the scope of a world-introducing predicate in the matrix clause that is in turn in the scope of the comparative. For example, *Jack expects the engine to be one boxcar longer than Jill does* can be true even if Jack and Jill are not sure about the length of a boxcar, a situation that is paradoxical on other analyses of the comparative. This analysis also goes some way toward explaining why languages draw heavily on vocabulary associated with movement in space or time in comparative constructions, as in the Navajo construction discussed in Bogal-Allbritten and Coppock's contribution. There, the standard phrase is introduced by the spatial preposition *lááh* 'beyond', which specifies the starting point of a segment in Schwarzschild's analysis of the comparative, just as it specifies the starting point of a vector in its spatial use.

In "Measuring Cardinalities: Evidence from Differential Comparatives in French," Rajesh Bhatt and Vincent Homer discuss a curious restriction on differentials in French that relates to the proper analysis of quantity comparatives. In French, quality comparatives with differentials bear a strong resemblance to English, but differentials in quantity comparatives fall into two groups. Differentials that are themselves degree quantifiers like *beaucoup* 'a lot' pattern like English (*beaucoup plus de livres que* 'many more [of] books than'), but cardinal differentials cannot appear pre-nominally like other dfferentials do in French (**trois livres plus que* corresponding literally to 'three books more than'). It is possible to rescue this structure by inserting *de* 'of' before *plus*, as in *trois livres de plus que*, literally 'three books of more than'. However, Bhatt and Homer show that this has an entirely different structure from *beaucoup plus que* 'many more than', namely one in which the differential *trois livres* is the head of the nominal construction, and *de plus* a modifier of this noun. They postulate that *plus* has the same interpretation as elsewhere, it is a degree quantifier that relates two degree sets. In a sentence like *Marie a lu trois livres de plus que Jean* 'Marie has read three books [of] more than John', quantifier raising of the whole object noun phrase derives an abstract over things Marie read. As such, this is not an appropriate argument for *plus*, which, like *-er*, relates degree sets. However, borrowing from Grosu & Landman (1998), they claim that an operator occurs in object position that converts the degree argument into the corresponding amount of 'stuff', which must be books in this case to be commensurate with the book restriction on *plus*. This allows them to treat the abstraction over books that Marie read instead as an abstraction over degrees corresponding to the amounts of books Marie read, which provides an appropriate argument for *plus*. This mechanism allows for degree argument abstraction over individual argument slots in the syntax, which may play a role in quantity comparatives and superlatives more generally. It also shows, like the preceding papers, that the same underlying semantic relation between degree sets may manifest itself in a flexible variety of syntactic structures.

Haley Farkas and Alexis Wellwood experimentally investigate the interpretation of adverbial *more* in "Quantifying Events and Activities". A sentence like *Ann jumped more than Betty* does not explicitly specify the dimension on which *more* should be interpreted. It could mean she jumped higher, more times, or for a longer duration, raising the question of how the dimension of degree quantification is determined when it is underspecified by the syntactic context. In a series of experiments, Farkas and Wellwood investigate the role of the aspectual character of the modified verb and the role of aspects of the visual scene so described in making this determination. They ask participants (in separate blocks) whether one object in a visual scene they viewed moved or jumped more than another object, and compare their responses to responses to questions that ask directly whether the first object moved or jumped more times, longer, or higher than the second. Participants tend to evaluate *jump more* as meaning *more times* while *move more* can mean *more times* or *higher*, but still resists a *longer duration* interpretation. Two additional experiments show that altering aspects of the visual scene does not significantly change the responses recorded in the earlier experiments (insofar as the description *jump/move* is still appropriate to the scene). The fact that *more* is interpreted equally readily as degree quantification over times and height means that participants do not simply display a 'quantity over quality' bias in the interpretation of the comparative. The dimension of measurement is analysed by Schwarzschild (this volume) as the sole contribution of the gradable predicate in comparative constructions. In cases where the predicate modified by *more* is not itself gradable, Farkas and Wellwood show that the choice of dimension of gradability is nonetheless more heavily influenced by the meaning of that modifyee than by other factors. The interaction between event structure and the choice of dimension for the comparative reported here also reflects a more general interaction documented by Stassen (2006) between the morphological components of the comparative and the vocabulary of time and space, as exemplified in Navajo as described by Bogal-Allbritten and Coppock (this volume).

The final two contributions to this volume deal with the persistently challenging problem of the interpretation of individual quantifiers within *than*-clauses. In "Split Semantics for Non-monotonic Quantifiers in *Than*-Clauses", Linmin Zhang addresses the problem of non-monotonic cardinality quantifiers like *exactly two boys* when they occur in *than*-clauses. She begins with a non-monotonic interval theoretic analysis where *Mary is tall* denotes the minimal set containing Mary's exact height and no other degrees. *Mary is taller than John* says that there is a positive difference between Mary's height interval and John's. *Mary is taller than everyone* says that there is a positive difference between Mary's height interval and the smallest interval containing the heights of everyone else. In order to deal with *exactly two* in the *than*-clause, Zhang marries the interval theoretic approach to a dynamic semantic treatment of uniqueness based on Bumford (2017). On this approach, discourse referents are introduced for a plurality of boys and the interval including their heights as the structure is built, and at the sentence level it is asserted that there is a positive difference between Mary's height interval and the height interval of the boys. Only at this point is the uniqueness of *exactly two* and of *than* imposed. The latter requires the interval that includes the two boys' heights to be maximal, in this case meaning it extends from the lower bound of Mary's height interval downward indefinitely, and the former requires that the boys that have their heights in this interval be exactly two in number. This excludes the possibility that there is any third boy who is shorter than Mary. All the other boys are taller than Mary, if there are any. This analysis therefore captures an enigmatic interaction between quantification and degree, that allows non-monotonic quantifiers to be interpreted within *than*-clauses without falling victim to the false predictions that standard monotonic degree semantic analyses of the comparative make in such cases.

Nicholas Fleisher presents another strategy for dealing with quantifiers in *than*-clauses in "Nominal Quantifiers in *Than*-Clauses and Degree Questions". He capitalizes on parallels between the behavior of quantifiers in *than* clauses and in embedded questions, and analyzes *than*-clauses accordingly along the lines of degree questions (that ask *how much, how many*, etc.). Just as a naive degree semantic account of *John is taller than every girl* expects it to mean that he is taller than the shortest girl, as discussed in section 3, the embedded question *John knows how tall every girl is* is expected to mean that he knows the height of the shortest girl. Chierchia (1992) and others argue that the attested reading of embedded questions with quantifiers is a pair-list reading (a pairing of girls and their heights representing what John knows). Fleisher shows how pair list readings can be generated for *than* clauses containing quantifiers on the model of Chierchia's approach to embedded questions in combination with Nouwen and Dotlačil's (2017) claim that the quantifier has wide scope within the *than*-clause. He also shows that of two other readings for embedded questions, one, the single-point reading that presupposes, in the example above, that all the girls have the same height, carries over to *than*-clauses, though the reading is inconspicuous for pragmatic reasons. Another reading of embedded questions, the functional reading that licenses the continuation 'taller than her mother' to the embedded question cited above, is not available for *than*-clauses. But Fleisher attributes this to independent differences between embedded questions and *than* clauses. Unlike embedded degree questions, *than* clauses involve an operator that converts the most informative answer to the question to the degree that makes it true, for the purposes of comparison with the matrix clause denotation. The functional reading is not type-compatible with this conversion process. In this manner, Fleisher collapses the *than*-clause enigma with existing accounts of the interpretation of embedded degree questions, a unification that various empirical parallels warrant.

Acknowledgements

I would like to express my gratitude to all of the contributors who have enriched this volume, as well as to Johan van Benthem, Keir Moulton and an anonymous reviewer for comments on a draft of this introduction. My own contribution to this project was generously supported by the Austrian Science Fund (FWF), grant #P30409-G30.

References

Abrusán, Márta & Benjamin Spector. 2010. A semantics for degree questions based on intervals: negative islands and their obviation. *Journal of Semantics* 28(1). 107–147.

Alrenga, Peter & Christopher Kennedy. 2014. *No more* shall we part: quantifiers in English comparatives. *Natural Language Semantics* 22(1). 1–53.

Anderson, Curt & Marcin Morzycki. 2015. Degrees as kinds. *Natural Language and Linguistic Theory* 33(3). 791–828.

Bach, Emmon. 1986. Natural language metaphysics. In Ruth Barcan Marcus, George J.W. Dorn & Paul Weingartner (eds.), *Logic, methodology and philosophy of science VII*, 573–595. Amsterdam: Elsevier Science Publishers.

Bartsch, Renate & Theo Vennemann. 1973. *Semantic structures: a study in the relation between syntax and semantics.* Frankfurt: Athenaeum Verlag.

Barwise, John & Robin Cooper. 1981. Generalized quantifiers and natural language. *Linguistics and Philosophy* 4(2). 159–219.

Beck, Sigrid. 2010. Quantifiers in *than*-clauses. *Semantics and Pragmatics* 3(1). 1–72.

Beghelli, Filippo & Tim Stowell. 1997. Distributivity and negation: the syntax of *each* and *every*. In Anna Szabolcsi (ed.), *Ways of scope taking*, 71–107. Dordrecht: Kluwer Academic Publishers.

van Benthem, Johan. 1982. Later than late: on the logical origin of the temporal order. *Pacific Philosophical Quarterly* 63(2). 193–203.

van Benthem, Johan. 1983. Determiners and logic. *Linguistics and Philosophy* 6(4). 447–478.

van Benthem, Johan. 1984. Questions about quantifiers. *The Journal of Symbolic Logic* 49(2). 443–466.

van Benthem, Johan. 1986. *Essays in logical semantics.* Dordrecht: D. Reidel Publishing Company.

van Benthem, Johan. 2002. Invariance and definability: two faces of logical constants. In Wilfried Sieg, Richard Sommer & Carolyn Talcott (eds.), *Reflections of the foundations of mathematics: essays in honor of Sol Feferman*, 426–446. Natick, Mass.: The Association for Symbolic Logic.

Bhatt, Rajesh & Roumyana Pancheva. 2004. Late merger of degree clauses. *Linguistic Inquiry* 35(1). 1–46.

Bhatt, Rajesh & Shoichi Takahashi. 2011. Reduced and unreduced phrasal comparatives. *Natural Language and Linguistic Theory* 29(3). 581–620.

Bobaljik, Jonathan. 2012. *Universals in comparative morphology: suppletion, superlatives, and the structure of words.* Cambridge, Mass.: MIT Press.

Bresnan, Joan. 1973. Syntax of the comparative clause construction in English. *Linguistic Inquiry* 4(3). 275–343.

Bresnan, Joan. 1975. Comparative deletion and constraints on transformations. *Linguistic Analysis* 1(1). 25–74.

Bruening, Benjamin. 2001. QR obeys superiority: frozen scope and ACD. *Linguistic Inquiry* 32(2). 233–273.

Bumford, Dylan. 2017. Split scope definites: relative superlatives and Haddock descriptions. *Linguistics and Philosophy* 40(6). 549–593.

Carlson, Greg. 1977a. A unified analysis of the English bare plural. *Linguistics and Philosophy* 1(3). 413–457.

Carlson, Greg. 1977b. Amount relatives. *Language* 53(3). 520–542.

Chierchia, Gennaro. 1992. Questions with quantifiers. *Natural Language Semantics* 1(2). 181–234.

Chierchia, Gennaro. 1998. Reference to kinds across language. *Natural Language Semantics* 6(4). 339–405.

Chomsky, Noam. 1977. On wh-movement. In Peter Culicover, Thomas Wasow & Adrian Akmajian (eds.), *Formal syntax*, 71–132. New York: Academic Press.

Chung, Sandra & William Ladusaw. 2004. *Restriction and saturation*. Cambridge, Mass.: MIT Press.

Cooper, Robin. 1996. The role of situations in generalized quantifiers. In Shalom Lappin (ed.), *The handbook of contemporary semantic theory*, 65–86. Oxford: Blackwell.

Coppock, Elizabeth & David Beaver. 2015. Definiteness and determinacy. *Linguistics and Philosophy* 38(5). 377–435.

Corver, Norbert. 1997. Much-support as a last resort. *Linguistic Inquiry* 28(1). 119–164.

Cresswell, Max. 1976. The semantics of degree. In Barbara Partee (ed.), *Montague grammar*, 261–292. New York: Academic Press.

Cresti, Diana. 1995. Extraction and reconstruction. *Natural Language Semantics* 3(1). 79–122.

Diesing, Molly. 1992. *Indefinites*. Cambridge, Mass.: MIT Press.

Dobrovie-Sorin, Carmen. 2013. Most: the view from mass quantification. In Maria Aloni, Michael Franke & Floris Roelofsen (eds.), *Proceedings of the 19th Amsterdam Colloquium*, 99–106. Amsterdam: Institute for Logic, Language & Computation.

Dobrovie-Sorin, Carmen. 2015. Two types of *most*. In Sarah D'Antonio, Mary Moroney & Carol Rose Little (eds.), *Proceedings of SALT 25*, 394–412. Washington, D.C.: Linguistic Society of America.

Dobrovie-Sorin, Carmen & Ion Giurgea. to appear. *Quantity superlatives and proportional quantification: a crosslinguistic analysis of* most. Oxford: Oxford University Press.

Dotlačil, Jakub & Rick Nouwen. 2016. The comparative and degree pluralities. *Natural Language Semantics* 24(1). 45–78.

Dummett, Michael. 1973. *Frege: philosophy of language*. New York: Harper & Row.

Dummett, Michael. 1991. *Frege: philosophy of mathematics*. Cambridge, MA: Harvard University Press.

Farkas, Donka & Katalin Kiss. 2000. On the comparative and absolute readings of superlatives. *Natural Language and Linguistic Theory* 18(3). 417–455.

Fauconnier, Gilles. 1975. Pragmatic scales and logical structure. *Linguistic Inquiry* 6(3). 353–376.

von Fintel, Kai. 1994. *Restrictions on quantifier domains*. University of Massachusetts, Amherst dissertation.

von Fintel, Kai. 1997. Bare plurals, bare conditionals, and *only*. *Journal of Semantics* 14(1). 1–56.

Fleisher, Nicholas. 2016. Comparing theories of quantifiers in *than* clauses: lessons from downward-entailing differentials. *Semantics and Pragmatics* 9(4). 1–23.

Fox, Danny. 2002. Antecedent-contained deletion and the copy theory of movement. *Linguistic Inquiry* 33(1). 63–96.

Fox, Danny & Martin Hackl. 2006. The universal density of measurement. *Linguistics and Philosophy* 29(5). 537–586.

Frege, Gottlob. 1884. *Die Grundlagen der Arithmetik*. Breslau: Koebner.

Gajewski, Jon. 2008. More on quantifiers in comparative clauses. In Jon Gajewski, Tova Friedman & Satoshi Ito (eds.), *Proceedings of SALT 18*, 340–357. Ithaca, NY: LSA.

Gawron, Jean Mark. 1995. Comparatives, superlatives, and resolution. *Linguistics and Philosophy* 18(4). 333–380.

Geurts, Bart & Rick Nouwen. 2007. At Least et al.: the semantics of scalar modifiers. *Language* 83(3). 533–559.

Grosu, Alexander & Fred Landman. 1998. Strange relatives of the third kind. *Natural Language Semantics* 6(2). 125–170.

Hackl, Martin. 2000. *Comparative quantifiers*. Massachusetts Institute of Technology dissertation.

Hackl, Martin. 2009. On the grammar and processing of proportional quantifiers: *most* vs. *more than half*. *Natural Language Semantics* 17(1). 63–98.

Hankamer, Jorge. 1973. Unacceptable ambiguity. *Linguistic Inquiry* 4(1). 17–68.

Heim, Irene. 1983. File change semantics and the familiarity theory of definiteness. In Rainer Bäuerle, Christoph Schwarze & Arnim von Stechow (eds.), *Meaning, use, and interpretation of language*, 164–189. Berlin: Walter de Gruyter.

Heim, Irene. 1985. Notes on comparatives and related matters. Ms., University of Texas, Austin.

Heim, Irene. 1999. Notes on superlatives. Ms., University of Texas, Austin.

Heim, Irene. 2001. Degree operators and scope. In Caroline Fery & Wolfgang Sternefeld (eds.), *Audiatur vox sapientiae. a festschrift for Arnim von Stechow*, 214–239. Berlin: Akademie Verlag.

Heim, Irene. 2006a. *Little*. In Masayuki Gibson & Jonathan Howell (eds.), *Proceedings of SALT 16*, 35–58. Washington, D.C.: Linguistic Society of America.

Heim, Irene. 2006b. *Remarks on comparative clauses as generalized quantifiers*. Cambridge, Mass.: Ms., MIT.

Heim, Irene & Angelika Kratzer. 1998. *Semantics in generative grammar*. Malden, MA: Blackwell.

Heycock, Caroline. 1995. Asymmetries in reconstruction. *Linguistic Inquiry* 26(4). 547–570.

Higginbotham, James & Robert May. 1981. Questions, quantifiers and crossing. *The Linguistic Review* 1(1). 41–80.

Higgins, Francis Roger. 1979. *The pseudo-cleft construction in English*. New York: Garland.

Hoeksema, Jack. 1983. Negative polarity and the comparative. *Natural Language and Linguistic Theory* 1(3). 403–434.

Hofweber, Thomas. 2005. Number determiners, numbers, and arithmetic. *The Philosophical Review* 114(2). 179–225.

Ionin, Tania & Ora Matushansky. 2006. The composition of complex cardinals. *Journal of Semantics* 23(4). 315–360.

Kadmon, Nirit. 1993. *On unique and non-unique reference and asymmetric quantification*. New York: Garland.

Kamp, Hans & Uwe Reyle. 1993. *From discourse to logic*. Dordrecht: Kluwer Academic Publishers.

Kayne, Richard. 2005. A note on the syntax of quantity in English. In *Movement and silence*, 176–214. Oxford: Oxford University Press.

Keenan, Edward & Jonathan Stavi. 1986. A semantic characterization of natural language determiners. *Linguistics and Philosophy* 9(3). 253–326.

Kennedy, Chris. 1999. *Projecting the adjective: the syntax and semantics of gradability and comparison*. New York: Garland Publishing.

Kennedy, Chris. 2013. A scalar semantics for scalar readings of number words. In Ivano Caponigro & Carlo Cecchetto (eds.), *From grammar to meaning: the spontaneous logicality of language*, 172–200. Cambridge: Cambridge University Press.

Kennedy, Chris. 2015. A "de-Fregean" semantics (and neo-Gricean pragmatics) for modified and unmodified numerals. *Semantics and Pragmatics* 8(10). 1–44.

Klein, Ewan. 1980. A semantics for positive and comparative adjectives. *Linguistics and Philosophy* 4(1). 1–45.

Krifka, Manfred. 1989. Nominal reference, temporal constitution and quantification in event semantics. In Renate Bartsch, Johan van Benthem & Peter van Emde Boas (eds.), *Semantics and contextual expression*, 75–115. Foris Publications.

Krifka, Manfred. 1999. At least some determiners aren't determiners. In Ken Turner (ed.), *The semantics/pragmatics interface from different points of view*, 257–291. Elsevier Science.

Ladusaw, William A. 1979. *Polarity sensitivity as inherent scope relations*. Amherst, MA: University of Massachusetts, Amherst dissertation.

Landman, Fred. 2004. *Indefinites and the type of sets*. Oxford: Oxford University Press.

Landman, Meredith & Marcin Morzycki. 2003. Event-kinds and the representation of manner. In Nancy Antrim, Grant Goodall, Martha Schulte-Nafeh & Vida Samiian (eds.), *Proceedings of the Western Conference on Linguistics (WECOL)*, 136–147. Fresno: California State University.

Larson, Richard. 1988. Scope and comparatives. *Linguistics and Philosophy* 11(1). 1–26.

Lechner, Winfried. 2001. Reduced and phrasal comparatives. *Natural Language and Linguistic Theory* 19(4). 683–735.

Lechner, Winfried. 2004. *Ellipsis in Comparatives*. Berlin/New York: Mouton de Gruyter.

Lindenbaum, A. & A. Tarski. 1936. Über die Beschränktheit der Ausdrucksmittel deduktiver Theorien. *Ergebnisse eines mathematischen Kolloquiums* 7. 15–22.

Lindström, Per. 1966. First-order predicate logic with generalized quantifiers. *Theoria* 32(3). 186–195.

Link, Godehard. 1983. The logical analysis of plurals and mass terms: a lattice-theoretical approach. In Rainer Bäuerle, Christoph Schwarze & Arnim von Stechow (eds.), *Meaning, use and interpretation of language*. DeGruyter.

Lønning, Jan Tore. 1987. Collective readings of definite and indefinite noun phrases. In Peter Gärdenfors (ed.), *Generalized quantifers: linguistic and logical approaches*, 203–235. Dordrecht: D. Reidel.

Matushansky, Ora. 2002. Tipping the scales: the syntax of scalarity in the complement of *seem*. *Syntax* 5(3). 219–276.

Mautner, F. 1946. An extension of Klein's Erlanger Program: logic as invariant-theory. *American Journal of Mathematics* 68(3). 345–384.

May, Robert. 1977. *The grammar of quantification*. Massachusetts Institute of Technology dissertation.

May, Robert. 1981. Movement and binding. *Linguistic Inquiry* 12(2). 215–243.

May, Robert. 1985. *Logical form: its structure and derivation*. Cambridge, Massachusetts: MIT Press.

Moltmann, Friederike. 2013. Reference to numbers in natural language. *Philosophical Studies* 162(3). 499–536.

Montague, Richard. 1969. On the nature of certain philosophical entities. *The Monist* 53(2). 159–194.

Montague, Richard. 1973. The proper treatment of quantification in ordinary English. In Jaakko Hintikka, Julius Moravcsik & Patrick Suppes (eds.), *Approaches to natural language: proceedings of the 1970 Stanford Workshop on Grammar and Semantics*, 221–242. Dordrecht: D. Reidel Publishing Company.

Mostowski, Andrzej. 1957. On a generalization of quantifiers. *Fundamenta Mathematicae* 44(1). 12–36.

Nouwen, Rick & Jakub Dotlačil. 2017. The scope of nominal quantifiers in comparative clauses. *Semantics and Pragmatics* 10(15). 1–20.

Partee, Barbara. 1987. Noun phrase interpretation and type-shifting principles. In Jeroen Groenendijk, Dick de Jongh & Martin Stokhof (eds.), *Studies in discourse representation theory and the theory of generalized quantifiers*, 115–143. Dordrecht: Foris Publications.

Peters, Stanley & Dag Westerståhl. 2006. *Quantifiers in language and logic*. Oxford: Clarendon Press.

Postal, Paul. 1974. On certain ambiguities. *Linguistic Inquiry* 5(3). 367–425.

Rett, Jessica. 2006. How *many* maximizes in the Balkan sprachbund. In Masayuki Gibson & Jonathan Howell (eds.), *Proceedings of SALT XVI*, 190–207. Ithaca, NY: Cornell University.

Romero, Maribel. 2012. Modal superlatives: a compositional analysis. *Natural Language Semantics* 21(1). 79–110.

van Rooij, Robert. 2008. Comparatives and quantifiers. In Olivier Bonami & Patricia

Cabredo Hofherr (eds.), *Empirical issues in syntax and semantics 7*, 423–444. Paris: Colloque de Syntaxe et Sémantique à Paris.

Schwarzschild, Roger. 2005. Measure phrases as modifiers of adjectives. *Recherches linguistique de Vincennes* 34. 207–228.

Schwarzschild, Roger. 2006. The role of dimensions in the syntax of noun phrases. *Syntax* 9(1). 67–110.

Schwarzschild, Roger. 2008. The semantics of comparatives and other degree constructions. *Language and Linguistics Compass* 2(2). 308–331.

Schwarzschild, Roger & Karina Wilkinson. 2002. Quantifiers in comparatives: a semantics of degree based on intervals. *Natural Language Semantics* 10(1). 1–41.

Scontras, Gregory. 2014. *The semantics of measurement*. Cambridge, Mass.: Harvard University dissertation.

Seuren, Pieter. 1973. The comparative. In Ferenc Kiefer & Nicholas Ruwet (eds.), *Generative grammar in Europe*, 528–564. Dordrecht: D. Reidel Publishing Company.

Sharvit, Yael & Penka Stateva. 2002. Superlative expressions, context, and focus. *Linguistics and Philosophy* 25(4). 453–504.

Snyder, Eric. 2017. Numbers and cardinalities: what's really wrong with the easy argument for numbers. *Linguistics and Philosophy* 40(4). 373–400.

Solt, Stephanie. 2011. How many *mosts*? In Ingo Reich, Eva Horch & Dennis Pauly (eds.), *Proceedings of Sinn und Bedeutung 15*, 565–579. Saarbrücken: Saarland University Press.

Solt, Stephanie. 2015. Q-adjectives and the semantics of quantity. *Journal of Semantics* 32(2). 221–273.

Sportiche, Dominique. 2005. Division of labor between merge and move: strict locality of selection and apparent reconstruction paradoxes. http://ling.auf.net/lingBuzz/000163.

Stanley, Jason. 2000. Context and logical form. *Linguistics and Philosophy* 23(4). 391–434.

Stanley, Jason. 2002. Nominal restriction. In Georg Peter & Gerhard Preyer (eds.), *Logical form and language*, 365–388. Oxford University Press.

Stanley, Jason & Zoltán Szabó. 2000. On quantifier domain restriction. *Mind and Language* 15(2–3). 219–261.

Stassen, Leonard. 2006. Comparative constructions. In Keith Brown (ed.), *Encyclopedia of language and linguistics*, 686–690. Oxford: Elsevier.

von Stechow, Arnim. 1984. Comparing semantic theories of comparison. *Journal of Semantics* 3(1). 1–77.

Strawson, P.F. 1974. *Subject and predicate in logic and grammar*. London: Methuen.

Szabolcsi, Anna. 1986. Comparative superlatives. In Naoki Fukui (ed.), *MIT working papers in linguistics, vol. 8*, 245–265. Cambridge, Mass.: MIT Press.

Szabolcsi, Anna. 2010. *Quantification*. Cambridge: Cambridge University Press.

Szabolcsi, Anna. 2012. Compositionality without word boundaries: (the) more and (the) most. In Anca Chereches (ed.), *Proceedings of SALT 22*, 1–25. Washington, D.C.: Linguistic Society of America.

Wellwood, Alexis. 2015. On the semantics of comparison across categories. *Linguistics and Philosophy* 38(1). 67–101.

Westerståhl, Dag. 1985a. Determiners and context sets. In Johan van Benthem & Alice ter Meulen (eds.), *Generalized quantifiers in natural language*, 45–71. Dordrecht: Foris.

Westerståhl, Dag. 1985b. Logical constants in quantifier languages. *Linguistics and Philosophy* 8(4). 387–413.

Williams, Edwin. 1977. Discourse and logical form. *Linguistic Inquiry* 8(1). 101–139.

Winter, Yoad. 2001. *Flexibility principles in Boolean semantics*. Cambridge, Mass.: MIT Press.

Zhang, Linmin & Jia Ling. 2015. Comparatives revisited: downward-entailing differentials do not threaten encapsulation theories. In Thomas Brochhagen, Floris Roelofsen & Nadine Theiler (eds.), *Proceedings of the 20th Amsterdam Colloquium*, 478–487. Amsterdam.

CHAPTER 2

Indeterminate Numerals and Their Alternatives

Curt Anderson

1   Introduction

Approximation in English can be expressed in various ways. For instance, the adverbials *almost* and *approximately* are some ways of expressing that a numerical expression should be construed approximately, that is, to express uncertainty regarding the precise number that expression should denote. Prepositions provide another way of expressing approximation.

(1)   a. around ten people
      b. between ten and twenty people
      c. close to ten people

In this paper, I look at a type of approximative construction in English involving numerals and an indefinite determiner, as in (2) below. With these numerals, which I call indeterminate numerals, *some* appears post-numerally, affixed to the preceding numeral. The interpretation in these examples is one where the indeterminate numeral expresses a range of possible numbers, but where the speaker doesn't know the precise number that satisfies the existential claim expressed by the sentence, as observed by Anderson (2015, 2016). These numerals are theoretically interesting due to their reliance on the epistemic indefinite *some*. This sets it apart syntactically from other instances of approximation, in that the element that is expressing approximation is not an adverbial or a preposition.

(2)   a. Twenty-some people arrived.
      b. His forty-some years of experience were devoted to human resources.
      c. I could have it entirely full of small icons and fit a hundred some icons on one screen.
      d. More than half of the expenditure of eighty-some thousand dollars is for soft costs.

However, these numerals are restricted syntactically. *Some* is not a simple ad-numeral affix, but seems to be integrated within the syntactic structure of

© KONINKLIJKE BRILL NV, LEIDEN, 2020 | DOI:10.1163/9789004431515_003 the numeral; only numerals which support additive composition can support *some*.

(3) a. *five-some
    b. *ten-some
    c. *fifteen-some

Interestingly, these numerals are also curious in that they simultaneously express both an upper-bounded and lower-bounded meaning. *Twenty-some*, for instance, expresses that any number between 20 and 30 is a possibility. In some ways, this makes them superficially similar to modified numerals such as *at least ten* and *not more than twenty*, but also different from them in having this sort of two-sided meaning.

Discussion of the semantics of numerals has often gone hand-in-hand with that of canonical quantificational determiners like *every* and *most*, with the question being of how and whether cardinal numerals differ from quantificational determiners in their type-theoretic properties. Possibilities include treating numerals as quantificational determiners (type $\langle et, \langle et, t \rangle \rangle$; e.g., Barwise & Cooper 1981, Hofweber 2005), as degree quantifiers (type $\langle dt, t \rangle$; see Kennedy 2015), as cardinality predicates (type $\langle e, t \rangle$; e.g., Landman 2003, Rothstein 2013) or predicate modifiers (type $\langle et, et \rangle$; e.g. Ionin & Matushansky 2006), and as degree-denoting terms (type d) with additional functional machinery mediating between the noun phrase and the numeral (e.g., Solt 2015).[1] Likewise, modified numerals like *at least sixty* and *no more than fifteen*, which indeterminate numerals bear some resemblance to, also have generated discussion as to their logical form, particularly about whether they are quantificational determiners (Barwise & Cooper 1981) or degree quantifiers (Nouwen 2010, Kennedy 2015). Indeed, some surveys of quantification devote space to discussion of both modified and unmodified numerals (for instance, Szabolcsi 2010: chapters 9 and 10).

These indeterminate numerals also bring into relief the way that degrees have been implicated in many areas of natural language meaning. That degree constructions such as comparatives and superlatives are degree quantifiers seems to now be the standard view (see Morzycki's (2016) textbook for discussion of these and other degree constructions, for instance), showing that there exist parallels between quantification over individuals and degrees. Degrees have also been implicated in many phenomena related to gradability and

---

1 See Geurts 2006 for additional discussion of these issues.

scalarity across lexical categories (not just gradable adjectives), again showing that degree variables and reference to degrees is as pervasive as that of individuals. The present chapter contributes to this view by showing that at least one indefinite determiner, *some*, can also quantify over degrees. Having degrees represented in the determiner system nudges this parallelism between degrees and individuals even further, and (as noted by Hallman (this volume)), reflects the way degrees have steadily worked their way into systems once thought to be reserved for operations over sets of individuals.

With the big picture in mind, I return to the matter at hand: indeterminate numerals. My analysis of indeterminate numerals makes use of a few key ingredients. First, I claim that the *some* in indeterminate numerals is the epistemic indefinite *some*. As an epistemic indefinite, *some* signals uncertainty regarding the precise referent that satisfies a description. *Some* has an identical flavor with numerals, in that it fails to commit the speaker to knowledge of the particular number that satisfies the numerical description. Second, the ignorance is derived from the properties of *some* itself. I take *some* to impose a requirement that there exists a non-singleton set of alternatives (in this case, numerical alternatives), with ignorance derived as an implicature. These alternatives are part of the compositional machinery of the sentence, following the framework developed by Kratzer & Shimoyama (2002). Third, I make a proposal for the syntax of indeterminate numerals, arguing that the numeral itself forms a constituent (to the exclusion of the NP, contra Ionin & Matushansky (2006)).

Looking at indeterminate numerals expands on our understanding of these groups of expressions and how quantificational elements like indefinite determiners interact with degrees denoted in domains other than the adjective phrase. Indeterminate numerals show an interaction of degree and quantification due to how properties of the indefinite determiner *some* (particularly, its ability to force the generation of multiple Hamblin alternatives) interact with the numeral to produce quantification over sets of alternatives that vary by degree. Additionally, looking at these numerals gives us insight into the division of labor between asserted and implicated meanings in complex numerals: I show that numerals modified by *some* assert their lower bound, but that the upper-bound is generated via implicature.

I structure this chapter in the following way. First, in section 2, I discuss additional background data on English indeterminate numerals as well as link them to the broader category of epistemic indefinites. Next, in section 3, I give a syntax for numerals in general that will be necessary to have for the analysis of indeterminate numerals. Section 4 lays out background on the alternative semantics used in the rest of the analysis in the paper. Section 5 develops an account of the semantics of ordinary numerals, while sections 6 and 7 develop the analysis of indeterminate numerals.

2 Background Data

2.1 *Expanding on the Phenomenon*

Modified numerals such as *at least 10* and *not more than 20* have bounded interpretations, either lower-bounded (like with *at least*) or upper-bounded (like with *not more than*). What sets indeterminate numerals apart from many other cases of modified numerals is that they are both lower-bounded and upper-bounded. For instance, the numerals in the examples in (2) are associated with the intervals as in (4). The salient fact about this interval is that its lower bound starts at the modified numeral, and has an upper-bound as determined by keeping the base of the modified numeral and increasing the multiplier by one unit. For instance, *twenty* is represented as 2 × 10, so by keeping the base 10 constant and increasing the multiplier from 2 to 3, we arrive at the upper-bound for *twenty-some*. Likewise, *hundred* is represented as 1 × 100, so the upper-bound of *hundred-some* is represented as 2 × 100.

(4) a. twenty-some ⤳ (20, 30)
    b. forty-some ⤳ (40, 50)
    c. hundred-some ⤳ (100, 200)

This makes indeterminate numerals different than approximators, such as *around* and *about*. Although they seem similar in that they involve a number that is close to what is being modified, *around* implicates a halo of numbers centered around the modified numeral (for instance, something like [18, 22] in (5)), while the interval for the indeterminate numeral is bounded on the lower end by the number denoted by the numeral.

(5) I saw around twenty dogs during my walk today.
    (= I saw between 18 and 22 days during my walk today.)

It's tricky to show that there is a particular number that sets the lower bound, due to the epistemic requirement that the speaker not know the precise number that satisfies the claim. But, if we pair an utterance with a fact about the world that the speaker learns later on, we can show that the utterance was either true or false. When we pair (6) with (7a), where the fact of the matter is that there was a number of dogs incompatible with *twenty-some*, namely 19 dogs, the sentence is judged false. However, if (6) is paired with (7b), where the fact is that there were actually 23 dogs the speaker saw, then the utterance is judged to be true. This shows that the utterance really is lower-bounded by the numeral that is being modified.

(6) I saw twenty-some dogs during my walk today.

(7) a. *Speaker later learns he saw only 19 dogs:*
    (6) is judged to have been false.
    b. *Speaker later learns he saw 23 dogs:*
    (6) is judged to have been true.

Moreover, the lower-bound is at the modified numeral, but does not include the denotation of said numeral. The examples in (8) and (9) are quite marginal, providing evidence that the lower-bound for e.g. *twenty-some* does not include the number 20, but rather starts at 21.

(8) ??I saw twenty-some dogs today, namely exactly twenty.

(9) (*Situation: John ate exactly twenty cookies.*)
    ??John ate twenty-some cookies.

Returning to the question of how and where *some* is licensed, what we observe is that indeterminate numerals in English are only possible if the modified numeral is one that can combine additively with another numeral. When the numeral cannot combine additively with another numeral, as is the case with *one* through *nineteen*, an indeterminate numeral is impossible.

(10) a. *ten-some
     b. *five-some

(11) a. *ten-five   (expected: 15)
     b. *five-one   (expected: 6)

Moreover, *some* does not have to occur after the entire phrase corresponding to the numeral. If a smaller constituent can combine additively with another numeral, *some* can appear in that position, as in (12).

(12) More than half of the expenditure of eighty-some thousand dollars is for soft costs.

A brief discussion of additivity is in order. What I mean by additivity is that the meaning of certain numerals is derived via addition of degrees. In the case of the numeral *twenty-five*, for instance, the meaning of *twenty-five* is derived via addition of the meanings for *twenty* and *five*, e.g. 20 + 5. Not all numerals support additive composition with a constituent to their right; *twenty* can combine additively with another numeral since the constituent immediately to its right (informally speaking) is semantically interpreted as being added to the meaning of *twenty*, but this is not a property of *ten*, since *ten* does not additive combine with a numeral to its right (e.g., **ten five* for 15). This contrasts with multiplicative composition, where some numerals combine with another numeral via multiplication of that numeral plus a base, such as with *ten thousand* or *two million*. These observations regarding the compositionality of the numeral system are not new, and go back at least to Hurford (1975), who provides an early phrase structural account of numerals in a variety of languages.

Perhaps unsurprisingly, these same facts are also found with measure phrases. This shows that we are looking at a phenomenon that is quite generally related to measurement and degree, and not only to counting constructions within the DP.

(13) a. The Empire State Building is 440-some meters tall.
 b. He is 20-some years old.

An understanding of the position of *some* in the syntax of the numeral, the lower and upper-bound of the scale, and the ignorance in the construction form the basic desideratum of an account of English indeterminate numerals.

2.2 Indeterminate Numerals as Epistemic Indefinites

The driving idea behind the analysis is that indeterminate numerals like *twenty-some* are a variety of epistemic indefinite. Epistemic indefinites are indefinites that convey ignorance on the part of the speaker as to the particular referent of some nominal expression. They are quite robustly attested cross-linguistically with examples in English (*some*), German (*irgendein*), Spanish (*algún*), Romanian (*vreun*), Hungarian (*vagy*), and Japanese (the WH *ka* series of pronouns).[2]

Rather than express ignorance as to the identify of an individual, however, what the indeterminate numeral does is express ignorance as to the precise number that satisfies a description. In other words, while ordinary epistemic indefinites contribute uncertainty as to the witnessing individual for a linguis-

---

2 See Haspelmath 1997 and Alonso-Ovalle & Menéndez-Benito 2013 for overviews.

tic description, indeterminate numerals contribute uncertainty with respect to the witnessing number. To motivate this view that indeterminate numerals really are epistemic indefinites, we have to first compare their properties with another well-known epistemic indefinite. The epistemic indefinites that I compare the indeterminacy-building element in indeterminate numerals to are *some* in its canonical determiner use, as well as Spanish *algún*.

Some implicates that the speaker doesn't know the precise identity of the person being referred to. The examples in (14) and (15) below (attributable to Strawson (1974)) demonstrate this contrast with *a* and *some*. While person B cannot ask the question about who was shot in the exchange in (14), due to person A having used *some*, this is allowed in (15), due to the indefinite *a* being compatible with knowledge on the part of the speaker.

(14) A: Some cabinet minister has been shot!
B: #Who?

(15) A: A cabinet minister has been shot!
B: Who?

Comparing the behavior of the indeterminate numeral to *some*, we can see that it requires the same expression of ignorance. This is illustrated in (16), where someone cannot follow-up an utterance that uses an indeterminate numeral by asking for an exact quantity.[3]

(16) A: Twenty-some students are taking my class this semester
B: #How many?

Alonso-Ovalle & Menéndez-Benito (2010) note that the ignorance inference with *algún* can be reinforced with other linguistic material. This sets it apart from presuppositional content and asserted content, which cannot be reinforced, due to being entailed. Thus, the fact that the ignorance inference can

---

3 Keir Moulton (p.c.) suggests that *precisely how many* is a better question for B to follow-up with than *how many*. My own judgements here aren't very firm, but I think that *precisely how many* can be acceptable if the implicature generated by *some* is not ignorance in this case, but rather relevance or indifference. It's probably generally the case that the implicature that can be generated by *some* is not just ignorance, but a variety of implicatures related to being unable or unwilling to name an individual or degree. That observation that ignorance is one member of a family of inferences is a point made by Condoravdi (2015) for *wh-ever* free relatives and Coppock (2016) for *at least* and *at most*.

be reinforced suggests that the inference is not entailed, but is rather an implicature. (17) demonstrates this with *algún*, where the clause following *pero* 'but' reinforces the ignorance expressed in the first clause. (18) demonstrates an equivalent sentence in English, where the epistemic indefinite determiner *some* is used.

(17) *María sale   con algún   estudiante del   departamento de*
    María goes out with ALGUN student   of the department   of
    lingüística, pero no sé   con quién
    linguistics, but   not I know with whom.
    'María is dating some student in the linguistics department, but I don't know who.' (Alonso-Ovalle & Menéndez-Benito 2010: (45d))

(18) Mary is dating some student in the linguistics department, but I don't know who.

Likewise, the expression of ignorance in the indeterminate numeral can be reinforced, drawing an additional parallel between known epistemic indefinites like *some* and *algún* on one hand, and indeterminate numerals.

(19) Mary cooked twenty-some pies, but I don't know exactly how many.[4]

Alonso-Ovalle & Menéndez-Benito (2010) argue that Spanish *algún* is compatible with partial ignorance. A speaker using *algún* is not committed to total ignorance regarding the witness of an existential claim (which individual(s) make the proposition true), merely that they cannot in principle narrow the domain of the indefinite to fewer than two choices. If *algún* required total ignorance, that all epistemic possibilities are available, examples such as the one in (20) would be malformed, due to restrictions being placed on the set of alternatives. As (20) shows, however, *algún* doesn't require that all possibilities be open, only that there be at least two. This also seems to hold for *some*, in that a similar example in English is also perfectly licit in the same scenario.

---

4 This example gets worse or even unacceptable if *exactly* is left off: **Mary cooked twenty-some pies, but I don't know how many*. My suspicion is that this is due to a clash between *twenty-some* committing the speaker to some measure of pies (just not an exact measure), and *I don't know how many* committing the speaker to total ignorance. Since the speaker does assert he knows some number, just not the precise number, he can't go on to further assert he doesn't know the number at all.

(20) SCENARIO: María, Juan, and Pedro are playing hide-and-seek in their country house. Juan is hiding. María and Pedro haven't started looking for Juan yet. Pedro believes that Juan is not hiding in the garden or in the barn: he is sure that Juan is inside the house. Furthermore, Pedro is sure that Juan is not in the bathroom or in the kitchen. As far as he knows, Juan could be in any of the other rooms in the house. Pedro utters:
Juan tiene que estar en alguna habitación de la casa.
Juan has to be in ALGUNA room of the house
'Juan must be in a room of the house.' (based on Alonso-Ovalle & Menéndez-Benito 2010: (14) & (15))

(21) Juan must be in some room in the house.

Mendia (2018) makes a similar observation for indeterminate numerals; these numerals are also compatible with partial ignorance regarding the witnessing number, as shown in (22). A score in basketball is usually two points, but a triple is worth three points; adding additional information about the manner of scoring in this way serves to narrow down the set of possibilities for how much Michael Jordan actually scored.

(22) That night Michael Jordan scored twenty-some points in triples. (Mendia 2018: (43))

To conclude this section, indeterminate numerals appear to pattern with other epistemic indefinites in that they also enforce an epistemic requirement on the speaker that the speaker not be able to make a precise claim as to the identity of the referent. With respect to numbers, this amounts to the speaker not being able to commit as to which particular number satisfies a description. This is similar to the behavior of *some* and *algún*. Moreover, like *algún* and *some*, the ignorance inference can be reinforced, making it pattern with implicatures rather than presuppositions and assertions. In the next sections, I'll develop an analysis of indeterminate numerals that uses insights from Alonso-Ovalle & Menéndez-Benito (2010)'s analysis of *algún*, and show how the ignorance inference can be generated as an implicature.

3 A Syntax for Numerals

3.1 Indeterminate Numerals Are in Specifiers

The syntax of numerals has largely revolved around two competing approaches, what Danon (2012) calls the head-complement construction and the spec-head construction. Although the precise details regarding various proposals for these types of approaches vary, what primarily differentiates them is whether multiplicative numerals, such as *two hundred*, are constituents (to the exclusion of the NP they appear along with) or are represented hierarchically along the spine of the noun phrase. The possibilities are schematically represented in (23) and (24). In (23), the head-complement approach, the numerals are located along the spine of the tree, with the base numeral *hundred* taking the NP as its complement. This contrasts with the spec-head approach in (24), where the numeral itself is a constituent, to the exclusion of the NP.

(23)  (head-complement)

(24)  (spec-head)

The facts regarding indeterminate numerals suggest that the appropriate structure in their case is a structure along the lines of (24), where the numeral (including *some*) form a constituent. The argument is as follows. First, suppose that the indeterminate numeral structure is as in (25), where *some* has as its complement the NP.

(25) (rejected analysis)

We observe that, in addition to *some*, English also allows for an equivalent structure containing *something*, as in (26).

(26) Similarly, Lauren and the other twenty-something people I observed had some structured group meals [...] (Google)

The ability of *something* to also appear in the indeterminate numeral construction is important, because it shows that *some* cannot be taking the NP as its complement. We are able to see that *something* cannot merge with an NP (possibly due to *some*'s complement already being filled by the noun *thing*). If the structure for indeterminate numerals were as in (25), with *something* in the same position as *some*, we would be forced to assume the existence of two separate instances of *something*: one that is incapable of appearing with an NP, and another that can have an NP as its complement, as in (28).

(27) some(*thing) people

(28) [twenty[something years]] old (rejected analysis)

Moreover, the existence of numeral internal *some* also points to *some* not taking the NP as a complement in examples such as *twenty-some people*.

(29) a. twenty-some thousand dollars
b. forty-some million Germans

(30) [twenty [some [thousand dollars]]] (rejected analysis)

We might have analyzed these as *some* taking the numeral as a complement again, but as I point out in Anderson (2014), examples like *some twenty people* have a kind of approximative interpretation: at first glance, *some twenty* has a meaning similar to *approximately twenty*, allowing for *some twenty* to refer to numbers close to twenty. I proposed that this is constructed via expanding the denotation of a numeral into its pragmatic halo (in the sense of Lasersohn (1999)) and then choosing from among this expanding denotation (see Sauerland & Stateva (2007) for an approach based on manipulating a granularity parameter and discussion of a variety of approximators, and also Stevens & Solt (2018), who argue that that examples like *some twenty people* have a different kind of semantics than *around twenty people*, *about twenty people*, and *approximately twenty people*). Thus, we would expect that the constituent *some thousand* get interpreted as an interval centered on 1000 (e.g., *some thousand* ≈ [990,1010]), and the entire indeterminate numeral have the interpretation "twenty counts of some thousand". But this is not what this means: *twenty-some thousand* is most naturally interpreted as a possible range of thousands, starting at twenty-one thousand and ending at twenty-nine thousand, as we would expect if *some* were a constituent with *twenty* and not *thousand*. Thus, the analysis in (30) must be rejected.

Based on these observations regarding *some*, I analyze *some* as forming a constituent with the numeral rather than the noun. This corresponds to the spec-head structure schematized in (24), rather than the complement structure in (23).

In order to link the numerosity denoted by the numeral up with the noun, I assume that a covert element is used in order to provide a degree argument. Some theories suppose a covert type-shift or adjective MANY/MUCH, which does the job of providing a degree argument via a measure function over individuals, returning their cardinality. Taking an approach closer to Solt (2015) and others who assume functional material in the DP mediating between numerals and the lexical NP, I syntacticize the measure function and place it in a functional head sister to the NP, Num (semantics to follow in later sections). The resulting structure thus looks like the following in (31).

(31)
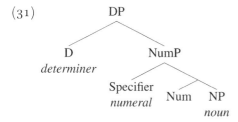

3.2   ADD *and Complex Numeral Structure*

In work on the syntax and semantics of numerals, Ionin & Matushansky (2006) argue that numerals largely have a structure where the numeral takes the noun as a complement, with parts of the numeral distributed along the spine of the tree rather than being in a specifier. (This corresponds to the head-complement analysis from the previous section.) Still, they need to address the fact that some numerals do have additional complexity that cannot be modeled in this way, such as with *two hundred twenty*. Ionin & Matushansky propose that these numerals are underlyingly coordinate structures.

Direct evidence can be found with languages that overtly realize this conjunction; for instance, as shown in (32), both Spanish and German overtly realize an element meaning *and* in at least some numerals with additive complements, and English even optionally allows for *and* in some environments, as shown in (33). (See Ionin & Matushansky 2006 for additional details.)

(32) a. *fünfundzwanzig*   *German*
       five.and.twenty

b. *treinta y   cinco*　　　　　　　　　　　　　　　　*Spanish*
   thirty and five

(33) one hundred (and) one

I take complex additive numerals to have the structure in (34), which follows Ionin & Matushansky (2006) in the use of a covert coordination element. Departing slightly from Ionin & Matushansky, I call this ADD. This use of ADD builds on even earlier work by Hurford (1975), who develops an early account using phrase structure rules for how numerals are constructed in English and a selection of other languages. Hurford observes that syntactic positions are correlated with particular modes of composition (additive or multiplicative), and the use of a coordination-like element encoding the mode of composition essentially syntacticizes this earlier insight.[5]

(34)

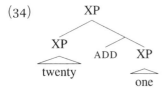

3.3   *NUMBER* as the Complement to *some*

As demonstrated previously, English indeterminate numerals are only possible with additive numeral constructions. I analyze the *some* component of the construction as being like a numeral, albeit an indefinite numeral. In keeping with the pragmatic parallels between *-some* in the indeterminate numeral and the more canonical determiner *some*, I analyze *some* in this construction as a determiner as well, taking an NP complement.

Being in a complex numeral construction, *some* is combined with the numeral that it modifies via the ADD coordinator described in the previous section. The structure for indeterminate numerals is as in (35). I assume that the NP complement to *some* is a silent noun NUMBER. A covert nominal of this sort has been proposed to be at work in other phenomena using numerals; Kayne (2005) proposes that *few* and *many* modify a silent noun NUMBER, while Zweig (2005) makes use of it in his syntax of numerals.

---

5 Hurford (1975) predates many contemporary syntactic notions; additive and multiplicative composition are rules for semantic interpretation assigned to particular phrase structure rules, rather than read off of terminals in the tree as in our current tradition. Regardless, he clearly has the view that structure plays a role.

(35)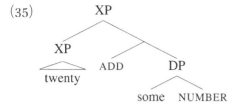

3.4 Blocking of Illicit Numerals

Before turning to the main analysis, I need to take a short detour to talk about how to rule out malformed numerals such as *twenty-eleven* (for *thirty-one*) and *forty-fifteen* (for *fifty-five*). The issue of how to constrain the compositionality of the numeral system has been vexing problem since at least Hurford (1975). The fundamental problem is that, while it is reasonably straightforward to describe the mathematical contribution of each individual component of a complex numeral, particular mathematically equivalent strings are ruled out; *twenty-eleven* and *thirty-one* should be able to name the same number, but only *thirty-one* seems to be a well-formed numeral in English.

One possibility that I speculate about in Anderson 2016 is the use of syntactic features corresponding to numerical bases (e.g., ones, tens, and hundreds). Additive numerals could use feature checking systems to ensure that the numerical base of their sister is smaller. Mendia (2018) independently develops a similar strategy, with the intention of generalizing to bases other than ten, but encodes this information in NUMBER rather than in features. I'm skeptical at putting too much of the machinery regarding compositionality and numerals in the syntactic component itself, though, due to a lack of direct evidence for particular proposals (my own feature-checking proposal included). Moreover, conventions regarding numerical well-formedness can sometimes be flouted (discussed more below), which suggests to me that it is not (entirely) the syntactic component determining what the numerical form for a number should be. Instead, I propose that at least some of the work in ruling out particular numerals is handled by the pragmatic system.

For instance, Bogal-Allbritten (2010) proposes a neo-Gricean principle called **Avoid Synonymy** (see (36)), meant to explain the distribution of evaluativity with comparative aspect and absolute aspect marked verbs in Navajo.[6] Perhaps we might consider the use of such a pragmatic principle in generally

---

6 See Rett 2007 for a similar (though unnamed) principle, and also Rett 2015 for additional discussion regarding evaluativity and markedness. A reviewer notes that this principle seems to be a manifestation of an elsewhere rule or Pāninian ordering rule, which prefers more specific rules before general rules (Kiparsky 1973, 1979).

ruling out illicit numerals, since these numerals have the same truth conditions as their competitor numerals (e.g., *thirty-one* and **twenty-eleven* have the same denotation, 31) but are marked due to violating the speaker's knowledge of the numeral paradigm.

(36) **Avoid Synonymy** (Bogal-Allbritten 2010)
Avoid a derivation producing an expression that has the same truth conditions as a competing derivation containing a less marked adjective.

More generally, we might consider the lack of forms such as *twenty-eleven* or *thirty-fourteen* as being ruled out by more general principles related to blocking, the phenomenon where marked forms are blocked by more unmarked forms. A canonical example is how the derivationally transparent but marked noun *stealer* is blocked by the lexicalized form *thief*; both have identical meanings, at least on a naive view, but the conventionalized form *thief* is preferred over the form *stealer*.

We might object that blocked forms do surface occasionally; *stealer* does have a meaning and occasionally surfaces, for instance. Blocked forms of numerals occasionally surface as well, although admittedly they are somewhat rarer. For instance, the numerical base for thousands in English can be re-expressed with a base for hundreds, provided the multiplicative numeral itself has an increase in its base (see (37)). Counting can be done incorrectly using numbers of too high a base (38a), and numerals constructed in this way can sometimes be used for humorous effect, such as when someone wants to make a comment on their age (38b).

(37) a. two thousand five hundred (= 2500)
 b. twenty-five hundred (= 2500)

(38) a. ..., thirty-nine, thirty-ten, thirty-eleven, ...
 b. Well Rob, I just turned thirty-eleven (and I do give you credit for the phraseology on that), and I saw my first silver hairs about 3 years ago. (Google)

Although how precisely blocking is to be formalized is still a matter of debate,[7] I do not think it is problematic to assume that blocking plays a role in the generation and subsequent filtering of possible numerals; it is the speaker's

---

7 See Embick & Marantz (2008) for discussion.

knowledge of the numeral paradigm that blocks illicit numerals from arising, just as it seems to be the speaker's knowledge of *thief* that blocks *stealer* from arising. I'm keen on highlighting this point here, since this sort of knowledge of the system itself seems to plausibly play a role in constraining the interpretation of indeterminate numerals.

4 Grammatical Alternatives

In order to model the ignorance implicature that characterizes indeterminate numerals, I make use of alternative semantics. Alternatives are familiar from Hamblin's (1973) and Karttunen's (1977) work on questions. In the kind of approach they develop, the meaning of a question is a set of propositions corresponding to answers to the question; a question such as *Who left?* might be represented as in (39), a set of propositions varying on the individual who did the leaving. What the meaning of question is, then, is a set of alternatives which raise an issue as to which alternative is the true alternative.

(39) $\llbracket \textit{Who left?} \rrbracket = \{\lambda w \exists x \,.\, \textbf{leave}_w(x) \mid \textbf{person}(x)\}$

I take the contribution of indeterminate numerals as expressing a set of alternatives. More about these alternatives will be discussed later in this paper, but for present purposes it's enough to suppose that sentences containing indeterminate numerals are related to a set of propositions corresponding to different values for the indeterminate numeral; in other words, the alternatives for a sentence containing an indeterminate numeral are propositions that vary with respect to the number that the indeterminate numeral is (in a sense) standing in for. In expressing a set of alternatives, the speaker raises the issue of which of the alternatives holds true in the actual world. By raising multiple possibilities, the speaker implicates their ignorance, uncertainty, or indifference as to which alternative is the true alternative.

I explicitly represent the alternatives as part of the compositional semantic meaning of the sentence. The best known system that does this is that of Kratzer & Shimoyama 2002, who consider denotations to be sets of alternatives. Systems like this have been used to model not just the familiar cases of questions (Hamblin 1973), and focus (Rooth 1985), but also topichood (Büring 1997), indefinites (Alonso-Ovalle & Menéndez-Benito 2003), pronouns (Kratzer & Shimoyama 2002, Kratzer 2005), modified numerals (Coppock 2016), and scalar implicatures (Chierchia 2004).

In a Hamblinized system such as this, where alternatives are represented as part of the compositional semantics, it's necessary to have a mode of composition separate from ordinary Function Application (Heim & Kratzer 1998) that can put sets of functions together with their arguments—namely, what's necessary is to have a mode of composition where we can act like we're working with functions, but in reality be composing sets of alternatives with each other. The intuition behind this mode of composition, Pointwise Function Application, is to apply all the objects from one set of alternatives to all the objects from another set of alternatives pointwise, creating another set of alternatives. This is formalized in (40) below.

(40) **Pointwise Function Application** (based on Kratzer & Shimoyama 2002)
If α is a branching node with daughters β and γ, and $[\![\beta]\!]^{d,C} \subseteq D_\sigma$ and $[\![\gamma]\!]^{d,C} \subseteq D_{\langle\sigma,\tau\rangle}$, then $[\![\alpha]\!]^{d,C} = \{c(b) \mid b \in [\![\beta]\!]^{d,C} \wedge c \in [\![\gamma]\!]^{d,C}\}$

Singleton sets of alternatives compose in more or less the usual way; one member of the set of alternatives applies to the member of the other set. Where things get more interesting is when multiple alternatives are present. Function application applies pointwise, so that each alternative in the first set is applied to each alternative in the second. In this way, these alternatives "fan outwards" (to borrow phrasing from Coppock (2016: 472)), creating expanding sets of alternatives.

The set of alternatives generated by repeated application of the Pointwise Function Application rule is existentially closed via an existential closure operator in the tree. This operator is associated with the following rule:

(41) **Existential Closure** (adapted from Alonso-Ovalle 2006)
Where $[\![A]\!] \subseteq D_{\langle st,t\rangle}$, $[\![\, \exists\, A\,]\!] = \{\lambda w \,.\, \exists p\, [p \in [\![A]\!] \wedge p(w)]\}$

This system will be put to use in the following sections in order to model the indeterminacy, with indeterminacy being related to a non-singleton set of alternatives.

5 Semantics of Ordinary Numerals

First, I assume a degree semantics for cardinal numerals, following a similar move by Solt for quantity words such as *few* and *many*. Departing from Solt (2015), however, I treat simple numerals as directly denoting degrees, objects of type *d*. This makes a cardinal such as *twenty* have the denotation in (42). Note that this denotation has already been Hamblinized; in a non-Hamblinized system, *twenty* would simply denote the degree 20. Here, it denotes the set containing only the degree 20.

(42) $[\![twenty]\!] = \{20\}$

Syntactically, numerals are inserted in the specifier of a NumP projection, as in (43), breaking with the syntax proposed by Ionin & Matushansky (2006) and more in line with proposals by Solt (2015) and others. NumP dominates the NP projection, but is still contained in DP. The role of Num head is to measure the cardinality of an individual (using a measure function for cardinality of individuals μ), and relate this to the denotation of the numeral in SpecNumP. How this is done is shown in (44).

(43)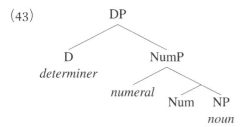

(44) $[\![Num]\!] = \{\lambda f_{\langle e,st \rangle} \lambda d_d \lambda x \lambda w \,.\, \mu_w(x) = d \wedge f_w(x)\}$

Putting these pieces together, the derivation for *twenty people* would look as in (46).[8] Num takes the NP headed by the lexical noun as an argument, and their denotations compose via the Pointwise Function Application rule. This merges with the numeral, and the numeral saturates the degree argument of Num, resulting in the singleton set containing the intensional property of being a plurality of people who measure twenty.

---

[8] It might be the case that *twenty* can be syntactically decomposed into *two* and *-ty*. This additional detail doesn't play a role in this paper, though see Mendia 2018 for discussion of multiplicative numerals with assumptions that are compatible with mine.

(45) $[\![people]\!] = \{\lambda x \lambda w \,.\, \mathbf{people}_w(x)\}$

(46)
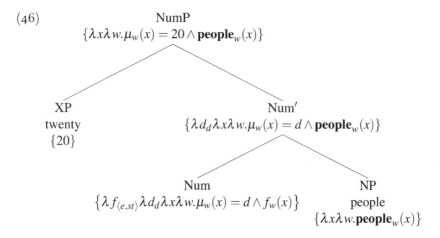

A complex, but non-indeterminate numeral can be given a similar analysis. First, the numeral is composed using ADD.

(47)
```
        XP
      {5+20}
      /    \
  twenty   {λd'.5+d'}
   {20}     /    \
          ADD     XP
     {λdλd'.d+d'} five
                  {5}
```

This numeral can then compose with its sister, an intermediate projection of NumP, via Pointwise Function Application.

(48)
```
                     NumP
         {λxλw.μ_w(x) = 5+20 ∧ people_w(x)}
              /                    \
            XP                      Num'
          {5+20}          {λd_d λxλw.μ_w(x) = d ∧ people_w(x)}
            △                        △
       twenty-ADD-five            Num people
```

In this way, no type-shift is necessary to get numerals to be an argument of Num. Numerals simply are names for degrees, and thus can directly serve as arguments to Num.

6   Analysis of Indeterminate Numerals

6.1   *Previous Analysis: Anderson (2015)*

Anderson (2015) provides an analysis of English indeterminate numerals with *some*. In this analysis, the *some* element in the numeral merges with a phonologically null noun NUMBER. Similarly, the *some NUMBER* constituent combines with an additive numeral using a covert coordinate element ADD. However, an important difference is that, due to a typeclash between the semantics of Num and the indeterminate numeral, they must be lifted to the type of a generalized quantifier over degrees ($\langle dt, t \rangle$) and must raise out of the DP via quantifier raising. Schematically, this is shown in (49), where the indeterminate numeral raises to the left edge of TP and leaves behind a trace of type d as in the familiar Heim & Kratzer (1998) mode of analysis, suitably extended to type d. QR is necessary in order to fix the typeclash generated when an epistemic numeral is used; as Anderson argues, Partee's (1987) BE type-shift is not available with indeterminate numerals due to the numeral not being expressible as a singleton: these numerals must be represented as a set of degrees. In order to have the indeterminate numeral be type-compatible with its sister, the indeterminate numeral needs to be lifted to the type of a generalized quantifier over degrees, $\langle dt, t \rangle$, and then undergo quantifier raising.

(49)   [*twenty-some*$_i$ λ_i [... [t_i [Num NP]]]]

However, this analysis has two problems. First, the DP itself is an island to movement, via familiar constraints on extraction out of definite DPs. Moreover, left-branch extraction of numerals is not generally permissible in English, and so it is suspicious that this construction would allow movement of the numeral, even if it is at LF; extraction of a numeral seems possible only when it pied-pipes the NP it counts over, as seen in (50).

(50)   a.   *[How many]$_i$ did John see [t_i dogs]? (John saw fifteen dogs.)
       How many dogs$_i$ did John see t_i?

Additionally, the analysis also runs aground due to what Bhatt & Pancheva (2004) call the Heim-Kennedy Constraint.[9] The Heim-Kennedy constraint is based on the observation that DegPs do not take scope over QPs. Bhatt & Pancheva (2004) suggest that is should be considered as a constraint on degree abstraction, and not simply DegP, as schematized in (52). Given this formulation, the analysis in Anderson (2015) would violate the constraint, as quantifier raising of indeterminate numerals out of the DP involves degree abstraction.[10]

(51) **Heim-Kennedy Constraint**   (as cited in Bhatt & Pancheva 2004: 15)
If the scope of a quantificational DP contains the trace of a DegP, it also contains that DegP itself.

(52) *λd ... QP ... d ...   (Bhatt & Pancheva 2004: (25))

Taken together, these problems point in a different direction for the analysis of indeterminate numerals. An analysis where numerals are properties of degrees and must QR out of the DP cannot be correct, due to it violating several well-known constraints on movement in English. The analysis of indeterminate numerals I build in the following sections solves this problem.

6.2   *The Meaning of* some

Based on the parallels that *some* shows with Spanish *algún*, I propose treating *some* in a similar way, in particular supposing that *some* triggers minimal domain widening via an anti-singleton constraint. This follows a proposal by Weir (2012), who analyzes the determiner *some* as making use of a subset selection function *f* that is constrained to have a non-singleton co-domain. In this way, *some* (like *algún*) can generate an implicature that the speaker cannot (or will not) narrow the domain to a single alternative, modeling the epistemic effect.

(53) $\llbracket some \rrbracket = \lambda f_{\langle et,et \rangle} \lambda P \lambda Q : \textbf{anti-singleton}(f) \, . \, \exists x \, [f(P)(x) \wedge Q(x)]$
(Weir 2012: (14))

Where I will depart from this analysis is in treating *some* as a quantificational determiner. Rather, building on previous work in alternative semantics (Kratzer & Shimoyama 2002, Szabolcsi 2015), I consider *some* to actually signal the presence of two operations. The first is an existential operator ∃ at

---

9   I thank Nicholas Fleisher (p.c.) for suggesting this line of thought.
10   This also relies on an assumption that a QP takes scope over material within the QP.

the clause level that provides existential closure over alternatives (flattening them into a single proposition). This operator has been mentioned already, as (41), repeated below as (54). An analysis of *some* as a quantificational determiner, as in Anderson (2015) and Weir (2012), requires that *some* introduce existential quantification. In a fully Hamblinized semantic system like the one I develop here, indefinites introduce sets of alternatives (see also Alonso-Ovalle & Menéndez-Benito (2003), AnderBois (2011)), with the existential closure operator performing the role that existential quantification provided in the determiner *some*.

(54) **Existential Closure** (adapted from Alonso-Ovalle 2006)
Where $[\![A]\!] \subseteq D_{\langle st,t \rangle}$, $[\![\,[\,\exists\,A\,]\,]\!] = \{\lambda w\,.\,\exists p\,[p \in [\![A]\!] \wedge p(w)]\}$

The second operation is marked by a morpheme ANTI-SINGLETON (abbreviated in trees as A-S). It has the role of ensuring that the alternatives generated by the constituent sister to ANTI-SINGLETON are a non-singleton set of alternatives. This mirrors in some respects the anti-singleton presupposition in Alonso-Ovalle & Menéndez-Benito's (2010) discussion of Spanish *algún*; where the anti-singleton presupposition in *algún* restricts the subset selection function in *algún* to having a non-singleton co-domain, ANTI-SINGLETON ensures that the set of alternatives generated at the point in the tree where ANTI-SINGLETON is merged are not a singleton. In English, ANTI-SINGLETON is spelled out as *some*.

To clarify this point, *some* is the spell-out of ANTI-SINGLETON in a particular syntactic configuration. When ANTI-SINGLETON is c-commanded by ∃, the phonological form for *some* is inserted at the syntactic position where ANTI-SINGLETON has been merged. This entails a realization theory of morphology, such as Distributed Morphology (Marantz 1997). What is most important to take away from this discussion is that the semantic work of *some*, the introduction of alternatives and the subsequent existential closure of them, is syntactically represented in two positions, with the phonological form for *some* being realized in the position of ANTI-SINGLETON.

Returning to the semantics of ANTI-SINGLETON, ANTI-SINGLETON is somewhat unusual: Because it needs access to the set of alternatives itself, rather than the individual alternatives within the set, it needs to exist in some sense "outside" of the normal composition rule in the semantic system I'm assuming, Pointwise Function Application. Instead, it combines with its argument via ordinary function application.[11] ANTI-SINGLETON takes a set of alternatives,

---

11   As a reviewer points out, there is a tension here in that this analysis needs both the usual

presupposes that a contextually defined subset selection function yields a non-singleton subset of the set of alternatives, and then passes that subset up the tree for computation. This is given in (55).

(55) ⟦ANTI-SINGLETON⟧ = $\lambda p_{\langle \sigma, t \rangle}$: **anti-singleton**(f) . $f(p)$

What makes ANTI-SINGLETON important in this analysis is that, by using it, the speaker signals that they are forcing the semantic derivation to include at least two alternatives, and hence signaling that there are multiple epistemic possibilities at issue. In this way, by forcing multiple alternatives, the speaker can generate the implicature that they are ignorant towards which possibility is the true possibility in the world of evaluation.

7 An Alternative Semantics for Indeterminate Numerals

7.1 Upper-Boundedness as Implicature

In Anderson 2015, I speculated that the upper-boundedness of indeterminate numerals comes from competition with other, larger numerals, and that an implicature can be used to derive the upper-boundedness. Anderson (2016) suggests that the upper-bound can be given syntactically through the use of syntactic features encoding the next lower base, although the strategy is also not fully fleshed out. In this approach, *twenty* would check a base feature on its sister that indexes it with base 10^0. In a similar move, Mendia (2018) proposes to fix the denotation of NUMBER in such a way so as to give it precisely the correct base for its position within the syntactic structure.

Here, I want to return to the original intuition that it is the form of the numeral that is fixing the upper-boundedness, once again deriving it as an implicature. The benefit of this approach is that the upper-bounded constraint on the indeterminate numeral can be constructed compositionally using familiar tools from the analysis of scalar implicatures, rather than treated as a constraint on the construction as a whole. The essential idea will be to treat the upper-bounded interpretation as a kind of Q (quantity) implicature, an implicature generated by flouting Grice's Maxim of Quantity, the communicative

---

Function Application rule as well as Pointwise Function Application. Moreover, this representation format also muddies the distinction between sets of alternatives and characteristic sets. Moving to a compositional system such as that proposed by Charlow (2014, 2019) might make resolve this situation, as a reviewer suggests. I'm sympathetic to such a move, but postpone the question of if and how my present analysis can be formulated with assumptions closer to Charlow's for another time.

principle that a speaker ought to be as informative as possible (Horn 1984, Grice 1957). In modifying one numeral rather than another, the speaker generates the inference, via the existence of a scale, that they could not commit themselves to the information content carried by members up the scale.

First, it is necessary to show that the lower-boundedness of indeterminate numerals is not an implicature, but is part of the asserted meaning of the sentence. This can be done by forcing a contradiction, as in (56).

(56) *There were thirty-some people at the party, and there weren't even thirty. (contradiction)

Next, (57) shows that the lower-bounded meaning component cannot be reinforced; these sentences sound redundant. This again suggests that it is part of the asserted meaning of the sentence. This is not surprising, I think, but showing this is necessary in order to make a distinction between the asserted and implicated components of indeterminate numerals.[12]

(57) a. ??There were thirty-some people at the party, definitely at least thirty.
b. ??I have a hundred-some stamps in my collection, definitely at least one hundred.

In comparison, the upper-bound of indeterminate numerals does seem to be reinforceable.

(58) a. There were thirty-some people at the party, definitely not more than forty.
b. I have a hundred-some stamps in my collection, definitely less than two hundred.

That the upper-bound is reinforceable, or at least more easily reinforceable than the lower-bound, suggests that it is not asserted as part of the conventional meaning of the indeterminate numeral; rather, the fact that it can be independently asserted and reinforced suggests that it behaves more like inferred meaning, e.g. an implicature.

---

12 There may be some ways of rescuing the sentences in (57), such as if the lower-bound is contextually relevant and the adverb *definitely* taken to be emphasizing meeting that bound. But, in out of the blue contexts, the preferred interpretation of (57) is one where *definitely* contributes information already asserted in the sentence, giving a sense of redundancy. I thank Ai Taniguchi (p.c.) for the observation that there is a context where these sentences are acceptable.

How is this implicature calculated? Minimally, we need to consider what the competitors to a numeral like *twenty* are. What we notice is that for *twenty-some*, of course, the upper bound is set by 30; for *two hundred-some*, the upper bound is set by 300. The competitors for a numeral involved in an indeterminate numeral, at least for English indeterminate numerals formed from *some*, are formed by abstracting over the multiplier for the largest base in the numeral. The immediately relevant alternative is the next higher multiplier for the base. For *twenty* (2 × 10), the relevant alternative for the implicature is calculated by picking the next highest multiplier (3 × 10). And, perhaps more generally, the upper bound can be related to the matter of blocking of illicit numerals (see 3.4). A speaker has knowledge of the numeral paradigm in their language, and this can be used to set an upper bound for an indeterminate numeral, in order to rule out truth-conditionally equivalent expressions that (if they were uttered) would not fit in the numeral paradigm. This seems to be easier said than done, but it may very well be that the same principles that rule out illicit numerals also play a role in constraining indeterminate numerals.

7.2 *Computation of Indeterminate Numerals*

The computation for an indeterminate numeral proceeds in largely the same fashion as for an ordinary numeral; both indeterminate numerals and ordinary numerals will be typed as degrees *d*, making them simply arguments to a Num head that mediates between the lexical NP and the numeral in SpecNumP. Where indeterminate numerals differ from ordinary numerals is in introducing into the derivation a non-singleton set of alternatives.

To begin, we'll consider the indeterminate numeral itself. First, ANTI-SINGLETON combines with NUMBER. I assume a weak semantics for NUMBER: it simply denotes the domain of degrees, D_d.[13] When ANTI-SINGLETON combines with NUMBER, it selects a subset of NUMBER. This set is guaranteed to have at least two members. For an indeterminate numeral such as *twenty-some*, the numeral will denote a set of degrees of the form 20 + *d*, where *d* is a

---

[13] It seems quite difficult for the indeterminate numeral to denote a fractional number, such as *twenty-some* denoting 25.5. If *some NUMBER* is just simply denoting the domain of degrees, it's somewhat unclear why this should be, given that some authors (e.g., Fox & Hackl (2007), for example) assume that the domain of degrees is a subset of the real numbers $\mathbb{R}$, and not of the integers. There's two options that come to mind here. One possibility would be to have NUMBER denote in the integers $\mathbb{Z}$ or in the natural numbers $\mathbb{N}$. A second possibility would be to have additional entailments stemming from a more general semantics of numerals that numerals necessarily count atomic individuals. An atomicity constraint of this type would then force *some NUMBER* to always denote an integer. I have very little else to say about these possibilities here, though, and leave the question for further research.

INDETERMINATE NUMERALS AND THEIR ALTERNATIVES   69

member of D_d, and this set will have at least two members. This derivation for *twenty-some* is given in (59).

(59)
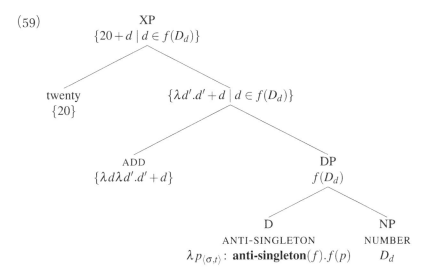

Next, Num' is applied pointwise to the denotation of the numeral; for each degree in the denotation of the numeral, Num' applies to it, saturating Num's degree argument. This allows the alternatives from the numeral to continue to fan outwards throughout the course of the semantic derivation.

(60)
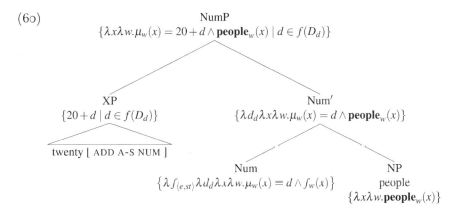

As argued for previously, the upper-bounded inference should be treated as an implicature. (As we can already see, it does not come directly from the semantics of the indeterminate numeral.) I assume that (for this example), at the level of NumP, an implicature is calculated based on competitors to the modified numeral. The relevant alternatives for the quantity implicature are given in (61b), where the next numeral "up" from the modified numeral, based on increasing the value of the multiplier in the numeral, sets an upper-bound for the measure function over individuals μ (see also section 7.1). The NumP and the implicature can be intersected to give the strengthened, upper-bounded interpretation in (62).

(61) a. NumP: $\{\lambda x \lambda w . \mu_w(x) = 20 + d \wedge \text{people}_w(x) \mid d \in f(D_d)\}$
  b. Implicature: $\{\lambda x \lambda w . \mu_w(x) < 30 \wedge \text{people}_w(x)\}$

(62) Strengthened: $\{\lambda x \lambda w . \mu_w(x) = 20 + d \wedge \mu_w(x) < 30 \wedge$
$\text{people}_w(x) \mid d \in f(D_d)\}$

Setting the upper-bound in this way ensures that, no matter what the subset selected from D_d is, the addition of any member of that subset with the modified numeral will never be larger than the competitor. A schematization of these alternatives is given in (63).

(63) $\begin{cases} \lambda x \lambda w . \mu_w(x) = 20 + 1 \wedge \mu_w(x) < 30 \wedge \text{people}_w(x), \\ \lambda x \lambda w . \mu_w(x) = 20 + 2 \wedge \mu_w(x) < 30 \wedge \text{people}_w(x), \\ \dots \\ \lambda x \lambda w . \mu_w(x) = 20 + 8 \wedge \mu_w(x) < 30 \wedge \text{people}_w(x), \\ \lambda x \lambda w . \mu_w(x) = 20 + 9 \wedge \mu_w(x) < 30 \wedge \text{people}_w(x) \end{cases}$

These alternatives percolate upward through the derivation, until arriving at the $\exists$ operator, which I will suppose is adjoined to CP. To recapitulate, the role of $\exists$ is to transform the set of alternatives it combines with into a singleton. To do this, it takes the alternatives which have been created in the course of the derivation, the set of epistemic possibilities, and asserts that one of them holds in the world of evaluation.

(64)
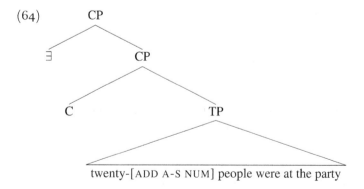

INDETERMINATE NUMERALS AND THEIR ALTERNATIVES   71

(65) ⟦∃ *twenty*-[ADD A-S NUM] *people were at the party*⟧
= {λw . ∃p[p ∈ ⟦*twenty*-[ADD A-S NUM] *people were at the party*⟧ ∧
$$p(w)]\}$$

In this way, indeterminate numerals generate a non-singleton set of alternatives, with the upper-bound given as a quantity implicature.

It's worth stressing at this point that it is not the values of NUMBER (or rather, *some* NUMBER) that are constrained in the course of the derivation for the indeterminate numeral. NUMBER itself is quite weak, simply the domain of degrees, and the value of *some* NUMERAL is a non-singleton subset of the domain of degrees. But, the value of *some* NUMERAL is not directly constrained by the other material in the numeral; there is no selection mechanism or anaphoric connection between *some* NUMERAL and the rest of the numeral. Rather, it is addition of the implicature that rules out certain alternatives. In the case of *twenty-some*, for instance, the "less than thirty" implicature causes any alternatives with a numerical value (computed by the addition of 20 plus members of the relevant non-singleton subset of the domain of degrees D_d) greater than 30 to be false.

How does this story fare with numerals other than *twenty-some*? The intuitions seem to be as expected from the analysis, though the picture for calculation of the upper-bounded implicature is somewhat complicated. Take the numerals in (66), along with their bracketings in (67). *Two million-some* has the upper-bound we might expect, 3 million, given its syntax. This is arrived at by generating an implicature based on increasing the multiplier for the base *million* from 2 to 3. *Six hundred thousand*'s upper-bound is generated by comparison with *seven hundred thousand*, and the upper-bounded implicature generated for *two million five hundred thousand-some* is *two million six hundred thousand*, with *six hundred thousand* being in competition with *five hundred thousand*, a move made by increasing the multiplier for 100 from 5 to 6.

(66) a. two million-some   (2 million, 3 million)
     b. six hundred thousand-some   (600000, 700000)
     c. two million 500 thousand-some   (2.5 million, 2.6 million)

(67) a. [[two × million] ADD *some* NUMBER]
     b. [[[six × hundred] × thousand] ADD *some* NUMBER]
     c. [[two × million] ADD [[[five × hundred] × thousand] ADD *some* NUMBER]]

This is not to say that the calculation of the implicature is trivial; there are a number of questions that remain about how the upper-bounded implicature is calculated, not all of which can be answered at this point.[14] For instance, why is it the multiplier (and not the base) that is involved in generating the implicature? The intuitive answer seems to be related to what numbers or numerals are contrastive with what has been spoken, with numerals of the same base but different multipliers generally being the most contrastive (e.g., *thirty* and *forty* form a more salient pair than *thirty* and *three hundred*), but this is admittedly not totally satisfying, nor straightforward to cash out formally. There is also the issue of how deep into the hierarchical syntax the mechanism for generating the upper-bounded implicature can see; *two* in (67a) is more embedded than *six* in (67b). And finally, the relevance of structure also feeds into the question of when the implicatures are calculated. For (66c), the implicature must be calculated internally to the numeral, due to the multiplier for the highest base not forming part of the implicature generation; the implicature is generated over *five hundred thousand*, rather than *two million*. Clearly, much work needs to be done in order to understand the semantics of indeterminate numerals more fully.

7.3 *Verbs of Saying and Indeterminate Numerals*

The analysis developed in the previous sections relies on a syntactically represented ∃ operator. This operator is adjoined to CP and scopes over all the alternatives, serving to close off the set of alternatives, e.g. to transform it into a set containing a single proposition. The effect of this is to anchor the ignorance implicature to the speaker, since it is the speaker who utters this proposition.

A quirk of this analysis is that closure of the alternatives generated by *some* could potentially occur at different syntactic levels; there is no principle that requires that ∃ be adjoined to the matrix CP. Put another way, the analysis predicts that closure of the alternatives could occur in (at least) two positions in a sentence with a finite embedded clause: at the highest CP, or at the CP corresponding to the embedded clause. These possibilities are schematized in (68), where (∃) marks a possible position for existential closure.

(68) [CP (∃) C [TP …[VP V [CP (∃) C …

With a verb that encodes an attitude towards a proposition, such as a verb of saying, this raises the possibility for an interpretational difference, depending on the height of ∃. Above the verb (at the highest CP), the ignorance will be anchored to the speaker, as in the cases discussed in previous sections. Under the verb, at the embedded CP, the ignorance will instead be anchored to the

---

14   I thank a reviewer for pressing me on some of these issues, and I regret that I'm not able to completely flesh out these details yet.

INDETERMINATE NUMERALS AND THEIR ALTERNATIVES 73

sentential subject. Thus, in a sentence with *some* in an embedded clause and under a verb of saying, we predict an ambiguity in which individual the ignorance implicature is anchored to.

This is what we find, as shown with example (69). This sentence is two-ways ambiguous, with ignorance being expressed by the sentential subject, the subject of the saying, or by the speaker; the paraphrases in (69a) and (69b) demonstrate this intuition, while (70) shows this via follow-ups that directly assert ignorance on behalf of either the speaker or subject. Thus, it seems that the analysis correctly predicts that sentences with an indeterminate numeral in the scope of an attitude verb are ambiguous.

(69) John said that there were twenty-some people were at the party.
    a. John said how many people were at the party, but I don't know precisely what he said.   (speaker ignorance)
    b. John said something and expressed ignorance as to the precise number of people at the party.   (subject ignorance)

(70) John said that there were twenty-some people at the party …
    a. … but I don't know exactly how many (he said there were).
        (speaker ignorance)
    b. … but he didn't know exactly how many.   (subject ignorance)

The anchoring of ignorance to different individuals can be essentially thought of as a relatively ordinary scope ambiguity; the relative scope of the $\exists$ operator with respect to the attitude verb determines when the set of propositional alternatives is flattened to a single proposition. If the operator scopes below the attitude verb, the alternatives are flattened into a single proposition, which is the proposition expressed by the one doing the saying.

(71)
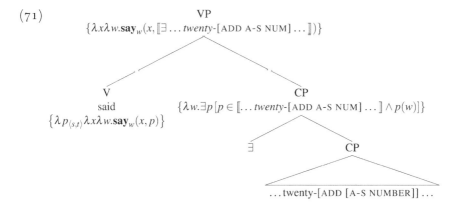

On the other hand, if the ∃ operator scopes above the verb, as in (72), then the alternatives from the indeterminate numeral persist to the top of the clause. Due to the Pointwise Function Application rule, the verbal meaning is factored into the alternatives generated by the indeterminate numeral. The resulting set of alternatives is a set of alternatives that vary by which proposition was said. By allowing the alternatives to persist past the level of the verb, what is constructed is a set of alternatives that express possible propositions that were said, as in (73). Effectively, this creates ignorance about which particular proposition was uttered by someone, but only commits the speaker of the root clause to ignorance, not the person who said (the content of) the embedded clause. The logical form for this is provided in (73).

(72)

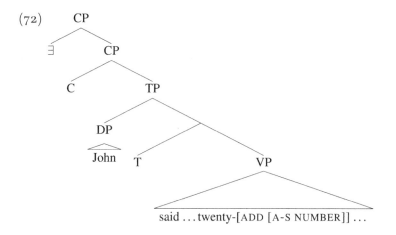

said ... twenty-[ADD [A-S NUMBER]] ...

(73) $\{\lambda w \, . \, \text{say}_w(\text{john}, \lambda w \exists x \exists d \, . \, \mu_w(x) = 20 + d \land \mu_w(x) < 30 \land \ldots)$
$\mid d \in f(D_d)\}$

To briefly summarize, the analysis of indeterminate numerals predicted that sentences with an indeterminate numeral in a clause embedded under an attitude verb such as *say* should be ambiguous, due to the set of alternatives being able to be closed off at the level of either the embedded CP or the matrix CP. This prediction was borne out, providing evidence for the claim that closure of the alternatives is contributed by a separate existential operator that can be variously merged at the level of either the matrix CP or the embedded CP.

8 Conclusion

This chapter investigated the use of *some* in forming approximate, uncertain meanings with numerals, what I call indeterminate numerals. These numerals have the structure and semantics of ordinary numerals (degree-denoting expressions), but are special in that they make use of a morpheme ANTI-SINGLETON (spelled out as *-some*) that forces the generation of at least two alternatives. The generation of multiple alternatives models the uncertainty inherent to these numerals. These numerals gain an additional upper-bounded inference via a second quantity implicature, based on the value of the numeral that *-some* attaches to. This work shows how morphemes associated with quantificational elements such as indefinite determiners can interact with degrees when placed in certain syntactic configurations, and sheds light on the quantificational mechanisms used in computing ignorance over sets of degrees.

Acknowledgements

I thank Marcin Morzycki, Peter Hallman, Keir Moulton, Ai Taniguchi, Adam Gobeski, Jon Ander Mendia, and two anonymous reviewers for their discussion and comments. I was funded by DFG Collaborative Research Center 991, projects B09 and C10, while writing this paper. Naturally, all errors are my own.

References

Alonso-Ovalle, Luis. 2006. *Disjunction in alternative semantics*. University of Massachusetts Amherst dissertation.

Alonso-Ovalle, Luis & Paula Menéndez-Benito. 2003. Some epistemic indefinites. In Shigeto Kawahara & Makoto Kadowaki (eds.), *Proceedings of the North East Linguistics Society (NELS) 33*, 1–12. Amherst, MA: GLSA.

Alonso-Ovalle, Luis & Paula Menéndez-Benito. 2010. Modal indefinites. *Natural Language Semantics* 18. 1–31.

Alonso-Ovalle, Luis & Paula Menéndez-Benito. 2013. Two views on epistemic indefinites. *Language and Linguistics Compass* 7. 105–122.

AnderBois, Scott. 2011. Sluicing as anaphora to issues. In Nan Li & David Lutz (eds.), *Semantics and Linguistic Theory 20*, 451–470.

Anderson, Curt. 2014. Approximation of complex numerals using *some*. In Claire Renaud, Carla Ghanem, Verónica González López & Kathryn Pruitt (eds.), *Proceedings of the Western Conference on Linguistics (WECOL) 2013*, 131–143.

Anderson, Curt. 2015. Numerical approximation using *some*. In Eva Csipak & Hedde Zeijlstra (eds.), *Proceedings of Sinn und Bedeutung 19*, 54–69.

Anderson, Curt. 2016. *Intensification and attenuation across categories*. Michigan State University dissertation.

Barwise, John & Robin Cooper. 1981. Generalized quantifiers and natural language. *Linguistics and Philosophy* 4(2). 159–219.

Bhatt, Rajesh & Roumyana Pancheva. 2004. Late merger of degree clauses. *Linguistic Inquiry* 35(1). 1–45.

Bogal-Allbritten, Elizabeth. 2010. Positively uninformative. In Michael Yoshitaka Erlewine & Yasutada Sudo (eds.), *Proceedings of the MIT workshop on comparatives 2010*, 19–34.

Büring, Daniel. 1997. *The meaning of topic and focus: the 59th Street Bridge accent*. London: Routledge.

Charlow, Simon. 2014. *On the semantics of exceptional scope*. New York University dissertation.

Charlow, Simon. 2019. The scope of alternatives: indefiniteness and islands. *Linguistics and Philosophy*.

Chierchia, Gennaro. 2004. Scalar implicatures, polarity phenomena, and the syntax/pragmatics interface. In Adriana Belletti (ed.), *Structures and beyond*, vol. 3, 39–103. Oxford University Press.

Condoravdi, Cleo. 2015. Ignorance, indifference, and individuation with wh-ever. In Luis Alonso-Ovalle & P. Menéndez-Benito (eds.), *Epistemic indefinites: exploring modality beyond the verbal domain*, 213–243. Oxford University Press.

Coppock, Elizabeth. 2016. Superlative modifiers as modified superlatives. In Mary Moroney, Carol-Rose Little, Jacob Collard & Dan Burgdorf (eds.), *Semantics and Linguistic Theory 26*, 471–488.

Danon, Gabi. 2012. Two structures for numeral-noun constructions. *Lingua* 122(12). 1282–1307.

Embick, David & Alec Marantz. 2008. Architecture and blocking. *Linguistic Inquiry* 39(1). 1–53.

Fox, Danny & Martin Hackl. 2007. The universal density of measurement. *Linguistics and Philosophy* 29(5). 537–586.

Geurts, Bart. 2006. Take five: the meaning and use of a number word. In Svetlana Vogeleer & Liliane Tasmowski (eds.), *Non-definiteness and plurality*, 311–329. John Benjamins Publishing Company.

Grice, H. Paul. 1957. Meaning. *The philosophical review*. 377–388.

Hamblin, Charles. 1973. Questions in Montague English. *Foundations of Language* 10(1). 41–53.

Haspelmath, Martin. 1997. *Indefinite pronouns*. Oxford University Press.

Heim, Irene & Angelika Kratzer. 1998. *Semantics in generative grammar*. Wiley-Blackwell.

Hofweber, Thomas. 2005. Number determiners, numbers, and arithmetic. *The Philosophical Review* 114(2). 179–225.

Horn, Laurence. 1984. Toward a new taxonomy for pragmatic inference: Q-based and R-based implicature. In Deborah Schiffrin (ed.), *Meaning, form, and use in context: linguistic applications*. Georgetown University Press.

Hurford, James R. 1975. *The linguistic theory of numerals*. Cambridge: Cambridge University Press.

Ionin, Tania & Ora Matushansky. 2006. The composition of complex cardinals. *Journal of Semantics* 23. 315–360.

Karttunen, Lauri. 1977. Syntax and semantics of questions. *Linguistics and Philosophy* 1(1). 3–44.

Kayne, Richard S. 2005. A note on the syntax of quantity in English. In Richard S. Kayne (ed.), *Movement and silence*, 176–214. Oxford: Oxford University Press.

Kennedy, Christopher. 2015. A "de-Fregean" semantics (and neo-Gricean pragmatics) for modified and unmodified numerals. *Semantics and Pragmatics* 8(10). 1–44. https://doi.org/10.3765/sp.8.10.

Kiparsky, Paul. 1973. 'Elsewhere' in phonology. In Stephen Anderson & Paul Kiparsky (eds.), *A festschrift for Morris Halle*, 93–106. Holt, Rinehart & Winston.

Kiparsky, Paul. 1979. *Pāṇini as a variationist*. Cambridge, MA: MIT Press.

Kratzer, Angelika. 2005. Indefinites and the operators they depend on: from Japanese to Salish. In Gregory Carlson & Francis J. Pelletier (eds.), *Reference and quantification: the Partee effect*. CSLI Publications.

Kratzer, Angelika & Junko Shimoyama. 2002. Indeterminate pronouns: the view from Japanese. In Yukio Otsu (ed.), *Third Tokyo Conference on Psycholinguistics*, 1–25. Tokyo: Hituzi Syobo.

Landman, Fred. 2003. Predicate-argument mismatches and the adjectival theory of indefinites. In Martine Coene & Yves D'hulst (eds.), *From NP to DP: the syntax and semantics of noun phrases*, vol. 1, 211–237. Amsterdam: John Benjamins Publishing Company.

Lasersohn, Peter. 1999. Pragmatic halos. *Language* 75(3). 522–551.

Marantz, Alec. 1997. No escape from syntax: don't try morphological analysis in the privacy of your own lexicon. *University of Pennsylvania Working Papers in Linguistics* 4(2). 201–225.

Mendia, Jon Ander. 2018. Epistemic numerals. In Sireemas Maspong, Brynhildur Stefánsdóttir, Katherine Blake & Forrest Davis (eds.), *Semantics and Linguistic Theory* 28, 493–511.

Morzycki, Marcin. 2016. *Modification*. Cambridge University Press.

Nouwen, Rick. 2010. Two kinds of modified numerals. *Semantics and Pragmatics* 3. 1–41.

Partee, Barbara. 1987. Noun phrase interpretation and type-shifting principles. In Jeroen Groenendijk, Dick de Jongh & Martin Stokhof (eds.), *Studies in Discourse*

Representation Theory and the theory of generalized quantifiers, 115–143. Foris Publications.

Rett, Jessica. 2007. Antonymy and evaluativity. In Tova Friedman & Masayuki Gibson (eds.), *Semantics and Linguistic Theory 17*, 210–227.

Rett, Jessica. 2015. *The semantics of evaluativity*. Oxford University Press.

Rooth, Mats. 1985. *Association with focus*. University of Massachusetts PhD Thesis.

Rothstein, Susan. 2013. A fregean semantics for number words. In Maria Aloni, Michael Franke & Floris Roelofsen (eds.), *19th Amsterdam Colloquium*, 179–186.

Sauerland, Uli & Penka Stateva. 2007. Scalar vs. epistemic vagueness: evidence from approximators. In Tova Friedman & Masayuki Gibson (eds.), *Semantics and Linguistic Theory 17*, 228–245.

Solt, Stephanie. 2015. Q-adjectives and the semantics of quantity. *Journal of Semantics* 32. 221–273.

Stevens, Jon & Stephanie Solt. 2018. The semantics and pragmatics of "some 27 arrests". In Ava Irani & Milena Šereikaitė (eds.), *University of Pennsylvania working papers in linguistics*, 179–188.

Strawson, P.F. 1974. *Subject and predicate in logic and grammar*. London: Methuen.

Szabolcsi, Anna. 2010. *Quantification*. Cambridge University Press.

Szabolcsi, Anna. 2015. What do quantifier particles do? *Linguistics and Philosophy* 38(2). 159–204.

Weir, Andrew. 2012. *Some*, speaker knowledge, and subkinds. In Rasmus K. Rendsvig & Sophia Katrenko (eds.), *Proceedings of the ESSLLI 2012 student session*, 180–190.

Zweig, Eytan. 2005. Nouns and adjectives in numeral NPs. In Leah Bateman & Cherlon Ussery (eds.), *Proceedings of the North East Linguistics Society 35*, 663–675.

CHAPTER 3

The Semantics of the Superlative Quantifier -*Est*

Barbara Tomaszewicz-Özakın

1   Introduction

Gradable predicates introduce degrees into the semantic representation (Cresswell 1976) and the comparative and superlative constructions, which express comparison, can be modelled as quantification over degrees. Two lexical entries have been proposed for the superlative quantifier -*est*: 3-place -*est* on which individuals are compared and 2-place -*est* comparing sets of degrees (Heim 1999, Romero 2010). We cannot judge by introspection whether in the semantics the comparison expressed by sentences like "Mary is taller than Bill" or "Mary is the tallest" is between individuals, Mary and Bill, or Mary and other people, or between degrees, i.e., the heights of Mary, Bill and others. In this paper, I present a novel superlative construction, found in Turkish and Polish, that explicitly calls for the comparison of degrees: superlatives with measure phrases and corresponding degree *wh*-questions. I will argue that the 2-place lexical entry for -*est*, comparing sets of degrees, is needed in the grammar to derive that construction. I will also show that cross-linguistically -$est_{2-place}$ is used only in cases of explicit comparison between degrees, while other readings are derived by -$est_{3-place}$. Thus, contra Heim (1999), I claim that there is a division of labor between the two lexical entries, because they are used in different, mutually exclusive contexts. Unlike what is proposed in Heim (1999), only -$est_{3-place}$ can associate with focus, because if we allow focus association for -$est_{2-place}$, it generates unattested readings (Pancheva and Tomaszewicz 2012, Tomaszewicz 2015a,b).

I will start out by presenting how the two entries for the superlative morpheme -*est* introduced by Heim (1999) can derive the range of readings available to a superlative sentence (section 2). To derive the different readings, -*est*, like other quantifiers, can scope outside the clause and associate with focus. Technically both mechanisms are available with both lexical entries, but Heim points out that the configuration with -$est_{2-place}$ is exactly parallel to that of other focus associators, such as *always* and *only*. Next, in section 3, I will present the Turkish and Polish data, where the superlative co-occurs with numeral modifiers, measure phrases and degree *wh*-question words. I will argue that these expressions explicitly require comparison between degrees and I will propose how $\textit{-est}_{2-\text{place}}$ is able to straightforwardly derive the right meaning. I will then discuss the role of definiteness in the availability of this construction cross-linguistically. I will show that the superlative DP needs to be indefinite, as it is in Turkish and Polish (unlike in English), to compositionally derive the comparison of degrees with $\textit{-est}_{2-\text{place}}$. In section 4, I will argue that $\textit{-est}_{2-\text{place}}$ does not associate with focus, although it technically can, because it overgenerates the range of readings found cross-linguistically (Tomaszewicz 2013, 2015a). This means that Heim's (1999) proposal that $\textit{-est}_{2-\text{place}}$ associates with focus on par with *always* and *only* is not supported empirically. In section 5, I will present arguments from Polish and Bulgarian that $\textit{-est}_{3-\text{place}}$ can associate with focus, but definiteness restricts the possible configurations for focus association (Tomaszewicz and Pancheva 2016, Tomaszewicz 2015a,b, 2016). $\textit{-Est}_{3-\text{place}}$ can QR when the superlative DP is indefinite as in Polish and Bulgarian, but the QR is blocked by the definite determiner in a language like English. This scoping mechanism together with focus association accounts for the different readings of definite and indefinite superlatives cross-linguistically, i.e., in Polish and Bulgarian a wider range of readings is found than in English.

The conclusion is that both lexical entries for *-est* and thus both comparison between individuals and between degress are needed in the grammar, but they occur in different contexts (definite vs. indefinite DPs, high vs. low scope of *-est*), some of which may not be available in a given language.[1]

2   Comparison between Degrees or Individuals?

2.1   *Two Lexical Entries for the Superlative*

A gradable predicate like *tall* expresses a relation between an individual (type e) and a degree of the relevant sort (type d)—the meaning of the adjective in (1) can be paraphrased as 'x is tall to degree d' or 'x is d-tall' (Cresswell 1976, von Stechow 1984, Heim 1985, 2000, a.o.). The presence of the degree argument entails that it can be quantified over, i.e., degree constructions such as the comparative and superlative, (2), are quantificational expressions and can undergo quantifier raising (QR).[2]

---

1 In some languages even the superlative morpheme itself may not be available, as in Navajo as discussed by Bogal-Albritten and Coppock in this volume. Superlative readings in Navajo are obtained from the combination of the comparative quantifier *-er* and an indefinite standard.
2 An alternative approach is advanced by Bale and by Schwarzschild in this volume: degrees are sets of possible individuals, and thus they are introduced by functional morphology, i.e. operators that quantify over them. Gradable adjectives themselves denote relations between

(1) $[\![\text{tall}]\!] = \lambda d_d. \lambda x_e.\text{tall}(d)(x)$

(2) a. *Mary is tall.*   POSITIVE
    b. *Mary is **taller** than Bill (is).*   COMPARATIVE
    c. *Mary is the **tallest**.*   SUPERLATIVE

We cannot judge by introspection whether the comparison expressed in the comparative sentence (2b) and the superlative sentence (2c) is between individuals, Mary and Bill in (2b), Mary and other people in (2c), or between degrees, i.e., the heights of Mary, Bill and others. In clausal comparatives ("... than Bill is."), the operator *-er* necessarily involves comparison of degrees, its two arguments are of the ⟨*d,t*⟩ type—see the lexical entry and the truth conditions in (3) (Seuren 1973, 1984, Cresswell 1976, Hoeksema 1983, von Stechow 1984, Rullmann 1995, Heim 1985, 2000, 2006).

(3) a. $[\![\text{-}er_{2\text{-place}}]\!] = \lambda P_{\langle d,t\rangle}. \lambda Q_{\langle d,t\rangle}. \exists d\, [\neg P(d) \wedge Q(d)]$
    b. $[\![\text{Mary is taller than Bill}]\!] = 1$ iff $\exists d\, [\neg\text{tall}(b, d) \wedge \text{tall}(m, d)]$

Phrasal comparatives, ("... than Bill."), can also be derived by the 2-place *-er* in (3) in many languages (via ellipsis). But in certain languages, e.g., in Hindi-Urdu, phrasal comparatives, (4b), require a 3-place *-er*, (5), which combines with two individual arguments and a predicate of individuals and degrees (Bhatt and Takahashi 2008, 2011).[3]

(4) a. [*Bill jitnaa lambaa hai*] [*John us-se   zyaadaa lambaa*
         Bill how tall   is   John that-than more   tall
         hai].   CLAUSAL COMPARATIVE
         is   Hindi-Urdu
         'John is taller than Bill is.' (Bhatt and Takahashi 2011:584)

    b. *John Bill-se   zyaadaa lambaa hai.*   PHRASAL COMPARATIVE
         John Bill-than more   tall   is
         'John is taller than Bill.' (Bhatt and Takahashi 2011:585)

---

    possible individuals. Schwarzschild further argues that degrees are used to construct scalar segments; gradable adjectives, measure phrases, and the comparative *-er* are all predicates of segments (the standard marker *than* performs the comparison).

3   The lexical entries in (3)–(6) require the assumption that gradable predicates are downward monotonic, (i):
      (i) A relation R between objects and degrees is downward monotonic iff: $\forall x \forall d \forall d'[R(x, d)=1 \wedge d'< d \rightarrow R(x,d')]$

(5) $[\![\text{-}er_{3\text{-place}}]\!] = \lambda x_e. \lambda P_{\langle d,et\rangle}. \lambda y_e. \exists d\,[P(d)(y) \wedge \neg(P(d)(x))]$

Heim (1999) introduced two lexical entries for the superlative -est morpheme with truth-conditionally equivalent meaning: the entry in (6) involving comparison between sets of degrees (the comparison class C is of type $\langle dt,t\rangle$),[4] and the entry in (7) comparing sets of individuals (C is of type $\langle e,t\rangle$). The sentence in (2c) is true if Mary's height exceeds the heights of all the other relevant individuals, (6), or, equivalently, if Mary is tall to degree d such that nobody else is tall to that degree, (7).

(6) $[\![\text{-}est_{2\text{-place}}]\!] = \lambda C_{\langle dt,t\rangle}. \lambda P_{\langle d,t\rangle}. \exists d\,[P(d) \wedge \forall Q\in C\,[Q\neq P \rightarrow \neg(Q(d))]]$
-$est_{2\text{-place}}$ $(C)(P)$ is defined iff (i) $P\in C$, and (ii) $\forall Q\,[[Q\in C \wedge Q\neq P]\rightarrow \exists d\,[Q(d)]]$

(7) $[\![\text{-}est_{3\text{-place}}]\!] = \lambda C_{\langle e,t\rangle}. \lambda P_{\langle d,et\rangle}. \lambda x_e. \exists d\,[P(d)(x) \wedge \forall y\in C\,[y\neq x \rightarrow \neg(P(d)(y))]]$
-$est_{3\text{-place}}$ $(C)(P)(x)$ is defined iff (i) $x\in C$, and (ii) $\forall y\,[y\in C \rightarrow \exists d\,[P(d)(y)]]$

Both entries in (6)–(7) can derive the well-known ambiguities that arise in superlative sentences. For instance, the sentence in (8) has two readings. That is because the superlative DP '*the tallest bookcase*' is interpreted relative to two different COMPARISON SETS, as specified in the *of*-PPs (this observation goes back to Ross (1964)). These different interpretations of superlatives are called the ABSOLUTE and the RELATIVE interpretation. In (8a), the comparison set is determined just on the basis of the DP containing the superlative expression. In (8b), what is taken into consideration is the expression external to the superlative DP, '*Mary*', and the property of building bookcases.

(8) *Mary built the tallest bookcase …*
   a. *… of all the relevant bookcases.*   ABSOLUTE
   b. *… of all the relevant bookcase building people.*   RELATIVE

The comparison set is the domain argument C in (6)–(7) and its value is restricted based on the context (as is the case with quantifiers in general) and in accordance with the presuppositions. Due to the presuppositions in (6)–(7) the comparison set is determined based on the denotation of the constituent to which -*est* adjoins as it QRs, and is then further contextually restricted.

---

[4] Technically, the variable C in (5) is the characteristic function of a set of sets degrees. I will refer to it as a set, for convenience. The same goes for C in (7).

The next section presents the details of the effects of the scoping mechanism on the comparison class with both -$est_{\text{2-place}}$ and -$est_{\text{3-place}}$ so that both absolute and relative readings can be derived. (As revealed above in the introduction, the main claim in this paper, however, is that the two lexical entries have nothing to do with the absolute/relative ambiguity, but that yet another superlative construction is available, where the comparison class is explicitly specified as containing degrees, and that this construction is derived by -$est_{\text{2-place}}$).

2.2 Scope of -est and the Comparison Class

The absolute and relative readings can be derived with both entries in (6)–(7). Assuming that -*est* can take scope inside or outside of the superlative DP (Szabolcsi 1986, 2012, Heim 1999),[5] comparison of individuals (using -$est_{\text{3-place}}$) gives us the comparison between bookcases on the absolute reading, (9a), and between people who built bookcases on the relative reading, (9b).[6] Degree comparison (using -$est_{\text{2-place}}$) involves comparison between different sets of degrees, depending on the scope of -*est*, (10a-b).[7] We cannot judge by introspection whether the comparison is between individuals (bookcases or bookcase builders), or between degrees: heights (Heim 1999, Farkas and Kiss 2000, Sharvit and Stateva 2002).

---

[5] The availability of the evidence for the QR of the comparative and superlative morphemes, -*er* and -*est*, has been debated. Kennedy (1999) argues that -*er* is non-quantificational because it does not participate in scopal ambiguities the way quantified noun phrases do. Heim (2000) and Stateva (2002) argue that the QR of -*er* is necessary to explain the scopal interactions with intensional verbs. Similarly on the basis of intensional contexts, Heim (1999) presents a quantificational analysis for -*est*. Stateva (2002), on the other hand, maintains that a quantificational approach to -*est* is not needed in contrast to -*er*. In Tomaszewicz (2015b) I show that the non-quantificational approach to -*est* makes the wrong predictions for the interaction of definiteness and the availability of the relative readings discussed here in Sections 4 5.

[6] Notice that in order for the truth-conditions to come out right in (8b) and (9b), the definite determiner on the relative reading has to be interpreted as indefinite. This is a stipulation on the Heim/Szabolcsi account. Szabolcsi (1986) proposes that on relative readings the superlative DP is necessarily indefinite for syntactic reasons, the movement of -*est* is allowed only if the DP is indefinite. Heim (1999) additionally observes that "definite DPs are generally islands for extraction" (p. 12), thus, on the QR Theory, the reason for having the indefinite determiner in the superlative DP when -*est* takes DP-external scope is syntactic. However, extraction from definite DPs is not universally precluded, as discussed in Tomaszewicz (2015a).

[7] The derivation of the absolute reading using -$est_{\text{2-place}}$ was proposed by Romero (2010, 2012). It involves the movement of the definite determiner not shown in (10a).

(9) a. Mary built [$_{DP}$ the [[-*est*$_{3-place}$ $C_{\langle e,t \rangle}$] λd [*d*-tall bookcase]]]
$C_{\langle e,t \rangle} \subseteq \{x: \exists d \, [x \text{ is a } d\text{-tall bookcase}]\}$ ABSOLUTE (11a)
b. Mary [[-*est*$_{3-place}$ $C_{\langle e,t \rangle}$] $\lambda d \, \lambda x$ [x built [$_{DP}$ A *d*-tall bookcase]]]
$C_{\langle e,t \rangle} \subseteq \{x: \exists d \, [x \text{ built a } d\text{-tall bookcase}]\}$ RELATIVE (11b)

(10) a. Mary built [$_{DP}$ the [[-*est*$_{2-place}$ $C_{\langle dt,t \rangle}$] λd [*d*-tall bookcase]]]
$C_{\langle dt,t \rangle} \subseteq \{D: \exists x \, [D = \lambda d \, [x \text{ is a } d\text{-tall bookcase}]]\}$ ABSOLUTE (11a)
b. [-*est*$_{2-place}$ $C_{\langle dt,t \rangle}$] λd [Mary λx [x built [$_{DP}$ A *d*-tall bookcase]]]
$C_{\langle dt,t \rangle} \subseteq \{D: \exists x \, [D = \lambda d \, [x \text{ built a } d\text{-tall bookcase}]]\}$ RELATIVE (11b)

(11) a. ABSOLUTE
'Mary built the bookcase that was taller than any other (relevant) bookcase.'
b. RELATIVE
'Mary built a taller bookcase than any other (relevant) person built.'

When -*est*$_{3-place}$ takes high scope, the contents of *C* on the relative reading are syntactically determined, depending on which constituent saturates its third argument, e.g. 'Mary' in (9b). But with -*est*$_{2-place}$ scope alone is not enough to derive the relative reading, (10b); the contents of *C* are established with respect to the context. For Heim (1999) this is desirable: like with all quantifiers, the superlative's domain variable is subject to pragmatic restrictions and can receive its value from the context in different ways, e.g., anaphorically (*Mary, Jane and Bill built bookcases. Mary built the tallest one.*). Crucially for Heim, the fact that the superlative is FOCUS SENSITIVE gets straightforwardly accounted for on the 2-place semantics: (12) and (13) illustrate how the alternatives contributed by focus contribute to the restriction of the domain of quantification of the adverb *always* and of the superlative (Rooth 1985, 1992, von Fintel 1994, Beaver and Clark 2008, a.o.). In (12a) and (13a) the focus is on the subject '*Mary*' and evokes a set of alternative people: with *always* the resulting meaning involves different occasions on which different people built bookcases; with the superlative, the comparison involves different people who built bookcases. Analogously, with focus on the adjunct '*for DVDs*' in (12b) and (13b), the meaning involves alternative purposes.

(12) a. [*Mary*]$_F$ *always built a bookcase for DVDs.*
'Whenever somebody built a bookcase for DVDs, it was Mary.'
b. *Mary always built a bookcase for* [*DVDs*]$_F$.
'Whenever Mary built a bookcase for some purpose, it was for DVDs.'

(13) a. *[Mary]$_F$ built the tallest bookcase for DVDs.*
'Mary built a taller bookcase for DVDs than anybody else did.'
b. *Mary built the tallest bookcase for [DVDs]$_F$.*
'Mary built a taller bookcase for DVDs than for any other purpose.'

However, in Tomaszewicz (2013, 2015a, 2015b) I showed that -$est_{2-place}$ with focus association overgenerates the relative readings attested cross-linguistically, while -$est_{3-place}$ can correctly derive the available range. Therefore, focus association is available for domain restriction of -$est_{3-place}$ but not of -$est_{2-place}$ (contra Heim 1999), which means that it is enough to have -$est_{3-place}$ in the grammar to derive the absolute/relative ambiguity. The novel claim in this paper is that -$est_{2-place}$ is needed in the grammar of languages that have a superlative construction where the comparison class is explicitly specified as containing sets of degrees, as in (14)–(15) in Turkish and Polish. To my knowledge, this kind of data has not yet been discussed in the literature. The sentences in (14)–(15) contain the superlative phrase '*tallest wardrobe*' modified by the measure phrase '*205 centimeters*'. This construction is not available in English; the English translations contain passive voice and a relative clause. In the Turkish and Polish sentences (14)–(15) 'tallest wardrobe' is the object, and I will provide arguments that -$est_{2-place}$ scopes at the edge of the DP and the measure phrase merges as the modifier of C, deriving the comparison as in (16).

(14) *En yüksek 205 cm gardırop satıyorum.*   Turkish
    est high   205 cm wardrobe I-sell
    'The tallest wardrobe I sell is 205 cm.'
    (Lit. '*I sell a tallest 205 cm wardrobe.*'—ungrammatical in English)

(15) *Najwyższą oferujemy szafę   na 205 centymetrów.*   Polish
    highest   we-offer   wardrobe at 205 centimeters
    'The tallest wardrobe we offer is 205 cm.'
    (Lit. '*We offer a tallest 205 cm wardrobe.*'—ungrammatical in English)

(16) LF for (14): I sell [$_{DP2}$ [-est_2 $_{place}$ [$C_{\langle dt,t\rangle}$ 205 m]] [$_{DP1}$ λd [d-tall wardrobe]]]
    $C_{\langle dt,t\rangle} \subseteq \{ D: \exists x [D = \lambda d.\ \text{wardrobe}(x) \wedge \text{tall}(x, d)] \}$
    $[\![DP2]\!] = \exists d. \exists x[\text{wardrobe}(x) \wedge \text{tall}(x, d) \wedge \forall Q \in C[C = \{D: \max(D) \leq 205\,\text{cm}\}$
    $\wedge\ Q \neq [\![DP1]\!] \rightarrow \neg(Q(d))]]$[8]
    I'm selling a wardrobe of 205 cm, which is higher than the height of any other relevant wardrobe.

---

8 We assume that in the indefinite DP the individual variable introduced by the predicate '*wardrobe*' is existentially closed off by a covert indefinite determiner. This allows for a simple

Due to the presence of the degree phrase in (14)–(15) the native speaker intuitions about the comparison set are clear: it contains different heights of wardrobes, i.e., sets of degrees. This provides direct evidence for $-est_{2-\text{place}}$, just like direct evidence for the existence of $-est_{3-\text{place}}$ in the grammar comes from the option of overtly specifying C as in (8a-b) above, where the PPs ("of all the bookcases", "of all the bookcase building people") explicitly define the relevant sets of individuals (Heim 1985).

A specialized role for $-est_{2-\text{place}}$ has been proposed by Romero (2010, 2012) who argues that it is necessary in the grammar to derive MODAL SUPERLATIVES (Larson 2000, Schwarz 2005). When the modal adjective *possible* is added as a modifier of the head noun, (17), the interpretation is that the object that Mary built is not actually a wardrobe but could be used as one. When *possible* accompanies a superlative adjective, (18), an additional special reading arises, (18b), where the wardrobe is an actual wardrobe that is as tall as it was possible for Mary to build.

(17) *Mary built a **possible** wardrobe.*
 'Mary built something that is possibly a wardrobe.'

(18) *Mary built the tallest **possible** wardrobe.*
 a. 'Out of objects that were possible wardrobes, Mary built the tallest one.'
 NOUN MODIFIER
 b. 'Mary built as tall a wardrobe as it was possible for her to build.' MODAL SUPERLATIVE

Romero (2010, 2012) adopts Larson's (2000) proposal that *possible* introduces a nonfinite complement that gets elided, leaving an antecedent-contained deletion (ACD) gap, but argues that (i) the constituent [possible ▲$_{\text{ACD}}$] is interpreted as an amount relative clause (19a) (Carlson 1977), and (ii) this constituent is plugged in as the comparison class argument of $-est_{2-\text{place}}$, (19b).

(19) a. LF for (18b):
 $[[-est_{2-\text{place}}]$ $[\lambda d$ possible $\langle$for Mary to build A d-tall wardrobe$\rangle]]$ $[\lambda d$ Mary built A d- tall wardrobe]
 b. $C_{\langle dt,t \rangle} = \text{SHIFT}^{\downarrow}_{\langle d,t \rangle} \rightarrow_{\langle dt,t \rangle} [\![\lambda d$ possible $\langle$Mary built A d-tall wardrobe$\rangle]\!]$
 $= \lambda D_{\langle d,t \rangle}. \exists d [\Diamond \exists x [\text{wardrobe}(x) \wedge \text{built}(m, x) \wedge \text{tall}(x, d)]] \wedge D = \lambda d'. d' \leq d$

---

combination of the DP with the rest of the clause. I discuss the role of null indefinite determiners in superlatives in sections 3–5.

The set of possible heights obtained from [λ*d* possible ▲$_{ACD}$] in (19a) is {..., 1m, 1.5m, 2m, ...} and it gets shifted to the set of corresponding degree sets {λ*d'. d'* ≤ 1m, λ*d'. d'* ≤ 1.5m, λ*d'. d'* ≤ 2m, ...} which functions as the comparison class *C*, (19b). The actual degree set is the meaning of [λ*d* Mary built a *d*-tall wardrobe] and so the meaning of the sentence is that Mary's actual degree set contains a degree that no other set in *C* has. Since for the modal superlative reading the constituent [λ*d* possible ▲$_{ACD}$] must be interpreted as overtly specifying *C*, when a *among/of*-PP is present, the comparison class is overtly specified and the degree reading disappears—the only available reading is the one where *possible* is just a noun modifier.

(20) *Among/of all the students, Mary built the tallest possible wardrobe.*

Romero (2010) shows that the modal superlative reading cannot be derived using -*est*$_{3-place}$. She concludes that just like the comparative morpheme -*er*, -*est* requires two different (but truth-conditionally equivalent) lexical entries in the grammar to account for the range of constructions found cross-linguistically.

In the next section, I discuss in further detail the data from Turkish and Polish where the superlative co-occurs with numeral modifiers and measure phrases, by which the comparison class is explicitly specified as containing sets of degrees. I then argue for a division of labor between the two lexical entries. Unlike proposed in Heim (1999), -*est*$_{2-place}$ does not derive relative readings with the use of the mechanism of focus association, its only job is to compare degrees (Section 4). -*Est*$_{3-place}$ derives relative readings by focus association, which accounts for the restrictions on the availability of those readings cross-linguistically (Pancheva and Tomaszewicz 2012, Tomaszewicz 2015a,b) (Section 5).

The division of labor between the two entries for -*est* predicts that some languages may have both of them and some only one. (Of course, some languages may not have a separate morpheme for the superlative at all. In this volume, Bogal-Albritten and Coppock discuss the superlative construction in Navajo that contains a morpheme with the semantics of the comparative quantifier -*er* and an indefinite standard.) However, other morpho-syntactic considerations also affect the cross-linguistic availability of various superlative constructions. In section 3.4, I show that the superlative DP needs to be indefinite, as it is in Turkish and Polish, to compositionally derive the comparison of degrees with -*est*$_{2-place}$. Thus, if English uses -*est*$_{2-place}$ for the modal readings as argued by Romero (2010, 2012), what typologically distinguishes Turkish/Polish from English is the definiteness of the superlative DP. In sections 3–4, I present arguments from Polish and Bulgarian (Tomaszewicz and Pancheva

2016, Tomaszewicz 2015a,b) that definiteness also restricts the possible configurations for focus association with -$est_{3-place}$. Table 3.1 below summarizes the facts. (Table 3.2, in section 5, will include the scope facts.)

3   -$Est_{2-place}$ Compares Degrees

3.1   New Data

As we saw in section 2.2 in the examples (14)–(15), repeated below as (21b) and (22b), in Turkish and Polish superlative phrases such as *'tallest wardrobe'* can be modified by MEASURE PHRASES, e.g. *'205 centimeters'*. Measure phrases occur with quality superlatives (21b-c), (22b-c) and numerals with quantity superlatives (21a), (22a). These expressions explicitly refer to degrees and, as we will see shortly, can be targeted by DEGREE *WH*-QUESTIONS. Such constructions are not possible in English and have not been reported in the literature.

(21) a. *Geçen hafta en[9] çok   5 tane çörek yedim*   Turkish
       last   week *est* many 5 *tane* donut I-ate
       'The most donuts I ate last week was 5.'

   b. *En yüksek 205 cm gardırop satıyorum.*
      est high 205 cm wardrobe I-sell
      'The tallest wardrobe I sell is 205 cm.'

   c. *Geçen hafta en yüksek B+ not   aldım.*
      last   week *est* high B+ grade I-got
      'The best grade I got last week was B+.'

(22) a. *W zeszłym tygodniu zjadłem najwięcej 5 pączków.*   Polish
       in last   week   I-ate   most   5 donuts
       'The most donuts I ate last week was 5.'

   b. *Najwyższą oferujemy szafę   na 2 metry.*
      highest   we-offer wardrobe at 2 meters
      'The tallest wardrobe we offer is 2 m.'

---

9   I am glossing *en* as the morpheme -*est* for clarity of exposition, though it corresponds to *most* in the English analytic form of the superlative, e.g., *'the most expensive'*, and is not a prefix like *naj-* in Polish. *En* can be accented, e.g, *'EN pahalı'*—*'the MOST expensive'*, and has to immediately precede the adjective/quantifier.

TABLE 3.1 Cross-linguistic variation

$-est_{2-place}$ (comparison of degrees)	definite/indefinite	modal superlatives	English
	indefinite	superlatives with measure phrases	Turkish, Polish
$-est_{3-place}$ (comparison of individuals)	definite	absolute readings	English, Turkish, Bulgarian, Polish
		relative readings with focus on DP-external constituents	English, Turkish, Bulgarian, Polish
	indefinite	relative readings with focus on DP-internal constituents	Turkish, Polish, Bulgarian

   c. *Najlepszą dostałem ocenę B+.*[10]
      best   I-got   grade B+
      'The best grade I got was B+.'

The numerals and measure phrases explicitly state what the highest degree in the comparison set is. Native speaker intuitions are clear: we are comparing different quantities of donuts eaten on different days/occasions in (21a), (22a), different heights of wardrobes in (21b), (22b) and different grades in (21c), (22c), i.e., different sets of degrees.

In order to demonstrate that these sentences explicitly state that degrees are compared, let's consider possible contexts in which they could appear. In the scenario in (23) there are different amounts of donuts and different days, so as in English, you can ask about the day on which the biggest amount was eaten,

---

10   In the examples (16b–c) the superlative adjective is topicalized, because without that a temporary ambiguity (garden path) obtains. In Polish, there is no definite determiner, so the following sentence out of the blue gets the absolute reading as indicated in the translation:

   Dostałem najlepszą ocenę B+.
   I-got   best   grade B+
   'I got the best grade, (it's) B+.'

(23 Target 1). Crucially, unlike in English, you can also ask about the amount itself using a SUPERLATIVE DEGREE QUESTION, (23 Target 2). In the question, the expression *'tek seferde'* ('in one sitting') emphasizes that we are asking about a single amount. The *wh*-word *'kaç'* together with the count noun classifier *'tane'* (Görgülü 2012, Sağ 2018) can be translated as *'how many'*, and its position is parallel to that of the numeral in the answer, (23A', identical to (21a) above) (Turkish is a *wh*-in-situ language). Of course, the question can also receive a short answer, (23A"), just like a regular question *'How many donuts did you eat?'*.

(23) SCENARIO: Turkish
Pazartesi 3, Salı   4, Çarşamba 5 çörek yedim. Yani en çok
Monday 3, Tuesday 4, Wednesday 5 donut I-ate. Thus *est* many
çöreği Çarşamba   yedim.
donut Wednesday I-ate
'I ate 3 donuts on Monday, 4 on Tuesday, and 5 on Wednesday. So on Wednesday I ate the most donuts.'

TARGET 1
Q: *Geçen hafta en çok   çöreği **hangi gün** yedin?*
    last week *est* many donut which day you-ate
    'On which day last week did you eat the most donuts?'

A: *Çarşamba.*
    Wednesday
    'On Wednesday.'

TARGET 2:
Q': *Geçen hafta tek   seferde en çok **kaç tane** çörek*
    last week single time *est* many how *tane* donut
    yedin?[11]   SUPERLATIVE DEGREE QUESTION
    you-ate
    'What was the most donuts that you ate last week in one sitting?'

A': *Geçen hafta en çok 5 tane çörek*
    last week *est* many 5 *tane* donut
    yedim.   QUANTITY SUPERLATIVE = (21a)
    I-ate
    'The most donuts I ate last week was 5.'

---

11   The phrase *'tek seferde'* ('in one sitting') helps to disambiguate between interpreting *'en çok'* as *'the most'* and *'at most'*. With adjectival superlatives there is no such ambiguity.

A": 5.

The same scenario is given in Polish in (24). In (24Q'), the wh-word *'ile'* is used exclusively for amounts and it undergoes *wh*-movement pied-piping the rest of the DP. In the answer, (24A'), the numeral follows *'most'* (like in (22a) above). *'Most'* can also be topicalized, (4A"), to match the information structural requirement to place old information first and new information last (Polish allows Left-Branch Extraction).

(24) SCENARIO: *Polish*
    W poniedziałek zjadłem 3 pączki, we wtorek 4, w środę 5.
    on Monday   I-ate   3 donuts, on Tuesday 4, on Wednesday 5
    Tak więc w środę   zjadłem najwięcej pączków.
    thus so   on Wednesday I-ate   most   donuts
    'I ate 3 donuts on Monday, 4 on Tuesday, and 5 on Wednesday. So on Wednesday I ate the most donuts.'

    TARGET 1:
    Q: *W jaki   dzień zjadłeś   najwięcej pączków?*
          on which day   you-ate most   donuts
          'On which did you eat the most donuts?'

    A: *W środę.*
          'On Wednesday.'

    TARGET 2:
    Q':   *Ile   najwięcej pączków zjadłeś   na raz?*
          how most   donuts   you-ate at once
          'What was the most donuts that you ate in one sitting?'

    A':   *Zjadłem najwięcej 5 pączków.*   (- (22))
          I-ate   most   5 donuts
          'The most donuts I ate was 5.'

    A":   *Najwięcej zjadłem 5 pączków.*
          most   I-ate   5 donuts
          'The most donuts I ate was 5.'

What further indicates that the comparison is between amounts is that when you add the adverbial 'on Wednesday' to the degree question, (25), the interpretation is forced where donuts were eaten on multiple occasions in a single day, i.e., several separate amounts are compared.

(25) Ile   najwięcej pączków zjadłeś   w   środę?
     how most   donuts   you-ate on Wednesday
     'What was the most donuts that you ate on Wednesday?'

With adjectival superlatives, degree questions are also possible and the answers contain the measure phrases shown above in (21b-c) and (22b-c). The question in (26Q) contains the *wh*-phrase '*ne kadar*' which, unlike '*kaç (tane)*' above in (23Q'), allows mass nouns. When '*kaç*' is used, (26Q'), an overt unit of measurement is necessary. Both (26Q-Q') can be answered in the same way, (26A). '*Ne kadar*' is also the default form for a degree question with the positive form of the adjective, as in (27Q). Thus, so far we see that in Turkish degree *wh*-phrases (*how many, how much, how tall*), numerals and measure phrases occur with both superlative and positive forms.

(26) Q: *En yüksek **ne kadar** gardırop   satıyorsunuz?*   Turkish
          est high   what   wardrobe you-sell
          'What is the tallest wardrobe that you sell?'

     Q': *En yüksek **kaç santim**   gardırop   satıyorsunuz?*
          est high   how centimeter wardrobe you-sell
          'What is the tallest wardrobe, in centimeters, that you sell?'

     A: *En yüksek 205 cm gardırop   satıyorum.*   (= (21b))
          est high   205 cm wardrobe I-sell
          'The tallest wardrobe I sell is 205 cm.'

(27) Q: *Ne kadar uzun gardırop   satıyorsunuz?*
          what   long wardrobe you-sell
          'How tall a wardrobe are you selling?'

     A: *205 cm uzunluğunda gardırop   satıyorum.*
          205 cm in-length   wardrobe I-sell
          'I'm selling a 205 cm tall wardrobe.'

Polish reveals a crucial difference between the '*how tall*' and '*how tallest*' questions. With the superlative, the *wh*-phrase shows agreement with the head noun (in case and gender), (28Q), but with the positive, it doesn't (29Q). Only with the superlative does the degree question word need to carry its own inflectional suffix '*jak-ą*'. This fact suggests that the two *wh*-elements do not originate in the same position. The details of this contrast will be discussed in the next section.

(28) Q: *Jaką   najwyższą   szafę*
       how*Acc.Fem* highest*Acc.Fem* wardrobe*Acc.Fem*
       oferujecie?   Polish
       you-offer
       'What is the tallest wardrobe that you offer?'

     A: *Najwyższą   oferujemy szafę   na*
       highest*Acc.Fem* we-offer   wardrobe*Acc.Fem* at
       2 metry.   (= (22b))
       2 meters
       'The tallest wardrobe we offer is 2 m.'

(29) Q: *Jak wysoką   szafę   oferujecie?*
       how high*Acc.Fem* wardrobe*Acc.Fem* you-offer
       'How tall a wardrobe are you selling?'

     A: *Oferujemy szafę   na 2 metry.*
       we-offer   wardrobe*Acc.Fem* at 2 meters
       'We're selling a 2 m tall wardrobe.'

When the alternatives are ordered on a scale that is not an inherent scale of the predicate, the answers with the superlative and with the positive are different, showing that the degree *wh*-words have different functions. The predicate *high/tall* in (28)–(29) above is associated with a measurement scale whose units are centimeters, inches, etc. But *high* can also be used for orderings on less conventional and ad-hoc scales, without units. The superlative degree question in (30Q), about the highest school grade, contains '*kaç*' and can only be answered by telling which grade it was (30A-A'). Thus, in a superlative question the function of a *wh*-word is to pick a degree from a comparison set of degrees, here, a set of school grades. The question implies that you received different grades and one of them was the highest, and accordingly it is incoherent to answer that the grade was high, (30A"). In contrast, both '*high*' and '*B+*' are felicitous as answers to the question with the positive form, (31). The same is illustrated for Polish in (32) and (33).

(30) Q: *Geçen hafta en yüksek **kaç** not aldın?*   Turkish
last week est high how grade you-got
'What was the best grade that you got last week?'

A: *Geçen hafta en yüksek B+ not aldım.*   (= (21c))
last week est high B+ grade I-got
'The best grade I got last week was B+.'

A': *B+.*

A": *#Yüksek.*
high

(31) Q: *Ne kadar yüksek not aldın?*[12]
what high grade you-got
'How good a grade did you get?'

A: *Yüksek (bir) not aldım.*
high a grade I-got
'I got a high grade.'

A': *B+ aldım.*
B+ I-got
'I got B+.'

(32) Q: *Jaką najlepszą ocenę dostałeś?*   Polish
how best grade you-got
'What was the best grade that you got?'

A: *Najlepszą dostałem ocenę B+.*   (= (22c))
best I-got grade B+
'The best grade I got was B+.'

A': *#Całkiem dobrą.*
'Pretty good.'

---

12 Note that, just like the English translation, this is not a neutral way of asking *'What grade did you get?'*. You could say *'Nasıl bir not aldın?'* (lit. *How a grade did you get*) and the appropriate answer could also be *'pretty good/bad'* (lit. *'pretty high/low'*).

(33) Q: *Jak dobrą ocenę dostałeś?*
       how good grade you-got
       'How good a grade did you get?'

   A: *Całkiem dobrą.*
       'Pretty good.'

   A': B+.

To summarize, the Turkish and Polish data above shows that superlative degree questions and their answers with measure phrases are about degrees, but the function of the measure phrases (and thus location at LF) is different to that with the positive form. While the questions with the positive form in (31) and (33) ask about the degree to which the grade is high/good, the meaning of the superlative questions (30) and (32) is different. In the next two sub-sections, I present the semantics of measure phrases and degree questions, and I show that '*how*' in superlative degree questions cannot bind the same argument as in positive degree questions. I propose that '*how*' and measure phrases merge as modifiers of the domain restrictor C of $-est_{2-place}$.

3.3 The Semantics of Superlatives with Measure Phrases

A measure phrase can provide an answer to a degree question, (34). Consider the standard analysis of a positive degree question, (35). *Wh*-movement creates abstraction over the degree argument (von Stechow 1984) and the question denotes a set of propositions of the form 'The wardrobe is d-high' (Hamblin 1973, Karttunen 1977, Beck and Rullmann 1999, a.o.).

(34) Q: How high is the wardrobe?
   A: The wardrobe is 2 m high.

(35) a. [? [how_d [the wardrobe is d-high]]]
   b. $\lambda p. \exists d\ [p = \lambda w\ [$the wardrobe is d-high in $w]]$
   c. {The wardrobe is 2 m high, The wardrobe is 205 cm high, The wardrobe is 3 m high, ...}

The superlative morpheme binds the degree argument of the gradable predicate, as shown in (36a) for $-est_{3-place}$, and in (36b) for $-est_{2-place}$ (the superlative morpheme moves to the edge of the DP and the determiner is assumed to contribute existential quantification). So, obviously, how_d in superlative degree questions cannot bind the same argument (nor can a measure phrase of type

⟨dt,t⟩, as introduced shortly in (42)). Needless to say, a measure phrase of type d cannot saturate the degree variable, since the superlative morpheme quantifies over that variable.)

(36) a. [$_{DP}$ the [-$est_{3-place}$ $C_{⟨e,t⟩}$]$_{⟨d,et⟩}$ [$_{NP}$ d-high wardrobe]]
   b. [$_{DP2}$ [-$est_{2-place}$ $C_{⟨dt,t⟩}$]$_{⟨dt,t⟩}$ [$_{DP1}$ *the*/*a* d-high wardrobe]]

I propose a solution based on the observation above that in Polish how$_d$ in superlative degree questions must carry its own inflectional suffix (*jak-ą*) in superlative questions, (37Q), in contrast to questions with the positive form where how$_d$ shows no agreement with the head noun, (*jak-∅*), (39Q). The inflection on *jak-ą* shows that it is an independent modifier of the noun just like in the question (38Q), [[how$_d$ + *Infl*] [Adj + -*est* + *Infl*] N] vs. [[how$_d$ [Adj + *Infl*]] N]. Like (38Q), (39Q) can be answered by naming the wardrobe type, PAX, because it can be interpreted as 'Which wardrobe of the tallest kind do you sell?' (cf. 'which wardrobe of the wooden kind'). When how$_d$ with the positive form (39Q) does not carry inflection, (*jak-∅*), the answer has to provide a measure. When it is inflected, (40Q) the answer can either be the measure phrase or the name of the wardrobe. Therefore, the measure phrase in the answer to the superlative question, (37A) is an independent modifier, unlike the measure phrase with the positive form (39A).

(37) Q: ***Jaką/(*jak)***   *najwyższą*   *szafę*
   how*ACC.FEM*/how∅ highest*ACC.FEM* wardrobe*ACC.FEM*
   oferujecie? (= (28Q)) Polish
   you-offer
   'What is the tallest wardrobe that you sell?' → Answer A
   'Which tallest wardrobe do you sell?' → Answer A'

   A: *Najwyższą*   *oferujemy szafę*   *na 2 metry.*
   highest*ACC.FEM* we-offer wardrobe*ACC.FEM* at 2 meters
   'The tallest wardrobe we sell is 2 m.'

   A': *Najwyższą*   *oferujemy szafę*   PAX.
   highest*ACC.FEM* we-offer wardrobe*ACC.FEM* PAX
   'The tallest wardrobe we sell is PAX.'

(38) Q: ***Jaką***   *drewnianą*   *szafę*   *oferujecie?*
   how*ACC.FEM* wooden*ACC.FEM* wardrobe*ACC.FEM* you-offer
   'Which wooden wardrobe do you sell?'

THE SEMANTICS OF THE SUPERLATIVE QUANTIFIER -EST 97

A: *Drewnianą oferujemy szafę* PAX.
woodenAcc.Fem we-offer wardrobeAcc.Fem PAX
'The wooden wardrobe that we sell is PAX.'

(39) Q: *Jak wysoką szafę oferujecie?* (= (29Q))
how highAcc.Fem wardrobeAcc.Fem you-offer
'How tall a wardrobe are you selling?'

A: *Oferujemy szafę na 2 metry.*
we-offer wardrobeAcc.Fem at 2 meters
'We're selling a 2 m tall wardrobe.'

A': **Wysoką oferujemy szafę* PAX.
highAcc.Fem we-offer wardrobeAcc.Fem PAX

(40) Q: *Jaką wysoką szafę oferujecie?*
howAcc.Fem highAcc.Fem wardrobeAcc.Fem you-offer
?'How tall a wardrobe are you selling?' → Answer A
'Which tall wardrobe are you selling?' → Answer A

A: *?Oferujemy szafę na 2 metry.*
we-offer wardrobeAcc.Fem at 2 meters
'We're selling a 2 m tall wardrobe.'

A': *Wysoką oferujemy szafę* PAX.
highAcc.Fem we-offer wardrobeAcc.Fem PAX
'We're selling a tall wardrobe PAX.'

Recall that Romero (2012) proposed that in modal superlatives $-est_{2-\text{place}}$ takes as its complement the syntactic unit [1 possible ▲]. This accounts for Schwarz's (2005) observation that in German for the modal superlative reading to arise, the superlative adjective and *möglich* ('possible') need to "share" the inflection suffix, [Adj + *-st möglich*] + *Infl*, as opposed to behaving like two independent modifiers [Adj + *-st* + *Infl*] [*möglich* + *Infl*]. In Polish superlative questions, the inflected how$_d$ and the superlative adjective are two independent modifiers. I propose that how$_d$ and the measure phrase merge as modifiers of the domain restrictor C of $-est_{2-\text{place}}$ (41a-b).

(41) a. We sell [-*est* [$C_{\langle dt,t \rangle}$ 2 $m_{\langle dt,t \rangle}$]] [1 d_1-high wardrobe]
b. We sell [-*est* [$C_{\langle dt,t \rangle}$ how$_{\langle dt,t \rangle}$]] [1 d_1-high wardrobe]

According to Schwarzschild (2005) measure phrases can be interpreted as sets of sets of degrees (i.e., predicates over intervals, type ⟨dt,t⟩), (42). (In this volume, Schwarzschild argues that neither the treatment of measure phrases as of type d nor as of type ⟨dt,t⟩ can adequately account for all the ways in which they are used in degree constructions (e.g. '2m *long*' is possible, but '2m *short*' is not, and neither is '2kg *heavy*'; in contrast, '2m *longer*', '2m *shorter*', '2kg *heavier*' are all fine). For our present purposes, type ⟨dt,t⟩ is optimal.) The predicate 'meter' in (42b) is true of the elements of the set that can be partitioned into the number of subsets indicated by the numeral, here 2. The measure phrase can be type-shifted (Schwarzschild 2005) or, as in (42c), it can QR to avoid type clash (von Stechow 2005, Beck 2008).

(42) a. ⟦2m⟧= $\lambda D. \max(D) = 2$ m
 b. ⟦meters⟧= $\lambda d\, \lambda D. \max(D) = d$ meters
 c. [2m$_{⟨dt,t⟩}$][$_{⟨d,t⟩}$1 [the wardrobe is d_1-high]]

Analogously, plural nouns can be thought of as predicates of sums of individuals and '5 donuts' is a set of sums of donuts whose cardinality is five (Landman 1989). I use a simplified notation for that idea in (43a-b), which is exactly parallel to (42a-c). Simply put, a bare numeral '5' in 'I ate 5 donuts' can mean '5-units'. This meaning is expressed overtly in Turkish, where the classifier '*tane*' has a parallel role to that of 'meter' in (42b). When '*tane*' is present with plural countable nouns in (23Q'-A'), according to Sağ (2018) it introduces a presupposition for atomic properties. In (43c) '*tane*' tells us that donuts come in units, and, above in the superlative question about donuts in (23Q') the *wh*-expression '*kaç tane*' ('how many') was felicitous.

(43) a. ⟦5-*units*⟧= $\lambda D. \max(D) = 5$ units

 b. [5-*units*$_{⟨dt,t⟩}$][$_{⟨d,t⟩}$1 [I ate d_1-many donuts]]

 c. *5 tane çörek yedim.*
   5 tane donut I-ate
   'I ate 5 donuts.'

That '*tane*' presupposes atomic units is supported by fact that it cannot be used with other kinds of degrees. In the superlative question about the height of the wardrobe in (26Q') a unit of measurement such as centimeters, '*kaç santim*', needed to be used instead of '*tane*'. Similarly, in the school grades context in (30) above, '*tane*' is not possible, the *wh*-word '*kaç*' needs to combine with '*not*' ('grade') directly.

THE SEMANTICS OF THE SUPERLATIVE QUANTIFIER -EST   99

The semantics of $\textit{-est}_{2-place}$ offers a straightforward role for the numeral '5 tane'. Consider first the meaning derived with $\textit{-est}_{2-place}$ in the absence of a numeral. The LF is as in (44a). The DP is indefinite and existential closure applies before λ-abstraction (44b). The presupposition of $\textit{-est}_{2-place}$ determines that the comparison set C contains the sets of different quantities of donuts, (44c).

(44) a. I ate [$_{DP2}$ [$\textit{-est}_{2-place}$ C] [$_{DP1}$ 1 [d_1-many donuts]]]
 b. ⟦DP1⟧= λd. ∃x. donut(x) ∧ |x|≥ d
 c. $C_{\langle dt,t \rangle}$ ⊆ { D: ∃x [D = λd. donut(x) ∧ |x|≥ d] }
 d. ⟦DP2⟧= ∃d. ∃x [donut(x) ∧ |x|≥ d ∧ ∀Q∈C [Q≠⟦DP1⟧→ ¬(Q(d))]]

The sentence is true if I ate a quantity of donuts that is larger than any other relevant quantity, (44a-d). But saying "I ate the largest quantity of donuts" is not very informative unless quantities of other sizes are salient in the context. The presupposition of $\textit{-est}_{2-place}$ is that the comparison class C contains the set determined by the scope of $\textit{-est}_{2-place}$, the set of quantities of donuts in (44b), and some other sets containing the relevant degrees (as specified in the lexical entry in (6) above). The meaning of '5-*units*' above in (43a) is that the maximum number of unit size partitions is 5. If the numeral merges as the modifier of C, as in (45a), the result could technically be C ={D: max(D) = 5}, meaning that the cardinality of all sets in C is 5, which is pragmatically odd because the assertion is about the degree d that only one of the sets in C has. Thus pragmatic relevance allows us to interpret the numeral as the highest cardinality of the sets in C, i.e., C ={D: max(D) ≤ 5}. Accordingly, the sentence asserts that I ate a quantity of donuts that was the largest quantity in C, namely 5.[13]

---

[13] We can also assume high scope for $\textit{-est}_{2-place}$, (i-a), which will explicitly derive the comparison between the different quantities that I ate. However, Heim (1999), Farkas and Kiss (2000), Sharvit and Stateva (2002) argue that when contextual specification alone is able to derive the relevant comparison set, we need a theoretical motivation for QR. While we see no need for $\textit{-est}_{2-place}$ for to QR, in Section 5, I present empirical data that $\textit{-est}_{3-place}$ must QR.
(i) a. [$_{CP2}$ [$\textit{-est}_{2-place}$ [C 5-unit]] [$_{CP1}$ I ate [$_{DP}$ 1 [d_1-many donuts]]]]
 b. ⟦CP1⟧= λd. ∃x [eat(I, x) ∧ donut(x) ∧ |x|≥ d]
 c. $C_{\langle dt,t \rangle}$ ⊆ { D: ∃x [D = λd. eat(I, x) ∧ donut(x) ∧ |x|≥ d] }
 d. ⟦CP2⟧= ∃d. ∃x [eat(I, x) ∧ donut(x) ∧ |x|≥ d ∧ ∀Q∈C [C ={D: max(D) ≤ 5} ∧ Q≠⟦DP1⟧→ ¬(Q(d))]]
 e. *I ate donuts in a quantity of 5 that was a larger quantity than any other relevant quantity that I ate.*

(45) a. I ate [$_{DP2}$ [-$est_{2-place}$ [C 5-unit]] [$_{DP1}$ 1 [d_1-many donuts]]]
   b. ⟦DP1⟧= $\lambda d.\ \exists x\ [\text{donut}(x) \wedge |x| \geq d\ ]$
   c. $C_{\langle dt,t \rangle} \subseteq \{\ D: \exists x\ [D = \lambda d.\ \text{donut}(x) \wedge |x| \geq d]\ \}$
   d. ⟦DP2⟧= $\exists d.\ \exists x\ [\text{donut}(x) \wedge |x| \geq d \wedge \forall Q \in C\ [C = \{D: \max(D) \leq 5\} \wedge Q \neq$ ⟦DP1⟧ $\rightarrow \neg(Q(d))]]$
   e. *I ate donuts in a quantity of 5 that was a larger quantity than any other relevant quantity.*

Superlative degree questions are derived in a parallel way. The question in (46a) is about the maximal quantity in C and not about the maximal quantity of the eaten donuts like in a regular *how-many* question, (46b) (for the different approaches to the 'maximality effect' in degree questions see Rullman 1995, Beck and Rullman 1999, Rett 2006, a.o.). C contains different quantities of donuts, eaten on different occasions, which is why the superlative question in (47a) with the adverbial 'last week' is most naturally interpreted as asking about quantities of donuts eaten on different days. For the same reason the question in (47b), with the adverbial 'on Wednesday' (seen above in (25)), implies that there were multiple occasions of donut eating on a single day.

(46) a. I ate [-$est_{2-place}$ [$C_{\langle dt,t \rangle}$ **how**$_{\langle dt,t \rangle}$]] [1 [d_1-many donuts]]]
   b. [**how**$_{\langle dt,t \rangle}$][1 [I ate d_1-many donuts]]

(47) a. *Ile   najwięcej pączków zjadłeś w zeszłym tygodniu?*
       how most donuts   you-ate in last   week
       'What was the most donuts that you ate last week?'

   b. *Ile   najwięcej pączków zjadłeś w środę?*   (= (25))
       how most donuts   you-ate on Wednesday
       'What was the most donuts that you ate on Wednesday?'

The *wh*-words '*kaç (tane)*', '*ne kadar*', '*ile*' and '*jak*' take a degree set and give its maximal degree, which by definition must be unique, (48). This meaning is compatible with the presupposition that C contains different measures for a given entity and the different forms of the *wh*-words select for the different kinds of degrees (cardinalities of donuts, school grades, heights of wardrobe). (Just like '*2 meters*' is composed of a numeral and the predicate '*meter*', (42b) above, these *wh*-words are underlyingly composed of a *wh*-element and predicate specifying the measure).

(48) ⟦ kaç (tane) / ne kadar / ile / jak ⟧= $\lambda D.\ \max(D)$

In a superlative question, (49a), the *wh*-word picks a set from the comparison set *C*, (49b). At LF, *-est* and its complement [*C* how] undergo *wh*-movement, (49a), and as a result both CP and the [*-est C* how] constituent are of type ⟨dt,t⟩. They get combined by pointwise functional application resulting in the set (49c) (Hamblin 1973). The set contains propositions with different maximal quantities in *C*, (49d).

(49) a. [*-est*₂₋place [*C*⟨dt,t⟩ how⟨dt,t⟩]] [CP 2 [I ate [DP2 t₂ [DP1 1 [*d*₁-many donuts]]]]]
   b. *C*⟨dt,t⟩ ⊆ { *D*: ∃*x* [*D* = λ*d*. donut(*x*) ∧ |*x*| ≥ *d*] }
   c. {⟦CP⟧(*D*) | *D* ∈ ⟦*-est C*⟨dt,t⟩ how⟨dt,t⟩⟧}
   d. { I ate *x1* ∧ ∃d [donut(*x1*) ∧ |*x1*| ≥ *d* ∧ ∀*Q*∈*C* [*C* ={*D*: **max(*D*) ≤ 5**} ∧ *Q* ≠ (λ*d'*. donut(*x1*) ∧ |*x1*| ≥ *d'*) → ¬*Q*(*d*)]]; I ate *x2* ∧ ∃d [donut(*x2*) ∧ |*x2*| ≥ *d* ∧ ∀*Q*∈*C* [*C* ={*D*: **max(*D*) ≤ 6**} ∧ *Q* ≠ (λ*d'*. donut(*x2*) ∧ |*x2*| ≥ *d'*) → ¬*Q*(*d*)]]; ...}

The LF for the degree question with *-est*₂₋place in (49) and the LF with the measure phrase as a modifier of *C* in (45) match the intuition of native speakers of Turkish an Polish that the comparison involves different amounts, a not individuals as on the absolute and relative readings discussed in the literature. In Tomaszewicz (2013, 2015a) I suggested that, cross-linguistically, *-est*₂₋place is used for cases of explicit comparison between degrees and not for focus association (contra Heim 1999). Here, I provided the data to back up that suggestion. In the next subsection, I discuss the role of definiteness in the availability of superlatives with measure phrases and corresponding superlative questions. I conclude that what allows these constructions in Turkish and Polish is the fact that in these languages superlative DPs can be indefinite. In sections 4 and 5, I present the arguments from Pancheva and Tomaszewicz (2012), Tomaszewicz (2013, 2015a,b) and Tomaszewicz and Pancheva (2016) that the definiteness of the superlative DP also constrains the range of relative readings derived by focus association and that this constraint can only be implemented using *-est*₃₋place. Thus, the two lexical entries are in complimentary distribution: *-est*₂₋place is used when the comparison class is explicitly specified as containing sets of degrees, *est*₃₋place is used when the comparison is between individuals, whose set can be established by focus association.

3.4 Cross-linguistic Predictions

The proposed derivations for superlatives with measure phrases and superlative degree questions rely on the ability of *-est*₂₋place to QR to the edge of the DP so that the derived gradable property can satisfy the presupposition *P*∈*C* and ∀*Q* [[*Q*∈*C* ∧ *Q*≠*P*] → ∃*d* [*Q*(*d*)]]. This is possible when the superlative DP is indefinite; if it is definite the specification of the comparison class C is anomalous. (Note that if $[-est_{2-place}\ C]$ raises to a position below the definite article, its second argument would not be of the right type; it would be $\langle d,et \rangle$, and not $\langle dt \rangle$ as required). Compare (50) with an indefinite and (51) with a definite: in (50b), existential closure applies below 1 and C contains degrees of grades of different "height" (e.g., A, B+, B, C+, ...) which allows for a compositional derivation of the truth conditions (50d-e). But in (51c) C contains degrees of a unique grade![14]

(50) a. I got $[_{DP2}\ [-est\ [C\ B+]]\ [_{DP1}\ 1\ [d_1\text{-high grade}]]]$
 b. $[\![DP1]\!] = \lambda d.\ \exists x\ [\text{grade}(x) \wedge \text{high}(x, d)]$
 c. $C_{\langle dt,t \rangle} \subseteq \{\ D: \exists x\ [D = \lambda d.\ \text{grade}(x) \wedge \text{high}(x, d)]\ \}$
 d. $[\![DP2]\!] = \exists d.\ \exists x\ [\text{grade}(x) \wedge \text{high}(x, d) \wedge \forall Q \in C\ [C = \{D: \max(D) \leq B+\} \wedge Q \neq [\![DP1]\!] \rightarrow \neg(Q(d))]]]$
 e. *I got a grade B+ that was a higher than any other relevant grade.*

(51) a. I got $[_{DP2}\ [-est\ [C\ B+]]\ [_{DP1}\ 1\ [\textbf{the}\ d_1\text{-high grade}]]]$
 b. $[\![DP1]\!] = \lambda d.\ \iota x\ [\text{grade}(x) \wedge \text{high}(x, d)]$
 c. $C_{\langle dt,t \rangle} \subseteq \{D: \iota x\ [D = \lambda d.\ \text{grade}(x) \wedge \text{high}(x, d)]\}$

The proposed account thus predicts that superlatives with measure phrases and superlative degree questions are only possible when the DP is indefinite, i.e., in the absence of the definite article. Empirical support comes from Turkish, where the addition of the definite morpheme makes the question uninterpretable (52Q), in contrast to (30Q). You can only ask *'Which highest grade did you receive?'*, (52Q' with *'hangi'* instead of *'kaç'*), and the answer receives the absolute reading, i.e., there is no comparison with other "heights" of grades that I received.

---

14 Romero (2010) proposes that the definite article can move leaving a trace of type e so that the absolute reading can be derived with $-est_{2-place}$, (i-a). (Romero 2010:36) notes that the "required trace t_2 could be obtained by positing an N'-internal PRO that moves and then deletes; see Heim and Kratzer (1998) on PRO, von Stechow (2009) on a similar use of PRO for tense.") However, she also postulates that the trace is focused and the set of focal alternatives works fine for the specification of C. We have no evidence for focus sensitivity of this construction, so focus marking on the trace would be completely unmotivated here, and without it the specification of C is not right, (i-d).
 (i) a. I got $[_{DP2}\ \text{the}\ 2\ [-est\ [C\ B+]]\ [_{DP1}\ 1\ [t_2\ [_{NP}\ d_1\text{-high grade}]]]]$
 b. $[\![NP]\!]^g = \lambda x\ [\text{grade}(x) \wedge \text{high}(x, g(1))]$
 c. $[\![DP1]\!]^g = \lambda d\ [\text{grade}(g(2)) \wedge \text{high}(g(2), d)]$
 d. $C_{\langle dt,t \rangle} = \{\ \lambda d\ [\text{grade}(g(2)) \wedge \text{high}(x, d)]\ \}$

(52) Q: *Geçen hafta en yüksek kaç notu$_{DEF}$ aldın?
last week *est* high how grade-the you-got

Q': Geçen hafta en yüksek hangi notu$_{DEF}$ aldın?
last week *est* high which grade-the you-got
'Which highest grade did you get?'

A: Geçen hafta en yüksek B+ notu$_{DEF}$ aldım.
last week *est* high B+ grade-the I-got
'I got the highest grade of B+'

It is worth noting that Krasikova (2012) suggests that the definite determiner could also be interpreted as ranging over degrees and not individuals (consider adverbial superlatives: '*I jumped the highest*'.) On Krasikova's account the definite indicates the presence of the maximality operator on C; in (53) we have a maximum of the set of sets of degrees.

(53) [**the** -*est* [C$_{\langle dt,t \rangle}$ how$_{\langle dt,t \rangle}$]] [$_{CP}$ 2 [I ate [$_{DP2}$ t$_2$ [$_{DP1}$ 1 [d$_1$-many donuts]]]]]

This could mean that in a language that has a *wh*-word dedicated to amounts (like the Turkish '*kaç (tane)*' and Polish '*ile*') the presence of the definite could still allow for the comparison class to contain amounts. Simply put, it is not possible to have '*how many the most* …' in English, but perhaps it is possible to have '*how*$_{\langle dt,t \rangle}$ *the most*'. French could be such a language, however, the question in (54) does not sound natural to native speakers.[15] It could have the same interpretation as the Turkish and Polish examples, on which different amounts of cookies are compared, but it does not sound grammatical.

(54) ?/*Combien de biscuits as-tu mangés le plus?   *French*
how-many of cookies have-you eaten the most
'What was the most cookies that you ate?'

I thus conclude that cross linguistically *est*$_{2-place}$ is used for constructions that explicitly call for comparison of degrees, through the presence of measure phrases or *wh*-words dedicated to amounts, but only if the comparison class C can be compositionally derived from the sister node of [-*est*$_{2-place}$ C]. If that

---

[15] I would like to thank Margot Colinet, Julie Belião, Sarah Ouwayda and Jérémy Zehr for their judgements about the French data.

node contains a definite determiner (quantifying over individuals) the resulting specification of C is anomalous.

4   -$Est_{2-place}$ Doesn't Associate with Focus

Heim's (1999) main motivation for the semantics of -$est_{2-place}$ is to account for the FOCUS SENSITIVITY of RELATIVE readings (Ross 1964, Jackendoff 1972, Heim 1985, Szabolcsi 1986, Gawron 1995, a.o.), but we will now see that this analysis overgenerates the range of relative readings available in a language like English where superlative DPs are definite (Tomaszewicz 2013).

The sentence we saw in (8) gets disambiguated in favor of the relative reading when prosodic focus is placed on the subject 'Mary', (55). The absolute reading is available irrespective of the presence of focus.

(55) [*Mary*]$_F$ *built the tallest bookcase (on Monday).*
Preferred reading:
a. '(On Monday,) Mary built a taller bookcase than anyone else did.'
RELATIVE

Also available:
b. '(On Monday,) Mary built a taller bookcase than all the relevant bookcases.'
ABSOLUTE

When we add an adverbial and place focus on it, the relative reading on which alternatives to Mary are compared is no longer available, (56).

(56) *Mary built the tallest bookcase* [*on Monday*]$_F$.
Preferred reading:
a. 'Mary built a taller bookcase on Monday than on any other day.'
RELATIVE

Also available:
b. 'Mary built a taller bookcase on Monday than all the relevant bookcases.'
ABSOLUTE

Not available:
c. 'On Monday, Mary built a taller bookcase than anyone else did.'
RELATIVE

Heim (1999) suggests that the truth-conditional effects of focus on the relative readings, (55a)–(56a vs. c), should be modeled as a contextual effect on the restrictor *C*, entirely parallel to the focus effects with *always*, which we saw in

(12) in section 1.2, and with *only*—the two sentences with pre-verbal *only* in (57a-b) differ only in the location of focus and it is focus that determines the interpretation of the whole sentence (Rooth 1985, 1992, von Fintel 1994, Beaver and Clark 2008, a.o.).

(57) a. *Mary **only** built a bookcase [on Monday]$_F$.*
'Mary built a bookcase on no other day but Monday.'
b. *Mary **only** built [a bookcase]$_F$ on Monday.*
'Mary built nothing else but a bookcase Monday.'

Rooth's (1985, 1992) theory of focus interpretation involves a focus operator, ~ ('squiggle'), which comes with its own restrictor variable, S. The ~ introduces the presupposition that S is a subset of the focus-value of the constituent to which [~ S] attaches, (59e), typically the clause. Following the condition on focus association, (58), when a quantificational element associates with focus, its restrictor variable C is set to be the subset of the same focus value, (59f), (60f).

(58) *Condition on focus association* (Rooth 1992)
$C \subseteq [\![\alpha]\!]^f$, or $C \subseteq \cup[\![\alpha]\!]^f$, where C is the restrictor of a quantificational adverb and α the sister to ~

(59) a. *Mary **only** built a bookcase [on **Monday**]$_F$.*
b. [Only C] [$_{TP2}$ [~ S] [$_{TP1}$ Mary built a bookcase [on Monday]$_F$]]
c. $[\![(59b)]\!] = \lambda w. \forall p[(p \in C \land p \neq [\![\text{Mary built a bookcase on Monday}]\!]) \rightarrow \neg p(w)]$
d. $[\![TP_1]\!]^f = \{p: \exists f\, \exists x\, \exists t\, [p = \lambda w\, [\text{build}(m, x)(\text{at } t)(\text{in } w) \land \text{bookcase}(x)(\text{in } w) \land f(t)(\text{in } w)]]\}$
e. $S \subseteq [\![TP_1]\!]^f$
f. $C \subseteq [\![TP_1]\!]^f$ (*focus association*, (58))

(60) a. *Mary **only** built [a **bookcase**]$_F$ on Monday.*
b. [Only C] [$_{TP2}$ [~ S] [$_{TP1}$ Mary built [a bookcase]$_F$ on Monday]]
c. $[\![(60b)]\!] = \lambda w. \forall p[(p \in C \land p \neq [\![\text{Mary built a bookcase on Monday}]\!]) \rightarrow \neg p(w)]$
d. $[\![TP_1]\!]^f = \{p: \exists f\, \exists x\, \exists t\, [p = \lambda w\, [\text{build}(m, x)(\text{at } t)(\text{in } w) \land \text{Monday}(t)(\text{in } w) \land f(x)(\text{in } w)]]\}$
e. $S \subseteq [\![TP_1]\!]^f$
f. $C \subseteq [\![TP_1]\!]^f$ (*focus association*, (58))

Heim's (1999) semantics for $\textit{-est}_{2-\text{place}}$ allows focus to determine what enters the comparison class via Rooth's focus association mechanism. Like *only*, $\textit{est}_{2-\text{place}}$ takes scope over the entire sentence and in (61a) the focus value of the sister of [~ S], TP$_2$, is a set of sets of degrees, (61c), hence S is of type ⟨dt,t⟩—the right type for C to associate with, (61e). Focus on 'Mary' specifies C as in (61f), while focus on 'on Monday' gives C the specification in (62b).

(61) a. LF for (55a): [$\textit{-est}_{2-\text{place}}$ $C_{\langle \text{dt,t} \rangle}$][$_{\text{TP1}}$ [~ $S_{\langle \text{dt,t} \rangle}$] [$_{\text{TP2}}$ 1 [**Mary**]$_\text{F}$ built A d_1-tall bookcase on Monday]]
  b. ⟦(61a)⟧ = 1 iff
    $\exists d\ \exists x\ \exists t$ [build(m, x)(at t) ∧ bookcase(x) ∧ tall(x, d) ∧ Mon(t)] ∧
    $\forall Q \in C\ [Q \neq ⟦\text{TP}_1⟧ \rightarrow \neg (Q(d))]$]
  c. ⟦TP$_2$⟧^{f} = {D: $\exists y\ \exists x\ \exists t$ [$D = \lambda d.$ build(y, x)(at t) ∧ bookcase(x) ∧ tall(x, d) ∧ Mon(t)]}
  d. $S \subseteq$ ⟦TP$_2$⟧^{f}
  e. $C \subseteq$ ⟦TP$_1$⟧^{f} (*focus association*, (58))
  f. $C_{\langle \text{dt,t} \rangle} \subseteq$ {D: $\exists y\ \exists x\ \exists t$ [$D = \lambda d.$ build(y, x)(at t) ∧ bookcase(x) ∧ tall(x, d) ∧ Mon(t)]}

(62) a. LF for (56a): [$\textit{-est}_{2-\text{place}}$ $C_{\langle \text{dt,t} \rangle}$][$_{\text{TP1}}$ [~ $S_{\langle \text{dt,t} \rangle}$][$_{\text{TP2}}$1 Mary built a d_1-tall bookcase [**on Monday**]$_\text{F}$]]
  b. $C_{\langle \text{dt,t} \rangle} \subseteq$ {D: $\exists f\ \exists x\ \exists t$ [$D = \lambda d.$ build(m, x)(at t) ∧ bookcase(x) ∧ tall(x, d) ∧ $f(t)$]}

Since focus marking is realized prosodically as intonational prominence, the configuration of ~ and $\textit{-est}_{2-\text{place}}$ predicts that focus is necessary to contribute propositional alternatives. As a consequence, the lack of focus effects on the absolute reading is compatible with Romero's (2010, 2012) proposal that $\textit{-est}_{2-\text{place}}$ scopes low, at the edge of the DP, and the definite moves while its trace is obligatorily focus marked deriving the right specification for the comparison class (e.g., other heights of bookcase for the absolute reading in (55b)-(56b)). As discussed in section 1.2, Romero (2010) provides evidence that only $\textit{-est}_{2-\text{place}}$ can derive the modal superlative readings, and I have shown above that $\textit{-est}_{2-\text{place}}$ straightforwardly derives the readings with measure phrases and superlative degree questions in Turkish and Polish. Is then the semantics of $\textit{-est}_{2-\text{place}}$ sufficient in the grammar to account for all the superlative readings, or is $\textit{-est}_{3-\text{place}}$ also necessary? In Tomaszewicz (2013) I observe that $\textit{-est}_{2-\text{place}}$ overgenerates the range of relative readings available in a language like English where superlative DPs are definite. Specifically, using $\textit{-est}_{2-\text{place}}$ we cannot account for the blocking effect of the definite determiner on focus association for a particular relative reading. Let's call it the 'extra' relative reading to reflect the fact that it had not been observed nor discussed in the literature prior to Pancheva and Tomaszewicz (2012) who reported its existence in Polish and Bulgarian. The 'extra' relative reading involves focus on a constituent inside the superlative DP and, as first observed in Pancheva and Tomaszewicz (2012), can be found only in languages where the superlative DP is indefinite. The blocking effect of the definite on the 'extra' relative reading is discussed in detail in the remainder of section 4, where I present the relevant data from Polish and Bulgarian vs. English and show how -$est_{2-place}$ makes the wrong predictions when the focus is DP-internal and the DP is definite. Next in section 5, I show that the interaction between definiteness and focus association is correctly accounted for using -$est_{3-place}$. Thus, it can be concluded that each lexical entry has its specialized role: -$est_{2-place}$ does not associate with focus (contra Heim 1999) but only compares degrees; -$est_{3-place}$ can associate with focus for relative readings.

The semantics of -$est_{2-place}$ makes the prediction that DP-internal focus, on 'bookcase' in (63), triggers the relative reading in (63b) with the comparison set (63e). This reading is not available in English, but it is available in Polish, (64) (although in English *only* in (60) can associate with the focus on 'bookcase'). Crucially, when focus is unambiguously marked on the DP-internal NP as in (65) where the superlative adjective is topicalized, this is the only reading available (Tomaszewicz 2013, 2015a).[16]

(63) a. *Mary built [$_{DP}$ the tallest [bookcase]$_F$].*
    b. 'Mary built a taller *bookcase* than *anything else she built.*'   RELATIVE
        'EXTRA'
    c. LF for (63a): [-$est_{2-place}$ C$_{\langle dt,t \rangle}$][$_{TP3}$ [~ S$_{\langle dt,t \rangle}$] [$_{TP2}$ 1 Mary built a d_1-tall [bookcase]$_F$]]
    d. $[\![TP_2]\!]^f \subseteq \{D: \exists f_{\langle e,t \rangle} \exists x [D = \lambda d.\ f(x) \wedge \text{tall}(x, d) \wedge \text{build}(m, x)]\}$
    e. $C_{\langle dt,t \rangle} \subseteq \{D: \exists f_{\langle e,t \rangle} \exists x [D = \lambda d.\ f(x) \wedge \text{tall}(x, d) \wedge \text{build}(m, x)]\}$

---

16   The superlative adjective in (59) is topicalized (optionally, a topic marker 'to' may be present) and the sentence has a neutral prosodic contour. The Left-Branch Extraction of the superlative adjective prevents the projection of the focus marked by the nuclear pitch accent on the last sentence constituent in (58) and (59). That is, LBE prevents a wide focus interpretation—the noun that remains in-situ and receives the nuclear pitch accent is necessarily interpreted as narrow focus (Tomaszewicz 2015a).

(64) *Maria zbudowała najwyższy regał.*   *Polish*
Maria built   tallest   bookcase
Available readings:
a. 'Mary built a taller bookcase than all the relevant bookcases.'
                                                                                       ABSOLUTE
b. 'Mary built a taller bookcase than anyone else did.'   RELATIVE
c. 'Mary built a taller bookcase than anything else she built.'   (= (63b))
                                                                                     RELATIVE 'EXTRA'

(65) *Najwyższy₁ Maria zbudowała* [$_{DP}$ t_1 [*regał*]$_F$].
tallest   Maria built   bookcase
Available readings:
c. 'Mary built a taller bookcase than anything else she built.'   (= (63b))
                                                                                      RELATIVE 'EXTRA'
Not available:
a. 'Mary built a taller bookcase than all the relevant bookcases.'
                                                                                        ABSOLUTE
b. 'Mary built a taller bookcase than anyone else did.'   RELATIVE

The contrast between Polish and English with respect to the relative reading in (63b) does not follow from the presence vs. absence of -$est_{2-\text{place}}$ in the language, because Bulgarian also allows relative readings with respect to a DP-internal constituent, but only when the superlative DP is indefinite, (67). When it is definite, the range of relative readings is exactly the same as in English, (66) (Pancheva and Tomaszewicz 2012, Tomaszewicz 2015a).

(66) *Maria postroi naj-visoka**ta** biblioteka.*   *Bulgarian*
Maria built   tallest-the   bookcase

Available readings:
a. 'Mary built a taller bookcase than all the relevant bookcases.'
                                                                                        ABSOLUTE
b. 'Mary built a taller bookcase than anyone else did.'   RELATIVE
Not available:
c. 'Mary built a taller bookcase than anything else she built.'   (= (63b))
                                                                                      RELATIVE 'EXTRA'

(67) *Maria postroi naj-visoka biblioteka.*
Maria built tallest bookcase
Available readings:
b. 'Mary built a taller bookcase than anyone else did.' RELATIVE
c. 'Mary built a taller bookcase than anything else she built.' (= (63b))
RELATIVE 'EXTRA'
Not available:
a. 'Mary built a taller bookcase than all the relevant bookcases.'
ABSOLUTE

Note that when the superlative DP is indefinite in Bulgarian, (67), the absolute reading is not available, which suggests that the definite and null indefinite determiners in Bulgarian superlatives are semantically contentful. Thus, Bulgarian contrasts with Polish, which does not have a definite determiner and so definiteness is always contextually determined.

The fact that the definite determiner prevents the 'extra' relative reading in English and Bulgarian (i.e., the definite prevents association with a focus inside the DP) and that it is required for the absolute reading in Bulgarian cannot be accounted with -$est_{2-place}$. In Tomaszewicz (2013, 2015a) I showed that if we assume that cross-linguistically the definite determiner blocks the QR of -$est_{2-place}$ outside of the DP, none of the three possible configurations for focus association results in a situation where only association with a DP-external focus (e.g., '*Mary*' or '*on Monday*' above) is possible. Allowing -$est_{2-place}$ to take sentential scope cannot handle the facts either.

This means that Heim's (1999) proposal that -$est_{2-place}$ associates with focus on par with quantifiers such as *always* or *only* is not supported empirically. Since -$est_{2-place}$ necessarily allows association with a DP-internal focus and generates a reading that is never available in the presence of a definite determiner, but *only* can associate with the same DP-internal focus, -$est_{2-place}$ should not be allowed to associate with focus in an entirely parallel way to *only*. Instead, as I proposed in section 2, the role of -$est_{2\ place}$ in the grammar is to compare degrees in constructions that explicitly call for the comparison of degrees, such as superlatives with measure phrases. Given that the presence of the definite article determines whether or not the 'extra' relative reading is available, in Tomaszewicz (2015a) I argued that -$est_{3-place}$ is used to derive **all the relative** readings cross-linguistically. I showed that only -$est_{3-place}$ allows us to account for the blocking effect of the definite determiner on association with DP-internal focus, as will now be discussed in the following section.

5 *-Est*$_{3-\text{place}}$ Associates with Focus

With *-est*$_{3-\text{place}}$ and the focus association mechanism, the presence of the definite determiner constrains the scope possibilities of *-est*$_{3-\text{place}}$ and thus the possible values for the comparison class variable C. In the presence of *the*, *-est*$_{3-\text{place}}$ is trapped inside the DP (Pancheva and Tomaszewicz 2012). This DP can QR and *-est* can associate from within with a DP-external focus (Heim 1999, Sharvit and Stateva 2002, Stateva 2002). This is shown in (68a) where the focus is on 'Mary' and *-est*$_{3-\text{place}}$ can associate with it given that the condition on focus association, (68d), and the presupposition of *-est*$_{3-\text{place}}$, (68e) match.

(68) a. *[Mary]$_F$ built **the tallest bookcase**.*
   b. [$_{\text{TP3}}$ [$_{\text{DP}}$ the [*-est*$_{3-\text{place}}$ $C_{\langle e,t \rangle}$) 2 [$_{\text{NP}}$ d_2-tall bookcase]]$_1$ [$_{\text{TP2}}$ [~ S] [$_{\text{TP1}}$ 1 [Mary]$_F$ built t_1]]]
   c. $S \subseteq [\![\text{TP}_2]\!]^f$, $[\![\text{TP}_2]\!]^f = \{P: \exists y \, [P = \lambda x \, [y \text{ built } x]\}$
   d. $C \subseteq \{x: \exists d \, [\text{bookcase}(x) \wedge \text{tall}(x, d)]\}$ (*presupposition of -est*$_{3-\text{place}}$ (7))
   e. $C \subseteq \cup S \subseteq \{x: \exists y \, [\text{build}(y, x)]\}$ (*focus association*, (58))

If focus were on some other DP-external constituent, e.g., 'on Monday' as we saw earlier in (56), the requirements of focus association and of the presupposition would also be compatible. But with focus on 'bookcase' the two requirements either clash, if ~ adjoins to the DP, (69), or focus has no effect on the contents of the comparison class, if ~ adjoins to the NP, (70) (the meaning is the same as on the absolute reading, (70f)). Therefore, the derivation of the 'extra' relative reading is not possible (Pancheva and Tomaszewicz (2012), Tomaszewicz 2015a).

(69) a. *Mary built **the tallest** [bookcase]$_F$.*
   b. [$_{\text{TP1}}$ Mary built [$_{\text{DP2}}$ [~ S] [$_{\text{DP1}}$ the [*-est*$_{3-\text{place}}$ $C_{\langle e,t \rangle}$] 1 [$_{\text{NP2}}$ d_1-tall [$_{\text{NP1}}$ bookcase]]]]]
   c. $S \subseteq [\![\text{DP}_2]\!]^f$, $[\![\text{DP}_2]\!]^f \subseteq \{x: x \text{ is the tallest bookcase}\}$
   d. $C \subseteq \{x: \exists d \, [x \text{ is a } d\text{-tall bookcase}]\}$ (*presuppositions of -est*$_{3-\text{place}}$ (7))
   e. $C \not\subseteq [\![\text{DP}_2]\!]^f$ (*focus association not possible*)

(70) a. *Mary built **the tallest** [bookcase]$_F$.*
   b. [$_{\text{TP1}}$ Mary built [$_{\text{DP}}$ the [*-est*$_{3-\text{place}}$ $C_{\langle e,t \rangle}$] 1 [$_{\text{NP3}}$ d_1-tall [$_{\text{NP2}}$ [~ S] [$_{\text{NP1}}$ bookcase]]]]]
   c. $S \subseteq [\![\text{NP}_1]\!]^f$, $[\![\text{NP}_1]\!]^f \subseteq \{f_{\langle e,t \rangle}: \exists x \, [f(x)]\}$
   d. $C \subseteq \{x: \exists d \, [x \text{ is a } d\text{-tall bookcase}]\}$ (*presuppositions of -est*$_{3-\text{place}}$ (7))

e. $C \subseteq \cup [\![NP_1]\!]^f \subseteq \{x\}$ (*focus association possible, but vacuous contribution to C*)
f. $[\![TP_1]\!] = 1$ iff Mary built the unique bookcase of some height such that no other bookcase in the comparison of bookcases of some height is taller than that bookcase

This account also correctly predicts that -*est*$_{3-\text{place}}$ trapped inside the DP does **not need** to associate with focus for relative readings—it is enough to contextually restrict the contents of the comparison class (Farkas and Kiss 2000, Sharvit and Stateva 2002, Coppock and Beaver 2014). We saw above in (68) that when -*est*$_{3-\text{place}}$ QRs into the clause, it can associate with the focus on Mary, but crucially, the same meaning can be derived without QR and without focus association. In (71), the comparison class is contextually restricted to contain bookcases of some height that someone built. We obtain the exact same relative reading as in as (68), where the comparison is among bookcase builders.

(71) a. *Mary built **the** tallest bookcase.*
 b. Mary built [$_{DP}$ the [[-*est*$_{3-\text{place}}$ $C_{\langle e,t \rangle}$] 1 [d_1-tall bookcase]]]
 c. $C_{\langle e,t \rangle} \subseteq \{x: \exists d\; \exists y\; [x \text{ is a } d\text{-tall bookcase} \wedge y \text{ built } x]\}$

The information added to the specification of C in (71c) can be inferred from the context or from the focus on '*Mary*' (given the anaphoric nature of C, in the absence of explicit context, the focus structure of the sentence can provide a clue about the implicit antecedent for C (Rooth 1992, von Fintel 1994)). The optionality of focus for relative readings was observed early on: elements that are not prosodically prominent (i.e., not foci), *who* or its trace in (72a) (from Szabolcsi 1986) and the null subject in (72b) (from Heim 1999), are relevant for the determination of the comparison set and the available relative reading. In (72a-b) actually other constituents are in focus, but the comparison class is still set with respect to *who* and the null subject. This lack of correspondence between prosodic focus and putative F-marking leads Szabolcsi (1986) and Heim (1999) to conclude that focus is not needed for the derivation of relative readings, and the present account is consistent with this conclusion.

(72) a. *We should console the girl who got the fewest* [LEtters]$_F$.
 b. *How does one win this contest?—By putting the tallest* [PLANT]$_F$ *on the table.*

Since both absolute and relative readings in English are derived with DP-internal QR of -*est*$_{3-\text{place}}$, the lack of obligatory focus association for -*est*$_{3-\text{place}}$

in this language follows. However, data from Bulgarian and Polish reveals that when -$est_{3-place}$ alone scopes into the clause ASSOCIATION WITH FOCUS is OBLIGATORY (Tomaszewicz 2015a, Tomaszewicz and Pancheva 2016). The facts are summarized below with the data in (73) and the crucial finding is that although the QR of -$est_{3-place}$ outside of the indefinite DP can derive the 'extra' relative reading without the mechanism of focus association, in Bulgarian and Polish focus is obligatory. Thus, although focus association is technically not needed, the empirical data indicates that it does take place.

The sentence in (73) has the 'extra' relative reading, where the comparison set contains alternatives to a constituent inside the superlative DP, the possessive pronoun 'its'. The -$est_{3-place}$ QRs into the clause and tucks in below the moved associate, 'its', (73b). As a result, the comparison class contains the different objects for which Ivan develops restoration methods, (73c).

(73) a. *Razraboti naj-evtin metod za nejnata*
 he-developed -*est*-cheap method for its-FULL.PRON-the
 restavracija.
 restoration
 'He developed the cheapest method for its restoration.'

 b. [$_{TP}$ its$_2$ [-$est_{3-place}$ $C_{\langle e,t \rangle}$]$_1$ [$_{TP}$ he developed [$_{DP}$ a [$_{NP}$ d_1-cheap method for t_2 restoration]]]]

 c. $C \subseteq \{x:$ he developed a method of some cost for the restoration of x$\}$

Consider first the scenario in (74) that supports this reading. Crucially, of all the superlative sentences in (74a-d), only one, (74a), is felicitous in the given context, because it is the only one that can express the relative reading '*Ivan developed a cheaper method for its restoration than any other method he developed for the restoration of the remaining objects*'.

(74) *Scenario*:
 Ivan is developing methods to restore a canvas, a sculpture, and a tapestry. He has very little money and so he has to prioritize which of these to restore first. (Tomaszewicz and Pancheva 2016)
 Šte započne săs skulpturata.
 will begin-3sg with sculpture-the
 'He will begin with the sculpture.'

THE SEMANTICS OF THE SUPERLATIVE QUANTIFIER -EST 113

    a. *Razraboti naj-evtin metod za **nejnata***
       he-developed -*est*-cheap method for her-FULL.PRON.POSS-the
       restavracija.   (= (73a))
       restoration
       'He developed the cheapest method for its restoration.'

    b. #*Razraboti naj-evtin metod za restavracijata*
       he-developed -*est*-cheap method for restoration-the
       i.
       her-CLITIC.POSS
       'He developed the cheapest method for its restoration.'

    c. #*Razraboti naj-evtin-ija metod za **nejnata***
       he-developed -*est*-cheap-the method for her-FULL.PRON.POSS-the
       restavracija.
       restoration
       'He developed the cheapest method for its restoration.'

    d. #*Razraboti naj-evtin-ija metod za restavracijata*
       he-developed -*est*-cheap-the method for restoration-the
       i.
       her-CLITIC.POSS
       'He developed the cheapest method for its restoration.'

This data shows that when the comparison class is set with respect to a constituent inside the superlative DP, the DP must be indefinite, ruling out (74c) and (74d). The only difference between the indefinite superlatives in (74a) and (74b) is the form of the pronoun—a full pronoun can function as the associate for the relevant relative reading, but a clitic pronoun cannot. This in turn shows that the associate must be focused. So although the LF in (73b) can derive the right reading, the empirical fact from Bulgarian indicates that focus on the associate is an obligatory ingredient. The focus operator attaches to the associate, the possessive pronoun, (75a), evoking the alternative set of individuals of which S is a subset, (75b). The focus association condition is satisfied, (75d), because there is no clash between the focal presupposition, (75b), and the specification of C resulting from the presuppositions of -$est_{3-\text{place}}$, (75c).

(75) a. [$_{TP}$ [[its$_2$]$_F$ [~ S]] [[-$est_{3-\text{place}}$ C]$_1$ 1 2 [$_{TP}$ he developed [$_{DP}$ a [$_{NP}$ d_1-cheap method for t_2 restoration]]]]

b. $S \subseteq [\![\text{its}_F]\!]^f, [\![\text{its}_F]\!]^f \subseteq \{\iota x\,[\text{canvas}(x)], \iota y\,[\text{sculpture}(y)], \iota z\,[\text{tapestry}(z)], \ldots\}$

c. $C \subseteq \{x: \exists d\,[\text{he developed a } d\text{-cheap method for } x\text{'s restoration}]\}$ (*presuppositions of* -$est_{3-\text{place}}$)

d. $C \subseteq [\![\text{its}_F]\!]^f$ (*focus association*, (58))

The need for focus on the associate of DP-external -$est_{3-\text{place}}$ does not seem to follow from any independent constraint. The theory of focus association predicts that focus effects are optional. (That is because according to the condition in (58) focus effects on quantifier domains are the result of the anaphoric dependence on the same background context, i.e. (75d) holds when both C and S have an antecedent in explicit or implicit discourse). It then follows that phonologically reduced material can play a role in the specification of the domain of a quantifier as a result of contextual effects on domain restriction. For cases where operators require phonological focus (e.g. *only*), focus association needs to be lexically stipulated, otherwise, irrespective of the presence of ~, the domain variable can be contextually resolved (Rooth 1992, Beaver and Clark 2008). The Bulgarian data concerning the availability of clitics as associates of -$est_{3-\text{place}}$ when it QRs into the clause indicates that focus is required. In indefinite superlatives, the associate of DP-external -$est_{3-\text{place}}$ must be F-marked, so that its focus alternative value is congruent with the comparison set. We thus need to treat **DP-external** -$est_{3-\text{place}}$ similar to adverbial *only*: they both **obligatorily** associate with focus. In a parallel way, **DP-internal** -$est_{3-\text{place}}$ (in definite superlatives) and DP-internal *only* **optionally** associate with focus (Tomaszewicz 2015a).

In Table 3.2, I extend Table 3.1 summarizing the cross-linguistic variation from section 1, by adding the scope facts. -$Est_{2-\text{place}}$ does not associate with focus; it operates in contexts where comparison of degrees, and not of individuals, is required. -$Est_{3-\text{place}}$ can associate with focus when it is DP-internal, but doesn't have to. DP-internal -$est_{3-\text{place}}$ can derive relative readings where comparison involves a constituent outside the superlative DP (e.g., C contains bookcases that different people built, or C contains bookcases that Mary built on different days, etc.). It can associate with focus for those readings, or the constraint on C can be established contextually. This is how relative readings are derived in English, where the superlative DP is definite trapping -$est_{3-\text{place}}$ inside it.[17] DP-external scope for -$est_{3-\text{place}}$ (i.e., QR into the clause) is required for the 'extra' relative reading that is found with indefinite superlatives in Bul-

---

17 In Tomaszewicz (2016) I conclude that cross-linguistically DP-internal scope of -$est_{3-\text{place}}$ is preferred for DP-external relative readings, because the intermediate movement step in the derivation of the DP-external relative readings violates the principle of Scope Econ-

THE SEMANTICS OF THE SUPERLATIVE QUANTIFIER -EST 115

TABLE 3.2 Cross-linguistic variation (*extended version of Table 3.1*)

$-est_{2-\text{place}}$ (comparison of degrees)	definite/indefinite DP-external scope	modal superlatives	English
	indefinite DP-internal scope	superlatives with measure phrases	Turkish, Polish
$-est_{3-\text{place}}$ (comparison of individuals)	definite DP-internal scope	absolute readings	English, Turkish, Bulgarian, Polish
		relative readings with focus on DP-external constituents	English, Turkish, Bulgarian, Polish
	indefinite DP-external scope	relative readings with focus on DP-internal constituents	Bulgarian, Polish, Turkish[a]

a In this paper, the Turkish data illustrating these relative readings has not been presented.

garian and Polish,[18] where the comparison involves a constituent inside the superlative DP (e.g., C contains different objects that Mary built). These readings require focus, thus DP-external $-est_{3-\text{place}}$ must associate with focus.

---

omy that constrains optional QR (Fox 2000, Reinhard 2006). In (i-a) there is no truth conditional difference between the LF before and after the movement of 'Mary' because the movement has no effect on C. In (ii-a) the movement has an effect on C.

(i) a. 1st Step of the derivation of the relative reading of: '[Mary]$_F$ built a tallest bookcase.'
   Mary$_1$ [$_{TP}$ t_1 built [$_{DP}$ a [$-est\ C$]$_2$ [$_{NP}$ d_2-tall bookcase]]]
   b. $C \subseteq \{x: \exists d\ [x \text{ is a } d\text{-tall bookcase}]\}$

(ii) a. 1st Step of the derivation of the relative reading of: 'Mary built a tallest [bookcase]$_F$.'
   bookcase$_1$ [Mary built [$_{DP}$ a [$-est\ C$]$_2$ [$_{NP}$ d_2-tall t_1]]]
   b. $[\![2\ [t_2\text{-tall } t_1]]\!]^g = \lambda d\ \lambda x\ [\text{tall}(x,d) \wedge g(1)(x)]$
   c. $C \subseteq \{x: \exists d\ [\text{tall}(x,d) \wedge g(1)(x)]\}$

18 As established in section 4, the absence of the absolute reading with indefinite superlatives in Bulgarian indicates that the null indefinite determiner is semantically contentful. Note that the indefinite determiner is null in all 3 languages, Bulgarian, Polish and Turkish, that allow the extra relative reading, whereas in English and other Germanic languages, as well as in Romance, indefinite determiners are overt and this reading is unavailable.

6 Conclusion

The superlative and comparative morphemes, *-est* and *-er*, have been analyzed as degree quantifiers (Cresswell 1967, von Stechow 1984, Heim 1985, 1999, 2000, Szabolcsi 1986, a.o.). Both constructions can be modeled in two ways, as comparison between individuals or as comparison between degrees (Heim 1985, 1999). In the comparative, the syntax of phrasal vs. clausal comparatives can determine which version of the lexical entry for *-er* is necessary (Heim 1985, Bhatt and Takahashi 2008, 2011). For the superlative, focus sensitivity of the relative readings was the motivation for Heim (1999) to introduce the 2-place semantics for *-est* (comparing degrees) where focus association could be modeled in a parallel way to the focus associating *only* (Rooth 1992). Romero (2010, 2012) found a new role for $-est_{2-place}$ showing that only $-est_{2-place}$ can derive the modal superlative readings.

In this paper, I presented a novel construction found in Turkish and Polish, superlatives with measure phrases and corresponding superlative degree questions, and I argued that its semantics can be straightforwardly accounted for as modification of the comparison class argument C of $-est_{2-place}$. This data supports my conclusion in Tomaszewicz (2013, 2015a) that $-est_{2-place}$ is used for cases of explicit comparison between degrees and not for focus association, contra Heim (1999). The focus association mechanism with $-est_{2-place}$ overgenerates the range of relative readings cross-linguistically, because it cannot account for the blocking effect of the definite determiner on the relative reading established with respect to a focus inside the superlative DP. Since the presence of the definite determiner limits which relative readings are available, it is desirable to assume that all the relative readings are derived with the same lexical entry and that the definite determiner at LF blocks some of the derivations. This can be achieved with $-est_{3-place}$ (Pancheva and Tomaszewicz 2012, Tomaszewicz 2015a,b).

Theoretically, the two issues, focus sensitivity and the two "modes of comparison", to use Kennedy's (1999) term, can be treated independently. The empirical facts, however, show that association with focus is necessary to account for cross-linguistic differences in the availability of relative readings, and that $-est_{2-place}$ is used in contexts where focus association does not take place, but where comparison of degrees is required by the presence of measure phrases. The role of $-est_{3-place}$ is to derive absolute and relative readings (in combination with contextual effects such as focus association). The grammar appears to be using the two modes of comparison for the superlative in different, mutually exclusive contexts.

Acknowledgements

I would like to thank Roumi Pancheva and Yael Sharvit for encouraging me to work on the topic of superlatives with measure phrases. I also thank Roumi for the Bulgarian data. Very special thanks are due to Yaman Özakın who patiently provided all the Turkish examples and spent hours with me discussing this data. I am also grateful for the comments to the anonymous reviewers and to Peter Hallman whose review helped to greatly improve the text. Any errors are mine.

References

Beaver, David and Brady Clark. 2008. *Sense and Sensitivity: How Focus Determines Meaning*. Oxford: Wiley-Blackwell.
Bhatt, Rajesh and Shoichi Takahashi. 2007. Direct comparisons: Resurrecting the direct analysis of phrasal comparatives. *Proceedings of Semantics and Linguistic Theory (SALT) 17*, 19–36. Cornell University, Ithaca: CLC Publications.
Bhatt, Rajesh, and Shoichi Takahashi. 2011. Reduced and unreduced phrasal comparatives. *Natural Language & Linguistic Theory* 29.3: 581–620.
Beck, Sigrid, and Hotze Rullmann. 1999. A flexible approach to exhaustivity in questions. *Natural Language Semantics* 7.3: 249–298.
Carlson, Greg. 1977. Amount relatives. *Language* 53: 520–542.
Coppock, Elizabeth and David Beaver. 2014. A Superlative Argument for a Minimal Theory of Definiteness. *Proceedings of Semantics and Linguistic Theory (SALT) 24*, ed. by Todd Snider, 177–196. Cornell University, Ithaca: CLC Publications.
Cresswell, Max J. 1976. The semantics of degree. In Barbara Partee (ed.), Montague grammar, 261–292. New York: Academic Press.
Farkas, Donka and Katalin É. Kiss. 2000. Comparative and absolute readings of superlatives. *Natural Language and Linguistic Theory* 18: 417–455.
von Fintel, Kai. 1994. *Restrictions on Quantifier Domains*. Doctoral Dissertation, University of Massachusetts, Amherst: Graduate Student Linguistics Association (GLSA).
Fox, Danny. 2000 *Economy and semantic interpretation*. Cambridge: MIT Press.
Fox, Danny and Martin Hackl. 2006. The universal density of measurement. *Linguistics and Philosophy* 29(5): 537–586.
Gawron, Mark. 1995. Comparatives, superlatives, and resolution. *Linguistics and Philosophy* 8: 333–380.
Görgülü, Emrah. 2012 *Semantics of Nouns and the Specification of Number in Turkish*. Diss. Arts & Social Sciences: Department of Linguistics.
Hamblin, Charles. 1973. Questions in Montague English. *Foundations of Language* 10: 41–53.

Hackl, Martin. 2000. *Comparative Quantifiers*. MIT, Cambridge: Doctoral Dissertation (MITWPL).
Hackl, Martin. 2009. On the grammar and processing of proportional quantifiers: most versus more than half. *Natural Language Semantics* 17: 63–98.
Heim, Irene. 1985. Notes on Comparatives and Related Matters. University of Texas, Austin: MS.
Heim, Irene. 1987. Where does the definiteness restriction apply? Evidence from the definiteness of variables. *The representation of (in)definiteness*, ed. by Eric J. Reuland and Alice G.B. ter Meulen, 21–42. Cambridge: The MIT Press.
Heim, Irene. 1999. Notes on superlatives. MIT, Cambridge: MS.
Heim, Irene. 2001. Degree operators and scope. In Caroline Féry & Wolfgang Sternefeld (eds.), Audiatur vox sapientiae. A Festschrift for Arnim von Stechow, 214–239.
Jackendoff, Ray. 1972. *Semantic Interpretation in Generative Grammar*. MIT Press.
Kennedy, Chris. 1999. *Projecting the Adjective: The Syntax and Semantics of Gradability and Comparison*. New York: Garland.
Krasikova, Sveta. 2012. Definiteness in superlatives, *Proceedings of the 18th Amsterdam Colloquium*, ed. by Maria Aloni, Vadim Kimmelman, Floris Roelofsen, Galit Weidman Sassoon, Katrin Schulz and Matthijs Westera, 404–413. New York: Springer.
Landman, Fred. 1989. Groups I & II. Linguistics and Philosophy 12: 559–605, 723–744.
Larson, Richard. 2000. ACD in AP? Paper presented at WCCFL 19, February 4–6, UCLA. Online: semlab5.sbs.sunysb.edu/~rlarson/wccfl19.pdf
Pancheva, Roumyana and Barbara M. Tomaszewicz, 2012. Cross-linguistic Differences in Superlative Movement out of Nominal Phrases. Proceedings of the 30th West Coast Conference on Formal Linguistics, ed. by Nathan Arnett and Ryan Bennett, 292–302. Somerville, MA: Cascadilla Proceedings.
Reinhart, Tanya. 2006. *Interface strategies: Optimal and costly computations*. Cambridge: MIT Press.
Rett, Jessica. 2006. How "many" Maximizes in the Balkan Sprachbund. *Semantics and Linguistic Theory*. Vol. 16.
Romero, Maribel. 2012. Modal Superlatives: A Compositional Analysis. *Natural Language Semantics* 21 (1): 79–110.
Rooth, Mats. 1985. *A Theory of Focus Interpretation*. University of Massachusetts, Amherst: Doctoral Dissertation.
Rooth, Mats. 1992. A Theory of Focus Interpretation. *Natural Language Semantics* 1: 75–116.
Rooth, Mats. 1996. On the Interface Principles for Intonational Focus. *Proceedings of Semantics and Linguistic Theory (SALT) 6*, ed. by Teresa Galloway and Justin Spence, 202–226. Cornell University, Ithaca, NY: CLC Publications.
Rooth, Mats. 1999. Association with focus or association with presupposition? *Focus:*

Linguistic, cognitive, and computational perspectives, ed. by Peter Bosch and Rob van der Sandt, 232–246. Cambridge Cambridge University Press.

Ross, John Robert. 1964. *A Partial Grammar of English Superlatives*. University of Pennsylvania: MA Thesis.

Rullmann, Hotze. 1995. *Maximality in the Semantics of Wh-Constructions*. University of Massachusetts, Amherst: Doctoral Dissertation.

Ruys, Eddy G. and Matushansky, Ora M. 2006. Meilleurs Voeux; Quelques notes sur la comparaison

Sağ, Yağmur (2018). The semantics of Turkish numeral constructions. In: Uli Sauerland and Stephanie Solt (eds.), Proceedings of Sinn und Bedeutung 22, vol. 1, ZASPiL 60, pp. 307–324. ZAS, Berlin.

Schwarz, Bernhard. 2005. Modal superlatives. *Proceedings of Semantics and Linguistic Theory (SALT) 15*, ed. by Efthymia Georgala, Jonathan Howell, 187–204. Cornell University, Ithaca, NY: CLC Publications.

Seuren, Peter. A.M., 1973, The Comparative, *Generative Grammar in Europe*, ed. by Ferenc Kiefer and NicolasRuwet, 528–564. Dordrecht: Reidel.

Selkirk, Elisabeth O. 1984. *Phonology and Syntax: The Relation between Sound and Structure*. Cambridge: MIT Press.

Sharvit, Yael and Penka Stateva. 2002. Superlative expressions, context, and focus, *Linguistics and Philosophy* 25: 453–504.

Stateva, Penka. 2002. *How different are different degree constructions?* University of Connecticut, Storrs: Doctoral dissertation.

Stateva, Penka. 2003. Superlative *more*. *Proceedings of Semantics and Linguistic Theory (SALT) 13*, ed. by Robert B. Young and Yuping Zhou, 276–291. Cornell University, Ithaca: CLC Publications.

von Stechow, Arnim. 1984. Comparing semantic theories of comparison. Journal of Semantics 3. 1–77.

von Stechow, Arnim. 2009. Tenses in compositional semantics. *The expression of time* (2009): 129–166. in Klein, Wolfgang, and Ping Li, eds. *The expression of time*. Vol. 3. Walter de Gruyter.

Szabolcsi, Anna. 1986. Comparative superlatives. *MITWPL* 8, 245–266.

Szabolcsi, Anna. 2012. Compositionality without word boundaries: (*the*) *more* and (*the*) *most*. *Proceedings of Semantics and Linguistic Theory (SALT) 22*, ed. by Anca Chereches, 1–25. eLanguage. Online: http://elanguage.net/journals/salt/

Tomaszewicz, Barbara. 2013. Focus association in superlatives and the semantics of *-est*. In Maria Aloni, Michael Franke and Floris Roelofsen, eds., *Proceedings of the 19th Amsterdam Colloquium*, 226–233. University of Amsterdam, Institute for Logic, Language and Computation.

Tomaszewicz, Barbara, 2015a. *Superlative ambiguities: a comparative perspective*. Ph.D. Dissertation, University of Southern California.

Tomaszewicz, Barbara, 2015b. Definiteness and degree morphology. In Błaszczak, J., Klimek-Jankowska, D., Migdalski, K. (eds.), Studies in Generative Grammar [SGG] 122: How Categorical are Categories? New Approaches to the Old Questions of Noun, Verb, and Adjective. De Gruyter Mouton. Pp. 197–232.

Tomaszewicz, Barbara, 2016. Relative readings of superlatives: scope or focus? In D'Antonio, S., Little, C.-R., Moroney, M.R., Wiegand, M. (eds.), *Proceedings of the 25th Semantics and Linguistic Theory Conference*. Ithaca, NY: LSA and CLC Publications.

Tomaszewicz, Barbara and Roumyana Pancheva, 2016. Focus association and the scope of superlative *-est*, In Nadine Bade, Sigrid Beck & Pritty Patel-Grosz (eds.), *Proceedings of Sinn & Bedeutung 20*.

CHAPTER 4

Quantification, Degrees, and *Beyond* in Navajo

Elizabeth Bogal-Allbritten and Elizabeth Coppock

1   Introduction

Intuitively, the comparison of objects along a gradient dimension seems like a cognitively basic ability that should be universally available and communicable (Sapir 1944).[1] However, we also find great diversity in the kinds of structures that individual languages use to express these meanings (Stassen 1985). Recent crosslinguistic investigation has found that even in languages that use rather similar morphosyntactic strategies to express comparison and related meaning, the semantics and syntax of structures in individual languages diverge in subtle, but still perceptible, ways (see, for example, Beck, Oda & Sugisaki 2004, Beck et al. 2009, Kennedy 2007, Bochnak 2015, and Rett's contribution to this volume).

A particularly rich line of investigation has probed the syntax of standards of comparison and its interplay with the semantics of the comparative marker (Hoeksema 1983, Heim 1985, Kennedy 1997, Lechner 2004, Pancheva 2006, Bhatt & Takahashi 2011, Beck, Hohaus & Tiemann 2012). In terms of syntax, the key question is whether the standard of comparison contains elided clausal structure in cases where it is not visible. Since Bresnan 1973, it has been usual to analyze sentences like (1) as containing an unpronounced instance of the adjective in the main clause.

(1)   Alice is taller than [$_{CP}$ Ben is ~~tall~~].

This kind of syntax is generally paired with a semantic analysis that treats comparative morphemes like *-er* as quantificational expressions on par with *every*.

---

[1] We thank Ellavina Perkins, Leroy Morgan, and Irene Tsosie for their patience and insight: All Navajo data not otherwise cited should be credited to them. We also thank Jessica Rett, Peter Hallman, Stephanie Solt, Wataru Uegaki, Peter Alrenga, Louise McNally, Michael Yoshitaka Erlewine, and an anonymous reviewer for helpful discussion which has strengthened the proposal. Any remaining errors are our own. This research was carried out with funding from the Swedish Research Council project 2015-01404 entitled *Most and more: Quantity superlatives across languages* awarded to PI Elizabeth Coppock at the University of Gothenburg.

Both compose with two predicate-type expressions, but where *every* composes with two sets of entities (2), *-er* instead composes with sets of degrees (3) (von Stechow 1984, Heim 2001, Beck 2011, among many others).

(2) *every* ⤳ $\lambda P_{\langle e,t \rangle} . \lambda Q_{\langle e,t \rangle} . \forall x . P(x) \rightarrow Q(x)$ $\qquad \langle \langle e,t \rangle, \langle \langle e,t \rangle, t \rangle \rangle$

(3) *-er* ⤳ $\lambda D_{\langle d,t \rangle} . \lambda D'_{\langle d,t \rangle} . \text{MAX}(D') > \text{MAX}(D)$ $\qquad \langle \langle d,t \rangle, \langle \langle d,t \rangle, t \rangle \rangle$

Applied to (1), the two sets of degrees (D, D') taken as arguments by *more/-er* correspond respectively to the degrees to which Ben is tall, and the degrees to which Alice is tall.

In a sentence like (4), by contrast, the standard lacks any overt clausal material. While there is debate as to the analysis of such strings (Lechner 2004, Bhatt & Takahashi 2011), one strategy is to treat the standard of comparison as denoting an entity rather than a set of degrees, without hidden clausal structure (Hoeksema 1983, Heim 1985, Kennedy 1997).

(4) Alice is taller than [$_{DP}$ Ben].

More recent crosslinguistic investigation has argued that this 'phrasal' analysis alone is available for standards of comparison in Mandarin, Japanese, Turkish, Hindi-Urdu, and Luganda (Xiang 2005, Kennedy 2007, Pancheva 2006, Hofstetter 2009, Bhatt & Takahashi 2011, Beck, Hohaus & Tiemann 2012).

A phrasal syntax for the standard of comparison is most often paired with a semantic analysis which does not treat *more/-er* and its reflexes in other languages as a quantifier. Instead, it composes directly with two entities (x, y) and a gradable predicate (g) determined by the adjective in the main clause. While the sentence in (4) would have the same truth conditions as its clausal counterpart in (1), these truth conditions would be derived differently.[2]

(5) *-er* ⤳ $\lambda y_e . \lambda g_{\langle d,et \rangle} . \lambda x_e . \text{MAX}(\lambda d . g(d,x)) > \text{MAX}(\lambda d . g(d,y))$
$\qquad\qquad\qquad\qquad\qquad\qquad\qquad\qquad\qquad\qquad$ (Heim 1985)
$\qquad\qquad\qquad\qquad\qquad\qquad\qquad\qquad\qquad\qquad \langle e, \langle \langle d, \langle e,t \rangle \rangle, \langle e,t \rangle \rangle \rangle$

This paper considers data from Navajo degree constructions like those in (6) which challenge this pairing of syntactic and semantic analyses. While Navajo

---

[2] While these analyses have been widely adopted and will be the focus of our paper, they are by no means the only analyses that have proposed for comparatives; see in particular Bale (this volume) and Schwarzschild (this volume) for two recent alternative proposals.

seems to be a clear case of a language with syntactically phrasal standards of comparison, we argue that it is nevertheless a language for which a quantificational semantics for comparative morphemes (or, as in Navajo, standard markers) is motivated.

(6) a. *Alice Ben yi-lááh   'áníłnééz.*
      Alice Ben 3-beyond 3.tall
      'Alice is taller than Ben.'

   b. *Alice 'a-lááh   'áníłnééz.*
      Alice UNSPEC-beyond 3.tall
      'Alice is tallest, Alice is taller than anyone.'

While a non-quantificational meaning for the comparative standard marker *-lááh* 'beyond' would suffice in (6a), the meaning of (6b) motivates us to posit (only) a quantificational meaning for *-lááh*. Superlative prompts are translated in Navajo by combination of the standard marker with the 'unspecified' object marker *'a-*. This type of strategy for expressing superlative meaning is crosslinguistically quite rare (Gorshenin 2012). We demonstrate that unless *-lááh* is given a quantificational meaning, we predict *'a-* to have scope over the comparative relation, giving rise to an unattested interpretation in which Alice need only be taller than a particular individual.

This paper addresses the interaction of quantification and degree in three ways. First, it provides evidence from a structure with a quantificational standard of comparison (*'a-* in (6b)) for a quantificational meaning for Navajo standard markers. Second, it considers how a phrasal syntax can be reconciled with a quantificational entry for comparative morphemes. We accomplish this by invoking application of a measurement operator to the standard. Third, it presents evidence that the Navajo lexicon includes expressions of quantificational determiner type $\langle\langle\tau, t\rangle, \langle\langle\tau, t\rangle, t\rangle\rangle$, in the domain of degrees. Navajo has generally been viewed as a language without meanings of this type (Faltz 1995, Faltz 2000, Speas & Parsons-Yazzie 1996). We suggest that Navajo allows this type of meaning in the domain of degrees because, unlike entity arguments of verbs more generally, the degree arguments of gradable expressions are not saturated by morphology on the verb itself, thus leaving property-type expressions available to compose with quantifiers.

2 Background

Navajo expresses gradable properties using verbs. While somewhat less morphologically complex than event-denoting verbs in Navajo, adjectival verbs such as those below still bear key morphological components otherwise associated with verbs, including a stem and a subject prefix.[3]

(7) a. *'áníłnééz*   3.tall
     b. *'ánísnééz*   1SG.tall
     c. *nineez*   3.tall
     d. *deesdoi*   3.hot
     e. *nohzhóní*   2PL.pretty

All Navajo verbs obligatorily bear prefixes to mark core nominal participants (subject, object). Adjectival verbs bear only a subject marker. As with all verbs, when the subject (or object, where relevant) is third person, a verb-external nominal expression can be optionally included.

(8) (*Alice*) *nineez*.
     Alice   3.tall
     'Alice (he, she, it) is tall.'

Bogal-Allbritten (2013, 2016) discusses at length differences in degree constructions that correlate with the morphological marking borne by adjectival verbs, for example *'áníłnééz* vs. *nineez* in (7). We follow Bogal-Allbritten in taking these differences to have syntactic, rather than semantic, sources. These differences will largely not be important for our purposes here and will only be mentioned when they are salient or useful to note.

Following proposals by Bogal-Allbritten (2013, 2016), we treat all adjectival verbs in Navajo as denoting, at an abstract level, relations between entities and degrees, as is familiar from analyses of gradable predicates in English (Cresswell 1976, von Stechow 1984, Heim 1985, Heim 2001, Kennedy & McNally 2005, and many others). The lexically-encoded semantic core of an adjectival verb is the measure function (e.g., height), which associates an entity with a degree along some scale. Scales can be defined by three parameters: a set of degrees, a dimension, and an ordering relation (Bartsch & Vennemann 1972, Bierwisch 1989, Kennedy 1997).[4]

---

3 For much more detail on the topics discussed here, see Bogal-Allbritten 2013, 2016.
4 It is more common to treat adjectives as denoting $\langle d, \langle e, t \rangle \rangle$ expressions. We reverse the entity

(9) $tall \rightsquigarrow \lambda x_e \ . \ \lambda d_d \ . \ \text{height}(x) \geq d$ $\equiv \lambda x \ . \ \lambda d \ . \ \text{tall}(d, x)$

Navajo verbs cannot appear without prefixes for all nominal arguments in place (Young & Morgan 1980, Faltz 1998). We therefore suggest that the denotation in (9) does not actually correspond to a verb form that can be pronounced in the language.[5] The verb's entity argument is saturated by the third-person pronominal subject prefix, which we treat as a pronoun, indicated with subscript i, translated as a variable with the same index (v_i). An adjectival verb as a whole denotes an expression of type $\langle d, t \rangle$.[6]

(10) *ánítnééz*$_i$ $\rightsquigarrow \lambda d \ . \ \text{height}(v_i) \geq d$ $\equiv \lambda d \ . \ \text{tall}(d, v_i)$
    3$_i$.tall

This view of Navajo verbs is consistent with analyses that take it to be a Pronominal Argument language, in which all nominal arguments of the verb are pronouns realized as morphologically dependent affixes on the verb (Jelinek 1984, Baker 1996, Willie & Jelinek 2000, Hale 2001). Verb-external nominal expressions do not themselves saturate the verb's argument positions but instead come to corefer with the pronominal prefixes through a binding process that we might think of as similar to clitic left dislocation in Romance (Baker 1996). The details of this process will not be critical to us. What is important is that typical verbs like in (11) do not denote relations of type $\langle e, t \rangle$ or $\langle e, \langle e, t \rangle \rangle$ but are instead treated like complete clauses would be (type t).

(11) *Yiyííyą́ą́!*
    3.3.eat.PFV
    'S/he/it ate it.'

We propose here that the key difference between ordinary verbs and adjectival verbs is that while the first express sentential meanings once fully inflected,

---

and degree arguments since we assume here the entity argument is obligatorily saturated first by verb-internal morphology in Navajo. The treatment in (9) is furthermore consistent with independent proposals for adjectival meaning in other languages, in particular Schwarzschild 2005 (Jessica Rett, p.c.).
5 Bogal-Allbritten (2016) suggests this to be the entry for the adjectival verb stems, which is the rightmost morpheme in the verb.
6 We place the index for the third-person subject prefix at the right edge of the verb in (10) as we are not showing the full morphological breakdown for these verbs here. The actual prefix would come towards the middle of the verb word.

adjectival verbs denote functions of type $\langle d, t \rangle$ since there does not exist an equivalent to subject and object prefixes in the domain of degrees.

We will be concerned with the semantics of elements found in Navajo degree constructions. In contrast with English, Navajo does not have both degree morphemes (e.g., *more/-er, less, as*) and standard markers (e.g., *than, as*). Instead, Navajo only uses standard markers to express comparative meaning. The standard markers are shown in bold below.[7] The comparative standard marker *-lááh* is the primary focus of discussion below, although all claims should be extendible to the other standard markers shown.

(12) *Alice (Ben) yi-lááh 'anítnééz.*
 Alice Ben 3-**beyond** 3.tall
 'Alice is taller than Ben/him/her/it.' [Comparison of superiority]

(13) *Alice shi-'oh 'anítnééz.*
 Alice 1-**short_of** 3.tall
 'Alice is less tall than me.' [Comparison of inferiority]

(14) *Alice (Ben) y-ee-nítnééz.*
 Alice Ben 3-**with**-3.tall
 'Alice is as tall as Ben/him/her/it.' [Equative, postpositional]

(15) *Alice Ben-gi 'anítnééz.*
 Alice Ben-**LOC** 3.tall
 'Alice is as tall as Ben.' [Equative, enclitic]

The Navajo standard markers shown above belong to two different morphosyntactic categories. Postpositions function as the comparative morphemes in comparisons of superiority (12), comparisons of inferiority (13), and the equative structure shown in (14). Postpositions in Navajo obligatorily bear object markers which indicate the person features of the object of the postposition (e.g., *yi-* in (12) and (14), and *shi-* in (13)). The standard marker in the equative construction in (15) is a locative enclitic which attaches to the independent nominal expression serving as the standard of comparison. Regardless of the category of the standard marker, the standard of comparison can never be omitted:

---

7 There are other degree constructions in Navajo which will not concern us here. See Bogal-Allbritten (2013, 2016) for discussion.

(16) a. *Alice lááh 'anítnééz.
    Alice beyond 3.tall
    (Intended: 'Alice is taller, Alice is taller than that.')

b. *Alice gi 'anítnééz.
    Alice LOC 3.tall
    (Intended: 'Alice is as tall, Alice is as tall as that.')

While all postpositional standard markers necessarily bear pronominal object marking, an additional expression can be added to provide more information about third-person standards of comparison. This additional expression can be a proper name as in the examples above. It can also be a measure phrase:

(17) a. *Alice hastą́ą-di 'adées'eez yi-lááh 'anítnééz.
    Alice six-LOC feet 3-beyond 3.tall
    'Alice is taller than six feet.'

b. Díí ńdíshchíí' hastą́ą-di 'adées'eez-gi 'anítnééz.
    this pine.tree six-LOC feet-LOC 3.tall
    'This pine tree is six feet tall.'

In addition, Navajo has a subcomparative construction in which the standard of comparison contains clausal material. In structures like (18), the clausal material in the standard is obligatorily marked by the nominalizer -ígíí, which is also found in internally-headed relative clauses in the language (Platero 1974, Willie 1989, Grosu 2012). We return to the analysis of subcomparatives in section 5.2.

(18) Ch'é'étiin bikáá'adání 'anítnééz-ígíí yi-lááh 'aníttéél.
    door table 3.tall-NMLZ 3-beyond 3.wide
    'The door is wider than the table is tall.'

Finally, it should be noted that the glosses given to each standard marker reflect the fact that none is only found in degree constructions. Their glosses reflect their meaning elsewhere in the language. For instance, -lááh can describe motion or position beyond some point in space, named by the object of the postposition. In these 'literal' uses, postpositions are frequently accompanied by additional locative markers such as -di in (19a), but this is not obligatory (19b).[8]

---

8 The marker -go (SUB) seen in (19b) is a subordinator or adverbializer whose distribution and

(19) a. *Tooh ńlíń-ígíí*   *bi-láah-di*   *shi-ghan*   *si'ą́.*
water 3.extend-NMLZ 3-beyond-LOC 1POSS-hogan 3.sit
'My place is over beyond the river.' (Young & Morgan 1987, 222)

b. *Ko̧'yee naagháhí dził*   *bi-láah-go*   *sh-ił* *dah diildo.*
balloon   mountain 3-beyond-SUB 1-with up 3.fly.PFV
'My balloon went flying up with me beyond the mountains.' (Young & Morgan 1987, 342)

This paper will not discuss how one might reconcile the entries that we give for standard markers with the use of the same expressions to convey various other types of meaning. For discussion of connections between comparative and locative meaning more generally, we refer the reader to Hohaus 2012. For discussion of this issue with particular respect to Navajo, see Schwarzschild 2013, 2014.

3 Clausal and Phrasal Analyses of Comparatives

3.1 Overview

There are two major approaches to a sentence with the shape in (20), both for English and for its counterparts in other languages. The key feature of (20) is that the standard appears to consist only of the DP *Ben*.

(20) Alice is taller than Ben.

One analysis of sentences like (20) is that the standard of comparison contains a clause which has been largely elided (Bresnan 1973, von Stechow 1984, Hackl 2000, Lechner 2004, Bhatt & Takahashi 2011), as in (21).

(21) Alice is taller than [$_{CP}$ Ben is tall].

This is the same kind of syntax as is given to standards with overt clausal structure:

(22) a. The door is wider than [$_{CP}$ the table is tall].
b. Alice is taller than [$_{CP}$ Ben is tall].

---

function will not be of interest to us here. For discussion, see Bogal-Allbritten 2013, Bogal-Allbritten 2016, and Schauber 1979.

A clausal syntax for the standard is most commonly paired with a semantic analysis of comparative and other degree morphemes as quantifiers over degrees (type $\langle\langle d,t\rangle,\langle\langle d,t\rangle,t\rangle\rangle$). The entry in (23) for *more/-er* is based on proposals by Cresswell (1976). The two properties of degrees taken as argument are both maximalized by the comparative morpheme such that comparison is ultimately between the maximal degrees in each set. Motivation for addition of maximalization can be found in von Stechow 1984 and Rullmann 1995.[9]

(23) $\textit{-er}_{clausal} \rightsquigarrow \lambda D_{\langle d,t\rangle} \,.\, \lambda D'_{\langle d,t\rangle} \,.\, \text{MAX}(D') > \text{MAX}(D)$
   where $\text{MAX}(D) \rightsquigarrow \lambda D_{\langle d,t\rangle} \,.\, \iota d \,.\, D(d) \,\&\, \forall d'[D(d') \rightarrow d' \leq d]$

The comparative morpheme takes as argument two sets of degrees: one contributed by the standard phrase and the other contributed by the main clause. The following LF is based on von Stechow 1984 as presented in Beck, Hohaus & Tiemann 2012.[10]

(24) $[[\textit{-er}_{clausal} \,[\text{than } [\lambda d_1 \,[\text{Ben is } d_1 \text{ tall}]]]] \,\lambda d_2 \,[\text{Alice is } d_2 \text{ tall }]]]$

As an aside, the proposals above have been criticized for English because all semantic work is done by *more/-er* while *than* is vacuous. Von Stechow (1984) and Rullmann (1995) suggest an alternative in which maximalization over the standard of comparison is accomplished by *than*, so that the comparative morpheme instead composes with a single degree followed by a property of degrees. Other approaches in this vein assign maximalization to a *wh*-operator and treat the standard as a free relative of degrees in the manner of Partee 1987 and Jacobson 1995.

(25) a. $\textit{-er}_{clausal} \rightsquigarrow \lambda d_d \,.\, \lambda D_{\langle d,t\rangle} \,.\, \text{MAX}(D) > d$
   b. $\textit{than} \rightsquigarrow \lambda D_{\langle d,t\rangle} \,.\, \text{MAX}(D)$

---

9   Alternative entries that are also of quantifier type include the following:
   (i) a. $\textit{-er}_{clausal} \rightsquigarrow \lambda D_{\langle d,t\rangle} \,.\, \lambda D'_{\langle d,t\rangle} \,.\, \exists d \,.\, D'(d) \land \neg D(d)$
       b. $\textit{-er}_{clausal} \rightsquigarrow \lambda D_{\langle d,t\rangle} \,.\, \lambda D'_{\langle d,t\rangle} \,.\, D \subset D'$
   Nothing about the claims made in the rest of this paper should change if either of these denotations is substituted for any instance of a comparative morpheme with the denotation in (23).
10 Abstraction over degree arguments in each clause is necessitated by the assumption that gradable predicates in English are expressions of type $\langle d,\langle e,t\rangle\rangle$. The LF will be simpler in Navajo since we take inflected adjectival verbs to already denote expressions of type $\langle d,t\rangle$.

While entries like (25) may be a good fit for a language like English, Navajo does not have separate comparative morphemes and standard markers. There is no overt element in Navajo which we might wish to treat as a separate maximality operator. Thus, when we consider the analysis of Navajo, we will focus on entries like (23)/(26) in which all meaning is contributed by a single morpheme, and where two sets of degrees are taken as argument.

(26) -*lááh*$_{clausal}$ ⤳ $\lambda D_{\langle d,t \rangle} \cdot \lambda D'_{\langle d,t \rangle} \cdot \text{MAX}(D') > \text{MAX}(D)$

Precedent for an entry like (26) for a standard marker comes from Alrenga, Kennedy & Merchant (2012), who observe that it is very common to find languages using only a standard marker to express comparative meanings.

The second major approach to the string in (20) treats the standard not as a reduced clause but instead as just a DP.

(27) Alice is taller than [$_{DP}$ Ben].

While this syntactic analysis has been long debated for English (Heim 1985, Kennedy 1997, Lechner 2004, Bhatt & Takahashi 2011), it has also been put forth for several other languages; see Xiang 2005 for Mandarin, Kennedy 2007 for Japanese (cf. Shimoyama 2012), Hofstetter 2009 for Turkish, Bhatt & Takahashi 2011 for Hindi-Urdu, and Bochnak 2013 for Luganda.

The syntax in (27) is compatible with the following denotation for -*er*. This entry is taken from Heim 1985; see Beck, Hohaus & Tiemann 2012 for comparison of it with an alternative from Kennedy 1997.

(28) -*er*$_{phrasal}$ ⤳ $\lambda y_e \cdot \lambda g_{\langle d,et \rangle} \cdot \lambda x_e \cdot \text{MAX}(\lambda d \cdot g(d,x)) > \text{MAX}(\lambda d \cdot g(d,y))$

Under this account, the comparative morpheme (type $\langle e, \langle \langle d, \langle e, t \rangle \rangle, \langle e, t \rangle \rangle \rangle$) does not take as argument two sets of degrees, but instead composes with two entities (or one entity and one degree) and a gradable predicate. As formulated here, the comparative relation still holds between the maximal degrees in two sets of degrees, but the sets of degrees are derived directly by *more/-er*.

As before, an account of Navajo on these lines would assign the meaning of *more/-er*$_{phrasal}$ to the standard marker -*lááh*. An entry of this kind is attributed to standard markers by Bhatt & Takahashi (2011) in their analysis of Hindi-Urdu.

(29) -*lááh*$_{phrasal}$ ⤳ $\lambda y_e \cdot \lambda g_{\langle d,et \rangle} \cdot \lambda x_e \cdot \text{MAX}(\lambda d \cdot g(d,x)) > \text{MAX}(\lambda d \cdot g(d,y))$

Not all analyses correspond fully to either of the two pairings described above. Of particular note for us is Pancheva's (2006) treatment of Slavic standards of the shape in (30), where the standard bears fixed (genitive) case and lacks an overt *wh*-operator. Pancheva argues that such standards neither originate as DPs nor derived from full clauses, but are instead derived from reduced small clauses (31).[11]

(30) *Germann   byl sil'nee   [$_{SC}$ svoego protivnika]*
      Germann.NOM was stronger   [own   adversary].GEN
      'Germann was stronger than his adversary.' (Pancheva 2006, (10b))

(31) a. Alice is taller than [$_{SC}$ Ben ~~d-tall~~]
     b. than [$_{SC}$ Ben Δ]

Standards of this shape can be contrasted with those of the shape in (32), which Pancheva argues are derived from full clauses that have undergone reduction.

(32) *Germann   byl sil'nee   [$_{CP}$ čem   (byl) ego protivnik]*
      Germann.NOM was stronger   what.INS was his adversary.NOM
      'Germann was stronger than his adversary.' (Pancheva 2006, (10a))

While a small clause account still treats standards as truly clausal structures, albeit of a smaller size, Pancheva suggests that it can explain certain differences between (30) and (32) while making it possible to maintain a single quantificational entry (23) for Slavic comparative markers.

In section 4, we consider the syntactic and semantic analysis of Navajo standards of comparison. To preview, we argue that by syntactic diagnostics, Navajo standards do not have reduced full clauses as their syntactic source. At the same time, we present evidence from quantificational standards that Navajo standard markers are quantificational expressions that take sets of degrees, rather than entities, as argument. The kind of narrative that this suggests for Navajo is thus quite similar to the narrative that Pancheva explores for Slavic, namely how to reconcile quantificational comparative morphemes with standards that are not derived from full clauses. Nevertheless, a small clause account is a non-

---

11   Further precedent for a small clause treatment of comparative standards comes from Lechner 2004. See also Pancheva 2010 for subsequent development of the account given in Pancheva 2006.

starter for Navajo. In contrast with Slavic and many other languages, there is no evidence that small clause structures exist in Navajo: All Navajo clauses consist of the same minimal element, namely a fully inflected verb marked for all nominal arguments and temporal information. Appealing to a small clause structure in only Navajo comparatives seems very stipulative. Thus, our focus as we develop an analysis in section 5.1 will be whether we can maintain a quantificational entry for comparative (standard) markers while not appealing to any clausal structure in the standard.

3.2 Diagnostics

There exist a number of structures that have been taken to support a phrasal analysis (syntax and semantics) over a clausal one, and vice versa. While some of these diagnostics were originally discussed for English (Hankamer 1973, Heim 1985, Kennedy 1997), we will illustrate them as applied to Hindi-Urdu by Bhatt & Takahashi (2011), who argue that only a phrasal analysis is appropriate for Hindi-Urdu. Hindi-Urdu comparatives are at least superficially similar to Navajo comparatives, making their comparison potentially instructive.[12] Like Navajo, Hindi-Urdu forms comparatives by marking a nominal standard of comparison with a postposition. The postposition -*se* is also used outside of comparative constructions to express temporal and locative notions of 'from' (Bhatt & Takahashi 2011, 591).[13]

(33) *John* [DP *Bill*]-*se* (*zyaadaa*) *lambaa hai*
     John   Bill-than   more   tall.M.SG be.PRES.SG
     'John is taller than Bill.'

The first diagnostic concerns the acceptability of multiple phrases within the standard of comparison. Hindi-Urdu does not permit the standard to contain any expression in addition to the DP. In the following example, a temporal adverb is permitted in the main clause but rejected in the standard:

---

12   A class of diagnostics that we do not consider here looks at the case of nominal expressions in the standard. Certain case markers have been taken to indicate the presence or absence of reduced full clausal structure (Heim 1985, Pancheva 2006). Since Navajo does not have nominal case, however, these diagnostics will not be instructive.

13   Unlike Navajo, Hindi-Urdu sentences like (33) can optionally contain the morpheme *zyaadaa* glossed here as a comparative marker 'more'. This morpheme becomes obligatory in certain comparative constructions, including comparisons of quantity. See discussion of its possible semantic function in Schwarzschild 2012.

(34) *Tina-ne aaj Pim kal-se zyaadaa kitaabẽ paRh-ĩ:
Tina-ERG today Pim yesterday-than more books.F read-PFV.F.PL
(Intended: 'Tina read more books today than Pim yesterday.')

The English translation shows that English, by contrast, permits multiple phrases in the standard of comparison. We expect the English sentence to be acceptable if the English standard derives from reduction of a full clause, which Bhatt & Takahashi (2011) argue it does. The absence of full clausal structure from Hindi-Urdu standards means that we correctly predict adverbs to be ungrammatical.[14]

The second diagnostic concerns the availability of reflexive standards of comparison. Hankamer (1973), Hoeksema (1983), and Napoli (1983) observe for English that a reflexive bound by the subject cannot function as the standard in clear cases of clausal comparison (35a). Reflexives become grammatical if the standard lacks any verbal material (35b).

(35) a. *No girl is taller than herself is.
 b. No girl is taller than herself.

Examples like these have been taken to suggest that English standards like (35b) are phrasal and do not derive from the reduction of a full clausal standard. If the standard is a full clause as in (35a), *herself* will not be locally bound and thus is correctly predicted to be ungrammatical. A phrasal syntactic analysis of (35b), on the other hand, puts *herself* in the same clause as the coreferential subject, making the reflexive not only licensed but obligatory on usual binding-theoretic assumptions (Chomsky 1981).

In Hindi-Urdu, by contrast, the standard in a *se*-phrase can, and indeed must, be a reflexive form when it is coindexed with the subject of the gradable predicate. This configuration suggests that Hindi-Urdu standards do not involve the reduction of full clausal standards.[15]

---

14   The Hindi-Urdu facts may also have an explanation on a small clause account of standards (Pancheva 2006, Pancheva 2010). Temporal adverbs would be blocked because of the absence of tense from small clauses. However, small clauses can contain other kinds of modifying phrases, for example *I consider her unattractive drunk* (Harley & Jung 2015). In contrast with Navajo, Hindi-Urdu has been independently claimed to possess small clauses (Shah 1995); if the Hindi-Urdu counterpart to, for example *Even when she's sober, Tina is louder than Pim drunk* is grammatical, this would suggest a small clause treatment might be appropriate for the language.

15   We note that Pancheva (2006) suggests that a small clause analysis is also consistent with these data: Reflexives seem to be licensed in small clauses, as in *I consider myself lucky*. If

(36) koi-bhii$_i$ apne   [$_{DP}$ aap]-se$_i$ / [$_{DP}$ us]-se$_{j/*i}$ lambaa nahĩ: ho
     anyone REFL.POSS   REFL-than   him-than   tall   NEG be
     sak-taa
     can-HABITUAL.M.SG
     'No one$_i$ can be taller than himself$_i$/him$_{j/*i}$.'

The final diagnostic we highlight concerns quantifier scope in standards. Bhatt & Takahashi (2011) show that in an English sentence like (37), the universal quantifier is permitted to take scope within the standard of comparison.[16]

(37) More students read every syntax paper than (read) every semantics paper.
     ≈ The number of students who read every syntax paper exceeds the number of students who read every semantics paper.

This reading would arise from the following LF, as given in Beck et al. 2012:

(38) [[-er$_{clausal}$ [than [λd . d-many students read every semantics paper]]]
     [λd . d-many students read every syntax paper]]

Bhatt & Takahashi (2011) give the following translation into Hindi-Urdu for sentence (37).

(39) [har syntax paper] [har semantics paper]-se zyaadaa
     every syntax paper every semantics paper-than more
     logõ-ne   paRh-aa
     people-ERG   read-PFV
     ≈ For every pair ⟨x, y⟩ of a syntax paper x and a semantics paper y, more people read x than y. (The least-read syntax paper was read by more people than any semantics paper) (paraphrase from Beck et al. 2012)

In contrast with the English sentence, however, (39) only has a reading in which the universal quantifier is interpreted with scope above the comparative relation. This meaning can be paraphrased in terms of 'pairwise comparison' as shown above. This reading corresponds to the following LF (Beck et al. 2012):

---

   so, then these Hindi-Urdu facts may be consistent with a treatment of standards either as simple DPs or as reduced small clauses.
16 Much has been written about quantifiers in English that appear to obligatorily scope outside of comparatives (Gajewski 2008, Larson 1988, Schwarzschild & Wilkinson 2002, Heim 2006, Alrenga & Kennedy 2014, Fleisher 2016).

(40) [every syntax paper λx [every semantics paper
  λy [x [[-er$_{phrasal}$ than y] [λd . λz . d-many people read z]]]]]

This difference between English and Hindi-Urdu is expected if English permits clausal standards while Hindi-Urdu does not. In English, the quantificational phrase *every semantics paper* ($\langle\langle e, t\rangle, t\rangle$) must undergo Quantifier Raising, leaving behind a trace of appropriate type (e) to compose with the unpronounced verb in the standard of comparison. Because QR can occur within the confines of the clausal standard of comparison, the quantificational phrase can take low scope with respect to the comparative operator. In Hindi-Urdu, by contrast, quantificational phrases cannot take scope within the standard of comparison. This makes sense if Hindi-Urdu has phrasal standards of comparison and the standard marker *-se* seeks a type e argument: *Every semantics paper* must QR out of the standard of comparison in order to resolve the type mismatch.[17]

4 Applying the Tests to Navajo

4.1 First Impressions

This section considers evidence for, and against, possible analyses of Navajo standards. We will not consider a small clause analysis along the lines of Pancheva 2006 since, as already noted, small clauses are not a structure for which there is independent motivation in Navajo grammar. This leaves us with two options: a phrasal analysis and a reduced (full) clausal analysis. A phrasal analysis of Navajo standards immediately suggests itself when we consider simple degree constructions like those below. The standard marker *-lááh* obligatorily bears pronominal marking corresponding to the standard of comparison. On verbs we treated prefixes for objects and subjects as saturating argument positions of their host: Why not say that *shi-* in (41) saturates the first argument of *-lááh*$_{phrasal}$?

(41) *Alice shi-lááh 'anítnééz.*
  Alice 1-beyond 3.tall
  'Alice is taller than me.'

---

17 Hindi combines a universal quantifier *sab* with standard marker *-se* to translate superlatives prompts, as well. As expected, *sab* can only take high scope.
  (i) *Atif sab-se lambaa hai*
    Atif all-ABL tall be.PRES.SG
    'Atif is the tallest.' (*Lit:* Atif is taller than everyone)

Despite the initial appeal of a phrasal syntactic analysis, subcomparative-like structures like (42) have been previously used to motivate a clausal analysis for Navajo standards of comparison. Bogal-Allbritten (2013, 2016) treats all Navajo standards as underlyingly clausal, extrapolating from complex structures like (42) to simple cases like (41).

(42) *Ch'é'étiin bikáá'adání 'anítnééz-ígíí yi-lááh 'aníłtééł.*
door table 3.tall-NMLZ 3-beyond 3.wide
'The door is wider than the table is tall.'

As we will see next, however, despite the apparent existence of subcomparatives other diagnostics point away from a clausal analysis of the standard.

4.2 Evidence for Syntactically Phrasal Standards

With respect to the majority of diagnostics applied by Bhatt & Takahashi (2011) to Hindi-Urdu, Navajo seems to pattern like a clear example of a language with phrasal standards of comparison. First, like Hindi-Urdu—and unlike English—Navajo disallows multiple phrases in the standard of comparison.

(43) **'Ahbínídą́ą́' Alice 'atní'ní'ą́ą́dóo Ben yi-lááh-go bááh łikaní*
morning Alice afternoon Ben 3-beyond-SUB cookie
yiyíí'ą́ą́'.
3.3.eat.PFV
Context: Alice ate 4 cookies this morning. Ben ate 2 cookies this afternoon. I tell you: Alice ate more cookies this morning than Ben ate this afternoon.

(43) is not ungrammatical because it compares quantities. Quantities can be compared as in (44), which differs from (43) only in the lack of adverbs.

(44) *Alice Ben yi-lááh-go bááh łikaní yiyíí'ą́ą́'.*
Alice Ben 3-beyond-SUB cookie 3.3.eat.PFV
'Alice ate more cookies than Ben did.'

We can conclude that (43) must be ungrammatical because of the temporal adverb *'atní'ní'ą́ą́dóo* 'afternoon' in the standard of comparison. The sentence again becomes grammatical if this adverb is removed:

(45) *'Ahbínídą́ą́' Alice Ben yi-lááh-go bááh łikaní yiyíí'ą́ą́'.*
morning Alice Ben 3-beyond-SUB cookie 3.3.eat.PFV
'Alice ate more cookies this morning than Ben did.'

Second, Navajo postpositional standard markers can bear the reciprocal object marker *'ahi-*. We illustrate with the comparative standard marker *-lááh* as well as the equative standard marker *-ee*.[18,19]

(46) *Alice dóó Mary doo ahi-lááh 'anítnééz da.*
Alice and Mary NEG RECP-beyond 3.tall NEG
'Alice and Mary are not taller than each other.' (i.e. they are the same height)

(47) *'Ah-ee-niilnééz.*
RECP-with-1PL.tall
'We are equally tall.'
Lit. 'We are as tall as each other.' (Young & Morgan 1987, 54)

Reflexive and reciprocal object markers are obligatorily locally bound by an appropriate (i.e. non-singular) subject in Navajo (Willie 1991). The reciprocal marker in the following sentence cannot be replaced with a third-person marker without changing the meaning (i.e. 'We are painting some third person(s).').

(48) *'Ahiidleesh.*
RECP.1DU.paint.IPFV
'We are painting each other.' (Willie 1991, 34)

Thus, the grammaticality of reciprocal markers as standards of comparison suggests strongly that the standard of comparison should not be analyzed as a full clause, of which the standard is the subject.

---

18 We do not find examples of structures in which the standard marker *-gi* combines with a reciprocal object marker. Such structures seem to be ruled out for independent reasons, namely that Navajo lacks a non-affixal reciprocal pronoun (Willie 1991), which would be what *-gi* would need to attach to.
19 It is also possible to find the reflexive object marker *'ádi-* with standard markers. However, the meanings here were a bit odd, as shown in (i) (Young & Morgan 1987, 61). Further work is needed to determine how the meaning of (i) arises from its components.
   (i) *Díí tsin 'ał-'oh neel'á.*
       this stick REFL-short_of 3.extend
       'These sticks aren't the same length.' *Lit:* These sticks extend short of each other.

4.3 Evidence from the Scope of a Quantificational Standard

A phrasal treatment of Navajo standards is challenged, however, by comparatives with indefinite standards, used to express superlative meaning. Navajo lacks a single superlative marker comparable to English *-est* but instead translates superlative prompts by combining the comparative standard marker *-lááh* seen above with an object prefix of the shape *'a*. Superlative meaning arises regardless of the morphological form of the adjectival verb (e.g., *'anítnééz* vs. *nineez*).[20] Crucially, this sentence only has one meaning: Alice is taller than anyone else is. It cannot mean that there is someone whom Alice is taller than.

(49) a. *Alice 'a-lááh   'anítnééz.*
   Alice UNSPEC-beyond 3.tall
   'Alice is tallest, Alice is taller than anyone.'

   b. *Alice 'a-lááh-go   nineez.*
   Alice UNSPEC-beyond-SUB 3.tall
   'Alice is tallest, Alice is taller than anyone.'

The *'a-* object marker can also be borne by the postpositional standard marker used in comparisons of inferiority, *-'oh*. The meaning here is identical to (49) except that the meaning is that Alice is shorter (less tall) than anyone else in the context.

(50) *Alice 'a-'oh   'anítnééz.*
   Alice UNSPEC-short_of 3.tall
   'Alice is shortest.'
   Lit: Alice is tall short of anyone.

Young & Morgan (1987) refer to the *'a-* prefix as the 'unspecified' or 'indefinite' object marker. Reflexes of *'a-* with the same characteristics are found in other Athabaskan (Dene) languages. In Navajo, *'a-* occupies the same position in the morphological template otherwise associated with the kind of object markers

---

20 This sentence has a true superlative interpretation in the sense that it means that the subject bears the property in question to a unique degree among all relevant competitors. That is, (49) does not merely express that Alice is tall to a high degree, but rather that she is taller than anyone else under comparison. This sentence was rejected in a context in which Alice and Ben were both exceptionally tall individuals but the same height as each other.

we have already seen (Young & Morgan 1987). As such, it is not possible for a verb to bear both 'a and a 'normal' object marker.

The 'a- prefix is by no means restricted to superlative constructions. Minimal pairs of verbs with unspecified objects ((a)-sentences) and third-person objects ((b)-sentences) are given below.[21]

(51) a. *Na'nitkaad.*
UNSPEC.3.herd.IPFV
'S/he is herding (something).'

b. *Neinitkaad.*
3.3.herd.IPFV
'S/he is herding it/them.'

(52) a. *'Asts'ééh.*
UNSPEC.1SG.eat_mush.IPFV
'I am eating (something).'

b. *Yists'ééh.*
3.1SG.eat_mush.IPFV
'I am eating it.'

The 'a- object marker is also found on postpositions outside of those used in superlative constructions.[22]

(53) a. *Shi-zhéé   '-ee   nástaaz.*
1POSS-father UNSPEC-with 3.wrap_up.PFV
'My father was wrapped up (in something).'

b. *Shi-chee   y-ee   nástaaz.*
1POSS-grandfather 3-with 3.wrap_up.PFV
'My grandfather was wrapped up in it.' (Young & Morgan 1987, 569)

---

21 As the translations suggest, the verb stem may impose particular kinds of physical attributes on both regular and unspecified objects to have particular physical attributes. For example, the verb stem *tsééh* requires that the patient of the verb be mushy matter; thus, the unspecified object in (52a) must be mushy even though it does not refer to any particular mushy matter in particular as the object marker in (52b) does. See Fernald & Willie 2001 for discussion.

22 The 'a- prefix surfaces as a glottal stop here.

Replacing a regular object marker with ʼa- has two concrete effects. First, the use of ʼa- blocks the use of verb-external nominal expressions, which are unremarkable with regular object markers.

(54) a. ʼAshkii (*dibé) naʼnitkaad.
    boy   sheep   UNSPEC.3.herd.IPFV
    'The boy is herding.'

  b. ʼAshkii dibé   neinitkaad.
     boy   sheep 3.3.herd.IPFV
     'The boy is herding sheep.'

Second, if a verb bears the ʼa- object prefix, a subsequent verb bearing a regular object prefix cannot refer back to the object involved in the event described by the first verb (Fernald et al. 2000).

(55) ʼAshkii léiʼ   naʼnitkaad.   #Éí   táididoogish.
     boy   INDF UNSPEC.3.herd.IPFV that.one 3.3.shear.FUT
     'A boy is herding. He will shear it/them.'

On the basis of these two behaviors, Fernald et al. (2000) and Fernald & Perkins (2018) treat ʼa- as a valency-reducing affix rather than a referential pronoun of the kind denoted by other subject and object prefixes in the language. We give ʼa- the following general and type-flexible meaning (compare Dowty's (1978) rule for Unspecified Object Deletion); ʼa- reduces the valency of the predicate to which it applies through existential closure.[23]

(56) Given predicate P and arguments $\alpha, \beta, \ldots \gamma \rightsquigarrow \lambda\alpha \, . \, \lambda\beta \ldots \lambda\gamma \, . \, P(\alpha, \beta, \ldots \gamma)$, then $ʼa\text{-}P \rightsquigarrow \lambda\beta \ldots \lambda\gamma \, . \, \exists\alpha \, . \, P(\alpha, \beta, \ldots, \gamma)$

The prefix ʼa- seems to saturate only internal argument positions of verbs: object positions in the examples above, or subject arguments of unaccusative verbs (e.g., *arrive*). This distribution is consistent with ʼa- being a valency reducing morpheme of the relevant sort.[24] Example (57) illustrates composition

---

23 This rule is type-flexible, such that the arguments of P can be of any type (entities, degrees, etc.). For simplicity, we show both subject and object arguments are part of the verb's basic meaning, rather than introduce the subject via a functional head (Hale 2000, Rice 2000). We also suppress situation arguments. Nothing hinges on this.

24 A different morphological passivization operation is used to remove subject arguments and promote object arguments (Fernald & Perkins 2018).

of *na'nitkaad* 's/he is herding (something)' through composition between the unspecified object marker *'a* and verb (or verb stem) followed by composition with the third-person pronominal subject.

(57) *na'nitkaad*$_i$ ⇝ $\exists x$. herd(x, v_i)
     UNSPEC.3$_i$.herd.IPFV

With this in hand, we return to the superlative construction. We stated above that (49) cannot be used in a context in which there is a particular individual whom Alice is taller than. However, this is precisely the truth conditions that are generated if we assign *-lááh* the denotation associated above with phrasal standards.[25]

(58) a. *-lááh*$_{phrasal}$ ⇝ λy . $\lambda g_{\langle d,et\rangle}$. λx . MAX$(\lambda d$. $g(d,x)) >$ MAX$(\lambda d$. $g(d,y))$
     b. *'a-lááh* ⇝ $\lambda g_{\langle d,et\rangle}$. λx . $\exists y$. MAX$(\lambda d$. $g(d,x)) >$ MAX$(\lambda d$. $g(d,y))$
     c. *Alice 'a-lááh 'anítnééz* ⇝
         $\exists y$. MAX$(\lambda d$. tall$(d,$ Alice$)) >$ MAX$(\lambda d$. tall$(d,y))$
         True iff there exists some *y*, such that Alice's maximal degree of height exceeds the maximal degree of height of *y*

If we instead permit Navajo to have clausal standards of comparison, we generate the right meaning. In the following derivation, *'a-* composes with the unpronounced copy of the gradable predicate in the standard of comparison and so has low scope.[26]

(59) a. *-lááh*$_{clausal}$ ⇝ $\lambda D_{\langle d,t\rangle}$. $\lambda D'_{\langle d,t\rangle}$. MAX$(D') >$ MAX(D)
     b. *Alice 'a-lááh 'anítnééz* ⇝
         MAX$(\lambda d$. tall$(d,$ Alice$)) >$ MAX$(\lambda d$. $\exists y$. tall$(d,y))$
         True iff Alice's maximal degree of height exceeds the maximal degree *d* such that for some *y*, *y* is tall to *d*

---

25 The translation in (58c) is a simplification. Since we assume that pronominal prefixes saturate the argument positions of verbs, *'anítnééz* would actually be translated as tall$(v_i)(d)$. The index *i* is associated with Alice via a binding process (Baker 1996).

26 As given, the truth conditions in (59b) are trivially false: Alice (a potential *y*) cannot be taller than herself. But verbs with *'a-* in place of a regular object prefix cannot generally describe the subject acting upon herself. Instead, the reflexive object marker (high tone, *'á-*) must be used, e.g., *'ádéshjoł* 'I am drying myself.' Thus, there seems to be a general requirement that the domain of entities quantified over by unspecified marker *'a-* be distinct from other actors in the sentence.

These results strongly suggest not only that Navajo can have a quantificational semantics for standard markers such as *-láàh*, but furthermore that it must. Admitting a phrasal semantics for *-láàh* would predict a high scope indefinite reading to be available for sentences in which *'a-* functions as the standard of comparison. Although *'a-* might seem like a prime candidate for a phrasal semantics for the standard marker—as *'a* consists of a nominal affix and nothing more—we never find *'a-* being interpreted with scope over the comparative relation. However, this conclusion about the semantics of *-láàh* and, by extension, other standard markers is in apparent conflict with earlier evidence that supported a phrasal syntax for the standard. The goal of the analysis will be to resolve this conflict.

4.4   Ruling Out an Alternative View of '*a-*

We motivated a quantificational semantics for the standard marker *-láàh* by appealing to a particular analysis of the prefix *'a-* as a valency-reducing existential closure operation. Before considering how to reconcile the semantic and syntactic claims made above, let us first briefly entertain an alternative analysis of *'a-* which would be compatible with a phrasal entry for *-láàh*..[27] The idea would be to treat *'a-* as ambiguous between a positive polarity item with existential force and a negative polarity item with universal force. The PPI form of *'a-* would be used in simple non-negated expressions like (60), repeated from above. The existential quantifier *'a-* would presumably undergo Quantifier Raising, leaving behind a type *e* trace. The resulting meaning would be identical to what we obtained on our earlier analysis.

(60) *na'nitkaad$_i$*   ⤳ $\exists x$. herd(x, v_i)
      UNSPEC.3$_i$.herd.IPFV

The NPI form of *'a-* would occur both in the scope of negation and in standards of comparison, which is also a downward-entailing environment. As an NPI, *'a-* would denote a universal quantifier; Shimoyama (2011) discusses Japanese NPIs with universal force that obligatorily scope above licensing negation. Like Japanese NPIs, Navajo NPI *'a-* would undergo Quantifier Raising and would be interpreted with scope above the comparative relation:

---

27   We thank Michael Yoshitaka Erlewine and Louise McNally for bringing this alternative view to our attention.

(61) *'a-lááh*   *'anítnééz$_i$*
    UNSPEC-beyond 3$_i$.tall
    ⤳ $\forall y$. MAX(λd . tall(d, v_i)) > MAX(λd . tall(d, y))

The truth conditions in (61) ($\forall > \neg$) are equivalent to the truth conditions in (59) ($\neg > \exists$). But while treating *'a-* as an NPI would allow us to maintain a phrasal entry for *-lááh*, such an analysis faces challenges which we believe rule it out from further consideration. First, this analysis forces us to make certain stipulative assumptions about *'a-*: Not only must we posit ambiguity for *'a-*, but we have to allow *'a-* to undergo covert quantifier raising. While such a move may be unproblematic for a scrambling language like Japanese, Navajo is reported to have fixed scope (Fernald et al. 2000, Bogal-Allbritten & Moulton 2017). Furthermore, scope of verbal affixes is claimed to be particularly rigid across the entire Athabaskan family (Rice 2000). We would have to say that NPI *'a-* is unique among Navajo morphemes in its ability to undergo covert movement.

Second, the distribution of *'a-* seems to be limited to internal argument positions. While this restriction is unsurprising on an analysis that treats *'a-* as a valency-reducing morpheme, it has no explanation on an account of *'a-* as a polarity item. Maintaining a polarity item analysis of *'a-* would mean stipulating its distribution.

Finally, if we posit ambiguity for *'a-*, it is not clear how to restrict the distribution of PPI existential *'a-*. If movement of quantificational *'a-* is available, then why can a sentence like (61) not contain an instance of PPI existential *'a-* that has raised out of the scope of negation? Such a structure would have the truth conditions repeated in (62), which we have already established as unavailable.

(62) $\exists y$. MAX(λd . tall(d, Alice)) > MAX(λd . tall(d, y))
    True iff there exists some y, such that Alice's maximal degree of height exceeds the maximal degree of height of y

With these considerations in hand, we set aside this alternative view of *'a-* and turn now to how we might reconcile syntactically phrasal standards with quantificational entries for standard markers in Navajo.

5 Quantificational Standard Markers, but Phrasal Standards

5.1 *Proposal*

We have seen evidence that suggests that Navajo standards are phrasal and part of the same clause as the rest of the degree construction, rather than deriving from reduced clausal structure. Nevertheless, we have also seen two kinds of evidence that challenge this view. First, subcomparatives; we will return to their analysis in sec. 5.2, where we argue that they in fact do not challenge a phrasal analysis. The second piece of evidence is the obligatory low scope of the quantificational prefix *'a-* in Navajo superlative constructions. This latter challenge is central to our main claim in this paper: Navajo standard markers must have quantificational entries. (We represent the class of standard markers with *-láah*, but the proposals made here should be able to be generalized to all postpositions and enclitics used in degree constructions.)

(63) *-láah* ⤳ $\lambda D_{\langle d,t \rangle} \lambda D'_{\langle d,t \rangle} \ . \ \text{MAX}(D') > \text{MAX}(D)$

Nevertheless, we will maintain that Navajo standards are syntactically phrasal.

In order to reconcile a quantificational semantics with a phrasal treatment of standards, we will need to associate the entities denoted by standard phrases with properties of degrees without adding actual clausal structure in the process. We propose that composition between an entity-denoting standard and a quantificational standard marker is mediated by MEAS, a null functional head. We adopt the entry assigned to MEAS by Solt (2009); see Rett 2014 for an entry that differs only in the order in which degrees and entities are taken as argument.

(64) MEAS ⤳ $\lambda x_e \ . \ \lambda d_d \ . \ \mu(x) \geq d$ where μ is a variable over measure functions

(Solt 2009, 105)

The measure function in MEAS associates an entity x with a scale (a set of degrees ordered along some dimension). Unlike other adjectival verbs whose measure functions are lexically determined (e.g., *tall*, height), however, the value of the measure function in MEAS is not specified. In applications of MEAS to phenomena in other languages, the measure function is determined both by the material it combines with (e.g., noun, measure phrase) and by context (Schwarzschild 2002, Solt 2009, Rett 2014). We return below to consider how this valuation can happen in Navajo.

There is significant precedent in the literature for measurement operators in a variety of constructions, although proposals vary as to whether the meaning of this operator is built into the meaning of nouns themselves or expressed by a separate head as we assume here (Cresswell 1976, Krifka 1989, Kayne 2005, Schwarzschild 2006, Svenonius & Kennedy 2006, Nakanishi 2007, Solt 2009, Rett 2014, Wellwood 2015, among others). Measurement operators are perhaps best known for being the semantic 'glue' which enables composition between nouns and measure phrases or numerals (e.g., *six cats, 5cm paperclips*), as well as between nouns and quantity adjectives (e.g., *many*) on analyses that treat them as relations between degrees and intervals (Rett 2008, Solt 2015).

In the Navajo degree constructions under discussion, MEAS mediates between an entity and a degree expression, in this case the standard marker *-lááh*. We illustrate the application of MEAS with the following simple sentence:

(65) *Alice yi-lááh 'ánítnééz.*
Alice 3-beyond 3.tall
'Alice is taller than him/her/it.'

The standard of comparison is the third-person pronominal prefix *yi-*. When *yi-* composes with the measurement operator MEAS, the referent of the pronominal prefix is mapped onto a scale (a set of degrees ordered along some dimension, to be determined).

(66) MEAS $yi_i \rightsquigarrow \lambda d \ . \ \mu(v_i) \geq d$

The set of degrees composes with the standard marker *-lááh*.

(67) *-lááh* [MEAS yi_i] $\rightsquigarrow \lambda D'_{\langle d,t \rangle} \ . \ \text{MAX}(D') > \text{MAX}(\lambda d \ . \ \mu(v_i) \geq d)$

The second set of degrees taken by *-lááh* is contributed by material from the main clause. The gradable predicate *'ánítnééz* bears a subject prefix which we have taken to saturate the entity argument position of the verb. We use the same simplification introduced earlier and show direct composition between the verb and *Alice*, the verb-external nominal expression which will ultimately come to value the subject pronominal prefix. The set of degrees to which Alice is tall is taken as argument by yi_1-*lááh* as it was defined in (67).

(68) *Alice yi_i-lááh 'ánítnééz* $\rightsquigarrow$
  $\text{MAX}(\lambda d \ . \ \text{height}(\text{Alice}) \geq d) > \text{MAX}(\lambda d \ . \ \mu(v_i) \geq d)$
  True iff the maximal degree to which Alice is tall exceeds the maximal degree associated with the referent of yi_i

The scale associated with MEAS is still unspecified in our truth conditions above, but it seems reasonable to assume that in a sentence like (65), the most accessible meaning is one in which μ is equated with the measure function from the main clause gradable predicate, namely height.

We now turn to the analysis of Navajo translations of superlative prompts, as repeated in (69):

(69) *Alice 'a-lááh   'ánítnééz.*
 Alice UNSPEC-beyond 3.tall
 'Alice is tallest, Alice is taller than anyone.'

The unspecified object prefix *'a-* composes first with MEAS. Composition returns the set of degrees d such that for any y, d is a degree associated with y on some scale whose dimension parameter remains to be determined.

(70) *'a* MEAS ⤳ $\lambda d \ . \ \exists y \ . \ \mu(y) \geq d$

This set of degrees is then taken as argument by the standard marker *-lááh*, just as before. The second set of degrees taken as argument by *-lááh* is determined by application of the main clause gradable predicate to the subject. Keeping the same notational simplifications from above in place, the final truth conditions are as follows. We once again assume that the measure function μ in MEAS is identified with the measure function, height, from the gradable predicate in the main clause.[28]

---

28 Our analysis of Navajo expressions of superlative meaning suggests another reason to avoid an alternative analysis on which *-lááh* is not of quantificational determiner type but is instead type $\langle d, \langle \langle d, t \rangle, t \rangle \rangle$, where its first argument is obtained by prior application of an independent MAX operator to the standard of comparison (von Stechow 1984, Rullmann 1995, Heim 2001). Earlier, we suggested that while such an approach may make sense for languages in which we find a standard marker (and/or *wh*-operator) in addition to a comparative morpheme, it is not parsimonious for Navajo, where we seem to only have a comparative operator at our disposal: Why not put all meaning related to comparison in the entry of a quantificational *-lááh*, then, as we have done?

However, there is another kind of analysis that would be consistent with a type $\langle d, \langle \langle d, t \rangle, t \rangle \rangle$ meaning for *-lááh*. What if we instead define MEAS as a measure function $(\langle e, d \rangle)$ as Wellwood (2015) does? This measure function would apply to entity-denoting standards and return the (maximal) degree associated with that entity on some scale. Thus, there would be no need to posit an extra MAX operator, which we found unappealing above. However, this alternative treatment of MEAS cannot be integrated with our analysis: Since we have defined *'a-* as an existential closure operation, it must compose with a set-type expression (i.e. the type ends in ...t)). We see no coherent way to define *'a-*

(71) *Alice 'a-lááh 'ánítnééź* ⤳
    $\text{MAX}(\lambda d \ . \ \text{height}(\text{Alice}) \geq d) > \text{MAX}(\lambda d \ . \ \exists y \ . \ \mu(y) \geq d)$
    True iff the maximal degree to which Alice is tall exceeds the maximal degree to which some *y* is tall

We recognize there to be a slight mismatch in morphological and semantic bracketing here. Although the prefixes *yi-* and *'a-* are taken as argument by MEAS, they are nevertheless morphologically realized as prefixes to the standard marker *-lááh*. A preference for matching the Logical Form with morphological bracketing might suggest that these two elements compose directly, as would be the case if *-lááh* had a non-quantificational meaning. But while regular object markers like *yi-* could in principle compose directly with *-lááh* so defined and still yield the right truth conditions, we have seen that the same is not true for *'a*. If *'a-* composes directly with *-lááh*, only the unattested high scope reading for *'a-* is expected.[29] We assume that *yi-* and *'a-* are realized as prefixes on *-lááh* despite composing first with MEAS because MEAS is not overt and therefore not an eligible host for prefixes.

Our account of Navajo is similar in spirit to the small clause account of certain Slavic comparatives developed by Pancheva (2006, 2010), who argues that it is possible to maintain a quantificational denotation for comparative markers without appealing to a full clausal syntax for standards of comparison. However, our analysis crucially differs from Pancheva's in that MEAS does not introduce (even small) clausal structure of the sort that might, for instance, license adverbs in the standard of comparison. As we noted already, it is not easy to see how a small clause account could be applied directly to Navajo, since there is no evidence that this is a structure in the language: All Navajo clauses consist of the same minimal element, namely a fully-inflected verb marked for all nominal arguments and temporal information. As such, we have developed an account that maintains quantificational entries for comparative (standard) markers while continuing to treat standards as syntactically phrasal.

---

such that it can compose with a measure function-type MEAS. This is, then, another strike against a type $\langle d, \langle \langle d, t \rangle, t \rangle \rangle$ treatment of Navajo standard markers.

29 Crucially, the truth conditions are incorrect for *'a-lááh* if we assume direct composition regardless of which entry we assign to *-lááh*. We have already seen that this is true for the phrasal analysis in (58); (i) demonstrates that the truth conditions are still wrong if *-lááh* is instead given a quantificational meaning but nevertheless composes with *'a-* directly:
 (i) a. *-lááh* ⤳ $\lambda D_{\langle d,t \rangle} \ . \ \lambda D'_{\langle d,t \rangle} \ . \ \text{MAX}(D') > \text{MAX}(D)$
     b. *'a-lááh* ⤳ $\lambda D'_{\langle d,t \rangle} \ . \ \exists D_{\langle d,t \rangle} \ . \ \text{MAX}(D') > \text{MAX}(D)$
     c. *Alice 'a-lááh 'ánítnééź* ⤳ $\exists D_{\langle d,t \rangle} \ . \ \text{MAX}(\lambda d \ . \ \text{tall}(d, \text{Alice})) > \text{MAX}(D)$
         'There exists a set of degrees D. Alice is taller than the maximal degree in this set.'

5.2 Accounting for Subcomparatives

Subcomparatives like (72) and (73) originally motivated Bogal-Allbritten (2013, 2016) to assume that Navajo must permit clausal standards.

(72) *Ch'é'étiin bikáá'adání 'anítnééz-ígíí yi-lááh   'aníłtééł.*
     door   table   3.tall-NMLZ   3-beyond   3.wide
     'The door is wider than the table is tall.'

(73) *Ch'é'étiin bikáá'adání 'anítnééz-í-gi   'aníłtééł.*
     door   table   3.tall-NMLZ-LOC   3.wide
     'The door is as wide as the table is tall.'

While Bogal-Allbritten did not assign any particular semantic function to -*ígíí*, it clearly plays some role in these sentences. If we remove -*ígíí* (or its morphological variant -*í* seen in (73)), the structure becomes ungrammatical:

(74) **Ch'é'étiin bikáá'adání 'anítnééz yi-lááh   'aníłtééł.*
     door   table   3.tall   3-beyond   3.wide

The marker -*ígíí* is also found on structures previously analyzed as internally-headed relative clauses (Platero 1974, Willie 1989). It marks the right edge of the relative clause, shown in brackets:

(75) [*K'ad 'ashkii 'ałhą́ą́'*]   -*ígíí*   *yádoołtih.*
     now boy 3.snore.IPFV -NMLZ   3.speak.FUT
     'The boy who is snoring right now will speak.' (adapt. Platero 1974)

While the bracketed structure above is clearly clausal, the addition of -*ígíí* allows it to occupy positions that can otherwise contain, for example, proper names as in *Alice yádoołtih* 'Alice will speak'.

On our analysis of standards developed above, MEAS composed with an entity and returned a property of degrees. In sentences like (75), the *ígíí*-marked clause occupies an argument position where we would expect to find type e expressions. Why not, then, claim that the *ígíí*-marked clauses in subcomparatives also denote a simple type d expression? Under this view, we could treat -*ígíí* as either a choice function or iota operator, which would apply to a set of degrees (as would be denoted by a gradable predicate inflected for subject) and return a single degree. We illustrate with the iota operator.[30]

---

30   Reason to prefer a choice function treatment of *ígíí*-marked clauses comes from cases in

(76) Bikáa'adání 'ánítnééz-ígíí
    table   3.tall-NMLZ
    ⤳ ιd . height(table) $\geq d$ $\equiv \iota d$. tall(d, table)

We have defined -*lááh* in such a way that it is not able to compose directly with a type d expression. However, we can obtain a property of degrees if we also permit MEAS to take a degree as first argument (77). Ambiguity between MEAS as defined in (77) and the original entry in (64) has precedent in Rett 2014.

(77) MEAS$_{\text{DEG}}$ ⤳ λd . $\lambda d'$. $\mu(d) \geq d'$

Application of MEAS to the length d of the table returns a set of degrees ordered along some dimension. This property of degrees would then go on to combine with -*lááh* and the rest of the clause in the familiar way. As before, we assume that the scale associated with MEAS is determined by the main clause gradable predicate. We illustrate below with the subcomparative structure from (72).

(78) Ch'é'étiin bikáá'adání 'ánítnééz-ígíí yi-lááh 'ánítééł ⤳
    MAX(λd . width(door) $\geq d$) $>$ MAX(λd . $\mu(\iota d$. tall(d, table)) $\geq d$)
    True iff the maximal degree to which the door is wide exceeds the maximal degree to which the table's height is wide.

It is a bit awkward to think about the *width* of a table's *height*, but this awkwardness seems to be a product of the paraphrase and not the original sentence. Just as is the case for the English translation, the Navajo sentence above is sensible because both *wide* and *tall* are associated with the dimension of linear extent (Kennedy 1997, Kennedy & McNally 2005). Of course, *wide* and *tall* are not synonymous, since the measure function that underlies each differs in whether a horizontal or vertical linear extent is measured. Nevertheless, because degrees of width and height are both degrees of linear extent, the degree correspond-

---

which these expressions do not appear to have the semantic attributes of definite noun phrases, such as in (i) from Grosu 2012, attributed to Ellavina Perkins. We will, however, leave this issue open for the time being.
(i) *Bilasáana hazhó'ó tánágis-ígíí   nisin.*
    apple   carefully   3.be_washed-NMLZ   3.1SG.want/think
    'I want an apple that is well-washed.'

ing to the table's height can be placed on the same scale as the degree corresponding to the door's width, and the two degrees ordered with respect to each other.[31]

This same entry for MEAS could also be used in measure phrase comparatives like (79), if we take measure phrases to denote degrees.[32]

(79) Alice hastą́ą-di 'adées'eez yi-lááh   'anítnééz.
     Alice six-LOC   feet   3-beyond   3.tall
     'Alice is taller than six feet.'

MEAS would apply to the measure phrase and return a set of degrees along some dimension. This set of degrees would then go on to compose with -*lááh* and the rest of the clause. This would be reminiscent of Hackl's (2000) analysis of measure phrase comparatives in English, which invokes an unpronounced quantity predicate in the standard of comparison. However, our account differs from Hackl's in that we do not invoke true clausal structure in Navajo standards of comparison.

5.3 Valuation of the Scale Associated with MEAS

To this point, we have only considered examples in which the main clause contains an overt gradable predicate. In our analysis of these structures, the measure function associated with MEAS was obligatorily identified with the measure function associated with the main clause gradable predicate. We have not found any evidence that a sentence like (80), for instance, can have a subcomparative interpretation, where the MEAS operator that composes

---

[31] The challenge will be to extend this view of -*ígíí* to its use in internally-headed relative clauses as in (75). When -*ígíí* is used in subcomparatives, it takes a property of degrees as argument. In the case of (75), however, it seems like -*ígíí* is combining with a complete clause rather than the type $\langle e, t \rangle$ expression that it seems we would need in order for the entire *ígíí*-marked expression to denote an entity. One possible direction is to take our analysis of *ígíí* as it occurs in subcomparatives as basic and reconsider Bogal-Allbritten & Moulton' 2017 analysis of Navajo internally-headed relative clauses as parallel to superficially similar structures in Japanese (Hoshi 1995, Shimoyama 1999). Instead, we might consider an account in which we abstract over one of the pronominal prefixes borne by the verb within the *ígíí*-marked clause. This process of abstraction would serve two functions: First, it would identify the head of the relative clause, and second it would create a property-type expression of the kind which *ígíí* can compose with. Precedent for this view of Navajo comes from Grosu 2012. However, we will leave resolution of this to future work.

[32] If measure phrases instead denote intervals ($\langle d, t \rangle$) as in Schwarzschild & Wilkinson 2002 and others, they could compose directly with -*lááh*.

with the standard is associated with a different measure function than the main clause predicate.[33]

(80) *Ch'éétiin bikáá'adání yi-lááh   'áníttééł.*
     door   table   3-beyond 3.wide
     Can only mean: 'The door is wider than the table.'
     Cannot mean: 'The door is wider than the table is tall.'   (viz. (72))

The apparent requirement that the scale associated with MEAS must match the scale associated with the overt main clause predicate strongly recalls the anaphoric predicate in Pancheva's (2006) small clause analysis of standards of comparison. Pancheva proposes that the anaphoric predicate is valued when the main clause predicate is copied at LF. A similar process could apply in Navajo to determine what measure function is associated with MEAS when the main clause contains a gradable predicate.[34]

At the same time, we expect that in the absence of a gradable predicate, the measure function associated with MEAS can be supplied by context, as is possible for MEAS in its other uses (Schwarzschild 2006, Solt 2009, Rett 2014). This expectation appears to be borne out. Ellavina Perkins volunteered the following sentence when asked about structures like (43), where the standard should contain a temporal adverb. In the context, it is clear that we are comparing quantities of cookies, and that is the interpretation that we get. There is no overt gradable predicate, however:

---

[33] Peter Alrenga (p.c.) suggests that this reading could be avoided if *-lááh* were redefined such that it takes the gradable predicate g as argument. The effect of this would essentially be to combine the standard marker with MEAS, where g would determine the scale. We see three challenges for such an approach. First, gradable predicates do not compose directly with comparative markers in Navajo; on our assumptions in section 2, obligatory composition with pronominal subject markers results in gradable predicates denoting sets of degrees at the point at which they compose with *-lááh*. Second, as we see in (81), there are at least some constructions where context, rather than a gradable predicate, appears to determine the scale. Finally, it is a challenge to define *-lááh* in such a way that it composes directly with the gradable predicate while also avoiding the undesirable high scope interpretation for existential *'a-*. One imaginable possibility is to define *-lááh* so that it composes directly with a quantifier (i). If we adopt (i), we will have to typeshift all standards other than *'a-* (i.e. pronominal prefixes) from type e to type $\langle\langle e, t\rangle, t\rangle$.
(i) *-lááh* ⤳ $\lambda g_{\langle e,dt\rangle} \cdot \lambda Q_{\langle et,t\rangle} \cdot \lambda D_{\langle d,t\rangle} \cdot \text{MAX}(D) > \text{MAX}(\lambda d \cdot Q(\lambda x \cdot g(x,d)))$
Given these challenges and the absence of compelling independent reasons to pursue this alternative analysis, we set it aside here.

[34] Pancheva (2006) does not provide more detail on this process; crucially, we do *not* mean a process by which clausal structure is copied at LF, but rather one which determines the measure function associated with MEAS.

(81) *'Ahbínídą́ą́' Alice bááh łikaní yiyíiyą́ą́'-ígíí   Ben 'ałní'ní'ą́ą́dóo*
    morning   Alice cookie   3.3.eat.PFV-NMLZ Ben afternoon
    yiyíiyą́ą́'-ígíí   t'áa bi-lááh.
    3.3.eat.PFV-NMLZ just 3-beyond
    Lit. 'The cookies that Alice ate this morning are more than the cookies that Ben ate this afternoon.'
    Prompt: Alice ate 4 cookies this morning. Ben ate 2 cookies this afternoon. I tell you: Alice ate more cookies this morning than Ben ate this afternoon.

If we take each *ígíí*-marked clause to denote a plurality of cookies—which we treat here as type *e* for the sake of illustration—an instance of MEAS would have to apply to each to yield the sets of degrees to be taken as argument by *-lááh*. In the context given, it was clear that we were comparing quantities of cookies. It makes sense, then, if μ projects entities onto the quantity scale.

(82) a. MEAS[ιx . x is cookies that Alice ate this morning] ⤳
    λd . μ(Alice-cookies) $\geq d$
    b. MEAS[ιx . x is cookies that Ben ate this afternoon] ⤳
    λd . μ(Ben-cookies) $\geq d$
    c. *-lááh*[λd . μ(Ben-cookies) $\geq d$][λd . μ(Alice-cookies) $\geq d$] ⤳
    MAX(λd . $\mu(d,$ Alice-cookies)) > MAX(λd . $\mu(d,$ Ben-cookies))

The potential flexibility of such examples remains underinvestigated, however. Future work must in particular ask if other measure functions or scales can be made sufficiently salient given an appropriate context. Our invocation of MEAS makes the prediction that while context may assist in determining the measure function of MEAS, only scales with monotonic dimensions will be available: Application of MEAS to other constructions demonstrates a general monotonicity restriction (Schwarzschild 2006, Solt 2009, Rett 2014). We leave further investigation of this point for Navajo to future work.

5.4   *Scope of Standard Phrases*
On our proposal, standard phrases in Navajo denote generalized quantifiers over degrees (type $\langle\langle d, t\rangle, t\rangle$).

(83) *yi$_i$-lááh* ⤳ $\lambda D'_{\langle d,t\rangle}$. MAX(D') > MAX(λd . $\mu(v_i) \geq d$)

As Heim (2001) discusses, Kennedy (1997) questions quantificational analyses of comparative structure given the absence of readings that we might expect if degree quantifiers could take scope with respect to other operators in the way that quantifiers over entities can. However, Heim argues that the apparent lack of scope-taking behavior by comparative structures does not necessarily rule against a quantificational analysis. Instead, she argues that many of the missing expected ambiguities can be attributed to certain systematic equivalences in truth conditions of sentences which might mask different scope positions of degree quantifiers. As she writes, these cases are consistent with a theory in which degree quantifiers can take high scope, as well as a theory in which they never move past the first position where they can be interpreted.

Heim suggests that the clearest cases where true scope ambiguities can be detected are *exactly*-differentials, of the shape in (84):

(84) John is 4′ tall. Every girl is exactly 1″ taller than that.
 a. $\forall x \,.\, \text{girl}(x) \rightarrow \text{MAX}(\lambda d \,.\, \text{tall}(d, x)) = 4'+1''$
  ≈ For every girl x, the maximum degree to which x is tall is 49″. Every girl is precisely 49″ tall.
 b. $\text{MAX}(\lambda d \,.\, \forall x \,.\, \text{girl}(x) \rightarrow \text{tall}(d, x)) = 4'+1''$
  ≈ The maximal degree d to which every girl is (at least) d-tall is 49″. The shortest girl is exactly 49″ tall.

Such examples get quite difficult to construct in Navajo since differential measure phrases are expressed using additional postpositional phrases; we have not yet tested them systematically.

Meanwhile, however, we can offer a few thoughts on what we might say if we do, ultimately, find that Navajo standard phrases are interpreted with lowest possible scope. Following Heim (2001), we suggest that this would not rule against a quantificational account of standard markers but would instead suggest that other factors in Navajo grammar are limiting scope possibilities. One such factor comes immediately to mind. As Bogal-Allbritten (2013, 2016) discusses at length, adjectival verbs of a certain morphological form—the form used in most examples in this paper—impose tight locality restrictions on the position of the standard phrase. While the negation frame *doo ... da* typically occurs directly adjacent to the verb (Faltz 2000), we see in (85) that the equative standard phrase cannot be separated from the adjectival verb even by negation.

(85) a. *Alice Ben-gi   doo 'anítnééz da.*
  Alice Ben-LOC NEG 3.tall NEG
  (Intended: 'Alice is not as tall as Ben.')

 b. *Alice doo Ben-gi   'anítnééz da.*
  Alice NEG Ben-LOC 3.tall NEG
  'Alice is not as tall as Ben.'

This contrasts with the normal flexibility in word order found for most verb-external expressions, in particular locative phrases used with non-adjectival verbs:

(86) *Baa' (Kinłání-di) bi-yáázh (Kinłání-di) naalnish.*
   Bah Flagstaff-LOC 3POSS-son Flagstaff-LOC 3.work.IPFV
   'Bah's son works in Flagstaff.' (Faltz 2000, 38–39)

Navajo seems to exhibit rigid surface scope with respect to other elements that might be treated as scope-bearing, such as the indefinite expression *ła'* and negation as shown below (Bogal-Allbritten & Moulton 2017).

(87) a. *Ła' t'áadoo yíyą́ą́' da.*
      INDF NEG 3.3.eat.PFV NEG
      'There was something I didn't eat.'

   b. *T'áadoo ła' yíyą́ą́' da.*
      NEG INDF 3.3.eat.PFV NEG
      'I didn't eat anything.'

Putting these pieces together, we may not find the kinds of ambiguities one might expect given quantificational meanings for standard phrases since Navajo both has rigid surface scope and imposes certain restrictions on the position of standard phrases. With respect to the search for scope ambiguities, the cases to focus on in the future will be those adjectival verbs that Bogal-Allbritten (2013, 2016) identifies as more permissive with respect to the position of standard phrases.

6   Conclusions and Looking Ahead: Quantification beyond Degrees?

Our primary claim is that despite having phrasal standards without reduced clausal structure, quantificational entries for Navajo standard markers are nonetheless appropriate given the scope of the existential prefix *'a-* in translations of superlative prompts. We can wed a phrasal syntax to quantificational entries like (88) if we allow a measurement operator MEAS to apply to type e (or d) standards and return a property of degrees.

(88) *-łááh*$_{clausal}$ ⇝ $\lambda D_{\langle d,t \rangle} . \lambda D'_{\langle d,t \rangle} . \text{MAX}(D') > \text{MAX}(D)$

Our analysis of Navajo suggests a novel strategy that might be employed in natural language to maintain quantificational meanings for comparative morphemes (or standard markers) even when there is evidence that standards of comparison lack clausal structure.

Our proposal that Navajo has degree quantifiers of type $\langle\langle d, t\rangle, \langle\langle d, t\rangle, t\rangle\rangle$ is notable in light of prior claims that Navajo lacks true quantificational determiners. That is, it has been claimed that Navajo lacks expressions that form syntactic constituents with phrases that determine a property-type meaning that can serve as the restrictor to a quantificational determiner (Faltz 1995, Faltz 2000, Speas & Parsons-Yazzie 1996). Faltz observes, for instance, that the Navajo expression *t'ááłá'í nitínígo* is sometimes translated into English as 'each'. In contrast with its English translation, however, this Navajo expression does not seem to form a constituent with the noun *'awéé'* 'baby' in the following sentences: The two expressions can be separated from each other by extraneous material, such as a temporal adverb.

(89) a. *'Awéé' 'adą́ą́dą́ą́' t'ááłá'í nitínígo deiłzhozh.*
baby   yesterday   each   3PL.1SG.tickle.PFV
'I tickled each baby yesterday.'

b. *T'ááłá'í nitínígo 'adą́ą́dą́ą́' 'awéé' deiłzhozh.*
each   yesterday baby   3PL.1SG.tickle.PFV
'I tickled each baby yesterday.' (Faltz 1995, 294)

Speas & Parsons-Yazzie (1996) also observe that *'ałtso*, often translated into English as 'every', can occur on its own without a nominal expression, in which case it is translated as an adverbial expression.

(90) (*'Ałk'ésdisíí*) *'ałtso yíyą́ą́'.*
candy   all   3.1SG.eat.PFV
'I ate it (the candy) all up.' (adapt. Speas & Parsons-Yazzie 1996: 44)

Examples like (90) were among the original cases that led Jelinek (1995) and other authors in the seminal Bach et al. 1995 volume on quantification to propose that some languages lack quantificational determiners (D-quantification), contra Barwise & Cooper's (1981) proposal that the kinds of structures and meanings involved in expressions like *every* or *every cat* are universally available.

One hypothesis for why Navajo lacks quantificational determiners could be that the Navajo language simply lacks the kinds of logical resources necessary to express meanings of the right kind. For instance, we might hypothesize Navajo to be a language with access only to first-order logic. In such a language, we would not expect to find quantificational determiners, which denote relations between sets of individuals and would therefore require access to second-order logic.[35]

However, Faltz (1995, 2000) suggests that perhaps Navajo lacks quantificational determiners because of independent facts about its grammar. If we take seriously the idea that the argument positions of Navajo verbs are saturated by prefixes, a Navajo verb will never denote a type $\langle e, t \rangle$ expression at the point at which it becomes 'syntactically visible', as Faltz puts it. Thus we do not find quantificational determiners because the kind of property-type expressions they need to compose with in the syntax are simply not present.

Our findings suggest that Faltz (1995, 2000) was exactly right in his reason for why Navajo lacks quantificational determiners over entities. We have argued that Navajo does, in fact, have quantificational expressions that denote relations between two sets. However, this type may be limited to the domain of degrees. This is expected given the grammar of Navajo: There are no pronominal prefixes that saturate the degree arguments of gradable predicates, so the right kind of property-type meanings—and the quantificational meanings that depend on them—will only be available in the domain of degrees.

---

35 As a reviewer observes, if Navajo only has the expressive power of first-order logic, we expect it to lack quantifiers that cannot be expressed using first-order logic, such as proportional *most* (Barwise & Cooper 1981). Indeed, Navajo, lacks a single dedicated lexical item comparable to English proportional *most*, instead using the paraphrase shown below.
   (i) *K'asdą́ą́' báah łikaní 'ałtso yíyą́ą́.*
   almost   cookie   all   3.3.eat.PFV
   'I almost ate all of the cookies.'
   As Coppock, Bogal-Allbritten & Nouri-Hosseini (2019) demonstrate, languages which lack a lexical counterpart to proportional *most* far outnumber languages with such an expression; previous observations in this spirit can be found in Hackl 2009, Živanović 2007, Bošković & Gajewski 2008, Pancheva 2015, and Dobrovie-Sorin & Giurgea (2015). While the absence of proportional *most* could be due to a lack of higher order quantifiers, other explanations may be available (Coppock, Bogal-Allbritten & Nouri-Hosseini 2019). Thus, the absence of such an expression in Navajo does not necessarily tell us that the language only has the expressive power of first-order logic.

References

Alrenga, Peter & Christopher Kennedy. 2014. *No more* shall we part: Quantifiers in English comparatives. *Natural Language Semantics* 22(1). 1–53.

Alrenga, Peter, Christopher Kennedy & Jason Merchant. 2012. A new standard of comparison. In *West Coast Conference on Formal Linguistics (WCCFL) 30*, 32–42.

Bach, Emmon, Eloise Jelinek, Angelika Kratzer & Barbara Partee. 1995. *Quantification in natural languages*. Vol. 54 (Studies in Linguistics and Philosophy). Dordrecht: Kluwer Academic Publishers.

Baker, Mark. 1996. *The polysynthesis parameter*. New York: Oxford University Press.

Bartsch, Renate & Theo Vennemann. 1972. *Semantic structures: a study in the relation between syntax and semantics*. Frankfurt: Athenäum Verlag.

Barwise, Jon & Robin Cooper. 1981. Generalized quantifiers and natural language. *Linguistics and Philosophy* 4(2). 159–219.

Beck, Sigrid. 2011. Comparison constructions. In Claudia Maienborn, Klaus von Heusinger & Paul Portner (eds.), *Semantics: an international handbook of natural language meaning*, 1341–1389. Berlin: de Gruyter Mouton.

Beck, Sigrid, Vera Hohaus & Sonja Tiemann. 2012. A note on phrasal comparatives. In *Semantics and Linguistic Theory (SALT) 22*, 146–165.

Beck, Sigrid, Svetlana Krasikova, Daniel Fleischer, Remus Gergel, Stefan Hofstetter, Christiane Savelsberg, John Vanderelst & Elisabeth Villalta. 2009. Crosslinguistic variation in comparison constructions. In Jeroen van Craenenbroeck & Johan Rooryck (eds.), *Linguistic Variation Yearbook*, vol. 9, 1–66. Philadelphia: John Benjamins.

Beck, Sigrid, Toshiko Oda & Koji Sugisaki. 2004. Parametric variation in the semantics of comparison: Japanese vs. English. *Journal of East Asian Linguistics* 13(4). 289–344.

Bhatt, Rajesh & Shoichi Takahashi. 2011. Reduced and unreduced phrasal comparatives. *Natural Language & Linguistic Theory* 29(3). 581–620.

Bierwisch, Manfred. 1989. The semantics of gradation. In Manfred Bierwisch & Ewan Lang (eds.), *Dimensional adjectives*, 71–262. Berlin: Springer-Verlag.

Bochnak, M. Ryan. 2013. *Cross-linguistic variation in the semantics of comparatives*. University of Chicago dissertation.

Bochnak, M. Ryan. 2015. The degree semantics parameter and cross-linguistic variation. *Semantics & Pragmatics* 8. 1–48.

Bogal-Allbritten, Elizabeth. 2013. Decomposing notions of adjectival transitivity in Navajo. *Natural Language Semantics* 21(3). 277–314.

Bogal-Allbritten, Elizabeth. 2016. *Building meaning in Navajo*. Amherst, MA: University of Massachusetts Amherst dissertation.

Bogal-Allbritten, Elizabeth & Keir Moulton. 2017. Navajo in the typology of internally-headed relatives. In *Semantics and Linguistic Theory (SALT) 28*, 700–720.

Bošković, Željko & Jon Gajewski. 2008. Semantic correlates of the NP/DP parameter. In *North East Linguistic Society (NELS) 39*, 121–134.

Bresnan, Joan. 1973. Syntax of the comparative clause construction in English. *Linguistic Inquiry* 4(3). 275–343.

Bruening, Benjamin. 2010. Ditransitive asymmetries and a theory of idiom formation. *Linguistic Inquiry* 41(4). 519–562.

Chomsky, Noam. 1981. *Lectures on government and binding*. Dordrecht: Foris.

Coppock, Elizabeth, Elizabeth Bogal-Allbritten & Golsa Nouri-Hosseini. 2019. Universals in superlative semantics. Ms., Boston University and University of Gothenburg.

Cresswell, Max J. 1976. The semantics of degree. In Barbara Partee (ed.), *Montague Grammar*, 261–292. New York: Academic Press.

Dobrovie-Sorin, Carmen & Ion Giurgea. 2015. *Quantity superlatives vs. proportional quantifiers: A comparative perspective*. 25th Colloquium on Generative Grammar, Bayonne.

Dowty, David R. 1978. Governed transformations as lexical rules in a Montague Grammar. *Linguistic Inquiry* 9(3). 393–426.

Faltz, Leonard M. 1995. Towards a typology of natural logic. In Emmon Bach, Eloise Jelinek, Angelika Kratzer & Barbara Partee (eds.), *Quantification in natural languages*, vol. 54 (Studies in Linguistics and Philosophy), 271–319. Dordrecht: Kluwer Academic Publishers.

Faltz, Leonard M. 1998. *The Navajo verb: a grammar for students and scholars*. Albuquerque, NM: University of New Mexico Press.

Faltz, Leonard M. 2000. A semantic basis for Navajo syntactic typology. In Theodore Fernald & Paul Platero (eds.), *The Athabaskan languages: perspectives on a Native American language family*, 28–50. Oxford: Oxford University Press.

Fernald, Theodore B., Lorene Legah, Alyse Neuendorf, Ellavina Tsosie Perkins & Paul Platero. 2000. Definite and indefinite descriptions in Navajo. In Theodore B. Fernald & Kenneth L. Hale (eds.), *Diné bizaad naalkaah: Navajo language investigations*, 31–54. Cambridge, MA: MIT Working Papers in Linguistics.

Fernald, Theodore B. & MaryAnn Willie. 2001. Navajo classification and coercion. In Ji-Yung Kim & Adam Werle (eds.), *Semantics of Under-represented Languages in the Americas (SULA) 1*.

Fernald, Theodore & Ellavina Perkins. 2018. Valence shifting operations in Navajo. In Rodica Ivan (ed.), *The leader of the pack: a festschrift in honor of Peggy Speas*. Amherst, MA: GLSA.

Fleisher, Nicholas. 2016. Comparing theories of quantifiers in *than* clauses: Lessons from downward-entailing differentials. *Semantics and Pragmatics* 9. 1–23.

Gajewski, Jon. 2008. More on quantifiers in comparative clauses. In *Semantics and Linguistic Theory (SALT) 18*, 340–357.

Gorshenin, Maksym. 2012. *The crosslinguistics of the superlative*. University of Bremen MA thesis.

Grosu, Alexander. 2012. Towards a more articulated typology of internally headed relative constructions: the semantics connection. *Language and Linguistics Compass* 6(7). 1–30.

Hackl, Martin. 2000. *Comparative quantifiers*. Boston, MA: Massachusetts Institute of Technology dissertation.

Hackl, Martin. 2009. On the grammar and processing of proportional quantifiers: *most* vs. *more than half*. *Natural Language Semantics* 17(1). 63–98.

Hale, Kenneth L. 2000. Remarks on the syntax of the Navajo verb. In Theodore Fernald & Ken Hale (eds.), *Diné bizaad naalkaah: Navajo language investigations*, vol. 3, 55–96. Cambridge, MA: MIT Working Papers in Linguistics.

Hale, Kenneth L. 2001. Navajo verb stem position and the bipartite structure of the Navajo conjunct sector. *Linguistic Inquiry* 32(4). 678–693.

Hankamer, Jorge. 1973. Why there are two *than*s in English. In *Chicago Linguistic Society (CLS)* 9, 179–191.

Harley, Heidi & Hyun Kyoung Jung. 2015. In support of the P-have analysis of the double object construction. *Linguistic Inquiry* 46(4). 703–730.

Heim, Irene. 1985. Notes on comparatives and related matters. Ms., University of Texas at Austin.

Heim, Irene. 2001. Degree operators and scope. In Caroline Féry & Wolfgang Sternefeld (eds.), *Audiatur vox sapientiae: a festschrift for Arnim von Stechow*, 214–239. Berlin: Akademie Verlag.

Heim, Irene. 2006. Remarks on comparative clauses as generalized quantifiers. Ms., Massachusetts Institute of Technology.

Hoeksema, Jack. 1983. Negative polarity and the comparative. *Natural Language and Linguistic Theory* 1(3). 403–434.

Hofstetter, Stefan. 2009. Comparison in Turkish: a rediscovery of the phrasal comparative. In *Sinn und Bedeutung 13*, 191–205.

Hohaus, Vera. 2012. Directed motion as comparison: Evidence from Samoan. In *Semantics of Under-represented Languages in the Americas (SULA) 6 and SULA-Bar*, 335–348.

Hoshi, Koji. 1995. *Structural and interpretive aspects of head-internal and head-external relative clauses*. University of Rochester dissertation.

Jacobson, Pauline. 1995. On the quantificational force of English free relatives. In Emmon Bach, Eloise Jelinek, Angelika Kratzer & Barbara H. Partee (eds.), *Quantification in natural languages*, vol. 54 (Studies in Linguistics and Philosophy), 451–486. Dordrecht: Kluwer Academic Publishers.

Jelinek, Eloise. 1984. Empty categories, case, and configurationality. *Natural Language & Linguistic Theory* 2(1). 39–76.

Jelinek, Eloise. 1995. Quantification in Straits Salish. In Emmon Bach, Eloise Jelinek, Angelika Kratzer & Barbara Partee (eds.), *Quantification in natural languages*, vol. 54 (Studies in Linguistics and Philosophy), 487–540. Dordrecht: Kluwer Academic Publishers.

Kayne, Richard S. 2005. Some notes on comparative syntax, with special reference to English and French. In Guglielmo Cinque & Richard S. Kayne (eds.), *The Oxford handbook of comparative syntax*, 3–69. Oxford: Oxford University Press.

Kennedy, Christopher. 1997. *The syntax and semantics of gradability and comparison*. University of California, Santa Cruz dissertation.

Kennedy, Christopher. 2007. Modes of comparison. In *Chicago Linguistic Society (CLS) 43*, 141–165.

Kennedy, Christopher & Louise McNally. 2005. Scale structure, degree modification, and the semantics of gradable predicates. *Language* 81(2). 345–381.

Krifka, Manfred. 1989. Nominal reference, temporal constitution and quantification in event semantics. In Renate Bartsch, Johan van Benthem & Peter van Emde Boas (eds.), *Semantics and contextual expression*, 75–115. Dordrecht: Foris.

Larson, Richard K. 1988. Scope and comparatives. *Linguistics and Philosophy* 11(1). 1–26.

Lechner, Winfried. 2004. *Ellipsis in comparatives*. Berlin, New York: Mouton de Gruyter.

Nakanishi, Kimiko. 2007. Measurement in the nominal and verbal domains. *Linguistics and Philosophy* 30(2). 235–276.

Napoli, Donna Jo. 1983. Comparative ellipsis: a phrase structure account. *Linguistic Inquiry* 14(4). 675–694.

Pancheva, Roumyana. 2006. Phrasal and clausal comparatives in Slavic. In *Formal Approaches to Slavic Linguistics 14*, 236–257.

Pancheva, Roumyana. 2010. More students attended FASL than CONSOLE. In *Formal Approaches to Slavic Linguistics 18*, 382–399.

Pancheva, Roumyana. 2015. Quantity superlatives: the view from Slavic and its cross-linguistic implications. In *Chicago Linguistic Society (CLS) 49*.

Partee, Barbara H. 1987. Noun phrase interpretation and type-shifting principles. In Dick de Jongh, Martin Stokhof & Jeroen Groenendijk (eds.), *Studies in discourse representation theory and the theory of generalized quantifiers*, 115–144. Dordrecht: Foris.

Pesetsky, David. 1995. *Zero syntax: experiencers and cascades*. Cambridge, MA: MIT Press.

Platero, Paul. 1974. The Navajo relative clause. *International Journal of American Linguistics* 40(3). 202–246.

Rett, Jessica. 2008. *Degree modification in natural language*. New Brunswick, NJ: Rutgers University dissertation.

Rett, Jessica. 2014. The polysemy of measurement. *Lingua* 143. 242–266.

Rice, Keren. 2000. *Morpheme order and semantic scope: word formation in the Atha-*

paskan verb (Cambridge Studies in Linguistics 90). Cambridge: Cambridge University Press.

Rullmann, Hotze. 1995. *Maximality in the semantics of wh-constructions*. University of Massachusetts Amherst dissertation.

Sapir, Edward. 1944. Grading, a study in semantics. *Philosophy of Science* 11(2). 93–116.

Schauber, Ellen. 1979. *The syntax and semantics of questions in Navajo* (Outstanding Dissertations in Linguistics). Champaign-Urbana: Garland Press.

Schwarzschild, Roger. 2002. The grammar of measurement. In *Semantics and Linguistic Theory (SALT)* 12, 225–245.

Schwarzschild, Roger. 2005. Measure phrases as modifiers of adjectives. *Recherches Linguistiques de Vincennes* 34. 207–228.

Schwarzschild, Roger. 2006. The role of dimension in the syntax of noun phrases. *Syntax* 9(1). 67–110.

Schwarzschild, Roger. 2012. Directed scale segments. In *Semantics and Linguistic Theory (SALT)* 22, 65–82.

Schwarzschild, Roger. 2013. Degrees and segments. In *Semantics and Linguistic Theory (SALT)* 23, 212–238.

Schwarzschild, Roger. 2014. Comparative markers and standard markers. In Michael Yoshitaka Erlewine & Yasutada Sudo (eds.), *Proceedings of the MIT Workshop on Comparatives*, 87–106. Cambridge, MA: MITWPL.

Schwarzschild, Roger & Karina Wilkinson. 2002. Quantifiers in comparatives: a semantics of degree based on intervals. *Natural Language Semantics* 10(1). 1–41.

Shah, Ara. 1995. *Complement clauses in Hindi and Gujarati*. University of Hyderabad dissertation.

Shimoyama, Junko. 1999. Internally headed relative clauses in Japanese and E-type anaphora. *Journal of East Asian Linguistics* 8(2). 147–182.

Shimoyama, Junko. 2011. Japanese indeterminate negative polarity items and their scope. *Journal of Semantics* 28(4). 413–450.

Shimoyama, Junko. 2012. Reassessing crosslinguistic variation in clausal comparatives. *Natural Language Semantics* 20(1). 83–113.

Solt, Stephanie. 2009. *The semantics of adjectives of quantity*. New York, NY: The Graduate Center—City University of New York dissertation.

Solt, Stephanie. 2015. Q-adjectives and the semantics of quantity. *Journal of Semantics* 32(2). 221–273.

Speas, Margaret & Evangeline Parsons-Yazzie. 1996. Quantification and the position of noun phrases in Navajo. In Eloise Jelinek, Sally Midgette, Keren Rice & Leslie Saxon (eds.), *Athabaskan language studies: essays in honor of Robert W. Young*, 35–80. Albuquerque, NM: University of New Mexico Press.

Stassen, Leon. 1985. *Comparison and universal grammar*. Oxford: Basil Blackwell.

von Stechow, Arnim. 1984. Comparing semantic theories of comparison. *Journal of Semantics* 3(1–2). 1–77.

Svenonius, Peter & Christopher Kennedy. 2006. Northern Norwegian degree questions and the syntax of measurement. In Mara Frascarelli (ed.), *Phases of interpretation*, 131–161. Berlin: Mouton de Gruyter.

Wellwood, Alexis. 2015. On the semantics of comparison across categories. *Linguistics and Philosophy* 38(1). 67–101.

Willie, MaryAnn. 1989. Why there is nothing missing in Navajo relative clauses. In Eung-Do Cook & Keren Rice (eds.), *Athapaskan linguistics: current perspectives on a language family* (Trends in Linguistics. State-of-the-Art Reports 15), 265–315. Berlin: Mouton de Gruyter.

Willie, MaryAnn. 1991. *Pronouns and obviation in Navajo*. Tucson, AZ: University of Arizona dissertation.

Willie, MaryAnn & Eloise Jelinek. 2000. Navajo as a discourse configurational language. In Theodore Fernald & Paul Platero (eds.), *The Athabaskan languages: perspectives on a Native American language family*, 252–287. Oxford: Oxford University Press.

Xiang, Ming. 2005. *Some topics in comparative constructions*. Michigan State University dissertation.

Young, Robert & William Morgan. 1980. *The Navajo Language*. Albuquerque, NM: University of New Mexico Press.

Young, Robert & William Morgan. 1987. *The Navajo Language*. Albuquerque, NM: University of New Mexico Press.

Živanović, Sašo. 2007. Varieties of *most*: on different readings of superlative determiners. In *2006 Conference on the formal description of Slavic languages*, 337–354.

CHAPTER 5

Separate but Equal: A Typology of Equative Constructions

Jessica Rett

1   Introduction to Degree Quantifiers

Bresnan (1973) observes the following parallels in the distribution of degree words:

(1) a. more people / more intelligent   *comparative*
     b. as many people / as intelligent   *equative*
     c. too many people / too intelligent   *excessive*
     d. that many people / that intelligent   *demonstrative*
     e. so many people / so intelligent   *resultative*
     f. how many people / how intelligent   *degree wh-word*

She took for granted that the quantity word *many* is an individual quantifier, so she characterized the degree words as determiners, and assigned them to a position of 'DegP' in the syntax.

In the decades since, both assumptions have been replaced in the degree-semantics literature. Quantity words like *many* do not behave like individual quantifiers in most respects (**too all people*, cf. (1c)), and are better characterized as degree modifiers (Rett 2007, 2008, 2018, Solt 2009, 2015). And degree words like the comparative *-er* and the equative *as* are best characterized as degree quantifiers, binding the degree arguments introduced by gradable adjectives or associated with nominals. In this paper, I focus on the consequences for this latter analysis on the semantics of equatives.

The degree-quantifier analysis of comparatives is based on the assumption that gradable adjectives denote relations between degrees and individuals, type $\langle e, \langle d, t \rangle \rangle$, as in (2) (Cresswell 1976).[1]

---

[1] Initially, the main evidence for the presence of this degree argument was the fact that measure phrases ('MPs') like *6ft* in constructions like *Jane is 6ft tall* value an adjective's degree argument. However, Schwarzschild (2005) convincingly argues that MPs are better analyzed as degree modifiers, type $\langle \langle d, t \rangle, \langle d, t \rangle \rangle$. This can explain why MPs—in English and other

(2) ⟦tall⟧ = λxλd . tall(x) ≥ d

It also takes for granted a syntax of comparison constructions—a term I will use to jointly refer to comparative and equative constructions—in which the degree arguments of adjectives are lambda-abstracted over by some mechanism that parallels *wh*-movement (Chomsky 1977, Heim 1985).[2]

(3) logical forms for comparison constructions
  a. *Jane is taller than Bill is*:
     -er([$_{CP}$ Op$_d$ Bill is ~~d-tall~~])([$_{CP}$ Op$_{d'}$ Jane is d'-tall])
  b. *Jane is as tall as Bill is*:
     as([$_{CP}$ Op$_d$ Bill is ~~d-tall~~])([$_{CP}$ Op$_{d'}$ Jane is d'-tall])

In (3), each degree morpheme relates two arguments: a set of degrees (*D*, type ⟨d, t⟩) corresponding to Bill's height, and a set of degrees corresponding to Jane's height. Semantically, therefore, it is a quantifier, but one that ranges over degrees instead of individuals: type ⟨⟨d, t⟩, ⟨⟨d, t⟩, t⟩⟩.

There are a variety of ways to define the meaning of these degree quantifiers precisely. (The same is true for the syntactic analysis of these constructions, especially when taking into account the embedders *than* and *as*, which are ignored in (3); Bhatt & Pancheva 2004.) For instance, a semantic analysis could be based on the 'at least' definition of gradable adjectives in (2), or it could analyze gradable adjectives as associating each individual with a single, maximal degree of height.

Assuming (2), a semantic account of degree quantifiers could have them relate points derived from sets of degrees, as in (4), or just relate the degree sets themselves, as in (5) (see Schwarzschild 2008 for a nice overview of the history of the two approaches).

(4) a point-based semantics for comparison constructions,
    where MAX(*D*) = ιd ∈ *D*[∀d' ∈ *D*[d' ≠ d → d' < d]]
    a. ⟦-er⟧ = λDλD'. MAX(D') > MAX(D)
    b. ⟦as⟧ = λDλD'. MAX(D') ≥ MAX(D)

---

languages—appear in adjunct rather than argument position; it can also be used to derive an intuitive semantic explanation for why MPs can never modify negative antonyms, as in *Jane is 4ft short*. This analysis of MP constructions also requires that gradable adjectives have a degree argument or output, and it suggests an ⟨e, ⟨d, t⟩⟩ type for gradable adjectives, which results compositionally in the degree sets manipulated by degree quantifiers in (4)–(5).

2 The lower degree operator is overt in some dialects of English, as in %*Jane is taller than what Bill is*; the upper degree operator is never overt (Rett 2013).

(5) a set-based semantics for comparison constructions
 a. ⟦-er⟧ = $\lambda D \lambda D'. D' \supset D$
 b. ⟦as⟧ = $\lambda D \lambda D'. D' \supseteq D$

These options are directly parallel to the literature on individual quantifiers, in which e.g. *all* can be defined in terms of individuals or sets, as in (6).

(6) a. ⟦all⟧ = $\lambda P \lambda Q \forall x\, [P(x) \rightarrow Q(x)]$ *individual-based*
 b. ⟦all⟧ = $\lambda P \lambda Q.\, P \subseteq Q$ *set-based*

The equative is defined in (4b)/(5b) as encoding a directional relation ($\supseteq$ or $\supseteq$), rather than an equivalence relation =. This is based on the long-standing observation that equatives seem to be compatible with both an 'at least' and an 'exactly' reading, depending on context; and the long-standing assumption that the latter is derivable from the former, but not vice-versa.

An equative like *Jane is as tall as Bill* is true and felicitous in a context in which Jane and Bill are both 5′10″. This context satisfies the strong, 'exactly' interpretation. But the sentence is also true and felicitous in contexts which only satisfy a weak, 'at least' interpretation. (7) is one such context.

(7) A: Bill doesn't want a bodyguard who is shorter than he is. Is Jane a possibility?
 B: Yes, Jane is as tall as Bill is (in fact, she's taller).

The relationship between the 'at least' and 'exactly' interpretation is generally viewed as one of pragmatic strengthening (Horn 1972), similar to the relationship between inclusive and exclusive *or*. Analyses like those above, in which the 'at least' reading is assumed to be semantically primary, also assume that the stronger, 'exactly' reading is derived via scalar implicature, in contexts in which the hearer has reason to assume that the speaker—if she in fact knows that Jane is taller than Bill—would be motivated by Gricean principles to utter the comparative *Jane is taller than Bill* instead of the equative. See Rett (2015a) for a more in-depth presentation of this type of analysis.

Modern semantic analyses of comparatives draw heavily from a strong tradition of cross-linguistic typology to differentiate between comparatives that are formed with degree quantifiers—like the English *Jane is taller than Bill* in (3a)—and comparatives that are likely not formed with degrees at all. These studies (discussed in §2.3) have stressed the need to look for subtle differences between different comparative strategies, and are clear indicators that synonymy in comparatives doesn't entail semantic identity. Given the strong morphosyntactic parallel between comparatives and equatives, I argue in §4 that similar typological distinctions need to be made for equatives, and consequently that not all equative constructions can and should be analyzed as involving degree quantifiers. As a result, I provide diagnostics for a new semantic typology of equatives, and argue that a few strategies shouldn't be analyzed as involving degree quantifiers.

There are two important distinctions covered in these typologies that I will not address here: the difference between phrasal and clausal comparatives and equatives; and the difference between specific and generic equatives. The former is addressed (for comparatives) in Pancheva (2006) and the latter is addressed in Rett (2013).

2 Comparative Typologies

2.1 *Descriptive Classes*

The first comprehensive typological studies of comparatives were conducted in Ultan (1972) and Stassen (1985). Stassen defined comparatives accordingly (p. 24): "A construction in natural language counts as a comparative construction if that construction has the semantic function of assigning a graded (i.e. non-identical) position on a predicative scale to two (possibly complex) objects." This includes comparatives like *Jane is taller than Bill*, but it also includes a sentence like *Compared to Bill, Jane is tall* or *Jane exceeds Bill in height*.

Stassen's typology classified comparative constructions into three broad categories—particle comparatives, exceed comparatives, and conjoined comparatives—each with their own subtypes (see also Kennedy 2007a). Several of these constructions are illustrated below. I will follow Stassen and others in identifying the subcomponents of a comparative with the following terms:

(8) Jane (is)   tall   -er   than   Bill
     TARGET OF   PARAMETER   PARAMETER   STANDARD   STANDARD OF
     COMPARISON   MARKER   MARKER   COMPARISON

2.1.1 Particle Comparatives

A particle comparative is one in which the standard is marked by a morpheme. These markers are often but not always homophonous with directional prepositions (see Schwarzschild 2013 for a semantic account of this polysemy). Crucially, particle comparatives may or may not include a parameter marker.

SEPARATE BUT EQUAL: A TYPOLOGY OF EQUATIVE CONSTRUCTIONS

The particle comparative in (9) is a separative comparative, whose standard marker means 'from'; other languages with separative comparatives include Amharic, Andoke, Classical Arabic, Aranda, Aymara, Bedauye, Bilin, Burmese, Burushaski, Carib, Cœur d'Alene, Eskimo, Guarani, Biblical Hebrew, Hindi, Japanese, Jurak, Kashmiri, Khalka, Korean, Lamutic, Laz, Manchu, Mandarin, Nama, Piro, Quechua, Tajik, Tibetan, Tupi, Turkish, and Vayu.

(9) *Sadom-ete hati mananga-i*   *Mundari*
    horse-from elephant big-pres.3sg
    'The elephant is bigger than the horse.'

Allative comparatives involve standard markers that, in other constructions, introduce goal phrases (like 'to' or 'for'). Other languages with allative comparatives include Basque, Breton, Dakota, Gumbainggir, Hungarian, Jacaltec, Kanuri, Latvian, Mandinka, Maori, Mapuche, Miwok, Naga, Nama, Navajo, Nuer, Salinan, Samoan, Siuslawan, Tamazight, Tamil, Tarascan, Tubu, and Ubykh.

(10) *Sapuk ol-kondi to l-kibulenkeny*   *Maasai*
     big.3sg the-deer to the-waterbuck
     'The deer is bigger than the waterbuck.'

Locative comparatives involve standard markers that mean roughly 'on', and are found in languages like Cebuano, Chuckchee, Miwok, Navajo, Salinan, and Tamil.

(11) *A ka gya ni ma*   *Mandinka*
     he is big me on
     'He is bigger than me.'

Finally, dedicated comparatives involve a construction-specific standard marker. English falls into this category, as do most European languages, as well as Ilocano, Javanese, Sranan, and Toba Batak.

(12) *Lehibe noho ny zana-ny Rabe*   *Malagasy*
     tall than the son-his R
     'Rabe is taller than his son.'

2.1.2 Exceed Comparatives

Exceed comparatives employ a verb to impose their strict ordering; the verb typically means something like 'exceed'. The standard is the direct object of the verb, the parameter is an adjunct. English has an exceed comparative; so does Aymara, Banda, Bari, Cambodian, Dagomba, Duala, Fulani, Gbeya, Hausa, Igbo, Jabem, Kirundi, Maasai, Margi, Nguna, Quechua, Sika, Sranan, Swahili, Tamazight, Thai, Vietnamese, Wolof, Yagan, and Yoruba.

(13) *To bi   ni   gao.*   *Mandarin*
     he exceed you tall
     'He is taller than you.'

2.1.3 Conjoined Comparatives

Conjoined comparatives use conjunction to associate the target and standard of comparison. They use either antonyms, as in (14) and (15), or a predicate and its negation, as in (16) and (17). Languages that do the former include Cayapo, Dakota, Mangarayi, Maori, Samoan, and Sika; languages that do the latter include Hixkaryana, Menomini, Mixtec, Shipibo, and Yavapai (see also Kubota & Matsui 2010). Other languages in this broad category include Abipon, Ekagi, Gumbainggir, Kobon, Monumbo, Nahuatl, and Pala.

(14) *Ua loa   lenei va'a, ua puupuu lena*   *Samoan*
     is long this boat is short that
     'This boat is longer than that boat.'

(15) *Yan kau   tukta, man almuk*   *Miskito*
     I   more young he old
     'I am younger than him.'

(16) *Kaw-ohra naha   Waraka, kaw naha*
     tall-not be.3sg.masc W   tall be.3sg.masc
     Kayweryé   *Hixkaryana*
     K
     'Kayweryé is taller than Waraka.'

(17) *Ina na namo herea una na dia namo*   *Motu*
     this is good more that is not good
     'This is better than that.'

There is a contrast within the pairs (14)–(15) and (16)–(17). In particular, the first member of the pair doesn't involve a comparative morpheme, while the second does: *kau* in (15) and *herea* in (17). This indicates that these morphosyntactic strategies are in principle independent from whether or not the construction involves a degree quantifier. This is the subject of the next subsection.

2.2   *Theoretical Classes*

Based largely on Stassen's typology, recent adaptations like Beck et al. (2004) and Kennedy (2007a) have differentiated between **explicit** and **implicit** comparatives (see also Sapir 1944). Informally, explicit comparatives involve specialized morphology (e.g. -*er*) that is in complementary distribution with other degree words as well as evaluativity (i.e. norm-relatedness). Implicit comparatives, on the other hand, involve the positive form of adjectives (e.g. *tall* as opposed to *taller*), and are evaluative (or norm-related).[3]

(18) IMPLICIT VS. EXPLICIT COMPARISON   (*Kennedy* 2007a)
   a. Implicit comparisons establish an ordering between x and y with respect to gradable property g using the positive form by manipulating the context or delineation function in such a way that the positive form is true of x and false of y.
   b. Explicit comparisons establish an ordering between objects x and y with respect to the gradable property g using morphology whose conventional meaning has the consequence that the degree to which x is g exceeds the degree to which y is g.

Beck et al. (2004) and Kennedy (2007a) also identify another parameter along which comparative constructions can vary: **individual** and **degree** comparatives. Informally, individual comparatives strictly order two individuals with respect to a gradable property, while degree comparatives strictly order two degrees that correspond to the measure of two individuals.

---

[3] Pearson (2010) further differentiates between strong implicit comparatives and weak implicit comparatives. Strong implicit comparatives are as Kennedy describes: they are formed with the positive form of the adjective, and generally introduce the target and standard in an adjunct (e.g. *Compared to Bill, Jane is tall* or *Of Jane and Bill, Jane is the tall one*). Weak implicit comparatives also introduce the target and standard in an adjunct, but involve the comparative form of an adjective, or a parameter marker (e.g. *Compared to Bill, Jane is taller* or *Of Jane and Bill, Jane is the taller one*). This distinction is a real and important one, but I will not address it here.

These parameters interact: an implicit comparative construction can compare either individuals or degrees, although an explicit comparative construction must compare degrees. These possibilities are exemplified for English in (19).

(19) a. explicit degree comparative: *Jane is taller than Bill.*
   b. implicit degree comparative: *Compared to Bill, Jane is tall.*
   c. implicit individual comparative: *Jane exceeds Bill in height.*

Kennedy's (2007a) diagnostic criteria for implicit comparatives are clear and decisive. A comparative is explicit if and only if it exhibits a property called 'crisp judgment'; is acceptable with absolute adjectives; and can be modified by a measure phrase differential. I'll present these in turn (see Pearson 2010, Bochnak & Bogal-Allbritten 2015: for additional tests).

2.2.4   Crisp Judgments

Explicit comparatives, in contrast to implicit ones, are acceptable in 'borderline' cases: those in which the difference in measure between the target and standard is negligible. Such situations require crisp judgments, or clear opinions about small differences. Kennedy's illustrations of this difference are below.

(20) NON-BORDERLINE CASE: Essay A is 600 words; Essay B is 200 words.
   a. Essay A is longer than Essay B.   *explicit*
   b. Compared to Essay B, Essay A is long.   *implicit*

(21) BORDERLINE CASE: Essay A is 600 words; Essay B is 590 words.
   a. Essay A is longer than Essay B.   *explicit*
   b. #Compared to Essay B, Essay A is long.   *implicit*

While the explicit comparative is acceptable in either context, the implicit comparative in (21b) is unacceptable in a context in which the differences between the target and standard are negligible. This is intuitively because the implicit comparative involves the vague, context-sensitive positive form *Essay A is long*, which attributes to Essay A the evaluative property of being longer than the salient standard in the context of utterance. (See Sawada 2009 and Bochnak 2015b for formal analyses of implicit comparatives.)

2.2.5 Compatibility with Absolute Adjectives

There are several subclasses of gradable adjectives. A key difference between relative adjectives (like *tall, long*) and absolute adjectives (like *dry, bent*) is the adjectives' behavior in definite descriptions (Kennedy 2007b, Syrett et al. 2010). In a context in which there are several glasses, all differing in heights, a definite description formed with the relative adjective *tall* (22a) picks out the tallest individual, regardless of whether the individual counts as tall in the context. In contrast, a definite description formed with the absolute adjective *empty* (22b) has a referent only in a context in which a glass actually counts as empty. In a context in which there are several glasses, all containing different levels of liquid (but none empty), the definite description in (22b) fails to refer.

(22) a. Pass me the tall one.
b. Pass me the empty one.

A standard formal interpretation of the difference in (22) is that absolute adjectives are associated with scales with lexicalized endpoints (Kennedy & McNally 2005), while relative adjectives are associated with open scales, and therefore have to appeal to context for an endpoint, like the one required by the definite determiner.

This independent distinction between relative and absolute adjectives is also useful as a diagnostic for the difference between explicit and implicit comparatives. In particular, explicit comparatives can be formed with both relative and absolute adjectives, while implicit comparatives can only be formed with relative adjectives. This is illustrated in (23) and (24), interpreted in a context in which both rods are bent, but Rod A is only slightly bent (from Kennedy 2007a).

(23) a. Rod B is more bent than Rod A.
b. ??Compared to Rod A, Rod B is bent.

(24) a. Rod A is straighter than Rod B.
b. ?Compared to B, A is straight.

Kennedy attributes the difference in acceptability of the (b) examples to the fact that absolute adjectives with maxima (*straight* but not *bent*) are more likely to allow imprecise interpretations. This suggests that a theoretical account of the definite description test in (22) could extend to account for this distinction between explicit and implicit comparatives with respect to absolute adjectives.

2.2.6 Compatibility with Differential MPs

Finally, explicit comparatives can be modified by a measure phrase (MP), while implicit comparatives cannot. Because the MP modifies the gap between the target and standard values, this use of an MP is characterized as a differential use. The contrast is illustrated in (25), again from Kennedy (2007a).

(25) a. Kim is 10 cm taller than Lee.
    b. ??Compared to Lee, Kim is 10 cm tall.

The implicit comparative in (25b) does have an interpretation, but it's an odd one. The main clause has the form of a measure phrase construction, and attributes to Kim the implausible property of being 10 cm tall, but the 'compared to' phrase suggests incorrectly that this is a subjective proposition (i.e. '10 cm tall relative to'). There is no other place in the implicit comparative where the MP phrase could grammatically occur.

2.3 Interim Summary of Comparatives

The existence of two distinct comparative strategies has called for two distinct semantic analyses of comparative constructions.[4] The semantics for explicit comparatives, presented in (4) and (5), involves a degree quantifier, a relation between sets of degrees.[5]

In contrast, proposals for the semantic formalization of implicit comparatives have come from the degree-free 'comparison class' account originally proposed in Klein (1980, 1982).[6] Klein argued against the assumption that grad-

---

4 Although of course there are potentially much more. Bhatt & Takahashi (2008), for instance, analyze at least some phrasal comparatives as involving a 'three-place -er,' taking two individuals and a gradable adjective denotation as arguments.
5 While degree quantifiers are used to model the contribution of a comparative parameter marker in explicit equatives, it's not obvious that the absence of a comparative parameter marker entails the absence of a degree quantifier. Bhatt & Takahashi (2008, 2011) have argued that Japanese comparatives are explicit comparatives and involve a degree quantifier despite only having an optional parameter marker. We will see in §4.3 that Italian *tanto* equatives also have an optional parameter marker.
6 For languages that only have implicit comparatives, the question remains whether the language must be modeled using degrees. A great body of recent work has argued that languages like Motu (Beck et al. 2009), Fijian (Pearson 2010), Washo (Bochnak 2015a,b, Beltrama & Bochnak 2015, Bochnak & Bogal-Allbritten 2015), and Walpiri (Bowler 2016) don't have any words that refer to, modify, or quantify over degrees, and therefore do not (and arguably should not) be formally modeled using degrees. Beck et al. (2009) refer to this as the 'Degree Semantics Parameter'. See Bogal-Albritten and Coppock (this volume) for the argument that Navajo should be analyzed as involving degree quantifiers despite having only phrasal comparatives.

ability should be modeled using degrees, and his account of explicit comparatives in English is one that manipulates classes of (e.g. equally tall) individuals, rather than degrees. While there are many reasons to think this account won't work for explicit comparatives, Pearson (2010) and Bochnak (2015b) have adopted it to treat implicit comparatives in Fijian and Washo, respectively.

Effectively, in these Kleinian accounts, gradable adjectives are defined as evaluative individual properties; *tall* holds of Jane iff Jane counts as tall in the context of evaluation. Implicit comparatives modulate the comparison classes; an implicit comparative that expresses that A is taller than B presupposes that *A* and *B* are the only two individuals in the relevant comparison class, and asserts that *A* exceeds *B* in height. Due to metasemantic constraints on the calculation of the standard, the result is a comparative that strictly orders *A*'s height above *B*'s height while simultaneously ensuring that *A* counts as tall in the context of evaluation.

There are two crucial points here for the discussion of equatives to follow. First, these semantic accounts of implicit comparatives are accounts of comparative constructions that don't involve anything like a degree quantifier. There are different morphosyntactic strategies for expressing the same essential meaning—$A > B$ on some specific dimension—and there is overwhelming evidence (from Beck et al. 2004, Kennedy 2007a) that at least one does not involve a degree quantifier (and, at least in certain languages, does not even involve degrees as semantic objects).

Second, the presence of a degree quantifier cross-cuts at least to some extent the descriptive typology from Ultan (1972) and Stassen (1985) in § 2.1. Comparative degree quantifiers occur in a variety of comparative strategies listed above, including separative comparatives, allative comparatives, locative, and even conjoined comparatives, as illustrated in (15) and (17). This means that the semantic analysis of a comparative strategy is in principle independent from its syntax.

Equatives are the semantic duals of comparatives, and they exhibit the same sort of morphosyntactic variation. Consequently, it's reasonable to suspect that the degree-quantifier analysis in (4)–(5) is not appropriate for all constructions that carry the essential meaning '$A = B$ on some dimension'. In particular, a reasonable null hypothesis is that equatives differ along the same two morphosyntactic dimensions that comparatives do: they can be explicit or implicit, and they can equate degrees or individuals directly. In the next sections, I reproduce the efforts in Ultan (1972), Stassen (1985), Beck et al. (2004) and Kennedy (2007a) for equatives, and argue that some equatives should not be analyzed as involving degree quantifiers.

3 A Descriptive Typology of Equatives

There are two excellent typological studies of equative constructions: Haspelmath & Buchholz (1998) examines equatives across 52 languages, and Henkelmann (2006) discusses equatives in 25 European languages. I will present their descriptive morphosyntactic classes in this section, and discuss these constructions with respect to the explicit/implicit issue in §4.

Haspelmath & Buchholz (henceforth HB) characterize equatives as constructions that equate extent. They characterize similatives—a related construction—as those that equate manner. I will not address the typological observations they make about the relationship between equatives and similatives; see Rett (2013) for an overview.

In what follows, I'll focus primarily on the nature of the morphemes involved, loosely following the typology in Henkelmann (2006): relative equatives (§3.1); predicate equatives (§3.2); and conjoined equatives (§3.3). In §4, I'll address the issue of what constitutes an equative formed with a degree quantifier and what does not.

3.1 *Relative Equatives*

A relative equative is an equative whose standard is marked by a morpheme that appears elsewhere as degree relativizer, or has plausibly descended from a degree relativizer.[7] This is the largest and most diverse subclass of equative, and the vast majority of European languages fall into this type. See the Appendix for a list of examples of each subtype of relative equative.

3.1.1 SM-Only Relative Equatives

An SM-only (standard-marker only) relative equative is one whose only equative morphology is a relativizer standard marker, often a degree or manner *wh*-word in the language.[8] These are equatives in which the parameter is not marked.

---

[7] A degree relativizer can be independently diagnosed as the morpheme used to subordinate the relative clause in a sentence like *I make how (ever) much he makes*, although these have marginal acceptability in English. In languages whose relativizers are homophonous with *wh*-phrases, these morphemes can also be identified by their ability to head degree questions, like *How tall is Jane?* or *How much does Jane make?*.

[8] HB (p. 288) characterize these standard markers as an "adverbial relative pronoun that is generally based on an interrogative pronoun".

(26) *Ime motër ëstë e   bukur si   ti.*   *Albanian*
     my sister is   DET pretty how(SM) you
     'My sister is as pretty as you.' (HB 291)

(27) *Sestra mi e xubava kato   tebe.*   *Bulgarian*
     sister my is pretty how(SM) you
     'My sister is as pretty as you.' (HB 291)

(28) *I   adhelfí mu ine ómorfi san   (kj)   eséna.*   *Modern Greek*
     the sister my is pretty as(SM) (also) you
     'My sister is as pretty as you.' (HB 291[9])

(29) *Mia sorella è carina come   te.*   *Italian*
     my sister is pretty how(SM) you
     'My sister is as pretty as you.' (HB 291)

HB specify that relative equatives appear to have an aerial distribution in Europe; the full list from their sample has Serbo-Croatian in addition to those exemplified above.

3.1.2   PM-Marked Relative Equatives

These are equatives in which the standard marker is a relativizer, but which also include a parameter marker (PM) associated with the adjective. These equatives are quite well attested in Europe; they are exhaustively listed and exemplified in the Appendix.

(30) *A   minha irmã é tão   bonita quanto   você.*   *Portuguese*
     the my   sister is that(PM) pretty how(SM) you
     'My sister is as pretty as you.' (HB 286)

(31) *Ó ónna   caŋgaa ai jínnaa   ó   daa praà.*   *Punjabi*
     he so(PM) good   is how(SM) he GEN brother
     'He is as good as his brother.' (HB 286)

---

[9] HB discuss the relationship between the Modern Greek relative equative and its correlative equative counterpart (94) on p. 293: "In Greek, the parameter marker is diachronically based on a relative pronoun (*san* < *hōs án*, where *hōs* 'how' is a relative pronoun and *án* is a modal particle)".

As HB point out, the parameter marker and standard marker are quite clearly morphologically related and semantically correlated. I will return to discuss the semantic properties of these constructions in § 4.3, where I will argue for the differentiation of the two types of PM-marked relative equatives exemplified in (30) and (31).

HB characterize the English *as ... as* equative as a marginal PM-marked relative equative, claiming that its parameter and standard markers are diachronically but not synchronically related to the language's degree demonstrative and relativizer. Certainly, the relativizers *as* and *how* are synonymous in similatives, as exemplified in (32) (Haspelmath & Buchholz 1998, Rett 2013).

(32) a. Jane danced as Bill danced (that is, beautifully/en pointe).
 b. Jane danced how Bill danced (that is, beautifully/en pointe).

3.2   *Predicate Equatives*
3.2.1   Main Predicate Equatives

Some languages have 'equal-to' equatives, in which the main predicate is not the gradable adjective, but rather a verb meaning roughly *equals*. In the sense that the comparison relation is encoded in a verbal predicate, this equative strategy is the analog to 'exceed' comparatives like (19b) *Compared to Bill, Jane is tall*.

(33) *N-o-ingana   Mugasho oburaingwa.*   Nkore-Kiga
 PRES-you-equal M   height
 'You are as tall as M.' (lit. 'You equal M in height.') (HB 289)

(34) *M-toto   wa-ngu   ni hodari sawa   na   wa-ko.*   Swahili
 1sg-child 1sg-POSS.1sg be clever equal with(SM) 1sg-POSS.2sg
 'My child is as clever as yours.' (Henkelmann 386)

(35) *À-pol-o-t'   ayòŋ   nɪ-ka-rì-aan-à-ni ka' iyoŋ'.*   Turkana
 1sg-big-VRB-sg 1sg.NOM comparable   with 2sg
 'I am as big as you.' (Henkelmann 386)

(36) *Wagù-n   nân yaa   kai   t'ireelà-n   nân*
 wagon-LINK.M here COMPL.3sg.m reach trailer-LINK.M here
 doogoo.   Hausa
 length
 'This wagon is as long as this trailer.' (Henkelmann 388)

Other languages in this category include Indonesian, Maori, Vietnamese, and Yoruba.

3.2.2 Adverbial Predicate Equatives

Some equatives are formed with adverbs or adverbial phrases meaning roughly *equally* or *to the same extent*. HB classify these adverbials as parameter markers, but they are in principle distinct from them; more about this in §4. Some examples below; languages with equatives in this category also include Danish, Dutch, Estonian, Finnish, Faroese, Norwegian, Swedish, and Swiss German (HB 294–295).

(37) *Tā gēn nǐ yíyàng gāo.*   Chinese
 she with you one.manner tall
 'She is as tall as you.' (HB 284)

(38) *Ohxe rye naha honyko, koso yaoro.*   Hixkaryana
 good same is peccary deer with(SM)
 'Peccary is equally good, along with deer.' (Henkelmann 385)

(39) *Systir min et jafn stór og ég.*   Icelandic
 sister my is equally tall as(SM) I
 'My sister is as tall as I.' (HB 294)

(40) *Anak saya se-pandai anak dia.*   Indonesian
 child 1SG one(PM)-bright child 3SG
 'My child is as bright as hers.' (Henkelmann 381)

(41) *I ris mem degre ki nu.*   Seychelles Creole
 he rich same extent SM we
 'He is as rich as us.' (HB 284)

HB characterize these standard markers, where present, as relative particles (similar to the standard markers in relative equatives).

3.3 *Conjoined Equatives*

In direct analog to conjoined comparatives, some languages have conjoined equatives. They involve two parallel clauses joined together serially or with an explicit conjunction. They often include an additive particle (synonymous with English *too, also*) as a standard marker.

(42) ŋaya   ŋa-balayi ñaŋgi   wadij ña-balayi.   *Mangarayi*
    1SG.NOM 1SG-big   2SG.NOM also 2.SG-big
    'I am big, you are also big.' (Henkelmann 395)

(43) *Hwara' na*   *Xijam. Hwara' na*   *Orowao quem ca'*
    big   T/A.3SG X   big   T/A.3SG O   REF this
    na.   *Wari'*
    T/A.3SG
    'Xijam is as big as Orowao.' (ibid.)

3.4 Case-Marked Standards

Other languages employ a case marker or preposition as a standard marker. These strategies exist with (45) or without (46) a parameter marker. Three examples are below; other languages include Abkhaz, Arabic, Basque, Comanche, Ibabura Quechua, Japanese, Kabardian, Kalmyk, Krongo, Lezgian, Ndyuka, Tamil, Turkana, and Turkish (Haspelmath & Buchholz 1998:296, Henkelmann 2006:382–383).

(44) *Yen-ke   æymen pərpər, rey-ke-kwo.*   *Awtuw*
    2SG-POSS knife   sharp 3SG-POSS-SM
    'Your knife is as sharp as his.' (Henkelmann 382)

(45) *Ilit-tut   utuqqaa-tiga-aq.*   *Greenlandic Eskimo*
    thou-SM be.old-PM-3SG.IND
    'He is as old as you.' (HB 285)

(46) *Pani-i-mi   qam-naw shumaq.*   *Ancash Quechua*
    sister-1SG-DIR you-SM   pretty
    'My sister is as pretty as you.' (HB 285)

3.5 Dedicated Morphemes

Finally, some languages employ parameter markers and standard markers with "no transparent etymology," i.e. which are construction-specific. HB identify these as the rare case. Welsh in (47) has both a dedicated PM and SM; Modern Irish and Breton have dedicated PMs but co-opted SMs (the commitative and conjunction morphemes, respectively).

(47) *Mae e   cyn ddued â 'r frân.*   *Welsh*
    is he PM black SM the crow
    'He is as black as the crow.' (HB 285)

(48) Tá Máire chomh cliste le   Liam.   Modern Irish
     is M   PM   clever with(SM) Liam
     'Máire is as clever as Liam.' (HB 285)

(49) Ma c'hoar a   red ken buan ha   c'hwi.   Breton
     my sister PTL run PM fast and(SM) you
     'My sister runs as fast as you.' (HB 285)

4 A Theoretical Typology of Equatives

In what follows, I take for granted extant treatments of parameter-marked equatives (like the English *as ... as* construction) as involving a degree quantifier, and thus instantiating an analog to explicit comparatives: explicit equatives. The questions I take up in this section are: What tests can we use to differentiate between an explicit and implicit equative strategy? And, how can we determine whether a given implicit equative strategy encodes a degree quantifier?

HB addressed these questions obliquely, by using the terms 'comparative degree' and 'equative degree' to refer to the relevant DegP heads (or degree quantifiers): "A parameter marker may be synthetic or analytic. If it is synthetic, we speak of an equative degree, which is completely analogous to the familiar comparative degree in comparative constructions. Unlike the comparative degree, the equative degree is rare in European languages. It is attested only at the margins of Europe, in Kartvelian, Celtic, and Finno-Ugric" (HB 283). This suggests that morphological dependence—whether a morpheme is free or bound—is sufficient for characterizing a parameter marker as a degree quantifier. This is unlikely to be the right distinction, even for comparative parameter markers, as the synonymy of the English *-er* and *more* attests.[10] I will argue in § 4.3 that it is in fact wrong, and in particular that some parameter-marked relative equatives involve degree quantification, while others do not.

I will first introduce several diagnostic tests that differentiate between explicit equatives like the English *as ... as* construction and other equative strategies.

---

10   These forms are often but not always in complementary distribution (in English as well as other languages, like Russian), with both a synthetic and an analytic comparative morpheme. As argued in Pancheva (2006), Rett (2015b), when synthetic and analytic comparatives are in free variation, the analytic version is marked and therefore evaluative, or norm-related (i.e. presupposes that the degree be significantly high in context). Compare the synthetic *Jane is taller than Bill* to the analytic *Jane is more tall than Bill*.

4.1 Semantic Tests for Equative Strategies

Recall that English employs more than one type of equative strategy. Many are listed below, with labels from the previous section (see Hanink 2018 for a discussion of *same* constructions, which are often also called equatives).

(50) a. Jane is as tall as Bill. — *PM equative*
b. Jane is tall like Bill. — *SM-only equative*
c. Jane is tall; Bill is tall (too). — *conjoined equative*
d. Jane equals Bill in height. — *predicate equative*

The strong parallels between these morphological strategies and those in comparative constructions suggests that equatives, too, can be split into explicit and implicit categories. What follows are proposed diagnostics for making that distinction.[11]

4.1.1 Availability of Weak Reading

As discussed in §1, the English parameter-marked relative equative *Jane is as tall as Bill* can receive a weak, 'at least' interpretation in addition to the strong 'exactly' interpretation, depending on context. We can diagnose the ability of an equative to receive a weak reading by using the continuation 'in fact she's taller'. This point is reproduced in (51a), and extended to the other English equative strategies.

(51) a. Jane is as tall as Bill, in fact she's taller. — *PM relative*
b. Jane is tall like Bill, in fact she's taller. — *SM-only relative*
c. Jane is tall; Bill is tall (too). In fact she's taller. — *conjoined*
d. Jane equals Bill in height, #in fact she's taller. — *predicate*

This diagnostic clearly distinguishes between the non-predicate equatives in (51a)–(51d)—which can receive a weak interpretation—with the predicate equative in (51d), which cannot. The latter observation is no surprise, as the predicate involved in these strategies is the word *equals*, which is not compatible with an 'at least' interpretation.

---

[11] I will only use main predicate equatives to exemplify the class of predicate equatives, as the subtypes pattern together on these diagnostics.

4.1.2 Evaluativity Patterns

A construction is evaluative iff it requires that a degree exceed a contextually-valued standard. The constructions in (52) differ with respect to evaluativity; one diagnostic of this difference is their (in)compatibility with the negation of the relevant antonym, as in (52).

(52) a. Jane is as tall as Bill, but she's short.
b. Jane is as short as Bill, #but she's tall.

The equative in (52a), formed with the positive relative adjective *tall*, is not evaluative: it doesn't presuppose that Jane or Bill is tall, so it's compatible with Jane or Bill being short. In contrast, the equative in (52b), formed with the negative relative adjective *short*, is evaluative: it does presuppose that Jane and Bill are short, so it is incompatible with their being tall. Not every construction displays this antonymic evaluativity contrast with respect to relative adjectives; explicit comparatives do not, but implicit comparatives are always evaluative (Rett 2015b).

The constructions in (50) differ with respect to evaluativity, even with a positive-antonym relative adjective like *tall*.[12]

(53) a. Jane is as tall as Bill, but she's short.   PM *relative*
b. Jane is tall like Bill, #but she's short.   SM-*only relative*
c. Jane is tall; Bill is tall (too), #but she is short.   *conjoined*
d. Jane equals Bill in height, but she's short.   *predicate*

The predicate equative in (53d) is not evaluative. Within the class of non-predicate equatives, we see an additional piece of evidence that there is a clear semantic difference between explicit and implicit equatives, defined in a way that is analogous to Kennedy's distinction in the comparative domain: equatives like (53a) that mark their parameters are explicit equatives, and are not evaluative when formed with positive-antonym relative adjectives. But equatives that do not mark their parameters, like (53b) and (53c)—implicit equatives—are evaluative.

---

12   In (53), the judgments should be evaluated in a context in which Jane and Bill are in the same comparison class, and therefore the hearer can take for granted that if one is tall (or short), than the other one is too.

4.1.3 Acceptability with Factor Modifiers

Recall that, in (18), Kennedy characterized the difference between explicit and implicit comparative strategies in terms of the forms of their adjectives. Implicit comparatives use the positive form of adjectives—the same as in positive constructions like *Jane is tall*—and explicit comparatives use the comparative form of adjectives. In English, the comparative forms of adjectives are just 'Adj-*er*,' for adjectives that take synthetic comparatives, but they can also be '*more* Adj.' This means, effectively, that there is a single necessary and sufficient condition for being an explicit comparative: that the construction have a parameter marker (either *-er* or *more* in English).

This seems to be a real distinction in equative strategies, as well; the ability of an equative to be modified by a factor modifier like *twice* or *half* differentiates even between equatives with parameter markers, as in (54a), and equatives without parameter markers, as in (54b).[13]

(54) a. Jane is twice as tall as Bill. *PM relative*
b. Jane is (*twice) tall like Bill. *SM-only relative*
c. Jane is (*twice) tall; Bill is tall (too). *conjoined*
d. Jane (*twice) equals Bill in height. *predicate*

In the case of (54d), the incompatibility of a factor modifier with the predicate *equals* is clearly unacceptable for the same reason that predicate equatives don't have weak, 'at least' interpretations: the truth conditions imposed by the equative strategy (equality of height) are semantically incompatible with the meaning encoded in the factor modifier.

But this is not true of the other equatives, in (54b) and (54c), the equative strategies whose subcomponents are positive constructions (*Jane is tall*). In these cases, just as with comparative strategies, the clear difference seems to be that the degree argument of the parameter *tall* is bound or valued by POS, or some other compositional mechanism that yields evaluativity (Rett 2015b). This suggests that the relevant degree of comparison is not available for degree quantification, and thus cannot be further restricted by a factor modifier.

---

13   These factor modifiers interact differently with negative antonyms than they do with positive antonyms; see Croft & Cruse (2004) for the original observation, and Rett (2015b) pp. 48, 114–115 for discussion.

SEPARATE BUT EQUAL: A TYPOLOGY OF EQUATIVE CONSTRUCTIONS

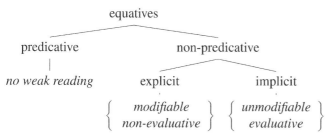

FIGURE 5.1 A typology of equatives (to be revised)

4.1.4 Summary

The diagnostics presented above yield roughly three different classes of equatives (shown in Figure 5.1): predicative equatives, formed by some version of a word like *equal*, like that in (50d), are equatives that do not receive weak, 'at least' interpretations.

Within the equatives that do receive 'at least' interpretations, there are two distinct types: explicit equatives, which are modifiable and non-evaluative (when formed with a positive relative adjective); and implicit equatives, which are not modifiable, and are evaluative (regardless of what type of adjective they're formed with). Because the explicit equative examined here (50a) has a parameter marker, and the implicit ones ((50b) and (50c)) do not, equatives seem to conform to Kennedy's explicit/implicit distinction for comparatives: non-predicate equatives with adjectives unbound by a degree quantifier are implicit equatives; those with adjectives bound by a degree quantifier (or a parameter marker) are explicit equatives.

In the next section I offer some evidence that this typology is cross-linguistically robust but incomplete. In § 5 I provide semantic analyses for two different types of relative equatives (the SM-only implicit equatives, and a second type of explicit, PM equative).

4.2 Semantic Diagnostics Cross-linguistically

In this section, I'll argue that the diagnostics reviewed above support the typology in Figure 5.1 across languages, with one exception: cross-linguistically, equatives with a parameter marker (PM equatives) fall into two distinct categories, one patterning with English explicit equatives, and the other with a slightly different semantic profile.

4.2.1 Predicative Equatives

Predicative equatives universally receive an 'exactly' reading, but no 'at least' reading. This is a definitional characteristic; predicate equatives are formed with predicates equivalent to 'equals'. I illustrate it below for Swedish and Dutch.

(55) #Thomas är lika lång som Christoffer; han är faktiskt
 T   is equal tall as C;   he is actually
 längre.   Swedish
 taller
 'Thomas is as tall as Christoffer; he is in fact taller.'

(56) #Jan is even lang als Piet. Hij is zelfs langer.   Dutch
 J   is equally tall as P. He is in.fact taller
 'John is as tall as Pete. He is in fact taller.'

The speaker reports that the equative in (55) is a contradiction of its continuation.

4.2.2 Implicit Equatives

SM-only relative equatives in other languages, too, qualify as implicit equatives according to the diagnostics below. I present two case studies, the first in Croatian, the second in Italian.

In Croatian, relative equatives can be formed with the relativizer *kao* ('as') but no parameter marker, as in (57).[14]

(57) *Ivan je visok kao Petar.*   Croatian
 John is tall as Peter
 'John is as tall as Peter.'

SM-only relative equatives in Croatian are not acceptable with factor modifiers, but they are evaluative. This first point is demonstrated in (58); the second in (59).

---

14 Croatian also has what appears to be a second relative equative strategy, with the *wh*-word meaning 'how much/many' but with a conjunction introducing the standard:
 (i) *Ivan je visok koliko i Petar.*
  John be tall how.much and Peter
  'John is tall as much as Peter.'
 I will not discuss this strategy here because it is not a canonical instance of either a relative equative or a conjoined equative.

(58) ??Ivan je dvostruko visok kao Petar.   Croatian
     John is twice   tall as Peter
     'John is twice as tall as Peter.'

(59) Ivan je visok kao Petar, a   Petar je   nizak!   Croatian
     John is tall as Peter, and Peter be short
     'John is as tall as Peter, and Peter is short!'

Italian also has an SM-only relative equative strategy, in (60).

(60) Gianni e alto come /quanto   Marco.   Italian
     G   is tall how /how.much M
     'Gianni is as tall as Marco.'

These equatives, too, are unmodifiable and evaluative; the former point is demonstrated below.

(61) *Gianni e due volte alto come /quanto   Marco.   Italian
     G   is two times tall how /how.much M
     'Gianni is twice as tall as Marco.'

4.3 A Closer Look at Explicit Equatives

The diagnostics outlined in §4.1 reveal an interesting difference within the descriptive class of parameter-marked relative equatives. In particular, these diagnostics show that parameter-marked relative equatives actually fall into two distinct subclasses: those whose parameter is marked by a degree demonstrative, like *that much*; and those whose parameter is marked by a resultative or sufficientive morpheme like *so*. In §5 I will suggest that only the latter involves degree quantification of the sort demonstrated in (4) and (5).

There are languages with equative strategies that mark parameters that do behave like the English explicit equative. Some are illustrated below; others are listed in the Appendix. The Dutch PM-marking equative in (62) behaves just like the English one in that it is modifiable (63), non-evaluative (64), and receives a weak interpretation (65).

(62) Jan is zo   lang als   Piet.   Dutch
     J   is so(PM) tall as(SM) P
     'John is as tall as Pete.'

(63) *Jan is twee keer zo lang als Piet.*   *Dutch*
     J is two times so(PM) long as(SM) P
     'John is twice as tall as Pete.'

(64) *Jan is zo lang als Piet, en hij is heel klein.*   *Dutch*
     J is so(PM) tall as(SM) P, and he is very small
     'John is as tall as Pete, and he is short.'

(65) *Jan is zo lang als Piet. Hij is zelfs langer.*   *Dutch*
     J is so(PM) tall as(SM) P. He is in.fact taller
     'John is as tall as Pete, in fact he is taller.'

The same is true for the Swedish PM-marked relative equative.

(66) *Thomas är dubbelt så lång som Christoffer.*   *Swedish*
     T is twice so(PM) tall as(SM) C.
     'Thomas is twice as tall as Christoffer.'

(67) *Thomas är så lång som Christoffer, men båda är*
     T is so(PM) tall as(SM) C, but both are
     korta.   *Swedish*
     short
     'Thomas is as tall as Christoffer, but both are short.'

(68) *Thomas är så lång som Christoffer, han är till och med*
     T is so(PM) tall as(SM) C, he is even
     högre.   *Swedish*
     taller
     'Thomas is as tall as Christoffer, in fact he is even taller.'

In contrast, there are other languages whose PM-marked relative equatives do not pattern with the English explicit equative strategy. In particular, they are non-evaluative and receive a weak interpretation—like the English relative equative—but they are not modifiable.

This is exemplified in Italian. (69) shows that the Italian PM-marked relative equative is not evaluative; (70) shows that it has a weak interpretation; and (71) shows that it is unmodifiable.

(69) *Gianni è tanto   alto quanto   Pietro, ma è
     G   is that.much(PM) tall how.much(SM) P,   but is
     basso.   Italian
     short
     'John is as tall as Peter, but he is short.'

(70) *G è tanto   alto quanto   P. Infatti, è più
     G is that.much(PM) tall how.much(SM) P. In fact, is more
     alto.   Italian
     tall
     'John is as tall as Peter. In fact, he is taller.'

(71) *Gianni è due volte tanto   alto quanto
     G   is two times that.much(PM) tall how.much(SM)
     Pietro.   Italian
     P
     'John is twice as tall as Peter.'

It's possible that Spanish also patterns with Italian in this respect; (72) shows that the PM-marked relative strategy is not evaluative, and (73) shows that it can receive a weak interpretation. (74), on the contrary, shows that it cannot be modified by a factor modifier.

(72) *Juan es tan   alto como   Pedro, pero Pedro es
     J   is that.much(PM) tall like(SM) P,   but P   is
     bajito.   Spanish
     short.DIM
     'John is as tall as Peter, but Peter is short.'

(73) *Juan es tan   alto como   Pedro. De hecho, él es más
     John is that.much(PM) tall like(SM) Peter. In fact, he is more
     alto.   Spanish
     tall
     'John is as tall as Peter. In fact, he is taller'

(74) ?Juan es dos veces tan alto como Pedro.   Spanish
     J   is two times as tall like P
     'John is twice as tall as Peter.'

TABLE 5.1 Subtypes of explicit equatives

Language	Parameter marker?	Modifiable?	Evaluative?	Weak reading?
English	*as*	yes	no	yes
Dutch	*zo*	yes	no	yes
German	*so*	yes	no	yes
Korean	*mankhum*	yes	no	yes
Swedish	*så*	yes	no	yes
Catalan	*tan*	no	no	yes
Italian	*tanto*	no	no	yes
Romanian	*tot*	no	no	yes
Slovenian	*tako*	no	?	?
Spanish	*tan*	no?	no	yes

My consultants reported (74) as unnatural, so there is a putative contrast with Italian, in which (70) is reported to be ungrammatical. It's possible that the distinction I'm making here between these two subclasses of explicit equatives is subject to dialectical variation or morphologic or semantic reanalysis.

A comprehensive list of relative equative strategies is in the Appendix. Table 5.1 lists the data I've collected on these two types of PM-marked relative equatives according to their behavior on these diagnostics.[15] The morphological patterns here suggest a subtypology: equatives whose parameter is marked with a morpheme meaning *so* or something similar behave one way—like the canonical English equative—and those whose parameter is marked with a demonstrative morpheme meaning *that much* behave another way. (There is a family resemblance here too, of course, with Germanic languages using one type of strategy and Romance and Slavic languages using the other.)

These data suggest that a more accurate cross-linguistic typology of equative strategies is as in Figure 5.2, with the category of explicit equatives—those equatives with parameter markers—divided into two distinct categories: those headed by sufficientives like *so*, and those headed by degree demonstratives, meaning roughly *that much*.

---

15 The Slovenian data are incomplete because I have drawn them from Crnič & Fox (2019), who give a very different explanation for why Slovenian equatives are not modifiable.

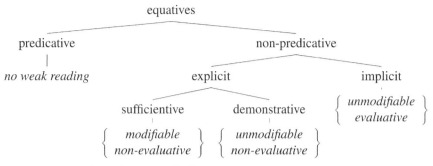

FIGURE 5.2 A typology of equatives (final)

This typology begs the question: if English equatives are best analyzed as involving degree quantifiers, and if English instantiates the sufficientive equative strategy, how are demonstrative equatives best analyzed semantically? What explains their inability to be modified (but their ability to receive a weak interpretation)? I take up these questions in the next section.

5   The Semantics of Non-Degree-Quantificational Equative Strategies

In this section, I'll provide a semantic analysis for SM-only relative clauses—taken from the treatment of generic equatives in Rett (2013)—and a semantic analysis of canonical demonstrative explicit equatives like Italian, borrowing from Brasoveanu (2009). The correct semantic analysis of sufficientive explicit equatives remains the same: I suggest they are the only equative strategy that involves degree quantification (although it is of course possible for one type of parameter marker to be reanalyzed as the other).

Not explicitly addressed in this section is the semantics of predicate equatives, conjoined equatives, case-marked equatives or dedicated-morpheme equatives. The semantics for predicate equatives are straightforward; they encode their equative relationship in a lexical item. A semantic analysis for the others will require further research.

5.1   *The Semantics of Implicit Equatives*

As Haspelmath & Buchholz (1998) showed, languages that have SM-only relative equatives form similatives—whose parameter is a verb, rather than an adjective, as in (75b)—with the same relativizer. An example below is from Serbo-Croatian.

(75) a. *On je visok kao   njegova sestra.*   Serbo-Croatian
       he is tall how(SM) his   sister
       'He is as tall as his sister.'

   b. *On piše   kao   njegova sestra.*   Serbo-Croatian
      he writes how(SM) his   sister
      'He writes like his sister.'

As Haspelmath & Buchholz also show, there is impressive cross-linguistic universality regarding these standard markers across similatives, specific equatives (the topic of this paper), and generic equatives, e.g. *Jane is white as snow* in English.

In Rett (2013), I argued that standard markers work the same way in generic equatives and similatives. They introduce relative clauses ranging over non-lexicalized arguments, associated with the parameter via a relation $\mathbb{R}$, encoded in some sort of type shifter ρ (Landman 2000).[16] As shown in (76a), it is strongly parallel to the null operator associating events with their runtimes, in (76b) (Davidson 1969). In the case of similatives, this type-shifter associates verbs with their manner; in the case of generic equatives, it associates adjectives with their evaluative or canonical properties.

(76) a. $[\![\rho]\!] = \lambda E_{\langle v,t \rangle} \lambda e . E(e) \wedge \mathbb{R}(e,m)$
     b. $[\![\tau]\!] = \lambda E_{\langle v,t \rangle} \lambda e . E(e) \wedge \mathbb{R}(e,t)$

I assume that the truth conditions in (77a) are the denotation of a sentence without this relation, and those in (77b) are a version that includes it. In this version, the eventuality introduced by the verb is associated with a manner m, in this case valued by context.

(77) a. $[\![\text{Jane danced}]\!] = \exists e[\text{dance}(e) \wedge \text{agent}(\text{jane},e)]$
     b. $[\![\text{Jane danced } \rho]\!] = \exists e[\text{dance}(e) \wedge \text{agent}(\text{jane},e) \wedge \mathbb{R}(e,m)]$
        shorthand: $\exists e[e = \text{dance}(\text{jane}) \wedge \mathbb{R}(e,m)]$

In English specific equatives, the equation of two degrees involves a degree quantifier, denoted by the parameter marker. Similatives and generic equatives

---

16 I think of $\mathbb{R}$ as semantically encoding some sort of pragmatic homomorphism, akin to what happens with deferred reference (more of that in Rett 2014). Another way of conceptualizing $\mathbb{R}$ is as a type-shifter along the lines of those in Partee & Rooth (1983)—i.e. the function from an individual to a set of its properties—but across semantic domains instead of types.

show that quantifiers aren't strictly speaking required to equate two things. We can do it using the compositional rules of Predicate Modification and Existential Closure, as demonstrated in (78).[17]

In (78), both the matrix and the subordinated clauses are relative clauses, and both are associated (via ρ) with a manner argument. The two clauses are combined semantically using Predicate Modification; this effectively equates the two manners. This variable is existentially bound at the end of the utterance using existential closure.

(78) Jane danced as Bill danced. *similative*
   a. $[\![$Jane danced$]\!] = [\![\text{Op}_\rho \text{ Jane danced } \rho]\!] =$
      $\lambda m \exists e [e = \text{danced}(\text{jane}) \land \mathbb{R}(e, m)]$
   b. $[\![$as Bill danced$]\!] = [\![$as Bill danced $\rho]\!] =$
      $\lambda m' \exists e' [e' = \text{danced}(\text{bill}) \land \mathbb{R}(e', m')]$
   c. *predicate modification*:
      $\lambda m \exists e, e' [e = \text{danced}(\text{jane}) \land \mathbb{R}(e, m) \land e' = \text{danced}(\text{bill}) \land \mathbb{R}(e', m)]$
   d. *existential closure*:
      $\exists m, e, e' [e = \text{danced}(\text{jane}) \land \mathbb{R}(e, m) \land e' = \text{danced}(\text{bill}) \land \mathbb{R}(e', m)]$

The same is true of generic equatives, as in (79), but in these constructions the type-shifter ρ associates the predicate with an evaluative property (in (79), the property of being significantly white). The same two mechanisms—Predicate Modification and Existential Closure—derive the equation of these two properties, so (79d) is true if some eventuality of Jane being white shares a property with some (generic) eventuality of snow being white.

(79) Jane is white as snow. *generic equative*
   a. $[\![$Jane is white$]\!] = [\![\text{Op}_\rho \text{ Jane is white } \rho]\!] =$
      $\lambda P \exists e [e = \text{white}(\text{jane}) \land \mathbb{R}(e, P)]$
   b. $[\![$as snow is white$]\!] = [\![$as snow is white $\rho]\!] =$
      $\lambda P' \exists e' [e' = \text{white}(\text{snow}) \land \mathbb{R}(e', P')]$

---

17   In all of these derivations, I assume that the matrix clause (including the target) forms a relative clause—just like the subordinated clause—via movement of a null operator. As discussed in Rett (2013), this is a standard assumption, although I know of no explanation for why the relativizers in subordinated clauses are sometimes pronounced, while those in matrix clauses never are.

c. *predicate modification*:
$\lambda P \exists e, e' [e = \text{white}(\text{jane}) \wedge \mathbb{R}(e, P) \wedge e' = \text{white}(\text{snow}) \wedge \mathbb{R}(e', P')]$

d. *existential closure*:
$\exists P, e, e' [e = \text{white}(\text{jane}) \wedge \mathbb{R}(e, P) \wedge e' = \text{white}(\text{snow}) \wedge \mathbb{R}(e', P')]$

As discussed in Rett (2013), this analysis works straightforwardly on SM-only relative equatives like the Italian *come* construction. (Italian, like Serbo-Croatian in (75), employs the same standard marker in its SM-only relative equative as it does in its similative and generic equative.) In the case of specific equatives, the type-shifter associates each clause with a property argument related to the (evaluative) eventuality of the subject being significantly tall (above s).[18]

(80) Gianni e alto come Pietro.　　　　　　　　　*Italian SM-only relative equative*

a. ⟦Gianni e alto⟧ = ⟦Op$_\rho$ Gianni e alto ρ⟧ =
$\lambda P \exists e [e = \exists d[\text{tall}(\text{gianni}, d) \wedge d > s] \wedge \mathbb{R}(e, P)]$

b. ⟦come Pietro e alto ρ⟧ =
$\lambda P' \exists e' [e' = \exists d'[\text{tall}(\text{pietro}, d') \wedge d' > s] \wedge \mathbb{R}(e', P')]$

c. *predicate modification*:
$\lambda P \exists e, e' [e = \exists d[\text{tall}(\text{gianni}, d) \wedge d > s] \wedge \mathbb{R}(e, P) \wedge e' = \exists d'[\text{tall}(\text{pietro}, d') \wedge d' > s] \wedge \mathbb{R}(e', P')]$

d. *existential closure*:
$\exists P, e, e' [e = \exists d[\text{tall}(\text{gianni}, d) \wedge d > s] \wedge \mathbb{R}(e, P) \wedge e' = \exists d'[\text{tall}(\text{pietro}, d') \wedge d' > s] \wedge \mathbb{R}(e', P')]$

The truth conditions in (80d) hold in any situation in which there is a property associated with the eventuality of Gianni being significantly tall and the eventuality of Pietro being significantly tall.

These constructions all share their semantic derivations with other relative clauses. They involve the association of two entities or properties by virtue of the juxtaposition of two relativized clauses, without any morphemes overtly encoding sameness, equation, or the ≥ relation we associate with explicit equative degree quantification. From this perspective, all relative clauses are equative-like; e.g. *Jane met who Bill met* equates the individual Jane met with the individual Bill met. In the vast quantity of languages that employ relativization, this is a natural equative strategy.

18　There are a number of ways to represent how these positive constructions come to be associated with an evaluative property; see Rett (2015b) for details.

5.2 The Semantics of Demonstrative Explicit Equatives

Demonstrative explicit equatives, too, repurpose morphology from elsewhere. In particular, the matrix clause is formed with a degree demonstrative, which is associated with the target, and the subordinate clause is formed with a relativizer, which is associated with the standard.

I propose to analyze these demonstrative explicit equatives transparently, i.e. involving the discourse introduction of a particular degree (by the degree demonstrative) and anaphora to that degree (by the relativizer). The semantic analysis will parallel in many ways the significantly more complicated analysis of degree correlatives from Brasoveanu (2009).

(81) *Pe cît   e Irina de frumoasă, (tot) pe atît   e de*
     PE how.much is I   DE beautiful   all PE that.much is DE
     deșteaptă.   Romanian
     smart
     'However much Irina is beautiful (to a certain, significant extent), she is that smart (i.e. to the same, equally significant extent).'

Degree correlatives like those in (81) are very similar to the demonstrative equatives we see in languages like Romanian, exemplified in (82). They differ in two ways: in degree correlatives, 1) the relative clause is left-dislocated; and 2) the relative clause is headed by a *wh*-phrase (*cît* in (81)) instead of a relativizer (*ca* in (82)).

(82) *Irina este tot atît   de înaltă ca   și   Maria.* Romanian
     I   is   all that-much(PM) of tall   as(SM) also M
     'Irina is as tall as Maria.'

The correlative in (81) has an added layer of semantic complexity because, like other comparisons of deviation (as in (37) Kennedy 2001, Bale 2008), it compares differential degrees. Rather than directly comparing Irina's degree of beauty to her degree of intelligence—which is arguably not semantically feasible, Kennedy (1999)—the comparison of deviation (or 'indirect comparison') compares the degree to which Irina's beauty differs from the contextually relevant standard of beauty to the degree to which Irina's intelligence differs from the contextually relevant standard of intelligence.

In contrast, the demonstrative explicit equative in (82) directly compares degrees of tallness. This obviates the need for a complicated homomorphism in the semantics, along the lines of those proposed in Bale (2008), Brasoveanu (2009). It also means that, whereas Brasoveanu's analysis of degree correlatives involves anaphora to differentials, the analysis of demonstrative explicit equatives can involve anaphora directly to (first-order) degrees.

As before, I will treat the embedded clause introducing the standard as a degree relative, headed by a relativizer (*ca* in the case of Romanian, *quanto* in Italian), repeated in (83) from (69). As with English equatives, the logical form of the standard clause in e.g. (70) will look like (83) (cf. (3b)).

(83) Gianni è tanto alto quanto Pietro:
[CP Gianni is [CP OP$_d$ how-much Pietro è̶ d̶-̶t̶a̶l̶l̶] that$_i$ tall]

I assume the relative clause is extraposed at LF, as it is in English comparison constructions (3b); I will discuss why this might be shortly.

Following Jacobson (1995), Caponigro (2004) and others since, relative clauses in many contexts are type-shifted to denote definites (and, in particular, maxima; in this case, a maximum degree).

(84) ⟦quanto Pietro è̶ a̶l̶t̶o̶⟧ = MAX(λd . tall(pietro, d))

The entire equative, as a result, will involve degree anaphora in the matrix clause, as in (85).

(85) ⟦Gianni è tanto alto quanto Pietro⟧ = tall(gianni, MAX(λd . tall(pietro, d)))

These demonstrative explicit equatives, especially in contrast to degree correlatives like (81), involve something much more closely resembling cataphora than traditional anaphora: the degree demonstrative linearly precedes its relativized modifier.

I have no explanation for why the correlatives have the order they do, but the extraposition of the standard-marking clause in these languages as well as languages like English seems to have a clear, non-optional discourse function. In particular, comparison constructions require their subject (or target) address the Question Under Discussion (Roberts 1996), even in equatives, in which the measure of the target provides information about the measure of the standard, and vice-versa. In Rett 2015b, I dub this the 'Equative Argument Asymmetry,' illustrated with data like (86) (p. 120): "A comparison construction with an external argument value x and an internal argument value y is felicitous iff x is relevant to the QUD."

(86) A: How tall/short is Doug?
    B: He's as tall/short as Adam.
    B′: #Adam is as tall/short as he is.

In other words, demonstrative explicit equatives may have the clausal syntax they do—specifically, an extra-posed relative clause—for information-structural reasons; the anaphoric phrase containing the demonstrative takes linear precedence because it addresses the QUD.

Most importantly for our purposes, the analysis of demonstrative explicit equatives in (85) correctly predicts the semantic behavior summarized in Table 5.1. Two of their properties come about by virtue of the fact that they're degree demonstrative constructions, similar to (87).

(87) A: How tall is Jane?
    B: (*gesturing*) This tall.

The degree demonstrative in (87) is not evaluative; it doesn't entail that Jane counts as tall in the context of utterance. When demonstrative explicit equatives are formed with positive-antonym relative adjectives like *tall* they, too, are not evaluative.

Degree demonstrative constructions also have a weak reading. This isn't evident in the context in (87), in which B's gesture is most naturally interpreted as setting a maximum height (arguably for Gricean Quantity reasons). But when the demonstrated height has an anaphoric link (van der Sandt 1992), as in (88), the degree demonstrative construction can receive a weak interpretation.

(88) A: How tall is Jane? (*gesturing*) Is she this tall?
    B: Yes (she's that tall), in fact she's taller.

In this way, too, degree demonstrative constructions parallel demonstrative explicit equatives.

Finally, a degree-demonstrative account of these equatives also predicts that they are unmodifiable by factor modifiers, in direct contrast to sufficientive explicit equatives. While sufficientive explicit equatives relate two sets of degrees, demonstrative explicit equatives are directly referring; they predicate one height of another.[19]

In languages like Italian and Spanish, degree demonstrative constructions cannot grammatically occur with factor modifiers, although there are some notable differences: the Italian degree demonstrative in (89) is formed with

---

19 There is a slight contrast, in my dialect, between the acceptable *twice as tall as that* and the marginal *twice that tall*, but it is admittedly not a strong contrast.

così; and (90) was marked by my Spanish consultants to be less acceptable than the equative version in (74).

(89) **Gianni è due volte così alto.*   Italian
      G   is two times that tall
      'John is twice that tall.'

(90) *??Juan es dos veces tan alto.*   Spanish
      J   is two times that tall
      'John is twice that tall.'

These data suggest that it's consistent with the present analysis of demonstrative explicit equatives that these constructions cannot be modified by factor modifiers.

In sum, the semantic properties of demonstrative explicit equatives are a lot like those of sufficientive explicit equatives: they both receive weak interpretations, and are non-evaluative when formed with positive-antonym relative adjectives. But I've suggested that these similarities—and other superficial syntactic similarities, including the extraposition of the standard clause—belie a fundamental difference: that the parameter marker in sufficientive equatives is a degree quantifier, while the one in demonstrative equatives is a degree demonstrative. This accounts for the inability of the latter to be modified by factor modifiers like *twice* and *half*.

6   Conclusions

The main goal of this paper has been to replicate the successful descriptive and theoretical typologies of comparatives for equative constructions, the morphosyntactic and semantic siblings of comparatives. There are a number of clear descriptive parallels across the two constructions: for each, languages differ with respect to how and whether they mark the constructions' adjectival parameter and standard, but none mark the constructions' target of comparison. And there are a few strategies available for each sort of construction: both comparatives and equatives, cross-linguistically, can be formed with explicit predicates ('exceed' or 'equal') and with conjoined or juxtaposed clauses.

In terms of semantic theory, comparatives fall into (at least) two classes: explicit and implicit equatives. Explicit comparatives involve a parameter marker (something binding or modifying the adjective, like the English *-er* or *more*); implicit comparatives do not (Kennedy 2007a). While implicit comparatives may or may not need to be represented in a degree semantics, explicit comparatives have been analyzed as involving degree quantifiers, type $\langle\langle d,t\rangle,$ $\langle\langle d,t\rangle,t\rangle\rangle$, and therefore must be represented in a degree semantics.

Equatives, too, differ with respect to whether they involve a parameter marker (something binding or modifying the adjective, like the first of the two *as* morphemes in the English *Jane is as tall as Bill*). Of the implicit equatives, predicative equatives are diagnosable by virtue of the fact that they can only receive a strong, 'exactly' interpretation. And relative-based implicit equatives can be diagnosed because they are evaluative regardless of which adjective they're formed with. This is due to the fact that they are formed from positive constructions like *Jane is tall*, just like their comparative counterparts (Kennedy 2007a). I've argued that predicative equatives can be analyzed quite easily based on the literal semantics of their predicates, while implicit equatives can be analyzed as degree relative clauses, as Rett (2013) does for generic equatives, their morphologic twins.

But I've also argued that, in contrast to explicit comparatives, there are two distinct strategies of explicit equatives. The first, exemplified by the English *as ... as* construction, involves two markers: a parameter marker (the first *as*), diachronically related to a sufficientive morpheme like *so*; and a standard marker (the second *as*), a degree relativizer. In keeping with tradition, the parameter markers in these languages seem best analyzed as a degree quantifier, relating the sets of degrees denoted by the matrix and embedded clauses. As a result, and by design, these constructions are not evaluative; have a weak interpretation; and can be modified by factor modifiers like *twice* and *half*.

In contrast, I've identified an explicit equative strategy in a handful of languages—Catalan, Italian, Romanian, Slovenian, and Spanish—whose parameter markers are degree demonstratives (the Romance *tan-* or the Slavic *tak-*). These explicit equatives differ from the English (and broadly Germanic) explicit equative strategy in that they cannot be modified by factor modifiers. I've argued that their near-similarity can be explained compositionally: these demonstrative explicit equatives are formed quite transparently from a degree demonstrative and a degree relative clause. This explains why these constructions are non-evaluative and receive weak interpretations; it also explains, I argue, why they cannot be modified by factor modifiers.

There's an interesting question of why there are two types of explicit equative strategies, but only one type of explicit comparative strategy. This is consistent with the broader typological claim that there are a wider variety of equative strategies of any sort than there are comparative strategies of any sort. It's possible that the equative relationship is more unmarked than the comparative semantically. In addition to being lexically encoded (in predicative comparatives or equatives) or functionally encoded in a quantifier (in explicit comparatives and sufficientive explicit equatives) we know, independently of equative constructions, that two entities can be equated by coreference (as in demonstrative explicit equatives); copredication (as in implicit equatives); and by mere juxtaposition (using something like the discourse coherence relation 'parallel,' Kehler 2002). In a perspective reminiscent of the morphological work in Bobaljik (2012), this suggests a prospective typology in which if a language uses a degree quantifier to form an equative it uses one to form a comparative, but not necessarily vice-versa.

7 Appendix: Relative Equatives

Below is a table of the three subtypes of relative equatives, based on that in Haspelmath & Buchholz (1998) (p. 292) and on my own data. In some places, my classification of languages into the latter two categories is speculative (i.e. a morphological decision, rather than a decision based on semantic diagnostics).

	Parameter marker	Standard marker
SM-only relative equatives		
Albanian		*si*
Bulgarian		*kato*
Greek, Modern		*san*
Imbabura Quechua		*shna*
Italian		*come*
Serbo-Croatian		*kao*
Syrian Arabic		*mitl*
Demonstrative relative equatives		
Armenian	*aynpes*	*inčpes*
Catalan	*tan*	*com*
Czech	*tak*	*jako*
Friulian	*tant*	*che*
Greek, Modern	*tóso*	*óso*
Hungarian	*annyira*	*mint*
Italian	*tanto*	*quanto*

(cont.)

	Parameter marker	Standard marker
Lithuanian	*toks/taip*	*kaip*
Occitan	*tan*	*coma*
Polish	*tak samo*	*jak*
Portuguese	*tão*	*como*
Romanian	*tot*	*ca*
Russian	*tak(oj) že*	*kak*
Slovak	*taká*	*ako*
Slovene	*tako*	*kot*
Sorbian	*tak*	*kaž*
Spanish	*tan*	*como*

Sufficientive relative equatives		
Dutch	*zo*	*als*
English	*as*	*as*
Finnish	*niin*	*kuin*
French	*aussi*	*que*
Friulian	*oussi*	*come/tanche*
Georgian	*ise(ti)ve*	*rogorc*
German	*so*	*wie*
Hungarian	*olyan*	*mint*
Punjabi	*ónna*	*jínnaa*
Swedish	*så*	*som*
Yiddish	*azoy*	*vi*

Some specific examples are below.

(91) *La meva germana ès tan bonica com tú.*   Catalan
 the my sister is so(PM) pretty how(SM) you
 'My sister is as pretty as you.' (HB 291)

(92) *Suomalaiset eivät anna kättä niin paljon kuin*
 Finns NEG.3sg shake hand so(PM) much how(SM)
 keskieurooppalaiset.   Finnish
 Central.Europeans
 'Finns don't shake hands as much as Central Europeans.' (HB 287)

(93) *Čemi da   isetive lamazi -a rogore   šen.*   *Georgian*
     my sister so(PM) pretty -is how(SM) you
     'My sister is as pretty as you.' (HB 287)

(94) *I adjelfí mu ine tóso   ómorfi óso   kj   esí.*   *Modern Greek*
     the sister my is so(PM) pretty how(SM) also you
     'My sister is as pretty as you.' (HB 287)

(95) *Claudia tam   docta   est quam   Julius.*   *Latin*
     C   so(PM) learned is how(SM) J
     'Claudia is as learned as Julius.' (HB 287)

(96) *Šiandien taip   šalta kaip   vakar*   *Lithuanian*
     today   so(PM) cold how(SM) yesterday
     'Today is as cold as yesterday.' (HB 284)

(97) *A minha irmã é tão   bonita quanto   você.*   *Portuguese*
     the my   sister is so(PM) pretty how(SM) you
     'My sister is as pretty as you.' (HB 286)

(98) *Ó ónna   caŋgaa ai jínnaa   ó daa pràà.*   *Punjabi*
     he so(PM) good is how(SM) he GEN brother
     'He is as good as his brother.' (HB 286)

(99) *Moja sestra je tako čedna kot   ti.*   *Slovene*
     my   sister is so pretty how you
     'My sister is as pretty as you.' (HB 288)

Acknowledgements

Many thanks to my consultants: Daniela Culinovic for Croatian; Jos Tellings for Dutch and Imbabura Quichua; Peter Hallman for German and Syrian Arabic; Nicoletta Loccioni for Italian; Jinyoung Jo and Hendrik Kim for Korean; Ed Keenan for Malagasy; Adrian Brasoveanu for Romanian; Victoria Mateu for Catalan and Spanish; Ingvar Lofstedt for Swedish; and Sozen Oksan for Turkish. Thanks also to the audience at my October 3, 2018 UCLA Syntax Seminar presentation.

References

Bale, Alan. 2008. A universal scale of comparison. *Linguistics and Philosophy* 31. 1–55.

Beck, Sigrid, Sveta Krasikova, Daniel Fleischer, Remus Gergel, Stefan Hofstetter, Christiane Savelsberg, John Vanderelst & Elizabeth Villalta. 2009. Crosslinguistic variation in comparison constructions. In J. van Craenenbroeck (ed.), *Linguistic variation yearbook*.

Beck, Sigrid, Toshiko Oda & Koji Sugisaki. 2004. Parametric variation in the semantics of comparison: Japanese vs. English. *Journal of East Asian Linguistics* 13. 289–344.

Beltrama, Andrea & M. Ryan Bochnak. 2015. Intensification without degrees crosslinguistically. *Natural Language and Lingusitic Theory* 33. 843–879.

Bhatt, Rajesh & Roumyana Pancheva. 2004. Late merger of degree clauses. *Linguistic Inquiry* 35. 1–45.

Bhatt, Rajesh & Shoichi Takahashi. 2008. Direct comparisons: resurrecting the direct analysis of phrasal comparatives. In Masayuki Gibson & Tova Friedman (eds.), *Proceedings of SALT XVII*. CLC Publications.

Bhatt, Rajesh & Shoichi Takahashi. 2011. Reduced and unreduced phrasal comparatives. *Natural Language and Linguistic Theory* 29. 581–620.

Bobaljik, Jonathan. 2012. *Universals in comparative morphology: suppletion, superlatives, and the structure of words*. MIT Press.

Bochnak, M. Ryan. 2015a. Degree achievements in a degree-less language. In J. Pasquereau (ed.), *Proceedings of semantics of underrepresented languages of the Americas (SULA) 8*, 17–32.

Bochnak, M. Ryan. 2015b. The degree semantics parameter and cross-linguistic variation. *Semantics and Pragmatics* 8. 1–48.

Bochnak, M. Ryan & Elizabeth Bogal-Allbritten. 2015. Investigating gradable predicates, comparison, and degree constructions in underrepresented languages. In M. Ryan Bochnak & Lisa Matthewson (eds.), *Methodologies in semantic fieldwork*, 110–134. Oxford University Press.

Bowler, Margit. 2016. The status of degrees in Walpiri. In Mira Grubic & Anne Mucha (eds.), *Proceedings of the semantics of African, Asian and Austronesian languages 2*, 1–17. Universitatsverlag Potsdam.

Brasoveanu, Adrian. 2009. Comparative correlatives as anaphora to differentials. In *Proceedings of SALT XVIII*. CLC Publications.

Bresnan, Joan. 1973. Syntax of comparative clause construction in English. *Linguistic Inquiry* 4. 275–344.

Caponigro, Ivano. 2004. The semantic contribution of wh-words and type-shifts: evidence from free relatives crosslinguistically. In Robert Young (ed.), *Proceedings of SALT XIV*, 38–55. CLC Publications.

Chomsky, Noam. 1977. On *wh*-movement. In *Formal syntax*, 71–132. Academic Press.

Cresswell, Max. 1976. The semantics of degree. In B. Partee (ed.), *Montague grammar*. Academic Press.

Crnič, Luka & Danny Fox. 2019. Equatives and maximality. In Daniel Altshuler & Jessica Rett (eds.), *The semantics of focus, plurals, degrees, and times*. Springer.

Croft, William & D. Alan Cruse. 2004. *Cognitive linguistics*. Cambridge University Press.

Davidson, Donald. 1969. The individuation of events. In Nick Rescher (ed.), *Essays in honor of Carl G. Hempel*, 216–234. Reidel.

Hanink, Emily. 2018. *Structural sources of anaphora and sameness*. University of Chicago PhD Thesis.

Haspelmath, Martin & Oda Buchholz. 1998. Equative and similative constructions in the languages of Europe. In Johan van der Auwera & Dónall Ó. Baoill (eds.), *Adverbial constructions in the languages of Europe*, 277–334. Mouton de Gruyter.

Heim, Irene. 1985. Notes on comparatives and related matters. Ms., University of Texas, Austin.

Henkelmann, Peter. 2006. Constructions of equative comparison. *Sprachtypologie und Universallenforschung* 59(4). 370–398.

Horn, Laurence. 1972. *On the semantic properties of the logical operators in English*. University of California, Los Angeles PhD Thesis.

Jacobson, Pauline. 1995. On the quantificiational force of English free relatives. In Emmon Bach, Eloise Jelinek, Angelika Kratzer & Barbara Partee (eds.), *Quantification in natural languages*, 451–486. Kluwer.

Kehler, Andy. 2002. *Coherence, reference, and the theory of grammar*. CSLI Publications.

Kennedy, Chris. 2007a. Modes of comparison. In Malcolm Elliott, James Kirby, Osamu Sawada, Eleni Staraki & Suwon Yoon (eds.), *Proceedings of CLS 43*.

Kennedy, Chris & Louise McNally. 2005. Scale structure, degree modification and the semantic typology of gradable predicates. *Language* 81(2). 345–381.

Kennedy, Christopher. 1999. *Projecting the adjective: the syntax and semantics of gradability and comparison*. Garland Press.

Kennedy, Christopher. 2001. Polar opposition and the ontology of degrees. *Linguistics and Philosophy* 24. 33–70.

Kennedy, Christopher. 2007b. Vagueness and grammar: the semantics of relative and absolute gradable predicates. *Linguistics and Philosophy* 30. 1–45.

Klein, Ewan. 1980. A semantics for positive and comparative adjectives. *Linguistics and Philosophy* 4. 1–45.

Klein, Ewan. 1982. The interpretation of adjectival comparatives. *The Journal of Linguistics* 18. 113–136.

Kubota, Yusuke & Ai Matsui. 2010. Modes of comparison and Question under Discussion: evidence from "contrastive comparison" in Japanese. In Nan Li & David Lutz (eds.), *Proceedings of SALT 20*, 57–75. CLC Publications.

Landman, Fred. 2000. Predicate-argument mismatches and the adjectival theory of indefinites. In Martine Coene & Yves d'Hulst (eds.), *From NP to DP*, chap. 8, 211–237. John Benjamins.

Pancheva, Roumyana. 2006. Phrasal and clausal comparatives in Slavic. In James Lavine, Steven Franks, Mila Tasseva-Kurktchieva & Hana Filip (eds.), *Formal approaches to Slavic linguistics 14: the Princeton Meeting*, 236–257.

Partee, Barbara & Mats Rooth. 1983. Generalized conjunction and type ambiguity. In Rainer Bäuerle, Christoph Schwarze & Arnim von Stechow (eds.), *Meaning, use and interpretation of language*, 361–383. Berlin: de Gruyter.

Pearson, Hazel. 2010. How to do comparison in a language without degrees. In Viola Schmitt & Sarah Zobel (eds.), *Proceedings of sinn und bedeutung 14*, 356–372.

Rett, Jessica. 2007. How *many* maximizes in the Balkan Sprachbund. In Masayuki Gibson & Jonathan Howell (eds.), *Proceedings of SALT XVI*. CLC Publications.

Rett, Jessica. 2008. *Degree modification in natural language*. Rutgers University dissertation.

Rett, Jessica. 2013. Similatives and the argument structure of verbs. *Natural Language and Linguistic Theory* 31. 1101–1137.

Rett, Jessica. 2014. The polysemy of measurement. *Lingua* 143. 242–266.

Rett, Jessica. 2015a. Measure phrase equatives and modified numerals. *Journal of Semantics* 32. 425–475.

Rett, Jessica. 2015b. *The semantics of evaluativity*. Oxford University Press.

Rett, Jessica. 2018. The semantics of *many, much, few* and *little*. *Language and Linguistics Compass* 12. 1–18.

Roberts, Craige. 1996. Information structure in discourse: towards an integrated formal theory of pragmatics. *OSU Working Papers in Linguistics* 49. 91–136.

van der Sandt, Robert. 1992. Presupposition projection as anaphora resolution. *Journal of Semantics* 9. 333–377.

Sapir, Edward. 1944. On grading: a study in semantics. *Philosophy of Science* 2. Reprinted in Sapir 1949, 93–116.

Sawada, Osamu. 2009. Pragmatic aspects of implicit comparison: an economy-based approach. *Journal of Pragmatics* 41. 1079–1103.

Schwarzschild, Roger. 2005. Measure phrases as modifiers of adjectives. *Recherches Linguistiques de Vincennes* 34. 207–228.

Schwarzschild, Roger. 2008. The semantics of the comparative and other degree constructions. *Language and Linguistics Compass* 2(2). 308–331.

Schwarzschild, Roger. 2013. Degrees and segments. In Todd Snider (ed.), *Proceedings of SALT XXIII*, 2122–238. CLC Publications.

Solt, Stephanie. 2009. *The semantics of adjectives of quantity*. City University of New York PhD Thesis.

Solt, Stephanie. 2015. Q-adjectives and the semantics of quantity. *Journal of Semantics* 32. 221–273.

Stassen, Leon. 1985. *Comparison and Universal Grammar: an essay in Universal Grammar*. Basil Blackwell.

Syrett, Kristen, Chris Kennedy & Jeff Lidz. 2010. Meaning and context in children's understanding of gradable adjectives. *Journal of Semantics* 27. 1–35.

Ultan, Russell. 1972. Some features of basic comparative constructions. In *Stanford working papers on language universals*, vol. 9, 117–162.

CHAPTER 6

Compounded Scales

Alan Bale

1 Introduction

Most semantic analyses of gradable adjectives have assumed that there is a direct link between adjectives and degrees, or alternatively between adjectives and delineations, extents, or intervals which exhibit many of the same formal properties as degrees (see Bartsch & Vennemann 1972, Seuren 1973, 1978, Cresswell 1976, Klein 1980, 1982, 1991, Hellan 1981, von Stechow 1984a,b, Heim 1985, 2000, Bierwisch 1987, Kennedy 1999, Hackl 2000, Kennedy & McNally 2005, Schwarzschild & Wilkinson 2002, Fox & Hackl 2006 among others—a notable exception is Wheeler III 1972). However, there are significant problems with this hypothesis when it comes to providing a compositional interpretation for comparative sentences that involve conjunction like those in (1).

(1)   a. Seymour is more handsome and talented than Patrick is.
       b. This floorboard is less long and wide than that floorboard is.

The problems are two-fold. First, adjectives like *handsome* and *talented* are not commensurable—they involve different types of degrees. This incommensurability becomes problematic when the two adjectives are combined by *and*. Second, even with adjectives that are commensurable (such as *long* and *wide*), interpreting the two adjectives as directly involving degrees yields truth conditions—as I will show in section 2—that are dependent on only one of the adjectives. In (1b), such truth conditions would be dependent solely on measurements of width—measurements of length would be inconsequential. Obviously such an analysis is not empirically supported.

One alternative to linking adjectives directly to degrees is to interpret them as more primitive building blocks from which scales and degrees can be constructed (see Bale 2006, 2011). This paper outlines such an alternative. It proposes that gradable adjectives should be treated as binary relations between individuals, not between individuals and degrees. As noted by Cresswell (1976) and Klein (1991) among others, such relations can be converted into scales as long as they are transitive and asymmetric. Furthermore, this conversion can be incorporated into the interpretation of the comparative morphemes (*more* and *less*) independent of the adjectives. Unlike the traditional degree analysis, this type of interpretation provides adequate truth conditions for the sentences in (1). Given the boolean interpretation of *and* as intersection, the conjunction of the two binary relations is itself a binary relation. This compounded binary relation can be converted into a scale by the comparative morphemes in much the same way that the non-compounded relations are converted. The result is a comparison that involves a compounded scale (a scale that encodes two gradable properties). Such comparisons accurately account for the truth conditions of the sentences in (1).

The outline of this paper is as follows. In section 2, I outline why the traditional degree analysis cannot straightforwardly account for sentences like those in (1). In section 3, I discuss whether gapping might be able to explain the interpretation of conjoined adjectives. Ultimately, I demonstrate that gapping does not make the correct empirical predictions. In section 4, I show how interpreting adjectives as binary relations provides a better account of conjoined adjectives. However, there are problems for this account as well, specifically when it comes to data with differentials and disjunction. In section 5, I discuss this type of data as well as a possible alternative solution which would involve interpreting *and* as a non-boolean operator (see Winter 1995). I further demonstrate that even if this alternative is viable, it cannot account for all of the data and thus, derived compounded-scale might be needed nonetheless. Finally, section 6 concludes this paper.

2 The Degree Approach to Conjoined Adjectives

Broadly speaking (and abstracting away from many important details), there are two main hypotheses about how adjectives connect degrees to entities like people, tables and couches: the measurement-function hypothesis (Bartsch & Vennemann 1972, Kennedy 1999) and the degree-relation hypothesis (Cresswell 1976). As demonstrated in this section, both approaches run into problems when trying to account for sentences with conjoined adjectives. However, before discussing such difficulties, let me first give a rough outline of both of these theories.

Kennedy (1999), following Bartsch & Vennemann (1972), suggests that adjectives should be interpreted as functions from entities to degrees. With such an interpretation, an adjective like *long* can apply directly to an entity like a couch yielding a measurement of length. In this type of theory, sentences like (2) would have truth conditions like those in (3), where t is the table, c is the couch, MAX is a function that picks out the greatest degree from a set, and $>_m$ and $\leq_m$ are the ordering relations.[1]

(2) This table is longer than the couch is.

(3) $\text{MAX}(\{d : d \leq_m [\![long]\!](t)\}) >_m \text{MAX}(\{d : d \leq_m [\![long]\!](c)\})$
  $= [\![long]\!](t) >_m [\![long]\!](c)$

These truth conditions state that the table is longer than the couch if and only if the measurement of the table's length is greater than the couch's.

In a slight variation of a similar approach, Cresswell (1976) proposes that adjectives should be interpreted as relations between individuals and degrees. For example, an adjective such as *long* can be interpreted as a set of ordered pairs where the first member is an entity and the second is a degree. With *long*, an entity is related to a degree if and only if the the measurement of the entity's length is equal to or greater than that degree.[2] Given this interpretation, a sentence like (2) can be assigned the truth conditions in (4).

(4) $\text{MAX}(\{d : [\![long]\!](t, d)\}) >_m \text{MAX}(\{d : [\![long]\!](c, d)\})$

Similar to (3), these truth conditions state that the table is longer than the couch if and only if the largest degree representing the table's length is greater than the largest degree representing the couch's length.

For the remainder of this section, the notation '*x is d-*ADJ' will be used to represent both the measurement function and degree-relation hypotheses. Thus, when considering the measure function approach '*x is d-*ADJ' will translate as $d \leq_{adj} [\![\text{ADJ}]\!](x)$. On the other hand, when considering the degree relation approach, '*x is d-*ADJ' will translate as $[\![\text{ADJ}]\!](x, d)$.

With this notational convention in mind, reconsider the two comparatives in (1), repeated in (5) below.

---

[1] The truth conditions of this simple sentence could also be represented by comparing the results of the measure functions directly. In fact this is what Bartsch & Vennemann (1972) do. However, as discussed in Kennedy (1999) abstracting a degree variable and forming a set is needed to account for more complex sentences.
[2] Cresswell actually proposes that the relation of entities to degrees is one to one. An entity is related to a degree if and only if the individual's length is equal to that degree. However, others who adopt this type of interpretation usually adopt the relation specified here (see von von Stechow 1984a).

(5) a. Seymour is more handsome and talented than Patrick is.
    b. This floorboard is less long and wide than that floorboard is.

The sentence in (5a) can be roughly paraphrased as stating that Seymour is more handsome than Patrick and more talented. The sentence in (5b) can be roughly paraphrased as stating that "this floorboard" is less long than "that floorboard" and also less wide. Applying the degree analysis to these sentences in the same way that we applied it to the sentences without conjoined adjectives would yield truth-conditions like the ones given in (6a) and (6b). (Note, for the sake of simplicity, we will represent the truth conditions of *less* using the "less-than" symbol instead of the "greater-than" symbol.)

(6) a. MAX({d : Seymour is d-handsome and d-talented}) > MAX({d : Patrick is d-handsome and d-talented})
    b. MAX({d : this floorboard is d-long and d-wide}) < MAX({d : that floorboard is d-long and d-wide})

However these truth conditions do not accurately reflect speaker intuitions. The problem for (6a) is that the set of degrees would be empty. To put it intuitively, there are no degrees such that Seymour is handsome to that degree and talented to that degree. Degrees of handsomeness and talent are assumed to belong to different scales. To put it more formally, if *and* is interpreted as intersection (Boolean meet) then when the two adjectives are conjoined the result would be an empty set. The interpretations of the adjectives would have disjoint co-domains and hence the ordered pairs that represent the relation or function would also be disjoint. The emptiness of the conjoined adjectives would trivially entail that Seymour is not related to any degree within the conjoined adjectives. Hence, the function that picks out the maximal degree would have nothing to pick-out. As a result the sentence should be odd or undefined. Yet the sentence in (5a) is perfectly interpretable.

The problem becomes even more interesting when we consider adjectives that are commensurable such as the ones in (5b). Although we no longer necessarily have a problem with the empty set as we did with (5a),[3] the interpretation assigned to (5b) is nonetheless infelicitous. Consider the formula in (6b). Unlike the previous formula, there are degrees that are both degrees of length

---

[3] This is not quite true. If the relation between individuals and degrees is one to one (instead of one to many) then the result of intersecting *long* and *wide* would still be empty, unless there are individuals that are equally as wide as they are long. However, for the sake of argument, I will focus on the *one-to-many* interpretations of the adjectives.

and width. Thus there are degrees d where "this floorboard" is d-long and d-wide. In fact, if we assume that, like all floorboards, "this floorboard" is longer than it is wide, it follows that for any degree d such that "this floorboard" is d-wide, it is also d-long (although the opposite does not hold). Hence, the set $\{d :$ this floorboard is d-long and d-wide$\}$ is equivalent to the set $\{d :$ this floorboard is d-wide$\}$. By similar reasoning, the set $\{d :$ that floorboard is d-long and d-wide$\}$ is equivalent to the set $\{d :$ that floorboard is d-wide$\}$. To put this in more formal terms, the intersection of the relations *wide* and *long* when restricted to floorboards is identical to the relation *wide* when restricted to floorboards. As a result of these two equivalences, one can replace the truth conditions in (6b) with the equivalent formula in (7).

(7) MAX($\{d :$ this floorboard is d-wide$\}$) < MAX($\{d :$ that floorboard is d-wide$\}$)

However, the formula in (7) also represents the truth conditions for (8).

(8) This floorboard is less wide than that floorboard is.

In other words, both the formulae in (6b) and (7) describe truth conditions that are based on a comparison of width only. Length is not relevant. This is obviously a problem. Intuitively, (5b) expresses a comparison based on both length and width.

In summary, the problem for the degree approach to adjectives is two-fold. Combining two adjectives directly with Boolean *and* either predicts that sentences should be anomalous (when they are intuitively perfectly well-formed) or that the truth conditions should be based on only one of the gradable properties denoted by the adjectives.

3   Reasons to Think There Is No Ellipsis

One potential solution to the problem described in section 2 is to hypothesize that the conjunction is not conjoining two adjectives but rather is conjoining two comparative expressions. For example, a sentence such as (9a) might only differ from (9b) in that the second instance of *more* in the latter sentence is unpronounced due to some kind of gapping, otherwise the two sentences are syntactically and semantically identical.[4]

---

4   For exposition purposes, gapping will be discussed as if it involves elision, as hypothesized

(9) a. Seymour is more handsome and more talented than Patrick is.
    b. Seymour is more handsome and talented than Patrick is.

However, there are problems with a gapping analysis. In other types of gapping constructions, the addition of adjuncts and other material after the gapped and antecedent segments does not affect the acceptability of the sentences (as long as parallelism is maintained between the two conjoined phrases). Consider the sentences in (10).

(10) a. John fought with Betty and Fred with Suzan.
     b. John fought with Betty on Tuesday and Fred with Suzan on Wednesday.
     c. John fought with Betty in the mountain park on Tuesday and Fred with Suzan in the fountain park on Wednesday.

The sentence in (10a) is a typical example of gapping. The sentences in (10b) and (10c) are identical to (10a) except for the addition of time and/or location adverbials after the antecedent segment and the gapped segment respectively. This additional material does not affect the acceptability of the sentences. In fact, for some English speakers who find gapped-constructions slightly anomalous, such additions improve acceptability.

Other potential examples of gapping demonstrate similar kinds of effects. For example, consider the sentences in (11).

(11) a. This fork and knife are gifts from my mother.
     b. This fork and this knife are gifts from my mother.

As pointed out to me by Brendan Gillon (p.c.), there is some evidence supporting the hypothesis that (11a) is syntactically and semantically identical to (11b) except for an unpronounced determiner in the first sentence. The conjoined phrase in (11a) yields plural agreement when combined with an auxiliary: in (11a) the auxiliary is *are*. This is a common property of conjoined noun phrases, as shown in (11b). Furthermore the determiner in (11a) is singular. If the phrase *knife and fork* were responsible for the plural agreement marking on the auxiliary, then one would expect this conjoined noun phrase to combine with a plural determiner like *these*. The singular marking on the determiner in (11a) suggests that the determiner *this* is combining with the singular noun *fork*

---

by Ross (1970), Hartmann (2001) among others. However, the criticisms discussed in this section are theory independent. They are equally applicable to a theory such as Johnson's, 2009, which relies on movement and variable extraction.

rather than a conjoined phrase *fork and knife*. All of this evidence is consistent with the hypothesis that the sentence in (11a) has two demonstrative determiners underlyingly (for an alternative analysis, see Link 1983).

Given these facts, consider the sentences in (12).

(12) a. This fork and knife that I used this morning are gifts from my mother.
 b. This fork that I used yesterday and knife that I used this morning are gifts from my mother.

In (12a), the relative clause restrictor appears after the second noun in the conjunction. It is understood as restricting both of the nouns that precede it. This is similar to the *than*-clause in (5) which appears after the two adjectives. This similarity is even more striking given other parallels between *than*-clauses and relative clause restrictors (see Bhatt & Pancheva 2004). Notice that the elision of the determiner in (12b) remains acceptable when another relative clause restrictor is inserted immediately after the first noun.

These facts about gapping constructions contrast with the comparative constructions discussed earlier. If sentences such as (1) above—repeated in (13)—contain an elided comparative in the second half of the conjunction, then it would be expected that the addition of other material between the antecedent and the remnant would not affect the acceptability of the sentences.

(13) a. Seymour is more handsome and talented than Patrick is.
 b. This floorboard is less long and wide than that floorboard is.

This prediction is not borne out. Although the sentences in (13a) and (14a) are completely acceptable, the sentence in (14b) is not as acceptable.

(14) a. Seymour is more handsome than Dan is and more talented than Patrick is.
 b. ?Seymour is more handsome than Dan is and talented than Patrick is.

Most speakers find the sentence in (14b) to be odd. A few speakers accept the sentence only with a marked intonational pattern (a slight pause before the second adjective followed by heavy emphasis). By *marked* I mean that this intonational pattern is not required for the acceptability of (13a). This is an important point and bears repeating. The sentences in (13) do not require a pause before pronouncing the second adjective nor do they require that any intonational emphasis be put on the second adjective. Insofar as speakers accept (14b), a pause is required as well as intonational emphasis.

Similar to the sentence in (14b), speakers find the sentence in (15b) odd despite the acceptability of (13b) and (15a).

(15) a. This floorboard is less long than the floorboard by the table is and less wide than the floorboard by the chair is
b. ??This floorboard is less long than the floorboard by the table is and wide than the floorboard by the chair is

Unlike in (14b), a change in the intonational pattern does not have an effect on the acceptability of (15b). In fact, this seems to be the case in general with *less*-comparatives. Consider the sentences in (16a).

(16) a. Jen is less intelligent and beautiful than Morag is.
b. Jen is less intelligent than Betty is and less beautiful than Morag is.
c. ??Jen is less intelligent than Betty is and beautiful than Morag is.

As with the sentences in (15), the sentences in (16) demonstrate that it is possible to have an extra *than*-clause inserted after the first adjective, but only when the comparative morpheme *less* is repeated in the second clause (hence the contrast between (16b) and (16c)).

The degraded acceptability of (14b), (15b) and (16c) is unexpected if gapping were involved in these types of constructions. One might object at this point that comparing *than*-clauses to time adverbials and relative clauses is a bit misleading. Clearly there is a difference between these types of constructions. One might even object that adverbials and relative clauses are truly optional unlike *than*-clauses. However as those of us who work on comparatives know well, this is not a completely accurate description. *Than*-clauses are in fact syntactically optional. For example, consider the second sentences in (17).

(17) a. Morag is beautiful. However, Jen is more beautiful.
b. Morag is tall. However, Jen is taller.

These sentences have comparatives without any *than*-clause. The object of comparison is provided contextually via the preceding sentence. *Than*-clauses are more like adjuncts than it would first appear. However, the point about gapping and comparatives can be made even without using *than*-clauses. If we use gradable properties that can vary over time or space (e.g., aggression and carefulness), then we can construct examples using the same kind of adjuncts that were used in prototypical gapping constructions. Consider the sentences in (18).

(18) a. Bob is an inexperienced skier. He is not very careful on the sharp turns and not very comfortable on the moguls but ...
b. ... Jen is less careful on the sharp turns and less comfortable on the moguls.
c. ??... Jen is less careful on the sharp turns and comfortable on the moguls.

Unlike (18b), it is extremely difficult to get a reading of (18c) that implies that Jen is less comfortable than Bob on the Moguls. As with the previous examples, this oddity would not be expected if gapping or ellipsis were involved.

In addition to the evidence above, there is at least one other piece of evidence that speaks against a gapping analysis. In prototypical gapping constructions (constructions that involve the elision of an auxiliary), comparative morphemes cannot be elided without also eliding the adjectives they modify. Consider the sentences in (19) where '_' marks the gap.

(19) a. Donald and Patrick are quite handsome and talented but [Seymour is more handsome than Donald] and [Bill _ more talented than Patrick].
b. Donald and Patrick are quite talented but [Seymour is more talented than Donald] and [Bill _ than Patrick].
c. *Donald and Patrick are quite handsome and talented but [Seymour is more handsome than Donald] and [Bill _ talented than Patrick].

The sentence in (19b), where the comparative morpheme is elided along with the adjective it modifies, is as acceptable as the sentence in (19a), where only the copula is elided. However, the sentence (19c), where only the comparative morpheme is elided, is unacceptable. It appears as if canonical gapping constructions do not permit the elision of the comparative morpheme without also eliding the adjective. A gapping analysis of the sentence in (13) would have to hypothesize that such an elision would be permissible.

In summary, there are two challenges for a gapping analysis of sentences with conjoined gradable adjectives as in (1). First, unlike other gapping constructions the addition of adjuncts and other material between the two conjoined adjectives decreases the acceptability of the sentence. Second, in canonical gapping constructions, the comparative morphemes cannot be elided without also eliding the adjective.

4 Adjectives as Binary Relations

One alternative to interpreting adjectives as directly involving degrees is to interpret them as relations between two individuals. This alternative is foreshadowed in the work of Cresswell (1976), Klein (1991) and Bale (2006, 2008), and explicitly adopted in Bale (2011). Certain types of relations (namely transitive, asymmetric relations)[5] can be used to create scales. These scales, in turn, can be used as a basis for comparison in comparative sentences. In the current context, the importance of this alternative is that it provides a straightforward account of sentences with conjoined adjectives. The result of intersecting two transitive, asymmetric relations is another transitive, asymmetric relation. The intersected relation can be used to create a scale that provides adequate truth conditions for sentences with conjoined adjectives.[6]

4.1 The Basic Idea

Cresswell (1976), basing much of his discussion on measurement theory in mathematics (see, for example, Krantz, Luce & Tversky 1971), demonstrates that quotient structures—partial orders of sets—can be built from more basic relations and, furthermore that these quotient structures can serve as scales in the analysis of degree constructions.[7] The basic idea can be best demonstrated with an example.

Cresswell proposed that gradable adjectives are associated with an underlying binary relation, such as the following relation which expresses a strict weak ordering based on beauty (*strict weak orders* are transitive and asymmetric).

$\{\langle x, y \rangle : x$ has more beauty than $y\}$.

For convenience, let's label this relation as β.[8] By taking the quotient structure of this basic binary relation, a linear scale can be formed. Forming such a scale (aka, quotient structure) involves at least three steps.

---

5 Alternatively, the relations could be transitive and reflexive as discussed in Cresswell 1976 and Klein 1991 and proposed in Bale 2011.
6 It should be noted that much of the discussion in this section is non-coincidentally similar to the discussion of multidimensional adjectives like *clever* in Klein 1980.
7 An alternative way of deriving scalar meanings based on the same ideas expressed in this section—modulo the incorporation of possible worlds and the idea of a possible individual (pairings between worlds and entities)—is discussed in Schwarzschild, this volume. See also Schwarzschild 2013.
8 A quick note is required here to dispel a potential source of confusion. On the surface, from the way the relation β is stated and describe, it might seem a bit circular to use the language of comparison (words like *more*) to describe a relation that eventually will be used to provide a semantics for comparison. However, it should be kept in mind that the comparative language

1. **Form equivalence classes based on the original binary relation.** This can be done by associating each member in the domain with a set of elements that are indistinguishable from it, relative to the binary relation. Two elements x and y are indistinguishable if and only if there is no z that bears a relation to x but not y or vice versa (i.e., given a binary relation β, x and y are indistinguishable iff $\neg \exists z . (\langle x, z \rangle \in \beta \wedge \langle y, z \rangle \notin \beta) \vee (\langle z, x \rangle \in \beta \wedge \langle z, y \rangle \notin \beta) \vee (\langle y, z \rangle \in \beta \wedge \langle x, z \rangle \notin \beta) \vee (\langle z, y \rangle \in \beta \wedge \langle z, x \rangle \notin \beta))$.
2. **Use the set of equivalence classes to form the domain of the scale/quotient structure.** The domain of the quotient structure is the set of all equivalence classes that can be formed from the members of the original binary relation.
3. **Rank the equivalence classes in a way that is congruent to the original binary relation.** For any two equivalence classes X and Y, X is ranked above Y in the quotient structure iff for every member z of X and w of Y, $\langle z, w \rangle$ is a member of the original binary relation.

Consider the following example. Let's begin by outlining a particular transitive and asymmetric relation. To save time and space, such a relation can be specified graphically, as it is in the far left hand graph labelled as $>_\beta$ in (20).

(20)

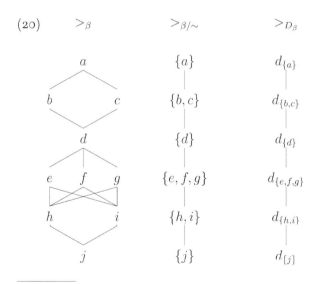

is being used to describe a non-linguistic concept. Although the comparative-language is useful in describing this concept, such a language is by no means necessary for having this concept. Even those without language (monkeys, cats, dogs) are able to compare two objects or individuals in terms of a certain property (to tell which food bowl has more, or which potential mates are more suitable/beautiful). The relation between individuals is formed from this language-independent concept of comparison rather than from the language dependent phrase *has more beauty than*. There is no circularity in basing a scale used to interpret comparative sentences on such an underlying concept (see Bale 2008 for a discussion).

The graph $>_\beta$ in (20) can be read in the following way. For any two members of the graph, call them x and y, if x appears above y and there is a downward path of lines from x to y, then x has as much beauty as y but not vice versa (i.e., $\langle x, y \rangle \in \beta$ but $\langle y, x \rangle \notin \beta$). For example, according to the graph in $>_\beta$, f has more beauty than h, i and j, (i.e., $\langle f, h \rangle \in \beta$, $\langle f, i \rangle \in \beta$, and $\langle f, j \rangle \in \beta$), but not more beauty than a, b, c, d, e, and g. However, only a, b, c and d have more beauty than f. e and g are not related to f (i.e., $\langle f, g \rangle \notin \beta$, $\langle g, f \rangle \notin \beta$, $\langle f, e \rangle \notin \beta$ and $\langle e, f \rangle \notin \beta$).

To construct a quotient structure from β (represented as $>_{\beta/\sim}$ above), one first needs to determine what the relevant set of equivalence classes is. As specified in step one, this is done by forming sets that contain all the members of the domain that are indistinguishable from one another. For example, e, f and g are indistinguishable since they relate to all other members of the domain in the same way in terms of beauty (only a, b, c and d have more beauty and only h, i and j have less beauty). Thus, they are put into one set $\{e, f, g\}$. Similarly, b and c are related to all other members of the domain in the same way and hence they are also put into one set $\{b, c\}$. However, a is the only element that that has more beauty than b or c (i.e., there is no $z \neq a$ such that $\langle z, b \rangle \in \beta$ and $\langle z, c \rangle \in \beta$), hence a is put into a set by itself (i.e., $\{a\}$ is an equivalence class). With respect to β, the set of equivalence classes would be $\{\{a\}, \{b, c\}, \{d\}, \{e, f, g\}, \{h, i\}, \{j\}\}$.

Once the set of equivalence classes is determined, the next step is to order these equivalence classes so that they are congruent to the original relation. This can be achieved by ordering the equivalence classes according to how their members relate to one another. If the members of one equivalence class A have more beauty than the members of another equivalence class B, then the set A is ordered above the set B. For example, since $\langle b, e \rangle$, $\langle b, f \rangle$, $\langle b, g \rangle$, $\langle c, e \rangle$, $\langle c, f \rangle$, and $\langle c, g \rangle$ are all members of β, the equivalence class $\{b, c\}$ is ranked above (is greater than) the equivalence class $\{e, f, g\}$. This resulting order of equivalence classes, one above the other, creates a scale which characterizes the quotient structure. For example, the relation β creates the quotient structure under the label $>_{\beta/\sim}$ in (20). These sets (or equivalence classes) can serve as degrees in this linear scale of beauty. For ease of notation, one can replace the set representation of the equivalence classes with d's and subscripts just to make the scalar use of these quotient structures clear. Klein (1991) sometimes follows this convention and I will do so here, as shown by the scale under the label $>_{D_\beta}$ in (20). Comparisons can be made through this scale using a semantics involving the manipulation of degrees without necessarily having to hypothesize language independent scales. Although the underlying relations are independent of language, the scales are derived from these simpler concepts.

Although Cresswell hypothesizes that these types of scales are only associated with adjectives that are not linked to an independently justified measurement system (the vast majority of adjectives as it so happens), it is clear that his derivation can be extended to all adjectives. Just as one can have relations based on underlying concepts of who/what has more beauty than another and who/what has more intelligence than another, one can also have underlying relations based upon who/what has more length than another or who/what has more width than another. The only difference between the former types of relations and the latter types is that relations based on width and height might have measurements in their domain as well as people and things, especially since one can be taller than six feet and six feet can be taller than five feet etc. In fact, one can manipulate the participation of measurements in the relation (and hence the equivalence classes) to provide a semantics for direct comparisons (*John is taller than Bill is wide*) and differentials (*John is two feet taller than Fred*). I will forgo the details for now, but the curious reader should read the discussion in Bale (2006, 2008) for some details on direct comparisons (see also the discussion in Klein 1991).[9]

4.2 Compounded Scales

Cresswell's (1976) idea about forming scales from relations can also be used to form scales from the intersection of two relations. For the purpose of this discussion, let's call such scales *compounded scales*. The key to forming compounded scales is that intersected relations preserve asymmetry and transitivity. Such intersected relations can then be converted into quotient structures just like the non-intersected relations. In this section, I first discuss the meaning of intersected relations before discussing how compounded scales can be built from such intersections.

To simplify matters somewhat, in this section and the rest of the paper I will assume contexts where all individuals are distinct from others in terms of the

---

[9] The fundamental concept of such a manipulation is simple. One can provide a semantics for differentials by calculating the difference between two measurements that are in two different equivalence classes, the equivalence classes containing the comparative subject and the comparative object respectively. One can provide a semantics for direct comparison by manipulating the fact that adjectives like *long* and *wide* are associated with the same measurement scale. The equivalence classes for height and width will be ordered with respect to the same measurement scale. Thus the derived scales will be isomorphic to one another as well as to the measurement scale. This isomorphism allows for a comparison by measurement. See Bale 2006 for details. For an alternative approach to differentials that is also compatible with interpreting adjectives as binary relations, see the vector analysis discussed by Schwarzschild in this volume.

basic gradable properties being considered. For example, every one will be distinct in length, width, beauty and intelligence. This will simplify the representations of the relations slightly and will also simplify the quotient structures. In fact, since every individual forms its own equivalence class (due to its distinctness), the quotient structures will be isomorphic to the underlying relation. I believe that this simplification will allow for a clearer understanding of what the intersection of two relations looks like.

To begin, let's consider the two relations η and τ as defined in (21).

(21) a. $\eta = \{\langle x,y \rangle : x$ is more handsome than $y\}$
b. $\tau = \{\langle x,y \rangle : x$ has more talent than $y\}$

Since these two relations have similar domains (whatever has handsomeness to a certain extent also has talent to a certain extent), they can be non-trivially intersected. The result of this intersection can be characterized as follows.

(22) $\langle x,y \rangle \in (\eta \cap \tau)$ iff $(\langle x,y \rangle \in \eta) \wedge (\langle x,y \rangle \in \tau)$

In other words, x is related to y through the intersected relation $(\eta \cap \tau)$ if and only if (i) x is more handsome than y and (ii) x has more talent than y. If either of these conditions fail then $\langle x,y \rangle$ is not a member of the intersection $(\eta \cap \tau)$.

It is important to note that since η and τ are transitive and asymmetric relations, so is their intersection. This can be shown by the following reasoning:

(23) a. **The intersection is asymmetric**: If x and y are both in the domain of η and τ then, by definition of asymmetry, it cannot be the case that both $\langle x,y \rangle$ and $\langle y,x \rangle$ are members of η. (Likewise for τ.) Hence, it cannot be the case that both $\langle x,y \rangle$ and $\langle y,x \rangle$ are in the intersection of η and τ. Thus, the intersection is asymmetric.
b. **The intersection is transitive**: Suppose that $\langle x,y \rangle$ and $\langle y,z \rangle$ are members of the intersected relation. By definition of intersection it follows that $\langle x,y \rangle$ and $\langle y,z \rangle$ are members of both η and τ. Since η and τ are transitive, $\langle x,z \rangle$ must be members of both η and τ. As a consequence $\langle x,z \rangle$ must be a member of the intersected relation. Hence the intersected relation is transitive.

Since taking the quotient structure of this relation preserves asymmetry and transitivity, it has all the properties necessary for forming a scale (although critically, the intersected relation need not be connected, more on this below).

COMPOUNDED SCALES

Having described the general outline, let's see how this works with a specific example. Consider a context where there are eight individuals represented by the letters *a* through *h*. Now their ranking in terms of handsomeness follows their ranking in terms of the alphabet: *a* is more handsome than *b*, *b* is more handsome than *c* and so on and so forth. Their ranking in terms of talent is a little more arbitrary. Using arrows to represent the relation of being more talented, consider the following ranking.

(24) $c \to a \to b \to f \to g \to h \to d \to e$

Thus, in this context, *c* has more talent than *a*, *a* has more talent than *b* and so on and so forth.

In this context, the relations η and τ can be represented by the graphs in (25) labeled $>_\eta$ and $>_\tau$. These diagrams are to be read similar to the previous diagrams where if an individual *x* is placed above another individual *y* and connected by a path, then $\langle x, y \rangle$ is a member of the relation. For example, according to the diagram, *b* is more handsome than *c* and *c* is more handsome than *h* but *c* is not more handsome than *b* nor is *h* more handsome than *c*.

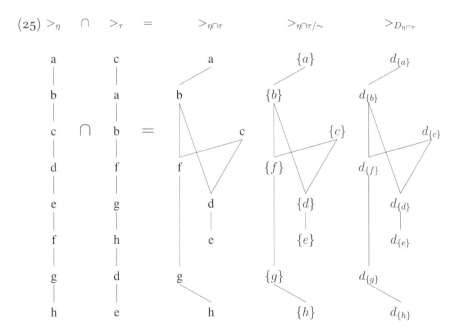

The diagram labeled as $>_{\eta \cap \tau}$ in (25) represents the intersection of η and τ. Note that for $\langle a, b \rangle$ to be a member of the intersected relation (or any other ordered pair), it has to be a member of both η and τ. Hence, *a* must be both more handsome than *b* and more talented than *b* in the relevant context. In other words, membership in the intersected relation encodes both the properties of talent and handsomeness in relating the two individuals.

This intersected relation can then be converted into the quotient structure represented under the label $>_{\eta \cap \tau/\sim}$. Unlike our previous quotient structure in (20), each element is part of its own equivalence class. This is because each element behaves differently with respect to the intersected relation. For example, although *f* and *d* are not related to each other, they are also not equivalent. This is because, within the intersected relation, *f* is related to *g* (i.e., $\langle f, g \rangle \in \eta \cap \tau$) but *d* is not related to *g* (i.e., $\langle d, g \rangle \notin \eta \cap \tau$). Hence, *f* and *d* are distinct despite not being ranked in comparison to one another. Unlike the quotient structure in (20), $>_{\eta \cap \tau/\sim}$ is not fully connected (i.e., it is not a linear order). There are some equivalency classes that are not related to one another (e.g., {*a*} and {*c*}, {*c*} and {*b*}, etc.).

Note, this is an empirical advantage, rather than a flaw. In terms of entailment relations, conjoined adjectives do not behave as if they are connected. Consider the difference between (26) and (27).

(26) a. John is more handsome than Patrick is.
  b. Patrick is more handsome than John is.
  c. John and Patrick are equally as handsome as one another.

(27) a. John is more handsome and talented than Patrick is.
  b. Patrick is more handsome and talented than John is.
  c. John and Patrick are equally as handsome and talented as one another.

If neither (26a) nor (26b) are true, then it seems reasonable to conclude that (26c) must hold. This is because the scale derived from *handsome* is connected. If for any two individuals, one is not more handsome than the other, then they must be equally as handsome. In contrast, this does not hold for the sentences in (27). All three sentences can be false, if, for example, John is more handsome than Patrick but Patrick is more talented John.

4.3 Details of the Potential Analysis

Having explained how Boolean conjunction can lead to the creation of compounded scales, let me now fill in the details of a semantic theory that can use these scales. The interpretation of *more* and *less* can be defined in a way that derives a scale from an underlying binary relation. (Recall that gradable adjectives, under this analysis, are interpreted as binary relations, c.f., Bale 2011.)

(28) a. $\llbracket more \rrbracket = \lambda P . \lambda d . \lambda x . (x_{P_{/\sim}} >_{P_{/\sim}} d)$
     b. $\llbracket less \rrbracket = \lambda P . \lambda d . \lambda x . (d >_{P_{/\sim}} x_{P_{/\sim}})$

The interpretations in (28) have three arguments. The *P* argument is the adjective which is a binary relation. This argument is converted into a quotient structure which serves to determine the ordering relation in the scale, represented as $>_{P_{/\sim}}$. The *x* argument is the subject of the comparative predicate. It is mapped to its equivalency class within the quotient structure, represented as $x_{P_{/\sim}}$. The *d* argument is the degree typically derived from the *than*-clause.

As in most analyses of comparatives (e.g., see Kennedy 1999), I will assume that the *than*-clause contains a copy of the adjectival predicate from the matrix clause. For example, a clause such as [*than Patrick is*] in a sentence such as [*Seymour is more talented than Patrick is*] contains a copy of the adjective *talented* (i.e., [*than Patrick is*] = [*than Patrick is talented*]). In contrast, in the sentence [*Seymour is more handsome and talented than Patrick is*], the *than*-clause contains a copy of the conjoined adjective [*handsome and talented*] (i.e., [*than Patrick is*] = [*than Patrick is handsome and talented*]). As is standard in many analyses, I will assume that the *than*-clause contains a phonologically null degree argument (see the arguments in Bresnan 1975) as well as a phonologically null operator that relates degrees to individuals, however, this operator will (non-standardly) serve to convert the adjectival phrase to a scale. For simplicity, I will label this operator *OP*. The interpretation of this operator is given in (29).

(29) $\llbracket OP \rrbracket = \lambda P . \lambda d . \lambda x . (x_{P_{/\sim}} >_{P_{/\sim}} d) \vee (x_{P_{/\sim}} = d)$

Essentially, this operator relates individuals to degrees such that the equivalency class associated with the individual in the scale formed from the quotient structure of the predicate *P* is either greater than *d* (in the quotient structure) or is equal to it. With this interpretation in mind, the template for interpreting a *than*-clause is given in (30), where *P* represents the interpretation of the elided adjectival phrase and *x* the interpretation of the subject.

(30) $\llbracket than\ x\ is\ d\ OP\ P \rrbracket$
     $= \text{MAX}\{d : (((\llbracket OP \rrbracket P) d) x)\}$
     $= \text{MAX}\{d : (x_{P_{/\sim}} >_{P_{/\sim}} d) \vee (x_{P_{/\sim}} = d)\}$
     $= x_{P_{/\sim}}$

As a result, in most cases, the maximal element of the set of degrees in the *than*-clause ends up being the degree/equivalence-class associated with the *than*-clause subject in the scale derived from the adjectival predicate.

Given this interpretation of the *than*-clause, we not only can interpret simple comparatives, but also comparatives with compounded scales. Let's first consider a simple comparative, as in (31).

(31) Where a is Seymour, b is Patrick, τ is the binary relation associated with talent:
⟦*Seymour is more talented than Patrick is*⟧
$= ((((\lambda P . \lambda d . \lambda x . (x_{P_{/\sim}} >_{P_{/\sim}} d))$⟦*talented*⟧)⟦than Patrick is d OP talented⟧)⟦*Seymour*⟧)
$= (a_{\tau_{/\sim}} >_{\tau_{/\sim}} b_{\tau_{/\sim}})$

Given the relation of τ defined in (25), where a has more talent than b, the sentence would end up being true. Next, consider the interpretation of the more complex comparative in (32).

(32) Where a is Seymour, b is Patrick, τ is the binary relation associated with talent, and η is the binary relation associated with handsomeness:
⟦*Seymour is more handsome and talented than Patrick is*⟧
$= ((((\lambda P . \lambda d . \lambda x . (x_{P_{/\sim}} >_{P_{/\sim}} d))$⟦*handsome and talented*⟧)
⟦*than Patrick is d OP handsome and talented*⟧)⟦*Seymour*⟧)
$= (a_{(\eta \cap \tau)_{/\sim}} >_{(\eta \cap \tau)_{/\sim}} b_{(\eta \cap \tau)_{/\sim}})$

Given the intersected relation defined in (25), the sentence would end up being true. More importantly, it is only true if Seymour is both more handsome and more talented than Patrick. If Seymour didn't exceed Patrick in either one of the qualities, then the ordered pair ⟨a, b⟩ would not be a member of the intersection and hence the degree associated with Seymour in the compounded scale (his equivalence class in terms of both qualities) would not be greater than the degree associated with Patrick.

Similar reasoning follows for sentences like *This floorboard is less tall and wide than that floorboard is*. The intersection of the two basic binary relations can be used to create a compounded scale. The sentence will be true if the degree associated with "this floorboard" on the compounded scale is ordered below the degree associated with "that floorboard". However, this is only possible if "this floorboard" is both shorter and narrower than "that floorboard". If "this floorboard" exceeds or equals "that floorboard" in either quality, the sentence will be false. For time and space reasons, I will forego the details.

5 Remaining Problems and an Alternative Solution

The main advantage of the solution sketched out in section 4 is that it maintains a standard boolean interpretation of conjunction while keeping the main ingredients of a degree analysis of comparatives. Importantly, when the adjectival phrase does not contain any conjunctions, the derived scale is isomorphic to the linear order of degrees that is at the heart of most degree analyses, even those that map individuals to measurements. This is important to emphasize and often overlooked. As discussed in Klein 1991 and Bale 2006, derived scales support all of the operations that are associated with numerical scales (including differentials that involve addition and/or multiplication), as long as the underlying binary relations include measurements.

However, despite the theoretical appeal of such an approach, compounded scales are not free of empirical difficulties. There are two main problems, one involving differentials and the other disjunction. The problem with differentials arises when one considers potential analyses for sentences like the one in (33).

(33) This floorboard is five centimetres less long and wide than that floorboard is.

If we assume that measurements are individuals, and that things can be longer than measurements and measurements can be longer than things, then both quotient structures derived from *long* and *wide* will be isomorphic to the linear order of measurements. Each individual will belong to an equivalence class that contains its measurement and the order of equivalence-classes will mirror the order of measurements. Hence, the operations of −, + and × can be defined for these scales.

However, the intersection of *long* and *wide* does not maintain this isomorphism. For example, let's suppose that that the floorboard f is five metres long and 10 centimetres wide. Thus, $\langle f, 4_m \rangle$ would be in the relation defined by *long* but not in the one defined by *wide* (i.e., f has more length than four metres but not more width). In contrast, $\langle 5_m, 4_m \rangle$ would be in both relations (i.e., five meters is longer than 4 meters and five meters is wider than four meters). As a result, $\langle 5_m, 4_m \rangle$ would be in the intersected relation but $\langle f, 4_m \rangle$ would not. Hence, f and 5_m would no longer be associated with the same equivalence class. If the compounded-scale analysis is to be maintained, one would need to provide a more complicated analysis of differentials: perhaps one that would manipulate the binary relations prior to conjunction. It might be possible to do this with movement and across the board extraction of a variable, but for reasons of time and space, I will not explore such an analysis here.[10] It might also be possible to address this problem through a vector analysis of differentials, such as the one discussed in Schwarzschild (this volume). However, once again due to limitation of time and space, I will not pursue this line of inquiry here.

The other empirical problem involves the distribution of disjunction. In general, disjunction and conjunction are intersubstitutable for one another, and this intersubstitutability holds for constructions that have conjoined adjectives as in (1). For example, the sentences in (34) are identical to (1) except that *and* has been replaced by *or*. The resulting sentences are perfectly acceptable.

(34) a. Seymour is more handsome or talented than Patrick is.
b. This floorboard is less long or wide than that floorboard is.

As with the sentences containing conjunction, the truth conditions of the sentences in (34) can be paraphrase by repeating the comparative morpheme.

(35) a. Seymour is more handsome or more talented than Patrick is.
b. This floorboard is less long or less wide than that floorboard is.

Furthermore, as with conjunction, it is unlikely that gapping could explain the interpretation of the sentences in (36). Unlike typical gapping, the insertion of material after the first disjunct leads to a decline in acceptability.

(36) a. ??Seymour is more handsome than Bill is or talented than Patrick is.
b. ??This floorboard is less long than the one by the table is or wide than the one by the chair is.

The problem with these disjoined adjectives is that they cannot receive an analysis like the one outlined in section 4. Disjunction is usually analyzed as Boolean union, but the union of two binary relations neither preserves transitivity nor asymmetry.[11] Hence, disjoined binary relations do not have a corresponding quotient structure and cannot be associated with any kind of scale.

---

10   The basic idea would be for the phrase *two inches* to influence the granularity of the binary relations before they are intersected. For example, if ω is the binary relation $\{\langle x,y \rangle : x$ has more width than $y\}$, then *two inches* would alter this relation to $\{\langle x,y \rangle : x$ has at least two inches more width than $y\}$.

11   For example, $\{\langle a,b \rangle, \langle b,c \rangle, \langle a,c \rangle\} \cup \{\langle b,a \rangle, \langle a,c \rangle, \langle b,c \rangle\} = \{\langle a,b \rangle, \langle b,c \rangle, \langle a,c \rangle, \langle b,a \rangle\}$. The resulting union is not transitive since it does not contain the pair $\langle a,a \rangle$ and it is not asymmetric since it contains the pairs $\langle a,b \rangle$ and $\langle b,a \rangle$.

However, the idea that *or* is directly interpreted as Boolean union has long been questioned in the literature. It has been widely noted that the semantic effects of disjunction seems to take place at a point that is not directly associated with the surface syntactic position of *or* (see Alonso-Ovalle 2006, 2008, Larson 1985, Schwarz 1999, Simons 2005a,b, Zimmermann 2000, Geurts 2005 among others). To explain these effects, it has been hypothesized that *or*, at its surface position, forms a set where each member corresponds to the semantic value of one of the disjuncts (i.e., $[\![A \text{ or } B]\!] = \{[\![A]\!], [\![B]\!]\}$). Further functions/elements combine with this set through point-wise composition (e.g., where X and Y are of type α and Z is of type $\langle \alpha, \beta \rangle$, $Z(\{X,Y\}) = \{Z(X), Z(Y)\}$, and where X and Y are of type $\langle \alpha, \beta \rangle$ and Z is of type α, $\{X,Y\}(Z) = \{X(Z), Y(Z)\}$). At some point latter in the derivation, the two members of the set are combined with boolean union (e.g., at some point in the derivation an operator applies such that $OP_\cup(\{X, Y\}) = X \cup Y$). It is easy to see that the data in (34), with the paraphrases in (35), fall out naturally from these types of hypotheses. I will not go over the details here, but it is sufficient to note that under this type of interpretation of disjunction, a sentence like [*Seymour is more handsome or talented than Patrick is*] will have a meaning that mirrors the sentence [*Seymour is more handsome than Patrick is or Seymour is more talented than Patrick is*], without hypothesizing any type of ellipsis or gapping.

However, if one adopts this type of analysis for disjunction, why not conjunction? Why couldn't *and* trigger set-formation and why couldn't point-wise composition apply in the same way it does for disjunction? One could hypothesize an operator that eventually combines two members of a set using Boolean intersection (e.g., $OP_\cap(\{X, Y\}) = X \cap Y$). Indeed, this hypothesis is explicitly adopted by Winter (1995), although it should be noted that such a hypothesis has often been rejected in the literature due to differences between the interpretation of *and* and *or* (i.e., *or* seems to be able to take wider scope than *and*; see in particular Hulsey 2006). This possibility also opens up a whole new can of worms. For example, one would have to think of constraints on when the operator $OP_\cap$ can apply. An unconstrained theory would predict that sentences like those in (37) could have an interpretation that could be paraphrased by the sentences in (38). This is not the case. For example, the sentence in (37a) is only true if John is more handsome and more intelligent than one and the same younger man. In contrast, (38a) can be true if John is more handsome than one younger man and more intelligent than another.

(37) a. John is more handsome and intelligent than a man who is ten years younger than him.

b. A man from Italy is less handsome and intelligent than John is.
c. John is less scared and proud of a dog that Bill owns than Mary is.

(38) a. John is more handsome than a man who is ten years younger than him and more intelligent than a man who is ten years younger than him.
b. A man from Italy is less handsome than John is and a man from Italy is less intelligent than John is.
c. John is less scared of a dog that Bill owns than Mary is and less proud of a dog that Bill owns than Mary is.

Similar observations hold for the contrast between the other sentences. The sentences in (38) have weaker truth conditions than the sentences in (37).

However, even if the proper constraints can be sketched out, and even if we accept that something like Winter's (1995) theory is on the right track, we still might need compounded scales. Consider the contrast between the sentences in (39a) and (40a).

(39) a. Seymour is more handsome and talented than how handsome and talented Patrick is.
b. Seymour is more handsome and talented than Patrick is.

(40) a. ??Seymour is more handsome or talented than how handsome or talented Patrick is.
b. Seymour is more handsome or talented than Patrick is.

The sentence in (39a) has the same truth conditions as the sentence in (39b). This follows straightforwardly from the compounded scale analysis: the phrase [*handsome and talented*] is treated as a single binary relation. In fact, the only difference between (39a) and (39b) is that (39a) overtly expresses the degree abstraction operator.

In contast, (39a) cannot be readily analyzed by using set formation and point-wise composition. There are two instances of conjoined phrases, one contained in the matrix clause and the other contained in the *than*-clause. The two instances would create two sets and one would have to arbitrarily stipulate how these two sets should be combined in order to get the correct truth conditions. Furthermore, even if one makes such a stipulation, then it would be predicted that the sentence in (40a) should have the same truth conditions as the sentence in (40b). This is not the case. First of all, (40a) sounds quite odd. Second of all, in so far as one can assign an interpretation to (40a), its truth conditions cannot be paraphrased by (40b).

In summary, even if one adopts an interpretation of *and* that parallels *or*, there is still some evidence that compounded scales might be needed nonetheless. Furthermore, adopting an interpretation of *and* where the semantic realization of conjunction (i.e., Boolean intersection) is displaced opens up a whole new set of problems and requires a new theory of constraints.

6 Conclusion

The data outlined in the paper minimally demonstrates that conjoined adjectives are a serious challenge to the traditional degree analysis of gradable adjectives. These challenges could not be adequately addressed through gapping or any other type of ellipsis. Although some of the problematic data could be accounted for by adopting a non-Boolean interpretation of *and*, certain problems still remain. At least on the surface—in many types of constructions—conjoined adjectives appear to function as a single unit. The advantage of the compounded-scale analysis is that it treats such constructions as units in that intersected binary relations serve as the building blocks for a single (potentially non-connected) quotient structure. Certain empirical difficulties still remain (such as differentials), but the empirical advantages of the compounded scale analysis suggest that this potential solution to conjoined adjectives is at least worth pursuing.

More generally, it is philosophically appealing to derive scales from more basic relations rather than having scales as semantic primitives. From a cognitive perspective, binary relations are simpler and, in principle, independent of language (in that even dogs and cats have the conceptual resources to rank individuals in terms of who is bigger or which food tastes better). Furthermore, as discussed in Cresswell 1976, even though mapping individuals to measurements seems intuitive with respect to heights and lengths, it is definitely unintuitive when it comes to properties such as beauty and talent. These philosophical considerations make it worthwhile to push, as far as it can go, the idea that scales are derived rather than primitive.

Acknowledgements

I would like to thank all the people who have discussed multidimensionality with me over the years, particularly Brendan Gillon, Bernhard Schwarz, Danny Fox, Irene Heim, Kai von Fintel, Kyle Johnson and all the participants in the International Conference on Adjectives (Lille, France) and the Workshop on

Representations of Gradability (Leiden, Netherlands). I would particularly like to thank Jenny Doetjes, Galit Sassoon, and Ora Matushansky for their comments on previous versions of this work. Finally, this work would not have been possible without the help of Peter Hallman and the support of the Social Sciences and Humanities Research Council of Canada (SSHRC), Insight Grant #435-2016-1376.

References

Alonso-Ovalle, Luis. 2006. *Disjunction in alternative semantics*. University of Massachusetts, Amherst dissertation.

Alonso-Ovalle, Luis. 2008. Innocent exclusion in an alternative semantics. *Natural Language Semantics* 16(2). 115–a28.

Bale, Alan. 2006. *The universal scale and the semantics of comparison*. McGill University dissertation.

Bale, Alan. 2008. A universal scale of comparison. *Linguistics and Philosophy* 31(1). 1–55.

Bale, Alan. 2011. Scales and comparison classes. *Natural Language Semantics* 19(2). 169–190.

Bartsch, Renate & Theo Vennemann. 1972. *Semantic structures: a study in the relation between semantics and syntax*. Frankfurt am Main: Athenäum.

Bhatt, Rajesh & Roumyana Pancheva. 2004. Late merger of degree clauses. *Linguistic Inquiry* 35(1). 1–45.

Bierwisch, Manfred. 1987. Semantik der graduierrung. In M. Bierwisch & E. Lang (eds.), *Grammatische und konseptuelle aspekete von dimensionsadjektiven*, 91–286. Berlin, Germany: Akademie Verlag.

Bresnan, Joan. 1975. Comparative deletion and constraints on transformations. *Linguistic Analysis* 1(1). 25–74.

Cresswell, M.J. 1976. The semantics of degree. In B. Partee (ed.), *Montague grammar*, 261–292. New York: Academic Press.

Fox, Danny & Martin Hackl. 2006. The universal density of measurement. *Linguistics and Philosophy* 29(5).

Geurts, Bart. 2005. Entertaining alternatives: disjunctions as modals. *Natural Language Semantics* 13(4). 383–410.

Hackl, Martin. 2000. *Comparative quantifiers*. Massachusetts Institute of Technology dissertation.

Hartmann, Katharina. 2001. *Right node raising and gapping: interface conditions on prosodic deletion*. John Benjamins.

Heim, Irene. 1985. Notes on comparatives and related matters. Unpublished manuscript, University of Texas-Austin.

Heim, Irene. 2000. Degree operators and scope. In Brendan Jackson & Tanya Matthews (eds.), *Proceedings of SALT X*, 40–64. Cornell University, Ithaca, NY: CLC Publications.

Hellan, Lars. 1981. *Towards an integrated theory of comparatives*. Tübingen: Gunter Narr.

Hulsey, Sarah. 2006. An argument from gapping for a hamblin semantics for disjunction. In E. Elfner & M. Walkow (eds.), *Proceedings of the 37th north east linguistics society (nels 37)*.

Johnson, Kyle. 2009. Gapping is not (VP-) ellipsis. *Linguistic Inquiry* 40. 289–328.

Kennedy, Christopher. 1999. *Projecting the adjective: the syntax and semantics of gradability and comparison*. New York: Garland.

Kennedy, Christopher & Louise McNally. 2005. Scale structure, degree modification, and the semantics of gradable predicates. *Language* 81(2). 345–381.

Klein, Ewan. 1980. A semantics for positive and comparative deletion. *Linguistics and Philosophy* 4(1). 1–46.

Klein, Ewan. 1982. The interpretation of adjectival comparatives. *Journal of Linguistics* 18. 113–136.

Klein, Ewan. 1991. Comparatives. In A. von Stechow & D. Wunderlich (eds.), *Semantik/semantics: an international handbook of contemporary research*, 673–691. Walter de Gruyter.

Krantz, D.H., R.D. Luce & A. Tversky. 1971. *Foundations of measurement*. New York, London: Academic Press.

Larson, Richard K. 1985. On the syntax of disjunction scope. *Natural Language and Linguistic Theory* 3(2). 217–264.

Link, Godehard. 1983. The logical analysis of plurals and mass terms: a lattice-theoretical approach. In R. Baeuerle, C. Schwarze & Arnim von Stechow (eds.), *Meaning, use and interpretation of language*, 302–323. DeGruyter.

Ross, John Robert. 1970. Gapping and the order of constituents. In Manfred Bierwisch & Karl E. Heidolph (eds.), *Progress in linguistics*, 249–259. The Hague: Mouton.

Schwarz, Bernhard. 1999. On the syntax of *either … or*. *Natural Language and Linguistic Theory* 17(2). 339–370.

Schwarzschild, Roger. 2013. Degrees and segments. In Todd Snider (ed.), *Proceedings of semantics and linguistic theory. salt xxiii*, 212–238.

Schwarzschild, Roger & Karina Wilkinson. 2002. Quantifiers in comparatives: a semantics of degree based on intervals. *Natural Language Semantics* 10(1). 1–41.

Seuren, A.M. 1973. The comparative. In F. Kiefer & N. Ruwet (eds.), *Generative grammar in europe*, 528–564. Dordrecht, Germany: D. Reidel Publishing Company.

Seuren, A.M. 1978. The structure and selection of positive and negative gradable adjectives. In W. Jacobson & K. Todrys (eds.), *Papers from the parasession on the lexicon, cls 14*, 336–346. Chicago: Chicago University Press.

Simons, Mandy. 2005a. Dividing things up: The semantics of or and the modal/or interaction. *Natural Language Semantics* 13(3). 271–316.

Simons, Mandy. 2005b. Semantics and pragmatics in the interpretation of 'or'. In Effi Georgala & Jonathan Howell (eds.), *Proceedings of SALT XV*, 205–222. Cornell University, Ithaca, NY: CLC Publications.

von Stechow, Arnim. 1984a. Comparing semantic theories of comparison. *Journal of Semantics* 3(1). 1–77.

von Stechow, Arnim. 1984b. My reaction to Cresswell's, Hellan's, Hoeksema's, and Seuren's comments. *Journal of Semantics* 3(1). 183–199.

Wheeler III, Samuel C. 1972. Attributives and their modifiers. *Nous* 6(4). 310–334.

Winter, Yoad. 1995. Syncategorematic conjunction and structured meanings. In M. Simons & T. Galloway (eds.), *Proceedings of semantics and linguistic theory, SALT V*.

Zimmermann, Thomas E. 2000. Free Choice Disjunction and Epistemic Possibility. *Natural Language Semantics* 8(4). 255–290.

CHAPTER 7

From Possible Individuals to Scalar Segments

Roger Schwarzschild

> the meaning of a sentence must be more like an arrow than a point.
> L. WITTGENSTEIN quoted in Portner (1992)

∴

1   Introduction

A comparative serves to locate two or more individuals on a scale associated with a particular gradable predicate. On most analyses, this involves quantification over abstract entities from an ordered realm. Theories differ on the nature of those entities and on their relation to the meanings of gradable predicates. My plan is to explore the consequences of adopting the following pair of theses:
(a) Degree constructions make use of quantification over scalar segments, parts of a scale.
(b) Gradable predicates denote relations between possible individuals. Degrees and segments are introduced with the functional vocabulary. They are defined in terms of possible individuals.
In §2, I introduce ingredients for a semantics based on segments with an analysis of simple phrasal comparatives.[1] The analysis is modeled on neo-Davidsonian event semantics, with segments existentially quantified in place of events. In §3, I show how degrees can be constructed from relations among individuals. The two theses jointly necessitate the presence in comparatives of operators that combine with individual-relational predicates and introduce segments. This necessity sets the stage for a brief discussion in §4 of a typology in which the functional lexicon is the locus of variation. In §5, the two theses

---

[1] A phrasal comparative is simple if the object of *than* corresponds to the subject of the gradable predicate. This includes *A is bigger than B*, *You are closer to Washington than me*, and it excludes *You are closer to Washington than Chicago*, *You threw the ball higher than me*, *You bought a bigger house than me*.

come together in a structure for clausal comparatives in English. At bottom is the comparative marker, *-er*, that combines with gradable predicates and introduces segments. The null *wh*-operator traditionally associated with comparatives is a predicate of segments, a segmental modifier (Izvorski 1995). It is raised, producing an expression denoting a set of sets of segments. *than* encodes the greater-than relation and combines two clauses both constructed with *-er* and the null operator (Alrenga, Kennedy, and Merchant 2012). By abstracting over modifiers denoting sets of segments, we account for the quantifier facts that motivated analyses based on degree intervals and degree pluralities (see Beck 2014, Dotlačil and Nouwen 2016, Fleisher 2016, this volume, and references therein). By allowing *-er* some scopal leeway, we gain a mechanism for capturing the facts about modals in comparative clauses for which the π operator was introduced (Heim 2006). The proposal will also allow us to address an empirical puzzle to do with ellipsis in differential comparatives ('10°' in (1) below is called a differential). Bresnan (1973) proposed that a comparative *than* clause, such as in (1) below, is generated as a sister to the comparative marker *-er*. If the *than* clause were generated where it is pronounced, that would require, given assumptions Bresnan made about ellipsis, that a copy of the differential be generated inside the comparative clause, a situation she deemed "semantically incorrect" (Bresnan 1973:388ff). In the meantime, Bhatt and Pancheva (2004) have adduced ample evidence that in fact *than* clauses must be generated where they are pronounced. But the judgment of semantic incorrectness persists and is taken to support the idea that DegP (differential+–*er*) is moved producing an antecedent for ellipsis, as in (2).

(1) It is 10° colder today than it was yesterday

(2) [It is t_1 cold today][10°–*er*]$_1$ [than OP$_1$ it was ⟨t_1 cold⟩ yesterday]

On the proposal to be advanced in §5, differentials that appear in the main clause can have corresponding instantiations in the comparative clause. This is due in part to the decision to quantify over segments, which can be described by differentials. As a result, a differential does not need to move to produce an antecedent for ellipsis. This becomes important when the differential is in the scope of an attitude verb with a de-dicto interpretation as in (3) below:

(3) {Jack and Jill are train enthusiasts. They've been discussing a high-speed freight train planned for their region. They wonder whether the boxcars will be 60 ft long, like on the Santa Fe line, or 50 ft long, like on the Caroliner. As far as the engine is concerned, Jack and Jill disagree. Jack's expec-

tation is that the engine will be 2 boxcars long. Jill expects it to be one boxcar long}

Jack expects the engine to be one boxcar longer than Jill does.

The differential *one boxcar* needs to be interpreted in the scope of *expect*: there is no actual length of a boxcar at issue here, only expected lengths. If *boxcar* is indeed in the scope of *expect*, it must lie between *expect* and *long* at LF and since both *expect* and *long* are elided in the comparative clause, I conclude that *boxcar* was elided as well. This implies the presence of a differential in the comparative clause.

The thesis in (a) above is closely related to proposals in Faller (2000) and Winter (2005). They analyze adjectives and comparatives in a semantics based on vectors, which have length and direction, like segments. An explanation of which adjectives can be modified by a measure phrase (e.g. *4 ft tall*) and which cannot (e.g **4 ft short*) is given in those works in terms of the contours of the vector space that the adjective denotes. The result interestingly extends the work begun in Zwarts (1997) on modification of locative prepositions (*2 ft behind the desk, *2 ft near the desk*). Relatedly, my initial motivation for developing a segmental semantics was the crosslinguistic recruitment of spatial vocabulary for the expression of comparatives and other degree constructions. Some of these facts are mentioned in §(2) below where I review the segmental semantics developed in Schwarzschild (2012,2013) and Thomas (2018). In that framework, components of a comparative meaning combine intersectively and so they can be rearranged and recombined. Thomas (2018) capitalizes on this feature in a distributive-morphology grammar in which morphemes which occur separated out in some languages are realized together in other languages, giving rise to crosslinguistically recurring polysemies in which additivity, continuity and comparison are colexified.

The thesis in (b) above also has antecedents. Hoeksema (1983:424) and Bale (2006, this volume) construct degrees outside the meaning of the gradable predicate via higher functional morphemes. When degrees are not introduced as primitives, but are built up in some way, the result is a theory in which one can ask questions about the nature of degrees, such as what kinds of degrees there are and how they get ordered. In § 3, I present a new way to derive degrees and I use it to address those questions as well as questions about measurement and degrees that I've always found intractable. What does it mean to say *two pounds* names a degree? Can degrees be added and if so, what does the addition represent? If we take degrees of weight and height to be things named by *two pounds* and *two meters*, what do we say about degrees associated with adjectives for which there aren't numerical measures or, worse, for which there could not be a meaningful numerical measure system? What does it mean to say that, when used as a differential, *five feet* measures the distance between two degrees? And how does that relate to its use as an adjectival modifier (*five feet tall*)?

Abstract entities—cardinalities, degrees, possible worlds, times—all come to life in the functional lexicon. In Klein (1994), this association is formalized by treating verb phrases as mere event predicates and introducing times via aspectual heads. Beck and von Stechow (2015) extend this logic to possible worlds. Similar to the *Asp* operator which locates an event temporally, they assume a *Modl* head which locates an event in a world. The thesis in (b) above extends this logic to degrees but with an important difference. Beck & von Stechow (2015) assume a primitive ontology with times and worlds and use functional morphemes to enter them into the computation. Here and in the abovementioned papers, the functional morphemes 'construct' degrees out of primitives, worlds and individuals.[2]

2 Scale Segments

A scale segment is a triple consisting of a measure function that assigns degrees and two degrees in the range of the function. The triple consisting of Anu's height, Raj's height and the height function (HT) is a scalar segment. The first element of the triple represents the **start** of the segment and the second element of the triple is the **end** of the segment. A segment is said to be **rising** if its end is higher than its start. To say that Anu is taller than Raj, is to say that the segment that starts with Raj's height and ends with Anu's height is rising. Using the notation defined in (4) below, we can formalize (5) as in (6):

---

[2] In fact, Wellwood (2015) fits the Kleinian model quite well. In that theory, adjectives are predicates of states, a degree domain is presupposed and functional morphemes relate the adjectival states to degrees. Yet another theoretical possibility is for adjectives to have degree-based meanings but not degree arguments. Svenonius & Kennedy (2006) hypothesize that "degree arguments are ... introduced by functional morphology in the extended projection of the adjective" by which they mean that an adjective of type $\langle e,d \rangle$ combines with a functional head to produce an expression of type $\langle d,\langle e,t \rangle\rangle$. Cresswell (1976), Klein (1991:679) and Rullmann (1995:125), on the other hand, show how degrees can be constructed out of individuals and worlds, and Anderson & Morzycki (2015) make the case for understanding degrees to be sets of possible states. In those papers, the construction is not associated with a step in the compositional semantics.

(4) Segmental semantic notation

    σ variable over scalar segments
    $\text{START}(\sigma)$ the first element of σ (a degree)
    $\text{END}(\sigma)$ the second element of σ (a degree)
    μ_σ the third element of σ (a measure function)
    $\nearrow(\sigma)$ σ is a rising segment

(5) Anu is taller than Raj.

(6) $\exists \sigma \, [\text{START}(\sigma) = \mu_\sigma(\text{Raj}) \wedge \text{END}(\sigma) = \mu_\sigma(\text{Anu}) \wedge \mu_\sigma = \text{HT} \wedge \nearrow(\sigma)]$

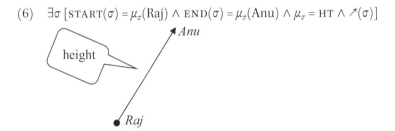

A semantics based on scalar segments allows for flexibility in how meanings are parceled out. The comparative marker, *-er*, in (5) above plausibly encodes the rise predicate, '$\nearrow$' of (6), while START is encoded in *than*. In many languages, these two meanings are jointly encoded. Compare the following Q'eqchi' examples[3] from Kockelman (2018) formed around the adjective *aal* 'heavy':

(7) *syen liibr aal li winq*
    100 pounds heavy the man
    'The man weighs 100 pounds.'

(8) *wib' liibr aal li winq* [*chi–r–u li ixq*]
    2 pounds heavy the man PREP–E3S–RN the woman
    'The man is two pounds heavier than the woman.'

The only indication that (8) is a comparative is the presence of the prepositional phrase *chiru li ixq*, in which the starting point of the comparative is introduced, so *chiru* plausibly encodes '$\nearrow$' and START.

One can discern a similarity between (5)/(6) and event semantic formalizations like in (9)–(10), with segments playing the role of events.

---

3   PREP = preposition, E = ergative case marker, RN = relational noun.

(9) Anu called Raj

(10) $\exists e\, [\text{Agent}(e) = \text{Anu} \wedge \text{Call}(e) \wedge \text{Patient}(e) = \text{Raj}]$

Pursuing this analogy, we adopt the structure and meanings below[4] in which we conceive of 'End' and *than* as akin to thematic role predicates:

(11)
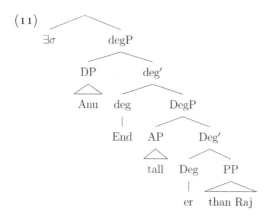

(12) $[\![than]\!]^{g,c} = \lambda x\, \lambda \sigma\, .\, \text{START}(\sigma) = \mu_\sigma(x)$

(13) $[\![-er]\!]^{g,c} = \lambda \sigma\, .\, \nearrow(\sigma)$

(14) $[\![tall]\!]^{g,c} = \lambda \sigma\, .\, \mu_\sigma = \text{HT}$

(15) $[\![End]\!]^{g,c} = \lambda x\, \lambda \sigma\, .\, \text{END}(\sigma) = \mu_\sigma(x)$

(16) $[\![\exists \sigma]\!]^{g,c} = \lambda P_{\langle \sigma, t \rangle}\, \exists \sigma\, P(\sigma)$

Using σ for the type of segments, we observe that the PP, the comparative marker *-er* and the adjective *tall* are all of type $\langle \sigma, t \rangle$ and can compose intersectively. Giving us:

(17) $[\![[_{\text{DegP}}\, \text{taller than Raj}]]\!]^{g,c} = \lambda \sigma\, .\, \mu_\sigma = \text{HT} \wedge \nearrow(\sigma) \wedge \text{START}(\sigma) = \mu_\sigma(\text{Raj})$

---

4 The structure is based on the one in Thomas (2018:61–62). The AP *tall* is merged in the specifier of DegP, following Lechner (2004). Thomas' chief interest lies in a particular pattern of syncretism across languages. Segmental semantics allows him to give meanings to the elements of an abstract syntactic structure. Heads in the structure undergo the restructuring operations of Distributed Morphology before being realized by morphophonological forms. I've simplified by replacing those heads with the morphemes that realize them.

Anu is the individual whose degree marks the endpoint of the segment. The phrase *Anu* is introduced in the Specifier of degP, just as the agent argument is introduced in the Specifier of *v*P in analyses of argument structure influenced by Kratzer's (1996) analysis of external arguments. To combine a VP meaning of type $\langle \varepsilon, t \rangle$ (function from events to truth-values) with the type $\langle e, \langle \varepsilon, t \rangle \rangle$ meaning of the agent thematic voice head at the Voice′ node in the structure below, Kratzer introduces a rule she calls 'Event Identification'.

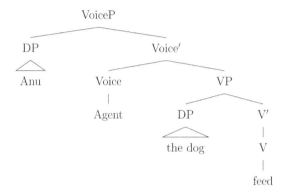

Following Thomas (2018), we'll employ a corresponding rule of 'Segment Identification' to combine 'End' with DegP at the deg′ node. The rule is stated as follows:

(18) Segment Identification
Let α be a node with two daughters, β and γ. Let β be of type $\langle e, \langle \sigma, t \rangle \rangle$ and γ of type $\langle \sigma, t \rangle$, then $[\![α]\!]^{g,c} = \lambda x \lambda \sigma . [\![β]\!]^{g,c}(x)(\sigma) \wedge [\![γ]\!]^{g,c}(\sigma)$

With (18) we now have:

(19) $[\![[_{\text{Deg}'} \text{ End taller than Raj}]]\!]^{g,c} =$
$\lambda x \lambda \sigma . \text{END}(\sigma) = \mu_\sigma(x) \wedge \mu_\sigma = \text{HT} \wedge \nearrow(\sigma) \wedge \text{START}(\sigma) = \mu_\sigma(\text{Raj})$

From there, by function argument application, we get the logical equivalent of (6):

(20) $\exists \sigma \, [\text{END}(\sigma) = \mu_\sigma(\text{Anu}) \wedge \mu_\sigma = \text{HT} \wedge \nearrow(\sigma) \wedge \text{START}(\sigma) = \mu_\sigma(\text{Raj})]$

In languages like Q'eqchi' in which the comparative is marked by the presence of an adpositional phrase introducing the starting point of the comparison, the adposition has a meaning like in (21) which includes $\nearrow$ and START:

(21) $\lambda x \lambda \sigma . \nearrow(\sigma) \wedge \text{START}(\sigma) = \mu_\sigma(x)$

The intersective architecture of event semantics was designed to account for the logic of modifiers, syntactic adjuncts to the verb that can be added or dropped without affecting grammaticality (Davidson 1967). Like Q'eqchi', Navajo has a postposition, *-lááh*, used in PPs marking the starting point of a comparison. *-lááh* introduces the starting point (START), but it also marks the clause as a comparative of superiority ($\nearrow$). Replacing *-lááh* 'beyond' with *=gi* 'at' leads to an equative meaning and replacement with *-'oh* produces a less-than comparative ($\searrow$). Bogal-Allbritten (2013:§3.3) establishes that these PPs can, and in many cases must, combine as adjuncts, occurring at some distance from the adjectival verbs they modify.[5]

Navajo standard marking *-lááh* has a spatial use with a meaning glossed as 'beyond'. Across a variety of languages, the starting point of a comparison is indicated with an adposition or a case marker, often one that can be used for a Source thematic role. I borrowed the phrase "the starting point of a comparison" from a discussion of Greenlandic languages in which the starting point is marked with ablative case (de Mey 1976). The proposal in (11) began as an attempt to make sense of these origins.[6]

In the Q'eqchi' comparative in (8) above, the measure phrase *wib' liibr* '2 lbs' describes the *difference* in weight between the man and the woman. This leads to formalization along the following lines:

(22) Raj is 2 lbs heavier than Anu.

(23) $\exists \sigma \, [\text{END}(\sigma) = \mu_\sigma(\text{Raj}) \wedge \mu_\sigma = \text{WT} \wedge \nearrow(\sigma) \wedge \text{START}(\sigma) = \mu_\sigma(\text{Anu}) \wedge 2\text{LBS}(\sigma)]$

---

5   For more on Navajo degree constructions, consult the paper by Bogal-Allbritten & Coppock in this volume and references therein.
6   Svenonius & Kennedy (2006) report Norwegian *kor gammel* 'how old' formed with locative *kor*, as in *Kor er han?* 'Where is he?'—another spatial source for scalar morphemes. Hohaus

In general, a measure phrase differential can be taken to be a predicate of type $\langle\sigma,t\rangle$ that describes the length of a segment. Given the conjunctive semantics and the rule of Segment Identification in (18), as far as the semantics is concerned, the measure phrase could be attached at various points in the structure below the final existential segment quantifier, '$\exists_\sigma$'. In Schwarzschild (2012), I provided evidence that in Hindi comparatives (at least those without *zyaadaa*), measure phrase differentials are attached to the adjective, which requires the adjective to be a segment predicate as in (14) above.

In this section, I've sketched a segmental analysis of simple phrasal comparatives. It was built around the idea that gradable adjectives are predicates of segments. In the next section, I'll propose a different kind of meaning for adjectives and we'll see how to reconcile the two ideas. The system of semantic types provides a handy way of marking progress. Here's the type system as it looks so far:

(24) Denotation domains
D_t = {TRUE, FALSE}
D_e = {$x : x$ is an individual}
D_d = {$d : d$ is a degree}
$D_{\langle a,b\rangle}$ = {$f : f$ is a function from D_a to D_b}
D_σ = {$\langle u,v,\mu\rangle \mid u \in D_d \wedge v \in D_d \wedge \mu \in D_{\langle e,d\rangle} \wedge u,v$ are in the range of μ}

Within this system, gradable adjectives, measure phrases, and the comparative markers *-er* and *more* are all type $\langle\sigma,t\rangle$. The standard-marking preposition *than* is type $\langle e, \langle\sigma, t\rangle\rangle$ as is the thematic role head *End*.

3 Constructing Degrees

As is customary in the degree semantic literature, up to now, I've presupposed the existence of a cornucopia of degrees, a different kind for each distinct kind of gradable predicate. And each variety has its own ordering. A tiredness degree is different from a height degree and they are not ordered with respect to one another. And in discussing measure phrases, I took for granted that it makes sense to talk about the *distance* between degrees of the same kind. My goal in this section is to assume an ontology based on individuals and possible worlds

---

(2018) charts the evolution of a directional particle ('forth, away') into a comparative marker in Samoan. English uses *way* and *far* as differentials (*far larger, way happier*).

and to construct degrees out of those ingredients. Doing this will make for a sharper understanding of the nature of degrees and of implicit assumptions we make about them.[7]

3.1 Relations

I am going to adopt a particular version of the idea that gradable predicates encode relations between individuals. On this version, the relation encoded by *heavy* holds between an object with weight and any other actual or possible object with equal or less weight. The various formulations in (25)–(28) below should serve to further illustrate the idea. Following Cresswell (1976:281), my meanings make use of entity-world pairs to be referred to as "possible individuals". I use two variables enclosed in angled brackets as a variable over such pairs. The reason for choosing a relational meaning of this particular type should become clear as we go along.

(25) $[\![heavy]\!]^{w,g,c} = \lambda \langle x,w' \rangle \lambda y.$ y in w is as heavy as, or heavier than x is in w'.

(26) $[\![expensive]\!]^{w,g,c} = \lambda \langle x,w' \rangle \lambda y.$ y's price in $w \geq x$'s price in w'.

(27) $[\![complicated]\!]^{w,g,c} = \lambda \langle x,w' \rangle \lambda y.$ y's level of complication in w meets or exceeds x's level of complication in w'.

(28) $[\![remarkable]\!]^{w,g,c} = \lambda \langle x,w' \rangle \lambda y.$ y is remarkable in w to the same or greater degree as x is in w'.

These relations represent the ability we have to compare a given entity with others, real or imagined, in terms of weight, price, complexity, exceptionality and so on.

As Faller (2000:168) and Bale (2007, this volume) point out, individual relational meanings have an advantage over more familiar $\langle d, \langle e, t \rangle \rangle$ meanings like in (29)–(30) when it comes to conjunctions of adjectives like in the comparatives in (31)–(33).

---

[7] Bale (2011) argued that degrees are derived from more basic relations between individuals. His argument was based on the effects of including *for* phrases in comparatives (*Esme is taller for a woman than Seymour is tall for a man*). Like Hoeksema (1983:423), Klein (1991:679) and Rullmann (1995:125), Bale equates Seymour's degree of height with the set of individuals whose height is *the same* as Seymour's. Schwarz (2010) challenged Bale's analysis with examples in which the *for* phrase was not local to the adjective (*Mia has a more expensive hat for a 3-year old than Sam does for a 9-year old*). The construction of degrees described here differs from Bale's. It arose as a response to Schwarz's challenge (Schwarzschild 2013).

(29) ⟦*expensive*⟧^{w,g,c} = λd. λx. d is x's price in w.

(30) ⟦*complicated*⟧^{w,g,c} = λd. λx. d is x's level of complication in w.

(31) This snake is more poisonous and aggressive than at least one of the others we examined.

(32) Hospital deaths are more expensive and intrusive than they once were.

(33) They made computing more expensive and complicated than we might have.

Interpreting *expensive and complicated* intersectively results in (34), on the proposed individual relational meaning, and it results in (35) assuming ⟨d,⟨e,t⟩⟩ meanings as input.

(34) λ⟨x,w'⟩ λy. y's price in w ≥ x's price in w' and y's level of complication in w meets or exceeds x's level of complication in w'.

(35) λd λx. d is x's price in w and d is x's level of complication in w.

(34) relates any entity y that has a price and a level of complication with any possible individual whose price and level of complication is the same or less than that of y. (35) is hopeless, assuming that a level of complication can't also be a price.[8] In (31)–(33), I chose examples with quantifiers in the comparative clause. This rules out a possible conjunction reduction analysis. (31) for example is not equivalent to (36) below.[9]

(36) This snake is more poisonous than at least one of the others we examined and this snake is more aggressive than at least one of the others we examined.

---

[8] The problem in (35) can be avoided along the lines of how Champollion (2015) solves a related problem in event semantics. Instead of *walk* being a predicate of walking events, you treat it as a predicate of sets that include walking events, then the meanings of *walk* and *talk* can be combined intersectively. Similarly here, one could replace the degree argument of *expensive* in (29) with a set containing x's price. This is in fact how Dotlačil and Nouwen (2016) interpret degree predicates.
   I am presupposing that *and* has a meaning that allows it to join two predicate meanings, a view that has come under fire recently in Schein (2017) and Hirsch (2017).

[9] See Bale (this volume) for further arguments against an ellipsis analysis.

The meanings offered in (25)–(28) above do not capture selectional restrictions associated with those adjectives. *heavy*, for example, is restricted to applying to objects with weight and so in place of (25) we should have:

(37) $[\![heavy]\!]^{w,g,c} = \lambda\langle x,w'\rangle : x$ has weight in w'. $\lambda y : y$ has weight in w. y in w is as heavy as, or heavier than x is in w'.

It's important to keep selectional restrictions in mind in assessing the developments in the next section, nevertheless we'll revert to (25), the version of (37) that's been edited for space and clarity.

3.2 Degrees

Using '@' to stand for the actual world, the actual extensions of *heavy* and *complicated* are given in (38) and (39):

(38) $[\![heavy]\!]^{@,g,c} = \lambda\langle x,w'\rangle\, \lambda y.\ y$'s weight in @ $\geq x$'s weight in w'.

(39) $[\![complicated]\!]^{@,g,c} = \lambda\langle x,w'\rangle\, \lambda y.\ y$'s level of complication in @ meets or exceeds x's level of complication in w'.

A man who weighs 70 kilo is related by (38) to the set of possible individuals whose weight is 70 kilo or less. If Jack's taxes have a certain level of complication, (39) relates his taxes to the set of possible individuals with that same level or less. I propose that we identify these sets of possible individuals with degrees of heaviness and complication respectively and that in general:

(40) A **degree** is a set of individual-world pairs.

Under this proposal, degrees are ordered by the subset relation. If Jack weighs 70 kilo and Jill weighs 60 kilo, then the degree assigned to Jill is a subset of the degree assigned to Jack.

(41) $\{\langle x,w'\rangle \mid$ Jill in @ is as heavy or heavier than x is in $w'\} \subset \{\langle x,w'\rangle \mid$ Jack in @ is as heavy or heavier than x is in $w'\}$

Using 'd_{Jill}' to stand for Jill's actual degree of heaviness, we can record the fact in (41) compactly as:

(42) $d_{\text{Jill}} \subset d_{\text{Jack}}$

Subset imposes a partial ordering on degrees. It holds between heaviness degrees but not between a degree of heaviness and a degree of complication or between a degree of heaviness and a degree of tallness. To see this, observe that (41) above says that for any possible individual u, if u'weight is less than or equal to Jill's, then u's weight is less than or equal to Jack's. Suppose now that Jill's *heavy* degree were ordered by subset below Jack's *tall* degree. In that case we would have:

(43) $\{\langle x,w'\rangle \mid$ Jill's weight meets or exceeds x's weight in $w'\} \subset \{\langle x,w'\rangle \mid$ Jack's height meets or exceeds x's height in $w'\}$

What (43) says is that for any possible individual u, if u's weight is less than or equal to Jill's, then u's height is less than or equal to Jack's. To say that is to say that it is not possible to weigh less than Jill but be taller than Jack. If Jill weighs 150 lbs and Jack's height is 5 feet, then (43) entails that it is *logically impossible* for a person to be 6 ft tall and weigh 140 lbs. But that can't be, height and weight just aren't correlated in that way. Nor are weight and degree of complication or redness or temperature. Based on this observation we can define what it means for two degrees to be commensurate:

(44) d and d' are **commensurate** *iff* $d \subset d' \vee d' \subset d \vee d = d'$

Using that definition we can define the relation '<' that orders degrees:

(45) '$d < d'$' is defined when and only when d and d' are commensurate. when defined: $d < d'$ iff $d \subset d'$

The ordering of degrees reflects the underlying ordering of individuals. If Jack is older than Jill, then Jack's *old*-degree is ordered above Jill's. In the previous section, we used the symbol '↗' to mean a rising segment. We can now define it more precisely:[10]

(46) $↗ \stackrel{\text{def}}{=} \lambda\sigma \; \text{START}(\sigma) < \text{END}(\sigma)$

In discussions of the semantics of comparatives and other degree constructions, one finds locutions such as "the degree to which the plane is high", "the

---

10 Incorporating commensurability as a definedness condition yields:
    $↗ \stackrel{\text{def}}{=} \lambda\sigma : \text{START}(\sigma)$ and $\text{END}(\sigma)$ are commensurate. $\text{START}(\sigma) \subset \text{END}(\sigma)$

extent to which Jack is funny", "John's degree of sloppiness", "John's coldness degree" or "Joe's degree of intelligence". These expressions presuppose a unique degree that a gradable adjective associates with an individual. Here's a recipe that underwrites this presupposition:[11]

(47) For any gradable predicate α and individual z,
$\{\langle x, w'\rangle \mid [\![\alpha]\!]^{w,g,c}(\langle x,w'\rangle)(z)\}$
is "the degree to which z is α in w" or "z's degree of α-ness in w"
EXAMPLE   Joe's actual degree of intelligence is:
   a. $\{\langle x, w'\rangle \mid [\![intelligent]\!]^{@,g,c}(\langle x,w'\rangle)(joe)\}$
   b. $\{\langle x, w'\rangle \mid$ Joe is of equal or greater intelligence in @ as x is in $w'\}$
   c. the set of possible individuals whose intelligence Joe's meets or exceeds.

Let's now explore some of the consequences of this conception of a degree. It turns out that on the proposed construction, Jack's degree of tallness is incommensurate with his degree of shortness. The incommensurability of tallness and shortness degrees is a building block of accounts of cross-polar anomaly (Seuren 1978, von Stechow 1984b, Kennedy 2001).

If a glass is full, every other possible container will be as full or less full. None will be more full. In that case, the glass has the maximal degree of fullness: the set of all possible containers. Not all adjectives give rise to maximal degrees. The distinction between those that do and those that don't is reflected in the distribution of proportional modifiers such as *mostly, completely* and *slightly* and it plays a role in the interpretation of the positive (Rotstein and Winter 2004, Kennedy & McNally 2005, 2010, Kennedy 2007a, for discussion and further references see Morzycki 2015:§ 3.7.2).

There is a standard way of assigning numbers to extended objects so that mathematical facts about the numbers reflect length-related facts about the objects. The sum of the lengths of two poles each expressed in numbers of meters will equal the length in meters of the result of placing them together **end to end**. Nothing of this sort has been done for *remarkability*. Whether it is even possible to do that is a question for measurement theory. In (25)–(28), I included the adjectives *complicated* and *remarkable* to emphasize the fact that

---

11   Degreehood is defined in a structurally similar way in Kamp & Partee (1995:153). Unfortunately, I haven't studied the recent work by Heather Burnett, Jenny Doetjes, Robert van Rooij and others building on Kamp (1975) and Klein (1980), but I suspect there is much there that parallels what I am doing here.

although degrees might sometimes be associated with expressions from established measurement systems, the existence of a system of measurement is not a prerequisite for defining degrees.[12] Still, we do use expressions that come from measurement systems in degree constructions. It is worth dwelling on some such uses to clarify how and where we rely on the measurement system to achieve the desired meaning. In (48), the phrase *10°C* is used as a differential, which in §2 was taken to mean it is a predicate of scale segments describing the distance between two degrees. This is indicated in the bolded conjunct in (49).

(48) The tea is 10°C hotter than the milk.

(49) $\exists \sigma \ [\text{END}(\sigma) = \mu_\sigma(\text{Tea}) \land \mathbf{10°C(\sigma)} \land \mu_\sigma = \text{HEAT} \land \nearrow(\sigma) \land \text{START}(\sigma) = \mu_\sigma \ (\text{Milk})]$

In order to develop an idea about what '$10°C(\sigma)$' says, it will help to first bring the discussion of comparatives like (48) in line with our new meanings for adjectives.

We begin by observing that the function named 'HEAT$_w$' defined below in (50) is in fact a measure function. To each individual y, it assigns a set of possible individuals, which, by the construction in (47) is the degree to which y is hot in w.[13]

(50) $\text{HEAT}_w \stackrel{\text{def}}{=} \lambda y. \ \{\langle x,w'\rangle \mid [\![hot]\!]^{w,g,c}(\langle x,w'\rangle)(y)\}$
   $\text{HEAT}_w \stackrel{\text{def}}{=} \lambda y. \ \{\langle x,w'\rangle \mid y\text{'s temperature in } w \geq x\text{'s temperature in } w'\}$

In the previous section we took gradable adjectives to be predicates of segments that established the measure function of the segment, for example:

(51) $[\![tall]\!]^{g,c} = \lambda \sigma. \ \mu_\sigma = \text{HEIGHT}$

To get to that kind of meaning in the new context we'll make use of an operator that combines with an adjective denoting a relation among individuals and

---

12 Sassoon (2010:176–177) agrees on this point even though, as that paper's title suggests, measurement is the foundation on which a degree semantics is built and conventional measurement systems, where they do exist, play a role in the interpretation of the relevant adjectives.

13 Strictly speaking, the meaning of *hot* is a function which is restricted to those entities that have a temperature and that selectional restriction is inherited by HEAT$_w$.

yields a predicate of segments. We'll realize that operator as a symbol composed of an 'S' for scale and a line through it representing a segment. The operator is defined in (52) below using 'R' as a variable over gradable adjective meanings. The label 'e×s' is the type of individual-world pairs—possible individuals:

(52) $[\![\$]\!]^{w,g,c} = \lambda R_{\langle e \times s,\langle e,t\rangle\rangle} \lambda \sigma. \mu_\sigma = \lambda y. \{\langle x,w'\rangle | R(\langle x,w'\rangle)(y)\}$

Combining that operator with *hot* we get:

(53) $[\![\$\,hot]\!]^{w,g,c} = \lambda\sigma. \mu_\sigma = \lambda y. \{\langle x,w'\rangle | [\![hot]\!]^{w,g,c}(\langle x,w'\rangle)(y)\}$

Using (50), we have:

(54) $[\![\$\,hot]\!]^{w,g,c} = \lambda\sigma. \mu_\sigma = \text{HEAT}_w$

Using our new $ operator, we have the following structure for (48):

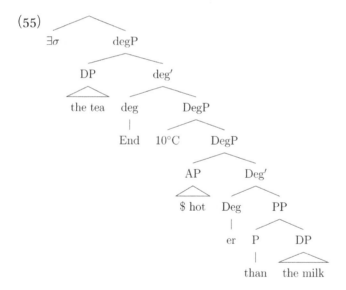

(56) $\exists \sigma\,[\text{END}(\sigma) = \mu_\sigma(\text{the.tea}) \wedge 10°C(\sigma) \wedge \mu_\sigma = \text{HEAT}_w \wedge \nearrow(\sigma) \wedge \text{START}(\sigma) = \mu_\sigma(\text{the.milk})]$

Our interest lies now in the conjunct '$10°C(\sigma)$'. We want to explain how a phrase, *10°C*, whose meaning relies on a particular system of measurement can be used to say something about a triple consisting of two degrees (sets of possible individuals) and a measure function. The analysis provided below in (57)–(59) is

FROM POSSIBLE INDIVIDUALS TO SCALAR SEGMENTS 247

designed to capture two intuitions behind the use of the statement '10°C(σ)': (a) the measure function in σ tracks those properties that the Celsius measurement system is designed to reflect and (b) any two individuals assigned the two degrees in σ will have Celsius temperatures whose scalar quantities differ by 10.

(57) Say that a measure function μ **correlates** with Celsius if the following holds:
Every entity in the domain of μ has a temperature.
For any x,y in the domain of μ, if the temperature of x on the Celsius scale is greater than that of y, then $μ(y) < μ(x)$

(58) Let CELSIUS be a partial function from *degrees* to *numbers* such that for any μ that correlates with Celsius, for any object x in the domain of μ, CELSIUS$(μ(x)) = n$ *iff* the temperature of x is n°C

(59) $[\![10°C]\!]^{w,g,c} =$
$λσ : μ_σ$ correlates with Celsius. |CELSIUS(START(σ)) − CELSIUS(END(σ))| = 10

'|n−m|' stands for the absolute value of $n − m$. Absolute value is needed here because the start of a segment could be higher or lower than the end. (48) describes a segment that begins with the milk's degree of heat and ends with the tea's degree of heat. And those degrees correspond in the sense of (58) to Celsius temperatures that differ by 10. In this analysis, degrees are not added or subtracted. Measurements are not added or subtracted either. Temperature is not like length in which addition and subtraction of measurements is meaningful. The subtraction in (59) is purely numerical. As an aside, the appeal to absolute value makes the welcome prediction that measure phrases formed with negative numbers can't serve as differentials (*−5° *colder*, *−2° *less hot*).

Nonce differentials like *a boxcar* in (60) below do not rely on a conventional system of measurement, so when we interpret them we rely on the context and on the world of evaluation to fill in the details of what counts as a standard and what the measurement procedure is.

(60) The new engine is a boxcar longer than the old engine.

a boxcar as used here describes a scale segment; as such it describes the distance between two degrees. If d_1 and d_2 are *long*-degrees and $d_1 < d_2$, then d_1 and d_2 "differ by a boxcar" as long as the following holds: For any object o whose *long*-degree is d_1, if *o* is concatenated with a boxcar, the result is an object having *long*-degree d_2. Exactly what that amounts to crucially relies on how long a boxcar is and the truth conditions of (60) will differ accordingly. In effect, a kind of contingent measurement system for length is assumed in which a boxcar is the standard and that measurement system plays the role that is played by Celsius in the analysis above.

Differential *a lot* is used in comparatives based on gradable adjectives of any variety. It does not rely on a particular system of measurement. In (62) below I offer a definition with the following idea in mind. If Carla is a lot nicer than Bob, then the difference between Carla and Bob's degrees of niceness is relatively large compared with Bob's degree. Like degrees, degree-differences are sets of possible individuals, so we'll need to make use of a contextually supplied measure on sets,[14] notated m_c, to assign a size to the difference. We'll make use of the following observations:

(61) (START(σ) ∪ END(σ)) is the larger of the two degrees making up σ.
(START(σ) ∩ END(σ)) is the smaller of the two degrees making up σ.

((START(σ) ∪ END(σ)) − (START(σ) ∩ END(σ))) is the difference between the larger and the smaller of the two degrees making up σ. It includes those possible individuals in the higher degree not in the lower one (if the degrees are equal this will be ∅).

(62) ⟦*a lot*⟧^{w,g,c}(σ) = 1 *iff* m_c((START(σ) ∪ END(σ)) − (START(σ) ∩ END(σ))) > $p_c(m_c$((START(σ) ∩ END(σ))))
m_c is a contextually supplied measure on sets.
p_c is a contextually supplied proportion.

A is a lot taller than B says that the set of possible individuals that are taller than B but not taller than A is big relative to the degree to which B is tall. A difference of 1-foot might be sufficient to be a lot taller than a person but insufficient to count as a lot taller than a building.[15]

---

[14] A *measure* is a way to talk about the relative 'size' of infinite sets. It's a function from sets to numbers. A measure needs to fulfill certain requirements, among them, for sets A, B, C in its domain, if $A \subset B$, then $m(A)$ is a smaller number than $m(B)$. If $(A \cap C) = \emptyset$, then $m(A)+m(C) = m(A \cup C)$. A *measure* is different from a *measure function*. The latter assigns degrees. I would have preferred the term "degree function", but that has been used to refer to meanings of modifiers like *quite* and *very*, moreover "measure function" is the standard term in the semantics literature for functions whose range is degrees.

[15] Differential *much* adds another layer of complexity, since it is a gradable predicate and

In addition to serving as differentials, measure phrases are employed on a limited basis as adjectival modifiers (Doetjes 2012, Faller 2000, Sawada & Grano 2011, Schwarzschild 2005, Svenonius & Kennedy 2006, Winter 2005). Differential and modifier uses cannot be reduced one to the other. In German, as in English, measure phrases formed with negative numbers cannot be used as differentials (*–5° *kälter* '–5°colder'), but they can modify adjectives (–5° *kalt* '–5° cold'). Going the other way, in English positive 5° cannot be used as an adjectival modifier (*5° *cold*), but it can serve as a differential (5° *colder*). To facilitate the combination of a measure phrase and an adjective, Svenonius & Kennedy (2006:105), following the logic of Kennedy (1999), posit a functional head 'Meas' that combines with an adjective to form a predicate of type $\langle d, \langle e, t \rangle \rangle$. Meas selects for *tall* and *old* but not for *heavy* and *cold*. Implementing this idea in the present system, gives us:

(63) $[\![Meas]\!]^{w,g,c} = \lambda R_{\langle e \times s, \langle e, t \rangle \rangle} \lambda d \, \lambda y. \, d = \{\langle x, w' \rangle | \, R(\langle x, w' \rangle)(y)\}$

This proposal presupposes that measure phrases themselves can name degrees. *Six feet* must be taken to stand for the degree of height possessed by those individuals whose length when correctly measured in feet in the vertical direction yields six. 5°*F* indirectly names the degree of coldness possessed by individuals whose Fahrenheit temperature is 5°. This nomenclature is familiar. It is usually employed without comment in the degree semantics literature.

This completes our discussion of degrees. The core idea is to conceive of degrees as sets of possible individuals and to introduce degrees, segments and measurements through functional heads that combine with gradable predicates. The segment introducing operator '$', defined in (52), is one of those functional heads as is the degree introducing 'Meas' in (63). In §5 below, the comparative marker *more/–er* that occurs in clausal comparatives will also be analyzed as a segment introducer.

Taking degrees to be sets allows us to identify the partial order that holds of degrees as the subset relation. Taking them to be sets of *logically possible* individuals, allows for comparison across worlds. The degree to which Terry is successful is ordered with respect to the degree to which he would have been successful had Charley looked out for him. We've also made clear how locutions whose interpretation flows from systems of measurement interact with degree talk without making measurement a precondition for degree talk.

so it has its own type $e \times s$ argument. For discussion of *much* in various contexts, see Rett (2018).

And we've discussed how mass quantifiers like *a lot* function as differentials. Deriving degrees in the syntax means that gradable adjectives are predicates of individuals and this allows for an account of adjective conjunctions ((31)–(34)) and it allows for a better account of *for* phrases in comparatives (footnote 7).

In (64) below, I've summarized the discussion to this point in the form of an assignment of denotation domains to semantic types. Up to now, I've been talking about degrees as sets of individuals because it's easier to think about them that way. But in carrying out a compositional semantics, it's better to take them to be the functions that characterize those sets, functions in the domain of type $\langle e \times s, t \rangle$.

(64) Denotation domains
D_t = {TRUE, FALSE}
D_e = set of individuals.
D_s = set of possible worlds.
$D_{\langle a,b \rangle} = (D_a \to D_b)$
$D_{e \times s} = \{\langle x, w' \rangle \mid x \in D_e \wedge w' \in D_s\}$ (possible individuals)
$D_d = D_{\langle e \times s, t \rangle}$ (degrees)
$D_\sigma = \{\langle u, v, \mu \rangle \mid u \in D_d \wedge v \in D_d \wedge \mu \in D_{\langle e, d \rangle} \wedge u, v \in \text{Range}(\mu)\}$ (segments)

4 Typological Landscape

In the previous two sections, I fleshed out the two hypotheses under investigation, repeated below:
(a) Degree constructions make use of quantification over scalar segments, parts of a scale.
(b) Gradable predicates denote relations between possible individuals. Degrees and segments are introduced with the functional vocabulary. They are defined in terms of possible individuals.

If theses (a) and (b) are universally valid, then any language that has a degree construction will perforce have an overt or covert operator such as $ or *Meas*. The presence of measure phrase modifiers and comparatives in Q'eqchi' exhibited in (7)–(8) above therefore implicates a null $ and *Meas* in that language. By contrast, Bochnak (2015) demonstrates the absence of degree constructions in Washo, which implies that it does without degree or segment introducing operators (Lassiter 2015:153). Bochnak argues that degrees as such are not part of the basic ontology of Washo, but he concludes (p. 41) with an argument for a thesis like in (b) "under my analysis, there are languages that simply lack a basic semantic type, namely degrees. This raises the question of why degrees should be subject to this kind of cross-linguistic variation. It is much less obvious that other logical types should be missing from a language (e.g., individuals, events, worlds), or what a language would look like if such a gap were to exist. I speculate that this point can be linked to the idea that degrees are not in fact basic on a par with other simple types. ... if degrees don't come 'for free' as basic elements in the model, then languages differ on whether they choose to derive them."

The $ morpheme was posited as a way to introduce segments when gradable predicates have type e×s arguments. A different option, to be explored in the next section, takes the comparative marker (er/more) to be of type $\langle d,\langle \sigma,t\rangle\rangle$:

(65) 〚-er〛 = λd λσ END(σ) = d

When this morpheme combines with a type $\langle e×s,\langle e,t\rangle\rangle$ predicate, there is a type mismatch which can be resolved through quantifier raising. -er is looking for an argument of type d, i.e. $\langle e×s,t\rangle$, so when it raises it leaves a trace of type e×s (compare, a generalized quantifier looks for an argument of type $\langle e,t\rangle$, so when it raises, it leaves a trace of type e):

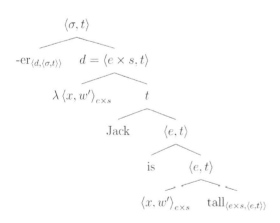

Suppose then that English makes do with -er and does not have a null $ operator. In that case, we have languages with null segment operators (Q'eqchi'), languages with overt segment operators (English) and languages with no such operators (Washo). A fourth possibility is a language that has both null and overt segment operators. In such a language, unlike in English, the overt comparative marker would be optional. Hebrew and Hindi are two such languages (Schwarzschild 2010, 2012). Both have an overt comparative marker but can form comparatives without it, although only with certain adjectives. In those languages, the null segment operator is selective, like the *Meas* operator discussed above.

Another parameter of variation that emerges from discussion to this point is the form and interpretation of the standard marker, the morpheme that introduces the START of the comparative. In the languages canvassed, START is indicated with a case-marker (Greenlandic), a preposition (Q'eqchi') and a postposition (Navajo). This task can also be performed by a verb (e.g. *surpass*) and in some cases by a particle derived from a conjunction (Stassen 2006). Comparatives formed in this way display syntactic properties characteristic of coordinations. Stassen points to gapping in Dutch. Lechner & Corver (2017:§ 4) discuss a range of such effects in English. Along these lines, in the following section, *than* will be understood to combine two identically constructed clauses.

A final parameter of variation is the locus of the ↗ operator. Recall, that in Navajo, it is unquestionably packaged together with the standard marker. Kennedy (2007b) argues that this is the norm cross-linguistically (see also Menon 2017). We'll adopt that proposal in the following section.

5 Clausal Comparatives

Von Stechow (1984a:55) treated comparative clauses as predicates of degrees in the scope of a maximality operator. This architecture successfully captured the meaning of comparative clauses containing the modal *can* and negative polarity *any*, and the semantics underwrites the claim that comparative clauses allow negative polarity items because they are downward entailing (von Stechow 1984a:70, Rullmann 1995:§ 2.4). In Schwarzschild & Wilkinson (2002), we proposed a semantics based on intervals (sets of degrees) which captured the meaning of comparative clauses containing quantifiers that are not negative polarity items. We also showed with examples using those quantifiers that comparative clauses are upward entailing. The two papers covered different data and were incompatible. Heim (2000, 2006) explained away the apparent contradiction by positing an operator inside the comparative clause that transitions from degrees to intervals. The environment below the operator is downward entailing. *can, have-to* and negative polarity items are situated there. The environment above the operator is upward entailing and non-NPI quantifiers are located there along with propositional attitude verbs and some modals. In this section, I hope to show that the bifurcation of the comparative clause that Heim discovered stems from the need to transition from predicates of possible individuals to predicates of segments.

FROM POSSIBLE INDIVIDUALS TO SCALAR SEGMENTS 253

Following Alrenga, Kennedy, and Merchant (2012), I take *than* to be a contentful expression that combines with two clauses both of which are formed with a comparative marker and a silent operator:

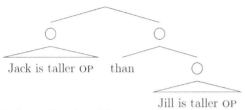

Jack is taller than Jill is

Izvorski (1995:15) suggests that the empty operator in comparatives is an adverbial amount/degree WH-expression. Adapting that suggestion to the current context, I take the operator to range over segmental modifiers and to therefore leave a trace of type $\langle \sigma, t \rangle$.[16] In syntactic structures, I'll use a Σ for type $\langle \sigma, t \rangle$ traces. The operator itself denotes the identity function, so the denotations for the nodes labeled ① is passed up to the dominating nodes, Ψ and Φ:

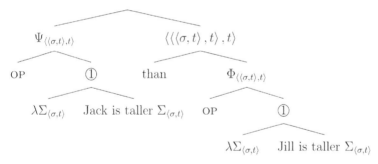

Jack is taller than Jill is

Turning now to the formation of the higher clause Ψ, we start with the structure below which features the segment existential '∃σ' from section 2:

---

16   $[\![\text{OP}]\!]^{w,g,c} = \lambda \psi_{\langle\langle\sigma,t\rangle,t\rangle}.\psi$. Being type $\langle\langle\langle\sigma,t\rangle,t\rangle t\rangle$, OP leaves a trace of type $\langle\sigma,t\rangle$, by analogy with WH expressions of type $\langle\langle e,t\rangle,t\rangle$ that leave type *e* traces. Based on a suggestion of Roger Higgins', Grimshaw (1987:668) posited "a phonologically null Adverb Phrase, something like *to a certain/great extent*, within the subcomparative clause". Izvorski adopted this idea and further proposed that this null phrase undergoes WH-movement.

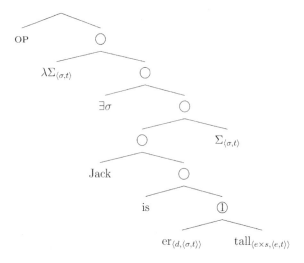

There is a type mismatch at ① which is resolved by raising -er and leaving a trace of type e×s.

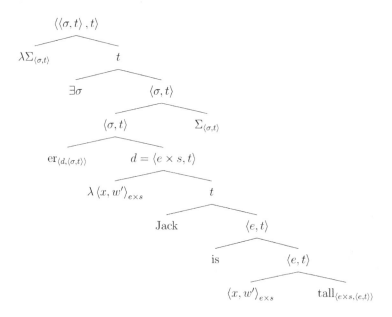

Given the definition in (47), the phrase labeled d denotes the degree to which Jack is tall, in other words, his height.[17] Given the meaning for -er introduced earlier,

---

17   More precisely, Jack's height in the world of evaluation. In building up the theory, I've sup-

(66) $\llbracket\text{-}er\rrbracket^{w,g,c} = \lambda d.\, \lambda\sigma.\, \text{END}(\sigma) = d$

the lower phrase labeled ⟨σ,t⟩ will have the meaning in (67) and the higher phrase labeled ⟨σ,t⟩ will have the meaning in (68) ('Σ' is used for traces in the object language and is the corresponding variable in the metalanguage)

(67) $\lambda\sigma\, \text{END}(\sigma) = $ Jack's height

(68) $\lambda\sigma\, [\text{END}(\sigma) = $ Jack's height $\wedge\, \Sigma(\sigma)]$

The entire clause denotes a predicate of sets of segments:

(69) $\lambda\Sigma\, \exists\sigma\, \text{END}(\sigma) = $ Jack's height $\wedge\, \Sigma(\sigma)$

The clause under *than* labeled 'Φ' above is formed in the exact same way, and parallel to (69), if it is true of a set, then that set includes a segment ending in Jill's height.

As discussed in § 2 and 3, differential measure phrases are type ⟨σ,t⟩ expressions. As such, they can be adjoined immediately above or below the WH operator:

(70)

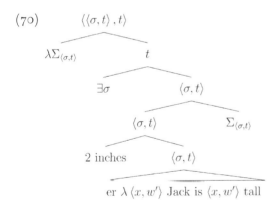

An alternative syntax, which I will not pursue here, keeps the differential and the WH operator inside the DegP. It would give us the structure in (71) below, interpretable through two applications of the rule of Segment Identification in (18) which would yield the meaning '$\lambda d\, \lambda\sigma\, 2\text{INS}(\sigma) \wedge \text{END}(\sigma) = d \wedge \Sigma(\sigma)$'.

---

pressed reference to the world of evaluation. The metalanguage 'height' in (68), (69) and subsequent formulas should be 'height$_w$'.

(71)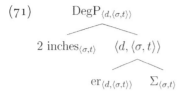

Summarizing now, the meaning of the comparative in (72) is arrived at by applying the meaning of *than* to the meanings in (73) and (74):

(72) Jack is 2 inches taller [than] Jill is.

(73) $[\![\text{OP } \lambda_2 \, \exists \sigma \, 2\text{ins} \, [\text{-}er \, \lambda_1 \text{ Jack is } t_1 \text{ tall}] \, t_2]\!]^{w,g,c} =$
$\lambda \Sigma \, \exists \sigma \, 2\text{INS}(\sigma) \wedge \text{END}(\sigma) = \text{Jack's height} \wedge \Sigma(\sigma)$

(74) $[\![\text{OP } \lambda_2 \, \exists \sigma \, [\text{-}er \, \lambda_1 \text{ Jill is } t_1 \text{ tall}] \, t_2]\!]^{w,g,c} =$
$\lambda \Sigma \, \exists \sigma \, \text{END}(\sigma) = \text{Jill's height} \wedge \Sigma(\sigma)$

The meanings in (73) and (74) both apply to a set of segments. If (73) is true of a set, that set includes a segment that ends with Jack's height and is 2inches long. If (74) is true of a set, that set includes a segment that ends with Jill's height.

The comparative in (72) is true under the circumstances illustrated below, in which a 2inch rising segment ending in Jack's height starts with the end of a segment ending in Jill's height.

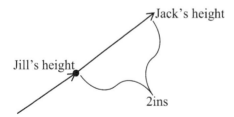

Jack is 2 inches taller than Jill is

What remains now is to arrive at a meaning for *than* that requires what is illustrated above in terms of the meanings in (73) and (74).

The sets that (73) and (74) pick out will contain many segments that are of no interest to us, having nothing to do with Jack or Jill. Since (74) merely requires that Σ contain a segment ending in Jill's height, it could hold of a set containing a segment ending in Jill's height along with another segment ending in the weight of the moon. For this reason, we'll makes use of the *min* operator in (75) adapted from Beck (2010, 2014) and Dotlačil & Nouwen (2016).

(75) $min(\Sigma_{\langle\sigma,t\rangle}, \Phi_{\langle\sigma t,t\rangle})$ iff $\Phi(\Sigma) \wedge \neg\exists\Sigma' [\Phi(\Sigma') \wedge \Sigma' \subset \Sigma]$

With (75), we can pick out the smallest sets that satisfy the clauses of the comparative. Sets satisfying (73) all contain at least one segment ending in Jack's height. A set that minimally satisfies (73) contains just one segment and that segment ends in Jack's height. Let's call such a segment, a *witness* for (73). Each set that minimally satisfies (73) contains such a witness. Each set that minimally satisfies (74) will contain a witness for (74), a segment that ends in Jill's height. What we want to require is that there be a witness ending in Jack's height that is rising and whose start is the end of a witness ending in Jill's height. The meaning for *than* in (76) below imposes that requirement ('Φ' corresponds to the meaning in (74) of *Jill is taller*):

(76) $[\![than]\!]^{w,g,c} = \lambda\Phi_{\langle\sigma t,t\rangle}.\lambda\Psi_{\langle\sigma t,t\rangle}.$
$\exists\Sigma_1 \, min(\Sigma_1, \Phi)$
$\wedge \, \forall\sigma_1 \in \Sigma_1 \, [\exists\Sigma_2 \, [min(\Sigma_2, \Psi) \wedge \exists\sigma_2 \in \Sigma_2 \, [\nearrow(\sigma_2) \wedge \text{END}(\sigma_1) = \text{START}(\sigma_2)]]]$

Since there is a differential in *Jack is 2 inches taller than Jill is*, all the witnesses for the main clause will be the same length, assuming '2' is construed as 'exactly 2'. If there were no differential, the witnesses could differ in length. In that case, one could start with Jill's height, but others wouldn't. Because of the existential '∃Σ₂', (76) correctly requires only that one of the witnesses start with Jill's height and end with Jack's.

Any set that minimally satisfies (74) will contain just one witness, just one segment ending in Jill's height, so the universal quantifier '∀σ₁' would appear to be superfluous. It becomes important once we turn to comparative clauses with individual or world quantifiers in them:

(77) a. Jumpy is more slippery than every other fish is.
 b. than OP λ_2 every other fish λx [$\exists\sigma$ [-er λ_1 x is t_1 slippery] t_2]
 c. $\lambda\Sigma \, \forall z$ fish(z) $\to \exists\sigma \, \text{END}(\sigma) = z$'s slipperiness $\wedge \Sigma(\sigma)$

(78) a. Jumpy is longer than I expected he would be.
 b. than OP λ_2 I expected [$\exists\sigma$ [-er λ_1 he would be t_1 long] t_2]

A set that minimally satisfies the comparative clause meaning in (77c) will contain, for each fish other than Jumpy, a segment ending in that fish's degree of slipperiness. (76) requires that for each one of those segments, there be a rising segment that ends in Jumpy's degree of slipperiness and that starts with the fish's degree. That means that for each fish, Jumpy is more slippery.

A set that minimally satisfies the clausal complement of *than* in (78b) will contain, for each world compatible with what I expected, a segment ending in Jumpy's length in that world. If my expectation covered a range, say from 2 to 4 inches long, then that minimal set will have segments ending in degrees ranging from 2 to 4 inches. (76) requires that for each one of those segments, there be a rising segment ending in Jumpy's actual length that starts with the expected length. That means Jumpy's length has to exceed my expectation: he must be more than 4 inches long.

In (72), there is a differential in the main clause which determines the lengths of the witness segments. The comparative clause is also given a segmental semantics, so differentials are interpretable there as well. This possibility is realized in the following example repeated from the introduction:

(79) Jack and Jill are train enthusiasts. They've been discussing a high-speed freight train planned for their region. They wonder about whether the boxcars will be 60 ft long, like on the Santa Fe line, or 50 ft long, like on the Caroliner. Jack and Jill disagree about the engine size. Jack's expectation is that the engine will be 2 boxcars long. Jill expects it to be one boxcar long:
Jack expects the engine to be one boxcar longer than Jill does.

(80) a. Jack expects the engine to be a boxcar longer than Jill does Δ.
b. OP λ_2 Jack expects [∃σ boxcar [$-er$ λ_1 the engine to be t_1 long] t_2]
c. than OP λ_2 Jill expects [∃σ boxcar [$-er$ λ_1 the engine to be t_1 long] t_2]
d. Δ = expects ∃σ boxcar [$-er$ λ_1 the engine to be t_1 long] t_2

The differential measure phrase in (80a) needs to be interpreted under the scope of *expect*: there is no actual length of a boxcar at issue here, only expected lengths. Since the ellipsis in the comparative clause includes *expect*, it must include the differential as well. So let's see how this works out given the information reported in (79). Consider a set Σ_{Jill} minimally satisfying the clausal complement of *than* in (80c). For each world compatible with Jill's expectation, there's a segment in Σ_{Jill} that is the length of a boxcar in that world (50 ft or 60 ft) and that ends with the length of an engine in that world (50 ft or 60 ft). So, there are two witnesses for Jill's expectation and they are depicted below as the lower arrows. Now, consider a set Σ_{Jack} minimally satisfying (80b). For each world compatible with Jack's expectation, there's a segment in Σ_{Jack} that is the

FROM POSSIBLE INDIVIDUALS TO SCALAR SEGMENTS 259

length of a boxcar in that world (50 ft or 60 ft) and that ends with the length of an engine in that world (100 ft or 120 ft). So Σ_{Jack} provides two witnesses for Jack's expectation depicted below as the upper arrows. As the meaning of *than* requires, for each witness σ_{Jill} in Σ_{Jill}, there is witness σ_{Jack} in Σ_{Jack} such that σ_{Jack} starts with the end of σ_{Jill}.[18]

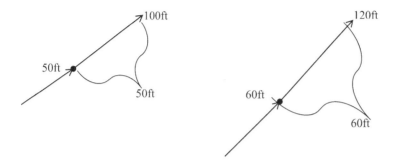

In (80d), the material elided in (80a) is shown to include a differential, *boxcar*. Another kind of example that requires elided measure phrases in the comparative clause involve conjunctions of compared adjectives:

(81) This rod is 2 lbs heavier and 1 inch longer than one of the tubes was.

Across the Board movement of the WH operator and of the subjects of both clauses produces these structures:

(82) a. OP λ_2 [The rod] λ_5 $\exists \sigma$ [2 lbs [–er λ_1 x_5 is t_1 heavy] t_2] and $\exists \sigma$ [1 inch [–er λ_1 x_5 is t_1 long] t_2]
b. than OP λ_2 [one of the tubes] λ_6 $\exists \sigma$ [2 lbs [–er λ_1 x_6 is t_1 heavy] t_2] and $\exists \sigma$ [1 inch [–er λ_1 x_6 is t_1 long] t_2]

---

18 This example has universal modal quantifiers in the two clauses joined by *than*. The example cited in Dotlačil & Nouwen (2016:64) and repeated below has universal individual quantifiers in the two clauses joined by *than*.
(i) The state economies of Ireland, the Netherlands and Australia **all** scored higher than they **each** scored in the mid-1980s.
Their example reveals a potential lacuna. Our meaning for *than* requires that for every 1980s score of one of the countries, there is a higher current score of one of the countries. This needs to be strengthened perhaps pragmatically to say "there is a higher current score of **that same** country" or more generally there is a corresponding score that is higher. Likewise, there is a sense in the build up to our (79) of a correspondence between Jack and Jill's expectations.

Consider a set Σ_{tube} minimally satisfying the clausal complement of *than* in (82b). It will include two segments, one with weights on either end and one with lengths on either end. This much follows from the meanings discussed in this section as well as the definition of a segment (64) and the constraint on measure functions imposed by measure phrases (59). There will be a different minimal set of segments for each one of the tubes (assuming they differ one from the other in weight or length). A set minimally satisfying the main clause will contain two witnesses, a weight segment and length segment. The meaning of *than* requires that we find one of the sets for the comparative clause (see '$\exists \Sigma_1$' in (76)) and relate both of its witnesses to the witnesses of the main clause. This will entail that:

(83) For one of the tubes, x_6, the rod is 2 lbs heavier than x_6 and the rod is 1 inch longer than x_6.

A possible verifying scenario is one in which the rod weighs 3 lbs and is 5 inches long, while one of the tubes weighs 1 lb and is 4 inches long. Let's call that tube x_6. Given that tube x_6 weighs 1 lb, a segment that ends in its weight could be 2 lbs-long, as (82b) requires, only if that segment is falling. That is possible. Although I've been drawing pictures in which the comparative clause segments are rising, nothing requires that. The rising predicate '$\nearrow$' is in the meaning of *than*, and not in the meaning of *-er*.[19] In both (80) and (81), a differential was found to be present in the comparative clause. Were it not there, ellipsis would not have been possible. Given the way the meaning of *than* is formulated, however, the differential has no truth conditional effect inside the comparative clause. So unless it's facilitating ellipsis, I assume its presence would violate a constraint that punishes verbosity.[20]

---

19 Williams (1977:132–133) took *than* to indicate the greater-than relation and he posited occurrences of *more* in both the main and subordinate clauses that quantifier-raise to create amount denoting expressions. von Stechow (1984a:8) thought that couldn't be right given that in his grandmother's German *wie* is used for the standard marker in both the comparative and the equative. He concluded that the greater-than relation must be encoded in the comparative marker. One could raise the same objection based on the use of English *than* in comparatives of inferiority and comparatives of superiority. However, if *-er* and *than* are related by agreement, as Alrenga & Kennedy (2014:43) suggest, the objection loses its force. Comparatives of inferiority might have a *than* that agrees with *less* and has '$\searrow$' in its meaning instead of '$\nearrow$'.

20 I have in mind something similar to Buccola & Spector (2016:165)'s pragmatic economy constraint, which says:

An LF φ containing a numeral n is infelicitous if, for some m distinct from n, φ is truth-conditionally equivalent to the result of substituting m for n in φ.

The conjunction in (81) has scope over the comparative, but, as anticipated in §3, the reverse is possible. Consider a tank that has been purchased to hold the wine produced in one day but is unfortunately not up to the task. The buyer laments:

(84) The tank is more shallow and narrow than it should to be.

The tank's depth would be ok, if only it were wider. Its width would be ok, if only it were deeper. So one might be reluctant to say that it's shallower than it should be or that it's narrower than it should be. Conjunction at the AP level with *more* attaching above that and then raising produces a predicate that names a shallow-narrow degree.

In the examples considered up to now, *-er* quantifier-raised coming to rest not far from the gradable predicate to which it is attached. But, as Heim (2001) showed, there are modals above which *-er* can raise and, depending on the choice of the modal, one will get 'maximum' or 'minimum' readings. In the example below, *-er* moves above the modal verb *had to*:

(85) a. The wire was longer than it had to be.
 b. than OP λ_2 [∃σ [*-er* λ_1 it had to be t_1 long] t_2]
 c. ⟦λ_1 *it had to be t_1 long*⟧^{w,g,c} = $\lambda \langle x,w' \rangle$[it had to be $\langle x,w' \rangle$ long]

(85c) gives the meaning for 'λ_1 it had to be t_1 long', the scope of *-er* in (85b). (85c) has a degree meaning, type $\langle e \times s, t \rangle$. It is true of possible individuals that the wire has to meet or exceed in length. If the wire is required to be at least 2 inches long, then (85c) will be true of any actual or possible individual 2 inches long or less. That set of possible individuals just is the degree of length that a 2-inch long individual has. In that case, (85a) says that the wire is more than 2 inches long. What (85) expresses is that the wire exceeds its minimum required length. Replacing *had to* with *allowed to*, we get:

(86) a. The wire was longer than it was allowed to be.
 b. than OP λ_2 [∃σ [*-er* λ_1 it was allowed to be t_1 long] t_2]
 c. ⟦λ_1 *it was allowed to be t_1 long*⟧^{w,g,c} = $\lambda \langle x,w' \rangle$[it was allowed to be $\langle x,w' \rangle$ long]

(86c) gives the meaning for 'λ_1 it was allowed to be t_1 long', the scope of *-er* in (86b). (86c) has a degree meaning, type $\langle e \times s, t \rangle$. It is true of possible individuals that the wire is allowed to meet or exceed in length. If the wire was allowed to be up to 4 inches long, then (86c) will be true of any actual or possible individual 4 inches long or less. That set of individuals just is the degree of length that a 4-inch long individual has. So (86a) says that the wire was more than 4 inches long. What (86) expresses is that the wire exceeded its maximum allowable length.

Having seen that -er scopes over modals in the comparative clause, we now expect to find -er scoping over modals in the main clause of a comparative. In fact, it was this context in which Heim (2001) first identified the effects of scoping above necessity and possibility modals. (87) below is one of her examples. Although its analysis has been questioned (Oda 2008 cited in Beck 2012:259ff), it is instructive to see how it works in the current context.

(87) (This draft is 10 pages.) The paper is allowed to be exactly 5 pages longer than that.

(88) "it is exactly 15pp long in the acceptable worlds where it is longest, which means it is not allowed to be longer than 15pp." (Heim 2001)

(87) has a kind of comparative different from the ones we've seen so far. The object of *than* is a pronoun referring to a previously mentioned degree. It requires a meaning for *than* as in (89). To produce the reading in (88), *than* would occur above *allowed* and -er would create a segmental predicate by moving to adjoin to the node labeled ①.

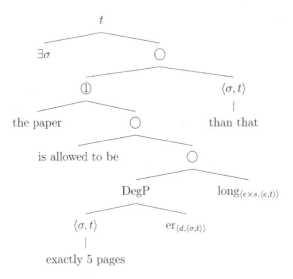

(89) $[\![than]\!]^{w,g,c} = \lambda d \, \lambda \sigma \, \nearrow(\sigma) \land \text{START}(\sigma) = d$

In this case, it's imperative that the measure phrase be generated inside DegP, otherwise it will be left behind when *-er* raises and will be interpreted in a non-segmental environment. So if Heim's analysis is correct, we have an argument for that syntax.

As observed in (86)–(88), when *-er* raises above an existential, it gives rise to a maximal reading. We can see this in the individual domain using negative polarity items. As long as there is no *exactly* differential in the main clause (Rullmann 1995:106), the scope of *-er* in the comparative clause is a downward entailing environment.[21] When a negative polarity existential is found there, it gives rise to a maximal reading. (90) says the box's weight exceeds the weight of the heaviest tube, unlike (91) which says only that it exceeded the weight of one of them.

(90) The box was heavier than any of the tubes were

(91) The box was heavier than one of the tubes was.

An important feature of the proposal made here has to do with the notion of "scope of comparison" (Williams 1974:217–218, Gawron 1995, Bhatt & Pancheva 2004). Compare the following:

(92) a. Jack wanted the coat to be more expensive than Jill did.
　　　b. Jack wanted [the coat to be more expensive than the sweater was].

In (92a), *want* is included in the scope of comparison. We compare prices that Jack wanted to the ones that Jill wanted. In (92b), we report on Jack's desires in which the price of the coat is compared to that of the sweater. In (92b), the scope of comparison does not extend past the clause embedded under *want*. Our logical forms have two mobile operators in them, OP and *-er*. OP defines the scope of comparison, while *-er* defines what we might call the scope of degree.

21　*-er* combines with a degree denoting expression, which is to say an expression that denotes a set of possible individuals. According to the semantics described above, *Jack is taller than Jill is* is true if Jill's height is a proper subset of Jack's. If we replace the expression denoting Jill's height with one that denotes a subset, then surely that smaller set will be also be proper subset of Jack's height. In other words, if the comparative statement $\varphi(A)$ is true, where A is the scope of *-er* in the comparative clause, and $[\![B]\!]^{w,g,c} \subseteq [\![A]\!]^{w,g,c}$, then $\varphi(B)$ is true.

　　I'm using *any* for illustration even though there is some question about its NPI status in this context (Aloni & Roelofsen 2014). There are uncontroversial cases of NPIs, verbs and adverbs, that appear in comparative clauses.

In (79), *Jack expects the engine to be one boxcar longer than Jill does*, the verb *expect* and the differential (*one boxcar*) are in the scope of comparison but not in the scope of degree. This presents a challenge to previous analyses for various reasons. For some, there is just one operator moving in the clause, which means that scope of comparison and scope of degree are conflated and that gives the wrong interpretation for *expect*. For some, there are two operators, but they differ between the main clause and the comparative clause. That means that to provide the right input for ellipsis, the scope-of-degree operator needs to be raised above *expect* (Alrenga & Kennedy 2014).

Summarizing now, the comparative marker, *-er*, turns out to be little more than a type shifter taking predicates of possible individuals into predicates of segments. Its presence is needed to form the input to the standard marker *than* in which the crux of comparison resides. In order to do its job, *-er* needs to move to take scope. In so doing, it divides the clause, giving rise to an interesting interaction of degree and quantification.[22] NPI quantifiers and some modals remain below *-er*, other modals and non-modal quantifiers raise above the segment-existential that binds the scalar segment argument introduced by *-er*.

6 Conclusion

Presumably we learn the meaning of *cold* by associating it with the physical sensation of coldness. Maybe at first, that's all there is to it. But eventually, to grasp its meaning we need to appeal to our ability to discriminate among those sensations and the objects that produce them to a greater or lesser degree. That's the message of our first thesis. *cold* is relational. According to our second thesis, when we communicate a comparative judgment we do so by reference to a scalar segment, which is a path of sorts connecting two points. It is natural then that we draw, by analogy, on vocabulary associated with movement in space or time.[23] Simultaneous adoption of these twin theses has led to a new

---

22 Unlike Heim (2006), the proposal here gives the wrong results when a DP of the form '*exactly* n NP' occurs in the comparative clause. In some ways the present proposal differs from Heim (2006) in the way that Gajewski (2009)'s E-theory differed from Schwarzschild & Wilkinson (2001) and those two theories also differed on the coverage of *exactly* DPs. Gajewski appealed to an implicature-generating mechanism taking scope over the comparative. Zhang (this volume) adopts this same strategy making use of developments in Bumford (2017) and Brasoveanu (2013) to separate out the upper bounding part of *exactly*'s content.

23 According to Stassen (2006), "the type(s) of comparative construction that a language

perspective on the interaction of degrees and quantifiers, a rudimentary typology, and a clarification of the use of measurement jargon and of degree structures. In working out the consequences of adopting these hypotheses, I've only covered a small part of what is known about gradable predicates and degree constructions. There are challenges awaiting in the various types of adjectives and many kinds of degree constructions left to be considered, including kinds of comparatives.

Acknowledgements

I wish to thank Peter Hallman for inviting my participation in this volume and for comments on the paper. I am indebted to the organizers of SALT 22 and SALT 23 and to participants in seminars at Rutgers and MIT. Comments from and discussions with the following friends and colleagues have led to considerable improvements: Pranav Anand, Alan Bale, Chris Barker, Sigrid Beck, Rajesh Bhatt, Jonathan Bobaljik, Ryan Bochnak, Elizabeth Bogal-Allbritten, Lisa Bylinina, Veneeta Dayal, Danny Fox, Itamar Francez, Jon Gajewski, Anastasia Giannakidou, Jane Grimshaw, Martin Hackl, Irene Heim, I-Ta Chris Hsieh, Magda Kaufmann, Chris Kennedy, Ezra Keshet, Ayesha Kidwai, Paul Kockelman, Manfred Krifka, Utpal Lahiri, Xiao Li, Joyce McDonough, Cecile Meier, Jason Merchant, Marcin Morzycki, David Nicolas, Paul Portner, Renate Raffelsiefen, Jessica Rett, Ken Safir, Galit Sassoon, Junko Shimoyama, Stephanie Solt and Anna Szabolcsi.

References

Aloni, Maria & Floris Roelofsen. 2014. Indefinites in Comparatives. *Natural Language Semantics* 22.2:145–167

Alrenga, Peter & Christopher Kennedy. 2014. No More Shall We Part: Quantifiers in English Comparatives. *Natural Language Semantics* 22.1:1–53 //dx.doi.org/10.1007/s11050-013-9099-4.

Alrenga, Peter, Christopher Kennedy, & Jason Merchant. 2012. A New Standard of Comparison. In James McCloskey (ed.) *Proceedings of WCCFL 30*, UC, Santa Cruz: West Coast Conference on Formal Linguistics.

may employ is argued to be limited by the options that the language has in the encoding of (simultaneous or consecutive) sequences of events."

Anderson, Curt & Marcin Morzycki. 2015. Degrees as Kinds. *Natural Language and Linguistic Theory* 33.3:791–828

Bale, Alan. 2007. Boolean *and* and the semantic correlates of gradable adjectives. Handout for International Conference on Adjectives. Lille. France, 13–15 September 2007.

Bale, Alan Clinton. 2006. *The Universal Scale and the Semantics of Comparison*, doctoral dissertation, Montréal: McGill University.

Bale, Alan Clinton. 2011. Scales and Comparison Classes. *Natural Language Semantics* 19.2:169–190. doi:10.1007/s11050-010-9068-0.

Beck, Sigrid. 2010. Quantifiers in *than*-Clauses. *Semantics and Pragmatics* 3.1:1–72

Beck, Sigrid. 2012. DegP Scope Revisited. *Natural Language Semantics* 20.3:227–272

Beck, Sigrid. 2014. Plural Predication and Quantified *than*-Clauses. In *The Art and Craft of Semantics: A Festschrift for Irene Heim*, vol. 1, MITWPL 70, ed. by Luka Crnič and Uli Sauerland, 91–115. Cambridge, MA: MIT Working Papers in Linguistics

Beck, Sigrid & Arnim von Stechow. 2015. Events, Times and Worlds—An LF Architecture. In *Situationsargumente im Nominalbereich, Linguistische Arbeiten 562*, ed. by Christian Fortmann, Anja Lübbe and Irene Rapp, 13–46. Berlin: de Gruyter

Bhatt, Rajesh & Roumyana Pancheva. 2004. Late Merger of Degree Clauses. *Linguistic Inquiry* 35.1:1–45

Bochnak, M. Ryan. 2015. The Degree Semantics Parameter and Cross-linguistic Variation. *Semantics and Pragmatics* 8.6:1–48

Bogal-Allbritten, Elizabeth. 2013. Decomposing Notions of Adjectival Transitivity in Navajo. *Natural Language Semantics* 21.3:277–314.

Brasoveanu, Adrian. 2013. Modified Numerals as Post-Suppositions. *Journal of Semantics* 30.2:155–209

Bresnan, Joan. 1973. The Syntax of the Comparative Clause Construction in English. *Linguistic Inquiry* 4.3:275–343.

Buccola, Brian & Benjamin Spector. 2016. Modified Numerals and Maximality. *Linguistics and Philosophy* 39.3:151–199

Bumford, Dylan. 2017. Split-scope Definites: Relative Superlatives and Haddock Descriptions. *Linguistics and Philosophy* 40.6:549–593

Champollion, Lucas. 2015. The Interaction of Compositional Semantics and Event Semantics. *Linguistics and Philosophy* 38.1:31–66

Cresswell, Max J. 1976. The Semantics of Degree. In *Montague Grammar*, ed. by Barbara Hall Partee, 261–292. Academic Press.

Davidson, Donald. 1967. The Logical Form of Action Sentences. In *The Logic of Decision and Action*, ed. by Nicholas Rescher, 81–95. Pittsburgh: University of Pittsburgh Press

Doetjes, Jenny S. 2012. On the Incompatibility of Non neutral Adjectives and Measure Phrases. In *Sinn und Bedeutung 16: Volume 1*, ed. by Ana Aguilar Guevara, Anna

Chernilovskaya, and Rick Nouwen, 197–211. Cambridge, MA: MIT Working Papers in Linguistics

Dotlačil, Jakub & Rick Nouwen. 2016. The Comparative and Degree Pluralities. *Natural Language Semantics* 24.1:45–78, DOI 10.1007/s11050-015-9119-7

Faller, Martina. 2000. Dimensional Adjectives and Measure Phrases in Vector Space Semantics. In *Formalizing the Dynamics of Information*, ed. by Martina Faller, Stefan Kaufmann and Marc Pauly, 151–170. Stanford, CA: CSLI Publications

Fleisher, Nicholas. 2016. Comparing Theories of Quantifiers in *than* Clauses: Lessons from Downward-Entailing Differentials. *Semantics and Pragmatics* 9, doi:10.3765/sp.9.4.

Gajewski, Jon. 2009. More on Quantifiers in Comparative Clauses. In *18th Semantics and Linguistic Theory conference, held March 21–23, 2008 at The University of Massachusetts, Amherst*, ed. by Tova Friedman and Satoshi Ito, 340–357

Gawron, Jean Mark. 1995. Comparatives, Superlatives and Resolution. *Linguistics and Philosophy* 18.4:333–380.

Grimshaw, Jane. 1987. Subdeletion. *Linguistic Inquiry* 18.4:659–669

Heim, Irene. 2000. Degree Operator Scope. handout for SALT 10 at Cornell.

Heim, Irene. 2001. Degree Operators and Scope. In *Audiatur Vox Sapientiae. A Festschrift for Arnim von Stechow*, ed. by Caroline Féry and Wolfgang Sternefeld, 214–239. Berlin: Akademie

Heim, Irene. 2006. Remarks on Comparative Clauses as Generalized Quantifiers. MIT ms.

Heim, Irene & Angelika Kratzer. 1998. *Semantics in Generative Grammar: Blackwell Textbooks in Linguistics*. Oxford/Malden, MA: Blackwell.

Hirsch, Aron. 2017. *An Inflexible Semantics for Cross-Categorial Operators*, doctoral dissertation, Cambridge, MA: Massachusetts Institute of Technology

Hoeksema, Jacob. 1983. Negative Polarity and the Comparative. *Natural Language & Linguistic Theory* 1.3:403–434

Hohaus, Vera. 2018. How do Degrees Enter the Grammar? Language Change in Samoan from [−DSP] to [+DSP]. In *Proceedings of TripleA 4*, ed. by Elizabeth Bogal-Allbritten and Elizabeth Coppock, 106–120. Universitätsbibliothek Tübingen

Izvorski, Roumyana. 1995. A Solution to the Subcomparative Paradox. In *Proceedings of WCCFL 14*, ed. by José Camacho, Lina Choueiri, and Maki Watanabe, 203–219. Stanford, CA: CSLI Publications

Kamp, Hans & Barbara Partee. 1995. Prototype Theory and Compositionality. *Cognition* 57.2:129–191.

Kamp, J.A.W. 1975. Two Theories about Adjectives. In *Formal Semantics of Natural Language*, ed. by Edward Keenan, 123–155. Cambridge: Cambridge University Press

Kennedy, Christopher. 1999. *Projecting the Adjective: The Syntax and Semantics of Gradability and Comparison*. New York: Garland.

Kennedy, Christopher. 2001. Polar Opposition and the Ontology of Degrees. *Linguistics and Philosophy* 24.1:33–70.

Kennedy, Christopher. 2007a. Vagueness and Grammar: The Semantics of Relative and Absolute Gradable Adjectives. *Linguistics and Philosophy* 30.1:1–45

Kennedy, Christopher. 2007b. Modes of Comparison. In *43rd Annual Meeting of the Chicago Linguistic Society, Volume 1: The Main Session*, ed. by in Malcolm Elliott, James Kirby, Osamu Sawada, Eleni Staraki and Suwon Yoon, 139–163, Chicago: Chicago Linguistic Society.

Kennedy, Christopher & Louise McNally. 2005. Scale Structure, Degree Modification, and the Semantics of Gradable Predicates. *Language* 81.2:345–381

Kennedy, Christopher & Louise McNally. 2010. Color, Context and Compositionality. *Synthese* 174:79–98

Klein, Ewan. 1980. A Semantics for Positive and Comparative Adjectives. *Linguistics and Philosophy* 4.1:1–45.

Klein, Ewan. 1991. Comparatives. In *Semantik/Semantics An International Handbook of Contemporary Research*, ed. by Arnim von Stechow and Dieter Wunderlich, 673–691, Berlin, New York: de Gruyter.

Klein, Wolfgang. 1994 *Time in Language*, London, New York: Routledge.

Kockelman, Paul. 2018. The Role of *mas* (< Sp. *más*) in Q'eqchi': a History of Comparison and Degree in a Mayan Language. ms.

Kratzer, Angelika. 1996. Severing the External Argument from its Verb. In, *Phrase Structure and the Lexicon*. ed. by Johan Rooryck and Lauri Zaring, 109–137. Dordrecht: Kluwer.

Larson, Richard. 1988. Scope and Comparatives. *Linguistics and Philosophy* 11.1:1–26.

Lassiter, Daniel. 2015. Adjectival Modification and Gradation. in *Wiley-Blackwell Handbook of Contemporary Semantics*, 2nd Edition, Chapter 5, ed. by Shalom Lappin and Chris Fox, 143–167, Wiley-Blackwell

Lechner, Winfried. 2004. *Ellipsis in Comparatives*. Berlin, New York: de Gruyter

Lechner, Winfried & Norbert Corver. 2017. Comparative Deletion and Comparative Subdeletion. In *The Wiley Blackwell Companion to Syntax, 2nd Edition*, edited by Martin Everaert and Henk van Riemsdijk, Malden: Blackwell.

Menon, Mythili. 2017. The Standard Marker in Malayalam Encodes Comparative Semantics. In *34th West Coast Conference on Formal Linguistics*, ed. by Aaron Kaplan et al. 379–386. Somerville, MA: Cascadilla Proceedings Project.

Mey, Jacob. 1976. Comparatives in Eskimo. In *Papers in Eskimo and Aleut Linguistics*, ed. by E.P. Hamp, 159–178. Chicago Linguistic Society

Morzycki, Marcin. 2015. *Modification*. Cambridge: Cambridge University Press.

Oda, Toshiko. 2008. *Degree Constructions in Japanese*, doctoral dissertation, University of Connecticut.

Portner, Paul. 1992. *Situation Theory and the Semantics of Propositional Expressions*, doctoral dissertation, Amherst, MA: University of Massachusetts

Rett, Jessica. 2018. The Semantics of *many, much, few*, and *little*. *Language & Linguistics Compass*, 12.1:1–18

Rotstein, Carmen & Yoad Winter. 2004. Total Adjectives vs. Partial Adjectives: Scale Structure and Higher-Order Modifiers. *Natural Language Semantics* 12.3:259–288.

Rullmann, Hotze. 1995 *Maximality in the Semantics of WH-Constructions*, doctoral dissertation, Amherst, MA: University of Massachusetts

Sassoon, Galit. 2010. Measurement Theory in Linguistics. *Synthese* 174:151–180. DOI 10.1007/s11229-009-9687-5

Sawada, Osamu & Thomas Grano. 2011. Scale Structure, Coercion, and the Interpretation of Measure Phrases in Japanese. *Natural Language Semantics* 19:191–226

Schein, Barry. 2017. '*And*': *Conjunction Reduction Redux*, Cambridge, MA.: The MIT Press.

Schwarz, Bernhard. 2010. A note on *for*-phrases and derived scales. Handout for talk at Sinn und Bedeutung 15, September 9–11, 2010.

Schwarzschild Roger & Karina Wilkinson. 2002. Quantifiers in Comparatives: A Semantics of Degree based on Intervals. *Natural Language Semantics* 10.1:1–41

Schwarzschild, Roger. 2005. Measure Phrases as Modifiers of Adjectives. In *L'adjectif, Recherches Linguistiques de Vincennes*, vol. 34, ed. by Patricia Cabredo Hofherr and Ora Matushansky, 207–228. Paris: Presses universitaires de Vincennes.

Schwarzschild, Roger. 2012. Directed Scale Segments. In *22nd Semantics and Linguistic Theory Conference, held at the University of Chicago in Chicago, Illinois, May 18–May 20, 2012*, ed. by Anca Chereches, 65–82

Schwarzschild, Roger. 2013. Degrees and Segments. In *23rd Semantics and Linguistic Theory Conference, held at the University of California, Santa Cruz, May 3–5, 2013*, ed. by Todd Snider, 212–238

Seuren, P.A.M. 1978. The Structure and Selection of Positive and Negative Gradable Adjectives. In *Parasession on the Lexicon, Chicago Linguistics Society*, ed by Donka Farkas, Wesley M. Jacobsen and Karol W. Todrys, 336–346. Chicago: Chicago Linguistic Society.

Stassen, Leonard. 2006. Comparative Constructions. In. *Encyclopedia of Language & Linguistics. Second Edition*, ed. by Keith Brown, 686–690, Elsevier, Oxford DOI 10.1016/B0-08-044854-2/00181-4

Svenonius, Peter & Christopher Kennedy. 2006. Northern Norwegian Degree Questions and the Syntax of Measurement. In *Phases of Interpretation*, ed. by Mara Frascarelli, 133–161. The Hague: de Gruyter,

Thomas, Guillaume. 2018. Underspecification in Degree Operators. *Journal of Semantics* 35.2:43–93

van Rooij, Robert. 2008. Comparatives and Quantifiers. In *Empirical Issues in Syntax and Semantics 7*, ed. by Olivier Bonami and Patricia Cabredo Hofherr, 423–444. Paris: Presses de l'Université de Paris-Sorbonne.

van Rooij, Robert. 2011. Measurement and Interadjective Comparisons. *Journal of Semantics* 28.3:335–358

von Stechow, Arnim. 1984a. Comparing Theories of Comparison. *Journal of Semantics* 3:1–77

von Stechow, Arnim. 1984b. My Reaction to Cresswell's, Hellan's, Hoeksema's and Seuren's Comments. *Journal of Semantics* 3:183–199

Wellwood, Alexis. 2015. On the Semantics of Comparison across Categories. *Linguistics and Philosophy* 38.1:67–101

Williams, Edwin Samuel. 1974 *Rule Ordering in Syntax*, doctoral dissertation, Cambridge, MA: Massachusetts Institute of Technology

Williams, Edwin S. 1977. Discourse and Logical Form. *Linguistic Inquiry* 8.1:101–139.

Winter, Yoad. 2005. Cross-Categorial Restrictions on Measure Phrase Modification. *Linguistics and Philosophy* 28.2:233–267. DOI 10.1007%2Fs10988-004-1469-4

Zwarts, Joost. 1997. Vectors as Relative Positions: A Compositional Semantics of Modified PPs. *Journal of Semantics*, 14.1:57–86.

CHAPTER 8

Measuring Cardinalities: Evidence from Differential Comparatives in French

Vincent Homer and Rajesh Bhatt

1 Introduction

In this article, we show that comparatives of cardinality (e.g., *more books*) are special: cardinality differs from other dimensions, e.g., tallness, in that it can only be measured out using strictly numerical measures. Our primary data in this paper comes from nominal comparatives in French, e.g., *plus de livres* 'more books' (where one compares numbers of books): certain differentials cannot straightforwardly combine with the degree head *plus*. Those are numerically quantified noun phrases (Num NP), for example *trois livres* 'three books', which cannot combine with the degree head in a nominal comparative the same way that measure phrases, e.g., *trois centimètres* 'three centimeters', combine with the degree head in adjectival comparatives.[1] We derive the inability of Num NP differentials to combine with nominal comparatives from the fact that nominal cardinality comparatives quantify over pure cardinalities while Num NP only gives cardinalities of NP. We also show how French circumvents the problem of combining Num NP with the degree head *plus* by resorting to a special structure, signaled by the presence of the preposition *de* before *plus*, where the differential is a verb argument (in many languages cardinality comparatives with differentials end up with a surface syntax that is quite different from their differential-less siblings, see Bhatt & Homer 2018). In this structure, the degree quantifier lacks sortal information since it does not combine with an NP. It therefore ranges over unspecified degrees, information about which is provided by the differential phrase. French shows us that there is flexibility in the way a quantificational head (the degree quantifier *plus*) combines syntactically with its semantic arguments. Depending upon the kind of degrees this quantifier quantifies over, its semantic arguments enter different syntactic structures.

---

1 The distinction between adjectival and nominal comparatives is also known as the degree comparative/quantity comparative distinction (Gawron 1995).

Section 2 provides the empirical background: we show that combining *plus* in a nominal comparative with a differential is subject to strict limitations: Num NP measure phrases (e.g., *trois livres*) are excluded, while 'quantity words', i.e., words like *beaucoup* 'much', which can be used as degree quantifiers or as comparative modifiers, are possible (a non-exhaustive list of quantity words in English is: *few, little, much, many*). In Section 3, we offer an explanation for the dichotomy between measure phrases and bare quantifiers. Section 4 describes the syntactic properties of the special construction, labelled '*de plus* differential comparative', that French uses to introduce Num NP measure phrases in nominal comparatives; a semantic analysis is also provided. Some outstanding problems are discussed in the last section.

2 The Problem: Measure Phrases in Nominal Comparatives

2.1 *Adjectival Comparatives*

French comparative constructions are superficially similar to the better studied English comparatives. The similarity is obvious in so-called adjectival comparatives, with or without a differential ((1a) and (1b)):

(1) *Adjectival comparatives*
   a. Without a differential:
      Marie est plus grande que Jean.
      Marie is more tall   than Jean
      'Marie is taller than Jean.'

   b. With a differential:
      Marie est trois centimètres plus grande que Jean.
      Marie is three centimeters more tall   than Jean.
      'Marie is three centimeters taller than Jean.'

In French, positive adjectives never take a measure phrase; but comparative adjectives can:[2]

---

[2] Here we do not count the measure phrases introduced post-nominally with *de*, which Schwarzschild (2005) talks about:
   (i) a. **cinq kilos lourd*
          five kgs heavy
       b. *lourd de cinq kilos*
          heavy of five kgs

(2) a. *trois centimètres grande
　　　three centimeters tall
　　　Intended: 'three centimeters tall'

　　b. trois centimètres plus grande
　　　three centimeters more tall
　　　'three centimeters taller'

2.2 Nominal Comparatives

In so-called nominal comparatives without a differential, the similarity still holds (note that *plus* is followed by the preposition *de* in nominal comparatives with a degree quantified NP; more on this in Section 3.1):

(3) Marie a lu plus de livres que Jean.
　　Marie has read more of books than Jean
　　'Marie read more books than Jean.'

With a differential, the situation is significantly more complex. The only differentials that can straightforwardly fit in the canonical position, i.e., right before *plus*, are differentials that consist of just a 'quantity word', e.g., *beaucoup* 'much, a lot':

(4) Marie a lu beaucoup plus de livres que Jean.
　　Marie has read much   more of books than Jean
　　'Marie read many more books than Jean.'

Similarly:

(5) a. un peu plus de livres
　　　a little more of books
　　　lit. 'a little more books'[3]

　　b. infiniment plus de livres
　　　infinitely more of books
　　　'infinitely more books'

3　*Un peu* cannot combine with count nouns (**un peu de livres*), but it can be used as a differential with a count nominal comparative.

c. *tellement plus de livres*
   so.much more of books
   lit. 'so much more books'

d. *trois fois plus de livres*
   three times more of books
   lit. 'three times more books'

Differentials that consist of only a bare numeral are out (while they are not in English):

(6) **Marie a lu trois plus de livres que Jean.*
    Marie has read three more of books than Jean
    Intended: 'Marie read three books more than Jean.'

Also out are differentials of the form Num NP, e.g., *trois livres* 'three books':

(7) **Marie a lu trois livres plus (de livres) que Jean.*
    Marie has read three books more of books than Jean
    Intended: 'Marie read three books more than Jean.'

The way French would render what is intended in (7) involves the preposition *de* before *plus* (notated de_{pre}), and no noun following it:

(8) *Marie a lu trois livres de_{pre} plus que Jean.*
    Marie has read three books of more than Jean
    'Marie read three books more than Jean.'

Compare with the Num-NP-more order in English (English also has a Num-more-NP order; we will discuss both orders in due course): no equivalent of *de* can intervene between the measure phrase and *more*, and, like in French, no noun can follow *more*:

(9) Marie read three books (*of) more (*books) than John.

(8) is an instance of what we will call the *de plus* differential comparative. All differentials that contain an NP (in other words, a sort denoting expression, e.g., *livres*) require the *de plus* differential comparative:

(10) a. *trois   livres   *(de) plus/ *trois   livres plus   de livres*
       three books   of   more   three books more of books
       'three books more'

   b. *plusieurs livres *(de) plus/ *plusieurs livres plus   de livres*
      several   books   of   more   several   books more of books
      'several books more'

   c. *quelques livres *(de) plus/ *quelques livres plus   de livres*
      some   books   of   more   some   books more of books
      'a few books more'

   d. *au   moins trois livres *(de) plus/ *au   moins trois livres*
      at.the less three books   of   more   at.the less three books
      plus   de livres
      more of books
      'at least three books more'

But differentials that do not contain an NP cannot enter the *de plus* differential comparative. We thus have an interesting pair: when *beaucoup* composes with an NP sort complement (11a), the presence of de_{pre} is mandatory, in other words, the *de plus* differential comparative is required; when it doesn't (11b), the *de plus* differential comparative is barred:

(11) a. *beaucoup de livres   *(de_{pre}) plus*
        a.lot   of books   of   more

   b. *beaucoup (*de_{pre}) plus de livres*   [=(4)]
      a.lot   of   more of books

The following paradigm sums up what we have seen so far, about count nominal comparatives in French:

(12) No differential:
     plus de livres

(13) Differential present, and *plus* followed by an NP:
     a. *trois plus de livres   *Num-plus-de-NP
     b. *trois livres plus de livres   *Num-NP-plus-de-NP
     c. *trois livres de_{pre} plus de livres   *Num-NP-de-plus-de-NP

    d. beaucoup plus de livres   ✓Quantity_word-plus-de-NP
    e. *beaucoup de$_{pre}$ plus de livres   *Quantity_word-de-plus-de-NP

(14) Differential present, and *plus* not followed by an NP:
    a. *trois livres plus   *Num-NP-plus
    b. trois livres de$_{pre}$ plus   ✓Num-NP-de-plus
    c. *beaucoup de livres plus   *Quantity_word-de-NP-plus
    d. beaucoup de livres de$_{pre}$ plus   ✓Quantity_word-de-NP-de-plus

Without a differential, *plus* can combine with a degree quantified NP (through the preposition *de*), e.g., *plus de livres* (12). If *plus* is to be followed by a degree quantified NP (a 'restrictor'), the only possible differentials are 'quantity words', i.e., ones that are not bare numerals and do not contain a sortal NP (13a)–(13d); *de$_{pre}$* is not available ((13c) and (13e)). In the absence of a degree quantified NP, *plus* can take a measure phrase as long as it is preceded by *de$_{pre}$* ((14a) vs. (14b) and (14c) vs. (14d)): (14b) and (14d) exemplify the *de plus* differential comparative, characterized by *de$_{pre}$* and no noun after *plus*. The term 'measure phrase' as we use it here covers Num-NP and quantity_word-de-NP phrases.

    We thus have the following generalization about bare *plus* and about *de$_{pre}$*:

(15) **Generalization:** In count nominal comparatives, bare *plus*, i.e., *plus* not preceded by *de$_{pre}$*, is possible either with a differential consisting of a quantity word, or with a following NP. *De$_{pre}$* is only possible with a preceding measure phrase (=a Num-NP phrase or a quantity_word-de-NP phrase) and no NP following *plus*.

This generalization is about count nominal comparatives; we will address mass nominal comparatives later (Section 5.2); in adjectival comparatives, all differentials, including measure phrases, can immediately precede *plus* (1b), in fact *de$_{pre}$* is impossible there:

(16) *Marie est trois centimètres de$_{pre}$ plus grande que Jean.
      Marie is three centimeters of   more tall   than Jean.
      Intended: 'Marie is three centimeters taller than Jean.'

In the next section, we propose an explanation for the restrictions on differentials with bare *plus* in count nominal comparatives.

3 Bare *plus* and Differentials

In order to understand the first part of the generalization in (15), we need to answer three questions: Why are bare numerals excluded with bare *plus?* Why are differentials with a sortal NP excluded? Why is the rest (e.g., *beaucoup*) possible? The three questions are taken up (not necessarily in that order) after a foray into the structure of nominal comparatives.

	Can bare *plus* be preceded by…	
trois	*trois livres/ beaucoup de livres*	*beaucoup*
No	No	Yes
(13a)	(13b)	(13d)

3.1 Hidden Structure

Following Bresnan 1973, we assume that in English, adjectival comparatives, as well as nominal comparatives with a degree quantified NP, are formed by combining *-er* with an adjective (*-er* heads a DegP projection which is adjoined to AP). In the adjectival comparative case, it is clear that there is an adjective (the case is maybe less straightforward in suppletion cases, *better*), e.g., *tall* as in *Mary is 3 centimeters tall-er than John.* In the nominal comparative case, the morphology is not fully transparent but the adjective is assumed to be *many/much: more* spells out *many-er/much-er*, as in *Mary read three many-er books than John.* The AP formed by *-er* and *many/much* is adjoined to an NP, e.g., *books*.

(17) *Standard representation of an adjectival comparative in English*

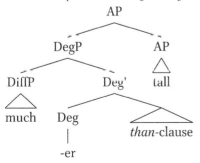

(18) *Standard representation of a nominal comparative in English*[4]

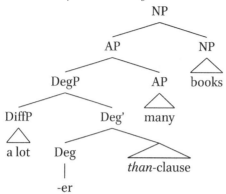

In the adjectival comparative case, French can combine *plus*, a counterpart of -*er*, with an adjective, e.g., *grande*, as in *Marie est plus grande que Jean*, in a similar fashion to English. In the nominal comparative case, e.g., *Marie a lu plus de livres que Jean*, there is no overt adjective: the morpheme *plus* which seems to semantically play the same role as -*er*, appears to have no adjective to combine with, in apparent contravention of Bresnan's rule. If the rule is in fact obeyed, a covert adjective has to be present in the structure. But an equivalent of the adjective *many/much*, used to form nominal comparatives in English, cannot be found in French. The closest that French has to *many/much*, *beaucoup*, is indeed an N/NP, not an adjective,[5] unlike *many/much*.

---

4 An anonymous reviewer notes two problems for this standard representation of nominal comparatives: (i) it leaves unexplained the fact that the *than*-clause cannot surface *in situ* (**more than Mary … books*), and (ii) it doesn't say why the *than*-clause can, unlike other adjunct contained material, extrapose (*She met more people yesterday than Mary* vs. **She met a {proud t_1} man {proud t_1} yesterday [of his daugther]$_1$*). A proposal that avoids these complications is Lechner 2004.

5 *Beaucoup* is etymologically formed with the noun *coup* 'knock' modified by the adjective *beau* 'beautiful' (Carlier 2011 a.o.). It doesn't combine with an NP directly the way an adjective would: the preposition *de* is necessary, which could signal noun complementation:
(i)   a. *beaucoup *(de) livres*
             a.lot   of   books
       b. *beaucoup *(de) vin*
             a.lot   of   wine
Unlike *many* or the adjective *nombreux* 'numerous', *beaucoup* cannot be used as a predicate or as an NP modifier:
(ii) a. *Les problèmes sont *beaucoup/ nombreux.*
             the problems   are   a.lot   numerous
       b. The problems are many.

We propose that French uses abstract formatives to construct *many/much*:

(19) *French nominal comparative:*
UN [[_{AP} [_{DegP} plus] GRAND] [_{NP} NOMBRE de_{post} livres]]

(20) *French nominal comparative (without a differential)*

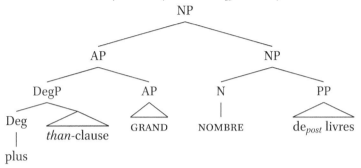

In this structure we find a covert occurrence of the adjective *grand* 'great' (notated: GRAND) and a covert occurrence of the noun *nombre* 'number' (notated: NOMBRE). The AP formed by *plus* and GRAND is adjoined to an NP headed by NOMBRE. The presence of the adjective is in accordance with Bresnan 1973. The motivation for postulating the covert noun NOMBRE is not just semantic, it also comes from the presence of the preposition *de*_{post}, which we take to be a signal of noun complementation: we analyze the overt NP, e.g., *livres*, as the complement of the silent N NOMBRE,[6] while in English the NP is

---

(iii) a. *les *beaucoup (de)/ nombreux problèmes que ...*
the a.lot   of   numerous problems that
b. the many problems that ...

Beaucoup cannot be modified by the adverb *infiniment* 'infinitely', unlike French adjectives, and unlike *many*:

(iv) a. **infiniment beaucoup de livres*
infinitely a.lot   of books
b. *infiniment grand*
infinitely great
c. infinitely many

6 The overt noun *number* requires the preposition *de* before its complement:
(i) *un nombre *(de) livres*
a number of books

Granted, there are many usages of the preposition *de*, so our claim that it is used here to introduce a complement of a noun is by no means the only plausible hypothesis. It doesn't seem to be required by case reasons at any rate: bare nouns can be used after certain quantifiers, e.g., *quelques livres* 'a few books'.

simply comprised of the visible N. To sum up, the structure corresponding to the English *many-er books* literally says the equivalent of *a greater number of books*, which is *un plus grand nombre de livres*, with three covert elements. This is to be compared with:

(21) *English nominal comparative:*
[[AP [DegP -er] many] [NP books]]

3.2 Ruling Out Differentials with a Sortal NP

When we try to degree quantify the overt noun *nombre/number* with a measure phrase, ungrammaticality ensues, in a way parallel to (13b). This seems to set it apart from other nouns, e.g., *girl/fille, book/livre*, etc.

(22) **trois livres plus de livres*   [=(13b)]
    Analyzed as:
    UN trois livres plus GRAND NOMBRE de livres[7]

(23) *French:*
    a. *une fille trois centimètres plus grande*
        a   girl three centimeters more tall

    b. **un nombre trois livres plus grand (de livres)*
        a   number three books more great   of books

(24) *English:*
    a. a three cm taller girl
    b. a three hundred mile greater range
    c. *a three book greater number (of books)

The adjective is not at fault by itself: the adjective *grand* can admit a measure phrase ((23a), where it means *tall*), and so can *great* (24b). Is the noun *nombre/number* at fault then? The problem is not actually tied to nominal comparatives or to the noun *nombre qua* noun. We can replicate the deviance of (23b) with an adjectival comparative predicated of the noun *nombre*:[8]

---

[7] In the underlying order we have a noun, NOMBRE, after the adjective; for reasons that we do not explore here, in the surface order (23a), the noun comes before the whole AP; (23b), with the N-AP order, is out, and so is the variant with the flipped order.

[8] In fact, the order 'un NP Num NP plus A', exemplified in (23a), (23b) and (25), is potentially ambiguous in French between an 'adjectival' structure and a 'nominal' one. In the former,

(25) *Ce nombre (de livres) est trois livres plus grand que ce
    this number of books is three books more great than that
    nombre (de livres).
    number of books

The same deviance obtains in English:

(26) *This number (of books) is three books greater than that number (of books).

And the deviance also obtains with the adjective *nombreux* 'numerous':

(27) *Cette classe est trois élèves plus nombreuse que cette classe.
    this class is three students more numerous than that class
    Intended: 'There are three more students in this class than in that class.'

The problem with measure phrases appears to be conceptual: something about the cardinality dimension makes measure phrases unavailable. The restrictions on possible differentials described above come into play when the adjective *grand* is recruited to measure a cardinality. But the same measure phrase, *trois livres*, which cannot be used to measure out a cardinality, can be coerced to measure out a length:

(28) *Marie a une étagère trois livres plus large que Jean.*
    Marie has a shelf three books more wide than Jean
    'Marie has a three book wider shelf than Jean.'

We will come back to the English case in Sect. 5.1 (*three books more* is an apparent counterexample). But for the time being, we focus on French.
    Recall the ill-formedness of (13b):

(29) *Marie a lu trois livres plus (de livres) que Jean.
    Marie has read three books more of books than Jean
    Intended: 'Marie read three books more than Jean.'

---

the adjectival comparative is predicative and realized inside a reduced relative clause; in the latter, the comparative is attributive and extraposed to the right.

With the cardinality dimension, unlike other dimensions, i.e., length, weight, volume, temperature, etc., Num-NP and quantity_word-de-NP are not acceptable differentials. We believe that a simple explanation can be given by considering the specialness of cardinality.

First, we spell out our semantics for *plus*, based on the well-behaved adjectival comparative:

(30) *Marie est trois centimètres plus grande que Jean.*
    Marie is three centimeters more tall than Jean
    'Marie is three centimeters taller than Jean.'

Assume the following entry for *plus* (modeled after standard accounts of *-er*):

(31) 〚plus〛 = $[\lambda D_{1\langle d,t\rangle} . \lambda D_{\langle\langle d,t\rangle,t\rangle} . \lambda D_{2\langle d,t\rangle} . D(\lambda d_d . D_2(d) \wedge \neg D_1(d))]$

Plus composes with three arguments. Among them are two predicates of degrees (type $\langle d, t\rangle$), or, in set-talk, two degree intervals (connected sets of degrees), one of which corresponds to the *than*-clause, and the other corresponds to the lambda abstract created by Quantifier Raising (QR). The $\langle\langle d, t\rangle, t\rangle$ argument is the differential argument:[9] it is a predicate of predicates of degrees, or, in set-talk, and since we assume that the relevant sets are connected, a predicate of intervals. The relevant interval is made up of all the degrees that are in the set corresponding to the lambda abstract (here, the set of degrees of tallness that Marie has) and not in the set corresponding to the *than*-clause (here the set of degrees of tallness that Jean has). This interval is a gap, between two heights. A differential such as *trois centimètres* indicates the size of this height interval:

(32) 〚(30)〛 = $(\mathcal{M}(\text{〚centimètres〛})(\text{〚trois〛}))(\lambda d_d.$ Marie is d-tall and Jean is not d-tall)
    = the size of {d : Marie is d-tall and Jean is not d-tall} is three centimeters

---

9 We retain from Schwarzschild 2005 the idea that measure phrases do not denote degrees (type d); instead they denote predicates of degree gaps (type $\langle\langle d, t\rangle, t\rangle$). The $\langle\langle d, t\rangle, t\rangle$ meaning is derived by combining $\mathcal{M}$, a variant of a shifter introduced in Rett 2014, with the unit and then with the numeral i.e., $\mathcal{M}(\text{〚unit〛})(\text{〚numeral〛})$. $\mathcal{M}$ is defined as follows: $\mathcal{M} \rightarrow \lambda P . \lambda n . \lambda D_{\langle d,t\rangle} . M(D) = n_P$. See Sect. 4.2 for details.

This is in essence Schwarzschild's (2005) analysis of measure phrases as predicates of gaps (our implementation bears some resemblance to Rett's (2018) implementation). To make sense of the unavailability of *trois livres plus (de livres)*, we need to ask ourselves whether *trois livres* can be a cardinality measure phrase. Going back to the semantics of *plus* (31), we see that its differential looks to measure out a gap, which is an interval of degrees. Here we are dealing with an interval of degrees of cardinality: this is a requirement imposed by *nombre*. What are degrees of cardinality? Like degrees of length, they are numbers; but unlike units of measurement of length, the unit of measurement of cardinality is not expressed. Crucially a sort, e.g., *book, apple, orange*, is not a cardinality unit. While it is possible to add three centimeters to five feet, as long as one unit of measurement can be converted into the other (or both to a third) because they are measured along the same dimension, *viz* length, there is no conversion that could, without loss of meaning, allow one to add three apples to five oranges. In *trois livres, livres* is a sort, not a cardinality unit; if there is a cardinality unit, then it is implicit. Therefore *trois livres* or *beaucoup de livres* cannot be appropriate cardinality measure phrases. They cannot measure out a gap that is a gap between sets of numbers; another way of seeing the problem is that three books/many books cannot be added to 5.[10]

(33) *Marie a lu trois livres plus (de livres) que Jean.[11]   [=(13b)]

(34) $[\![(33)]\!] = (\mathcal{M}([\![\text{livres}]\!])([\![\text{trois}]\!]))(\lambda d_d.$ Marie read d-many books and Jean did not read d-many books)
   $= \#$

The result is deviant; and the same deviance is expected to occur with all differentials with a sortal NP (e.g., **beaucoup de livres plus (de livres)*).

3.3 Ruling in Quantity Words as Differentials

When they combine with a de-NP restrictor, quantity words like *beaucoup* function as cardinality measure phrases; but the absence of an NP restrictor makes them purely quantitative. For that reason, we can compute a meaning for (35),

---

10   In Sect. 4.2, we make explicit our assumptions about the meaning of *trois livres*.
11   In our analysis, the anomaly of (33) is semantic; we haven't derived a contradiction or a tautology, some of which are known to induce ungrammaticality (Gajewski 2002). We leave for future research a complete explanation of the perceived ungrammaticality of such a sentence.

with some simplifying assumption about the source of evaluativity introduced by *beaucoup*:

(35) Marie a lu beaucoup plus de livres que Jean. [=(13d)]

(36) ⟦beaucoup⟧ = $\lambda D_{\langle d,t \rangle}$. the size of D is large

(37) ⟦(35)⟧ = ⟦beaucoup⟧(λd_d. Marie read d-many books and Jean did not read d-many books)
= the size of {d : Marie read d-many books and Jean did not read d-many books} is large

(38) *French nominal comparative with a quantity word differential*

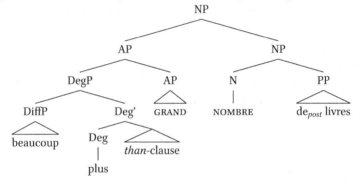

3.4 Bare Numerals

Bare numerals pose an interesting challenge. They are not acceptable as differentials, witness (39):

(39) *Marie a lu trois plus de livres que Jean. [=(13a)]

When cardinalities are explicitly compared, the deviance with bare numerals remains: this is shown by (40), a variant of (23b), and (41), a variant of (25):

(40) *Ceci est un nombre trois plus grand (de livres) que ça.
 this is a number three more great of books than that

(41) *Ce nombre (de livres) est trois plus grand que ce nombre
 this number of books is three more great than that number
 (de livres).
 of books

And yet, bare numerals do seem to be the right kind of object to measure out a gap between two cardinality intervals. If what we said in the previous subsection is on the right track, it seems that the source of the problem should not be conceptual, but rather syntactic. We do not have an explanation for the unacceptability of (39) through (41), but a way of looking at it might be to incriminate some constraint against free-standing numerals, an appearance of which would be in the ban on the constituency *more than Num/less than Num* for comparative numeral DPs (Arregi 2013).

Interestingly, English can say:

(42) Mary read three more books than John.

This Num-More-NP order is very rare cross-linguistically, and in fact, we cannot be absolutely certain that it is not the result of movement of the NP from Num-NP-More. Note that when cardinalities are explicitly compared, in a way parallel to (40)–(41) above, ungrammaticality ensues, which casts doubt on the Num-More-NP constituency (i.e., on the fact that the numeral is indeed a differential in (42)):

(43) *This is a three greater number (of books) than that.

(44) *This number (of books) is three greater than that number (of books).

With the intriguing exception of (42), bare numerals appear to not be suitable differentials. It stands to reason that it is the same (supposedly syntactic) constraint which applies to (39)–(41) and (43)–(44).

To sum up, in this section we've explained why bare *plus* cannot take measure phrases in nominal comparatives, because cardinality gaps cannot be measured out by measure phrases. Quantity words like *beaucoup* are suitable differentials because they are purely quantitative. Bare numerals are paradoxically ruled out: we proposed that a syntactic constraint explains this unexpected restriction. We can now turn to the *de plus* differential comparative.

4 The *de plus* Differential Comparative in French

After bare *plus*, we now discuss the *de plus* differential comparative, which is mandatory in nominal comparatives with a measure phrase and banned everywhere else:

(45) trois livres de_{pre} plus [=(14b)]

An obvious analytical challenge is the availability of a differential with a sort, given what we just explained about the cardinality dimension requiring a numerical measure; we will address the issue in Sect. 4.2 (and argue that the dimension of comparison is in fact not cardinality). Here we focus on the syntactic properties of the construction: we show that in this construction the differential is not a specifier of the Deg head. Instead, the differential *de plus* is adjoined to a projection of the differential NP, as shown in (46) below. What the verb combines with is thus a projection of the differential.

(46) De plus *differential comparative in French*

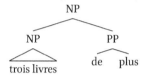

This stands in contrast to the structure of French nominal comparatives with a quantity word differential (38), which in turn conforms with standard assumptions about differential comparatives, namely that differentials sit in the specifier of the Deg head, and DegP is adjoined to an AP, e.g., *tall*, or *many* (the following trees illustrate those assumptions for English):

(47) *Adjectival comparative*

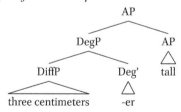

(48) *Nominal comparative*

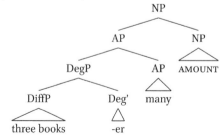

In the *de plus* construction, the presence of the preposition de_{pre} is hardly compatible with the view that the measure phrase occupies the specifier of *plus*. We present a set of additional facts which suggest that the measure phrase in the French *de plus* differential comparative (*trois livres de$_{pre}$ plus* (14b)) is a verb argument, and it is modified by a phrase containing the degree head (there simply is no degree quantified NP) as in (46).

4.1   Justifying the Special Constituency

4.1.1   Movement I: Quantitative *en* Cliticization

The first piece of evidence for (46) comes from the quantitative *en* cliticization test: the clitic *en* can be anaphoric to an NP preceded by a numeral or certain quantifiers (e.g., *beaucoup de* 'many'): for example in (49), *en* is anaphoric to *livres* 'books', an NP preceded by the numeral *cinq* 'five':

(49) *Jean a   lu   cinq livres et   Marie *(en)   a   lu   trois t.*
     Jean has read five books and Marie   of.it has read three
     'Jean has read five books and Marie has read three.'

The cliticization process must originate in a direct DP object. See, by contrast, how cliticization fails out of a PP adjunct:

(50) **Jean a   lu   cinq heures d'affilée et   Marie en   a   lu*
     Jean has read five hours in.a.row and Marie of.it has read
     trois t.
     three
     Intended: 'Jean has read for five hours on end and Marie has read for three hours.'

The cliticization test applies successfully to the *de plus* differential comparative (8)–(14b): the clitic originates in the differential DP (or what is semantically the differential) and the result is well-formed:

(51) De plus *differential comparative*
     *Jean a   lu   deux livres et   Marie en   a   lu   trois t *(de_{pre})*
     Jean has read two books and Marie of.it has read three   of
     plus que lui.
     more than him
     'Jean has read two books and Marie has read three more than him.'

This in fact, according to standard views, is a sub-extraction test (Ruwet 1972, Pollock 1998 a.o.) which is used to diagnose movement out of DPs in object position. And it supports the view embodied in tree (46): in a sentence like (8), what is semantically a differential is in fact an argument of the verb *lire* 'read', specifically its direct object. In an adjectival comparative, for which we do not postulate the special constituency whereby the differential is selected by the verb, but maintain an English-like constituency, as illustrated in (47), *en*-cliticization turns out to be impossible. In (52), *en* is intended as being anaphoric to the noun *kilogrammes* 'kilograms':

(52) *Adjectival comparative*
We are competing in a tug of war, and before that, there is a weigh-in; the other group weighs 5,000 kgs ...
*Nous en   sommes deux mille   t plus lourds qu'eux.
we   of.it are   two thousand   more heavy than-them
Intended: 'We are 2,000 kgs heavier than them.'

(53) *Control showing that the noun* kilogrammes *can antecede* en, *despite being a unit of measurement (and thus, a special noun somehow):*
Same context as above ...
Nous en   pesons deux mille   t.
we   of.it weigh two thousand
'We weigh 2,000 kgs.'

The discrepancy between *de plus* comparatives and adjectival comparatives with respect to the *en*-test is expected if our assumptions about constituency are correct. As additional confirming evidence, note that (54), a near synonym of (52) with a *de plus* differential comparative as direct object, is grammatical:

(54) *Same context as above ...*
Nous en   pesons deux mille   t de plus   qu'eux.
we   of.it weigh two thousand   of more than-them
'We weigh 2,000 kgs more than them.'

4.1.2   Movement II: Relativization

The NP that serves semantically as a differential in the *de plus* construction can be relativized (this process requires *wh*-movement, which is possible if the measure phrase is an object, but impossible if it is a specifier):

(55) De plus *differential comparative*
*Les trois prières que Marie a   dites   t *(de_{pre}) plus que*
the three prayers that Marie has said.FEM.PL   of   more than

Jean étaient en allemand.[12]
Jean were in German
'Marie said three more prayers than Jean; those prayers were in German.'

The same relativization is impossible with an adjectival comparative, in line with our expectations: this would amount to Left-branch extraction:

(56) *Adjectival comparative*
*Les trois centimètres que Marie est t plus grande que Jean
the three centimeters that Marie is more tall than Jean
comptent beaucoup.
mean a.lot
Intended: 'Marie is three centimeters taller than Jean; this difference means a lot.'

The near synonym with the transitive verb *mesurer* constructed with a nominal comparative is grammatical:

(57) *Control with a* de plus *differential comparative*
Les trois centimètres que Marie mesure t *(de_{pre}) plus que
the three centimeters that Marie measures of more than
Jean comptent beaucoup.
Jean mean a.lot
'Marie is three centimeters taller than Jean; this difference means a lot.'

In English we cannot sub-extract in order to express the equivalent of (55):

(58) The three prayers that Mary said more than John were in German.[13]

(58) is grammatical, but only under an irrelevant VP modifier reading (no sub-extraction). This is expected if the differential in English is not a verb argument, but sits in Spec,DegP.

---

12   Interestingly, the definiteness of *les trois prières* induces the following accommodation: Jean and Marie said the same n prayers, and Marie said a total of $n + 3$ prayers. It is asserted that those prayers that Marie said but Jean didn't were in German.
13   The closest we can get to the French sentence is:
(i) ?The three more prayers than John that Mary said were in German.
This is acceptable although marked; there is no sub-extraction, and the order is Num-More-NP. Note that the Num-NP-More order is worse:
(ii) *The three prayers more than John that Mary said were in German.

4.1.3 Movement III: *Wh*-sub-extraction

Wh-movement is possible in questions as well (sub-extraction out of the differential):

(59) *De quel vin Jean a-t-il bu trois bouteilles t *(de$_{pre}$) plus*
of what wine Jean has-he drunk three bottles of more
que Marie ?
than Marie
'What wine did Jean drink three more bottles of than Marie?'

Wh-sub-extraction is disallowed out of measure phrase differentials in English nominal comparatives (again this is a case of Left-branch extraction):

(60) a. ???What wine did John drink [[three bottles of *t*] more] than Mary?
b. What wine did John drink [three] more [bottles of *t*] than Mary?

English has two word orders for nominal comparatives, Numeral-NP-More and Numeral-More-NP. In (60), sub-extraction out of the differential is only attempted with the former order, shown in (60a); in the latter order (60b), the differential merely consists in the numeral *three*, and, for that reason, extraction is in fact done out of a right-branch NP, and is therefore allowed.

4.1.4 Agreement

In French, what appears to be a differential behaves like a DP argument with regard to agreement. We show this with a comparison bearing on amounts of mass objects, e.g., *trois litres de vin* 'three liters of wine'. If our constituency is correct, we predict that plural agreement is triggered by the plural DP *trois litres de vin*, in subject position. If on the other hand the English-style constituency (48) is correct, then the abstract AMOUNT will trigger singular agreement. Our test is about mass objects in order to avoid a confound: with a plural count noun, we would get plural agreement under either hypothesis, i.e., whether there is no quantified NP (46), or there is one, and it is an abstract noun triggering semantic plural agreement (48). The facts support our hypothesis, as only plural agreement is possible in the cases at hand:

(61) *Trois litres de vin de plus *a/ ont été vendus aujourd'hui*
three liters of wine of more has have been sold today
qu'hier.
than-yesterday
'Three liters more wine was sold today than yesterday.'

(62) is a control which indicates that the DP *trois litres de vin* in subject position triggers obligatory plural agreement; and (63) is a control without the differential, in which singular agreement is mandatory:

(62) Control:
*Trois litres de vin   *a/ ont   été   vendus aujourd'hui.*
three liters of wine   has have been sold   today
'Three liters of wine were sold today.'

(63) Control:
*Plus de vin   a/ *ont   été   vendu aujourd'hui qu'hier.*
more of wine   has   have been sold   today   than-yesterday
'More wine was sold today than yesterday.'

Another order is possible, with the phrase *de vin* following *plus*, but the agreement remains plural in that order; in fact, we believe that this second order results, not from a different construal of the degree head, but from the extraposition of *de vin*:[14]

(64) Trois litres de plus de vin *a/ont été vendus aujourd'hui qu'hier.

---

14   Spanish is similar to French in that, in nominal comparatives, only the Numeral-NP-More order is available with count nouns. Importantly, Spanish can show us something that French can't, because it has bare NPs, unlike French (where a plural/mass indefinite NP is formed with an NP preceded by *de* combined with a definite article, i.e., *des NP, du NP*):
(i)   a. *Bebió   (*de) vino.*
          he.drank   of   wine
      b. *Bebió   más   (*de) vino que Juan.*
          he.drank more   of wine than Juan
The preposition *de* mandatorily precedes a mass noun in a nominal comparative construction:
(ii) a. *Bebió   tres   litros más   *(de) vino que Juan.*
          he.drank three liters more   of wine than Juan
          'He drank three liters of wine more than Juan.'
      b. *Bebió   tres   litros *(de) vino más que Juan.*
          he.drank three liters   of wine more than Juan
We can conclude from this that *de vino* in (iia) and (iib) must be the object of the noun *litros* 'liters'. This is evidence that in Spanish, and probably also in French, the order observed in (iia) is the result of the extraposition of the object of the unit of measurement noun. Therefore even with mass nouns in Spanish/French, we observe limitations on the availability of the English construal with a degree head modified by a differential; we will return to the mass case in Sect. 5.2.

Assuming that there is an abstract degree quantified NP in (65a), i.e., the silent AMOUNT, we correctly expect that singular agreement is preferred for a mass amount in English (it is plausible that the word order in (65b) results from the extraposition of *of wine* past *more*, since *more of wine* is not otherwise well-formed):

(65) a. Three liters of wine more ?was/??were sold today than yesterday.
 b. Three liters more of wine was/??were sold today than yesterday.

This is so despite the fact that *three liters of wine* can trigger plural (or singular) agreement on its own in English, outside of comparative constructions:[15]

(66) Three liters of wine was/were sold yesterday.

To sum up, in the special construction which we call 'the *de plus*-differential comparative', used to form nominal comparatives with a measure phrase differential, what plays the role of a comparative differential is, syntactically, a verb argument. In order to syntactically combine this verb argument with *plus*, there is one route available, which is the detachable modifier strategy. French can use *de* to form post-nominal modifiers (Azoulay-Vicente 1985, Kayne 1994 a.o.):

(67) *quelque chose *(de) grand*
 something of big
 'something big'

(68) *J'en ai lu deux t *(de) passionnants.*
 I-of.it have read two of thrilling
 'I read two thrilling ones (books).'

We thus explain the presence of de_{pre} (14b) as introducing a detachable modifier (*de plus*). The resulting structure shown in (46) is repeated below:

(69) De plus *differential comparative*

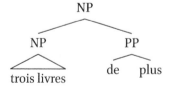

---

15 This optionality of agreement is discussed in Stavrou 2003 and Rett 2014.

4.2 Analysis of the de plus *Differential Comparative in French*

Because measure phrase differentials in the *de plus* construction are verb arguments, it is tempting to analogize them to the differential verbal comparatives in Mandarin discussed by Li (2015) (*bǐ* comparative construction).

(70) Marie a lu trois livres de plus que Jean.
 Marie has read three books of more than Jean
 'Marie read three more books than Jean.'

For a sentence like (70), an account along the lines of Li 2015 would involve a relation between three objects of type $\langle e, t \rangle$, namely the *than*-clause, the abstract formed by QRing the direct object *trois livres de plus que Jean* and leaving behind a trace of type e, and the differential. On this degreeless view, the *than*-clause denotes the set of books read by Jean and the predicate formed by QR denotes the set of books read by Marie. Between the two sets of books, we can establish a one-to-one mapping; once this is done, there is a remainder, namely three members of the set of books read by Marie, that are not covered by the mapping: this is the denotation of the differential.[16] We proposed such an account in Bhatt & Homer 2019. However we now think that it cannot be right, because there are some major differences between French and Mandarin.

Mandarin does not have straightforward counterparts of attributive comparatives, e.g., *a longer paper than ...*, *more books than ...*, so there is no direct counterpart of (3) and (12). Moreover we can get the usual scopal effects of Deg movement in French which have been shown to be unavailable in Mandarin (see Erlewine 2018 who argues that Mandarin lacks degree abstraction altogether):

---

[16] An entry for the degree head in the *de plus* differential comparative, along the lines of Li 2015 adapted for French, would be (assuming that *de* is semantically transparent):
 (i) $[\![\text{plus}_{\text{nomdiff}}]\!] = \lambda P_{\langle e,t \rangle} \cdot \lambda Q_{\langle e,t \rangle} \cdot \lambda R_{\langle e,t \rangle}. \exists f_{\langle e,e \rangle} [f: \{x: P(x) = 1\} \mapsto \{x: R(x) = 1\}$ is one-to-one $\wedge f$ preserves the taxonomic level introduced by $Q \wedge Q(\text{Max}(\{x: R(x) = 1\} \setminus \text{Range}(f)))]$
 This says that there is a one-to-one function f from the set of things that Jean read to the set of things that Marie read, such that the domain and codomain of f are sets of books (as required by the differential *trois livres*), and the difference of the range of f and the set of things read by Marie is a set whose maximum—a plural individual—has the property of being three books, i.e., the property denoted by the differential.

(71) Marie veut   lire   trois   livres de_{pre} plus   que   Jean.
     Marie wants read three books   of   more than Jean
     'Marie wants to read three books more than Jean.'
                                     'more ≫ want' reading is available

In order to be true, (71) does not require that there be particular books that Marie wants to read; it also does not require that she has a desire to outperform Jean. It can be true if the number of books that Marie wants to read exceeds the number of books that Jean wants to read by three. This 'more ≫ want' reading is derived by degree abstracting across the attitude *vouloir*. Li's treatment would leave an individual trace and that would not give us the intended reading.

For these reasons, Li's degreeless treatment of differential verbal comparatives with homomorphism cannot be ported to French. A degree-based account of the French differential comparatives is in order, one which preserves the fact that the differential has the syntactic status of a direct object. The syntactic relations and the semantic dependencies seem to come apart; moreover *plus* isn't directly degree quantifying anything.

(72) Marie a   lu   [[trois livres] [de [plus que   Jean]]].
     Marie has   read   three   books   of   more than Jean

Crucially, we make two stipulations: (i) there is no hidden structure after *de plus*, i.e., no silent adjective and noun, unlike in (19), and (ii) leaving *plus* without a following (hidden) AP is only possible with de_{pre}. In (72), *plus* combines with the following arguments (the entry is the same as in (31) for there is only one *plus* morpheme, but it can enter two syntactic structures): (i) the standard phrase; we assume that it is clausal underlyingly, having undergone ellipsis; it is of type $\langle d, t \rangle$ i.e., it is a degree predicate; (ii) the differential phrase, which we assume to be a predicate of sets of degrees ($\langle \langle d, t \rangle, t \rangle$); and (iii) another degree predicate which is created after QR of the entire direct object ($\langle d, t \rangle$). In this configuration, de_{pre} plays no semantic role:

(73) ⟦plus⟧ = $[\lambda D_{1\langle d,t \rangle} . \lambda D_{\langle \langle d,t \rangle, t \rangle} . \lambda D_{2\langle d,t \rangle} . D(\lambda d_d . D_2(d) \wedge \neg D_1(d))]$ [=(31)]

We see that Deg movement can take place (witness the scopal interaction with an attitude, (71)). This movement needs to take place because in our system, the object DP has the semantics of a degree quantifier and quantificational elements in object position must move. But this movement is not enough to allow composition to proceed. What we are moving is a degree quantifier which leaves behind a degree trace. A verb like *lire* 'read' cannot combine with a degree; it needs an individual. For this purpose, we need a 'degree-to-stuff' convertor. There is precedence for convertors between the degree and the individual domain. Grosu & Landman (1998) have a degree-to-stuff convertor while Rett (2014) argues for a convertor from stuff to degrees.[17]

(74) [[trois ℳ livres] [de [plus que Jean]]] λd Marie a lu degree-to-stuff(d)
plus: ⟨dt, ⟨dtt, dtt⟩⟩;
que Jean ...: ⟨d, t⟩;
trois ℳ livres: ⟨dt, t⟩;
λd Marie a lu degree-to-stuff(d): ⟨d, t⟩;
trois livres de plus que Jean: ⟨dt, t⟩

(75)

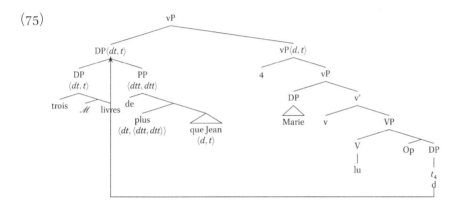

We assume that the degree-to-stuff convertor Op yields the following output:

(76) Main clause: $\lambda d\ .\ \exists x[\text{read'}(\text{marie},x) \land \mu(x) = d]$
(we will abbreviate this as: $\lambda d.\ \text{MARIE}(d)$)

The measure function μ is a free variable. We assume that conditions on ellipsis resolution ensure that the comparative clause receives a similar interpretation; in particular, it uses the same measure function μ.

(77) Comparative (que) clause: $\lambda d\ .\ \exists x[\text{read'}(\text{jean},x) \land \mu(x) = d]$
(we will abbreviate this as: $\lambda d.\ \text{JEAN}(d)$)

---

17 The output of our degree-to-stuff convertor is a quantificational object and hence must itself be moved. But for simplicity, we do not show this movement in our semantic derivation.

We adopt Schwarzschild's treatment of measure phrases as predicates of gaps; in the comparative this is the gap between the degrees in the main clause and the degrees in the comparative clause. In the case at hand, we have the following gap:

(78) $\lambda d.\ [\text{MARIE}(d) \wedge \neg \text{JEAN}(d)]$

This set is quite underspecified as it stands—it is the set of degrees such that Marie read objects with that degree and Jean didn't. But we don't know what μ is so we don't know what the dimension along which the objects that are read are being compared. It could be length, weight, literary significance, or as we will see number. The information about this μ is provided by the differential. In the case at hand, since the differential is *three books*, μ will have to be a function that maps objects to a degree scale on the *book* dimension. We can call this μ_{book}.[18]

We assume that *3 books* is a measure phrase, not very different from more canonical measure phrases like *4 centimeters* and *5 kilograms*. *4 centimeters* is the measure assigned by a length measure function (call it μ_{length}) to an object whose length is 4 centimeters, which 'has 4 centimeters' in it. In exactly the same way, *3 books* is the measure assigned by a measure function (call it μ_{book}) to a plural object which consists of 3 books. How are the degree *3 books* (type $\langle\langle d, t\rangle, t\rangle$) and the quantificational *3 books* (type $\langle\langle e, t\rangle, t\rangle$) related? We propose that they share the same core but that the derivation of the degree *3 books* involves a variant of Rett's M-OP$_d$ operator, which we call $\mathcal{M}$:

(79) Quantificational '3 books'
$\lambda P.\ \exists x [P(x) \wedge \text{book}'(x) \wedge \#(x) = 3]$

(80) Degree '3 books'
$\mathcal{M}(\llbracket \text{books} \rrbracket)(\llbracket 3 \rrbracket) =$
$\lambda D_{\langle d,t\rangle}.\ M(D) = 3_{book}$

---

18 The measure phrase can be any noun phrase that can represent a point on a scale. For example, it can be something like '3 kilos'. In that case, μ will be a function that maps stuff to a scale of weight. The one restriction we have identified is that the measure phrase cannot be a bare numeral. We believe this is so because a numeral by itself does not give us a dimension. There is no straightforward way to map stuff to a numerical scale while there is a way to map stuff to a scale of weight, length, books or socks. All of these mappings will impose restrictions of the kind of stuff we are dealing with but are reasonable given such restrictions. The problem with numerals on their own is that absent sortal information, there is no sensible way to count stuff.

$\mathcal{M}$ is defined as follows:

(81) $\mathcal{M} \rightarrow \lambda P . \lambda n . \lambda D_{\langle d,t \rangle}. M(D) = n_P$
(Following Rett 2014: 256, $M(D)$ will return the size of the gap; n_P is the point on the P-scale that corresponds to n.)

The semantic composition goes as follows, using the entry for *plus* in (73):

(82) $[\![\text{plus}]\!](\lambda d. \text{JEAN}(d))(\mathcal{M}([\![\text{books}]\!])([\![3]\!]))(\lambda d. \text{MARIE}(d)) =$
$(\mathcal{M}([\![\text{books}]\!])([\![3]\!]))(\lambda d. \text{MARIE}(d) \wedge \neg \text{JEAN}(d)) =$
$[M(\lambda d. \text{MARIE}(d) \wedge \neg \text{JEAN}(d)) = 3_{book}] =$
True *iff* the difference between what Marie read measured by μ_{book} and what Jean read measured by μ_{book} equals 3_{book} on the *book* scale.

Because (by our second stipulation) there is no hidden adjective or noun in the de_{pre} structure, there is no dimension for comparison provided by an adjective (e.g., *tall*), or an adjective plus a noun (as in *grand nombre*). Therefore we have to assume that *plus* quantifies over *unspecified* degrees. We start with an unspecified measure function μ which receives its value from the differential phrase.

The stipulation that leaving *plus* without a following (hidden) AP is only possible with de_{pre} ensures that we don't incorrectly rule in **trois livres plus* (14a): since we have a single lexical entry for *plus*, the only semantic difference between bare *plus* and the *de plus* differential comparative comes from the presence vs. absence of an AP (hence of a dimension of comparison). The bare *plus* involves a silent *grand nombre* and hence can only range over numbers; differentials like *trois livres* range over book degrees and are not possible.

4.3 Quantity Words

Lastly, we note that quantity words can be used as arguments:[19]

(83) Il   a   beaucoup   appris/ lu.
     he has   much   learned read
     'He learned/read a lot.'

---

[19] When they are used as an individual argument, quantity words undergo some movement, as is visible in example (83): *beaucoup* surfaces to the left of the past participle. In a simple present sentence (with no past participle), *beaucoup* surfaces to the right of the main verb (main verbs are higher than past participles in French, see Pollock 1989):

Although *beaucoup* can saturate a verb argument, it cannot, by itself, take part in the *de plus* construction:

(84) **Marie lit   beaucoup de plus   que Jean.*[20]
     Marie reads much   of more than Jean
     Intended: 'Marie reads much more than Jean.'

In light of the foregoing discussion, this is surprising. *Beaucoup* has the appropriate $\langle\langle d, t\rangle, t\rangle$ type (see (36) on p. 284) to compose with *plus* in the frame shown in (75). We want to submit that the absence of a sortal is what makes *beaucoup de plus* unacceptable, for *beaucoup de* NP *de plus* is perfect:

(85) *Marie lit   beaucoup de livres   de plus   que Jean.*
     Marie reads much   of books of more than Jean
     'Marie reads many more books than Jean.'

Without sortal information, the underspecification remains unresolved. Why this is a problem is not clear to us at the moment, but it seems to be a problem indeed.

5 Open Questions

5.1 *English*

We have already mentioned the cross-linguistically rare construction that English has, that is the Num-More-NP order (Sect. 3.4). Here we point out another challenge. English seems to have a counterpart to the ungrammatical **trois livres plus* (we stipulate that only de$_{pre}$ permits *plus* without a following AP):

(86) three books more

     (i) *Il apprend/ lit   beaucoup.*
         he learns   reads much
         'He learns/reads a lot.'

20 The way French can render what is intended in (84) is with bare *plus*:
     (i) *Marie lit   beaucoup plus   que Jean.*
         Marie reads much   more than Jean
         'Marie reads much more than Jean.'
     Since we stipulate that only in the *de plus* construction can there be no AP after *plus*, there has to be a hidden AP in (i), e.g., *grand nombre de choses* 'great number of things'.

We explained that, if the dimension of comparison is cardinality, a differential with a sortal NP causes a semantic anomaly (Sect. 3.2). We actually replicated the same anomaly in English (26). And it can be further demonstrated by the ungrammaticality of the following:

(87) *three books more books

If we analyze (86) as in (88), with a cardinality degree function, *many*, and a covert *books*, we incorrectly expect the same anomaly to occur:

(88) three books many-er BOOKS

But we don't have to postulate this underlying structure: we could instead suppose that English too can have a structure with no gradable predicate (no AP after *-er*), the way we did for the *de plus* differential comparative (with the unspecified degree analysis developed in Sect. 4.2):

(89) a. trois livres de plus
　　　b. three books much-er (with a dummy *much*)

Under this view, English still differs from French in that English doesn't use a preposition before *more*; and unlike French, the differential is not a verb argument, but sits on a left branch (hence the extraction and agreement facts in Sects. 4.1.3 and 4.1.4).

A further point worth noting here is that while *three books more books* and *three novels more books* are ungrammatical, measure phrases based on units of measurement (as opposed to sortals) are acceptable as differentials: *three centimeters more books* and *two kilos more socks*. Of course if the differential is a measure phrase based on a unit of measurement, then the comparative is an amount comparative even if it is based on a count noun. This generalization extends to amount comparatives which also do not permit measure phrases based on sortals (**two books more wine*) but permit measure phrases based on units as differentials (*two liters more wine*). This is not a syntactic restriction—if a sortal NP is interpreted as a unit, then it can function as a differential for both mass and cardinality comparatives (*two bottles more wine, two bottles more books*). Finally it is worth noting that this restriction does not extend to AP comparatives which freely allow for measure phrases based on sortals, albeit with coercion (*two books taller*).

5.2 Mass Comparatives in French

Surprisingly, the presence of a name of unit in a mass nominal comparative is incompatible with bare *plus:*

(90) *Marie a bu trois centilitres (d'eau) plus d'eau que
Marie has drunk three centiliters of-water more of-water than
Jean.
Jean
Intended: 'Marie drank three centiliters of water more than Jean.'

The *de plus* differential comparative is available:

(91) Marie a bu trois centilitres d'eau de_pre plus que Jean.
Marie has drunk three centiliters of-water of more than Jean
'Marie drank three centiliters of water more than Jean.'

This pattern is surprising, because if we analyze *plus d'eau* in a parallel way to *plus de livres* (19), we should postulate a silent occurrence of *quantité* 'amount':

(92) UNE [[_AP plus GRANDE] [_NP QUANTITÉ de_post eau]]

It seems plausible that degrees of quantity are not just numbers, but numbers with an amount unit, i.e., a unit of volume or weight. Therefore we cannot straightforwardly explain why *trois centilitres* is not an appropriate measure phrase. And yet, when we use an overt paraphrase, we again observe a degradation:

(93) a. ??une quantité trois centilitres plus grande d'eau
an amount three centiliters more great of-water

b. ??une quantité trois kilos plus grande de riz
an amount three kgs more great of rice

c. une quantité trois kilos plus lourde de riz
an amount three kgs more heavy of rice

Going from amount to weight causes a significant improvement ((93b) vs. (93c); the latter is perfect).

We also see that the presence of a sort forces the *de plus* differential comparative:

(94) Marie a   bu   beaucoup d'eau   *(de_pre) plus que Jean.
     Marie has drunk much   of-water of   more than Jean
     'Marie drank much more water than Jean.'

(95) Marie a   bu   beaucoup (*de_pre) plus d'eau   que Jean.
     Marie has drunk much   of   more of-water than Jean
     'Marie drank much more water than Jean.'

The facts with *beaucoup* (94)–(95) are intriguing. It might be that we are not analyzing the hidden elements correctly, or again that at some relevant conceptual level, *amount* and *number* do not differ significantly. The generalization for French does seem to be that nominal comparatives in French do not ever allow for measure phrase differentials irrespective of whether they are mass or cardinality comparatives.

6   Conclusion

An important distinction that has emerged in this paper is between cases where the degree head does not combine with a nominal restrictor and cases where it does. In cases where there is a nominal restrictor, both English and French block NP differentials with a sortal (e.g., *[three books] more books, *[trois livres] plus de livres). Our explanation is that in the presence of an NP restrictor the degree quantification is only over numbers and a differential like *three books/trois livres* denotes book degrees and not numbers.

We also proposed a semantics for the *trois livres de plus* construction in French, which we analyzed as lacking an NP restrictor. This we suggest allows for underspecified degrees in the syntax; this underspecification is resolved through the differential. We assigned essentially the same semantics to the English *three books more*. The link between the presence of a nominal restrictor and the inability to take count NP differentials is, we believe, significant. A structure with a count NP differential and a nominal restrictor ends up with unusable semantics; it does not deliver the meaning of a cardinality comparison with a differential. We believe that this is why the expression of nominal comparatives with count differentials crosslinguistically utilizes non-canonical structures. The next step is to study other languages from the angle of measure phrases in nominal comparatives, in search for a confirmation of our claims and for (possibly) different alternative strategies. Some preliminary research (Bhatt & Homer 2018) shows that in Hindi-Urdu comparatives the differential functions like an argument and the comparative directly modifies the predicate (while in French the differential functions like an argument and the comparative is a modifier of the differential).

References

Arregi, Karlos. 2013. The syntax of comparative numerals. In *North East Linguistic Society (NELS) 40*, vol. 1, 45–58. UMass Amherst: GLSA.

Azoulay-Vicente, Avigail. 1985. *Les tours comportant l'expression DE + adjectif*. Geneva: Droz.

Bhatt, Rajesh & Vincent Homer. 2018. Differential comparatives in Hindi-Urdu. In Ghanshyam Sharma & Rajesh Bhatt (eds.), *Trends in Hindi linguistics*, 27–46. Mouton de Gruyter.

Bhatt, Rajesh & Vincent Homer. 2019. Differentials crosslinguistically. In Daniel Altshuler & Jessica Rett (eds.), *The semantics of plurals, focus, degrees, and times: essays in honor of Roger Schwarzschild*. Cham: Springer.

Bresnan, Joan W. 1973. Syntax of the comparative clause construction in English. *Linguistic Inquiry* 4(3). 275–343.

Carlier, Anne. 2011. From *multum* to *beaucoup*: between adverb and nominal determiner. In Lucia Tovena (ed.), *Determiners in and across time*, 55–87. London: College Publications.

Erlewine, Michael Yoshitaka. 2018. Clausal comparison without degree abstraction in Mandarin Chinese. *Natural Language and Linguistic Theory* 36(2). 445–482.

Gajewski, Jon. 2002. On analyticity in natural language. Ms., University of Connecticut.

Gawron, Jean Mark. 1995. Comparatives, superlatives, and resolution. *Linguistics and Philosophy* 18(4). 333–380.

Grosu, Alexander & Fred Landman. 1998. Strange relatives of the third kind. *Natural Language Semantics* 6(2). 125–170.

Kayne, Richard S. 1994. *The antisymmetry of syntax*. The MIT Press.

Lechner, Winfried. 2004. *Ellipsis in comparatives*. Berlin: Mouton de Gruyter.

Li, Xiao. 2015. Degreeless comparatives: the semantics of differential verbal comparatives in Mandarin Chinese. *Journal of Semantics* 32(1). 1–38.

Pollock, Jean-Yves. 1989. Verb movement, universal grammar, and the structure of IP. *Linguistic Inquiry* 20(3). 365–424.

Pollock, Jean-Yves. 1998. On the syntax of subnominal clitics: cliticization and ellipsis. *Syntax* 1(3). 300–330.

Rett, Jessica. 2014. The polysemy of measurement. *Lingua* 143. 242–266.

Rett, Jessica. 2018. The semantics of *many, much, few,* and *little*. In *Language and linguistics compass*. Wiley Online Library.

Ruwet, Nicolas. 1972. La syntaxe du pronom *en* et la transformation de montée du sujet. In *Théorie syntaxique et syntaxe du français*. Le Seuil.

Schwarzschild, Roger. 2005. Measure phrases as modifiers of adjectives. *Recherches linguistiques de Vincennes* 34.

Stavrou, Melita. 2003. Semi-lexical nouns, classifiers, and the interpretation(s) of the pseudopartitive construction. In M. Coene & Y. d'Hulst (eds.), *From NP to DP: the syntax and semantics of noun phrases*, 329–353. Philadelphia: John Benjamins.

CHAPTER 9

Quantifying Events and Activities

Haley Farkas and Alexis Wellwood

1   Introduction

Expressions like *more* have been the target of early and sustained interest in formal semantics, from their occurrence as part of complex determiners (e.g., *more than three*; Barwise & Cooper 1981, Geurts & Nouwen 2007, etc.), as adjectival modifiers (e.g., *more intelligent*; Seuren 1973, Cresswell 1976, von Stechow 1984), and, more recently, as nominal and verbal modifiers (e.g., *more coffee*, *run more*). As the relevant empirical terrain has expanded, so are new questions raised about the relationship between quantification, broadly construed, and degree comparison. At the same time, research in cognitive psychology has revealed deep correspondences between comparative language and conceptualization, bringing to the fore certain foundational questions about how formal semantic analysis relates to language understanding. We examine the relationship between event structure (as encoded by verbs like *jump* and *move*) and conceptualization in the resolution of degree selection in comparatives.

The study of nominal and verbal comparatives has highlighted the general notion of 'measurement' in characterizing their meaning, where measurement is understood as a mapping μ_δ from an ordered set of entities E to degrees on a scale S_δ, where S_δ represents quantitative relationships along dimension δ that hold amongst the elements of E. In the case of *more coffee*, E is a set of portions of coffee ordered by inclusion, and it is a set of similarly-ordered stretches of running activity for *run more*. Which dimension for comparison δ is selected in any given case depends on whether μ_δ preserves strict ordering relationships on E (see e.g. Schwarzschild 2002, 2006, Wellwood, Hacquard & Pancheva 2012). Thus, part of the meaning of *more* in its nominal and verbal occurrences is a variable μ ranging over measure functions,[1] whereas adjectival *taller* and adverbial *faster/more quickly* lexically specify particular measure functions. Importantly, then, the prevailing theory of comparatives with bare

---

[1] A major question raised by this view is whether it is right to assume that *more* as it occurs in *more than three books* or *more books* can be assumed to directly encode a cardinality function; see Wellwood (2018) for relevant discussion.

more targeting N or V is that the specific interpretation of *more*—which dimension it involves—depends on the ontological properties of N and V.

Such a theory could ultimately only be tested, though, given an independent grasp on the relevant ontology. To see this, consider a novel verbal comparative ϕ based on *more* V, for novel V. We should like to say not only (i) under what conditions ϕ should be judged true, but (ii) whether, for any given state of affairs *s*, speakers will in fact say that ϕ is true in *s*. (ii) is a challenge for our semantic theory precisely whenever we multiply entities but fail to specify when or whether *s* in fact provides those entities. For example, it is common enough to assume that a given object *o* and its constituent matter *m* are distinct in our semantic domain *D* (cf. Parsons 1990, Link 1983), and to leverage such a distinction to help explain the intuitive asymmetry between *more matter* and ?*more object* (cf. Wellwood 2018). More often than not, though, semanticists contend that such distinctions in *D* merely reflect what competent speakers of the language 'talk *as if*' there is (see Bach 1986, Pelletier 2011, Bach & Chao 2012 for explicit defense of this position; cf. Moltmann 2017), disregarding what our best physical, metaphysical, or cognitive theories might say about the relation between *o* and *m*. In the extreme, we're free to posit entities (or representations of entities) with properties that no plausible independent theory would endorse. In contrast, only rarely will a semantic analysis be taken seriously if it fails to conform to the structural expectations of our best syntactic theories.

This chapter aims to correct, in small part, the theoretical retreat to mere 'talk *as if*.' We outline this perspective in somewhat more detail in the next section, along the way motivating our series of four experimental studies at the interface between language and vision.

2 Comparatives in Language and Mind

Semanticists often posit that the domain of entities to which we can refer or quantify over, *D*, distinguishes 'events' from 'activities,' analogously to its distinction between 'objects' and 'substances.'[2] Events, like objects, are importantly 'atomic', or indivisible for the purposes of reference and quantification;

---

2 Depending on one's terminology, 'activities' might be considered a subset of 'events'. Building on recent prior work testing the analogy *object : substance :: event : process* (Wellwood, Hespos & Rips 2018a,b), we understand the terms 'event' and 'activity'/'process' to be mutually exclusive.

activities and substances are non-atomic, or divisible. Evidence for these distinctions is primarily drawn from the distributional profiles of particular Ns and Vs in concert with an intuitive characterization of the semantic field invoked by N or V. In turn, these domain differences are put to semantic work, as in the noted analyses of nominal and verbal comparatives. Testing such theories, we contend, requires an explicit link between such theories and adjacent areas of cognitive psychology. Or at least, these are the points that this section aims to establish.

2.1 *Ontology in Semantic Explanation*

Semanticists often differentiate classes of NPs and VPs based on the kinds of relationships that hold (or fail to) between entities in their extensions.[3] Relevant data is typically drawn from (i) asymmetries in the intuitive naturalness/interpretability of NP/VP across a variety of grammatical environments, and (ii) the types of inferences (cumulativity, divisiveness, etc.) that they support.

For example, it has long been observed that concrete nouns differ in whether they comfortably appear in grammatical contexts that impose differing demands with respect to 'countability'. The nouns properly called 'count', (1a), are perfectly comfortable in the singular and plural form; they straightforwardly support distributive quantification, and counting language; and, they surface naturally with *many* as opposed to *much*, (1b). The nouns properly called 'mass' have the opposite distribution, (2).

(1) a. i. Ann bought a toy/some toys.
    ii. Each toy that Ann bought was shiny.
    iii. She bought three toys.
  b. i. Sue didn't buy many toys.
    ii. ?Sue didn't buy much toy.

(2) a. i. ?Ann bought a mud/some muds.
    ii. ?Each mud that Ann bought was blue.
    iii. ?She bought three mud(s).
  b. i. ?Sue didn't buy many muds.
    ii. Sue didn't buy much mud.

---

3 Our discussion is limited, for present purposes, to phrases that intuitively apply to concrete or 'basic level' entities like toys, mud, jumping, and moving.

Such nouns are also distinguished by the types of inference that they support. For example, the mass noun *mud* supports cumulativity inferences as in (3a), while the count noun *toy* does not, (3b).

(3) a. If this₁ is mud, and that₂ is mud, then this₁₊₂ is mud.
     b. ?If this₁ is a toy, and that₂ is a toy, then this₁₊₂ is a toy.

One way of explaining these patterns goes as follows (see Gillon 2012 for a more detailed overview and discussion). The extension of a count noun like *toy* is a set of entities, no proper subparts of which are in that same extension—i.e., a set of *atoms*.[4] In contrast, the extension of a mass noun like *mud* is a set of entities, any proper subpart of which *is* in that same extension. This difference in 'atomicity' can be understood in a couple of different ways; minimally, though, it has to do with whether the concept expressed by the noun supports non-arbitrary counts (see especially Koslicki 1997). That is, an array of four toys contains four toys no matter how they are arranged. But an array of portions of mud may, under rearrangement, end up being 8, or 2, or 17 portions. Singular and plural morphology, distributive quantifiers, and *many* impose a requirement for atomicity, which is plainly met by count nouns but not mass nouns.[5]

Similar observations and explanations have been made in relation to verbs, as well, though matters are more delicate here.[6] Certainly, it is straightforward to talk about single or multiple jumps, to pair jumps with commands to do so, to count some jumps, (4a), and to say that they weren't many in number, (4b). The pattern is different when we talk about what is happening *as* movement rather than *as* jumping, (5), though any jump would appear to be a movement of a particular sort. Movement *per se* can only be counted non-arbitrarily via, e.g., maximal episodes of continuous movement, or transitions from not moving to moving.[7]

---

[4] Whether this is understood as a lexically-determined extension or that of *toy*+SG, for some zero singular morpheme, depends on the theory.

[5] At least, not by the sort of mass nouns that are under discussion. Superordinate mass nouns like *furniture* have atomic minimal parts in their extensions, e.g. the individual chairs, tables, etc. We do not consider these cases here, but we also do not suggest the view that mass syntax implies *anti*-atomicity; see Bale & Barner 2009, Gillon 2012.

[6] Testing the verb *qua* verb is challenging; in the text, we illustrate the hypothetically parallel patterns using semelfactive *jump* versus activity *move*, as these provide the clearest possible contrasts in English.

[7] It is important for our purposes that *move* in sentences like (5b) not be read as in 'move house' or 'make a move', which we take to be related but independent from the sense of interest.

(4) a. i. Ann jumped once/again and again.
　　　ii. Ann jumped whenever Sue told her to.
　　　iii. She jumped three times.
　　b. i. Sue didn't jump many times.
　　　ii. ?Sue didn't jump much. [?distance]

(5) a. i. ?Ann moved once/again and again.
　　　ii. ?Ann moved whenever Sue told her to.
　　　iii. ?She moved three times.
　　b. i. ?Sue didn't move many times.
　　　ii. Sue didn't move much. [✓distance]

Extended consideration of such data motivates the idea that the mass/count distinction in the nominal domain and the atelic/telic distinction in the verbal domain are semantically parallel. And indeed, atelic or 'unbounded' *move* supports cumulativity inferences, (6a), while telic or 'bounded' *jump* does not, (6b).[8]

(6) a. If Ann moved for 30 seconds, and then moved for 30 seconds, then she moved for a minute.
　　b. ?If Ann jumped in 30 seconds, and then jumped again in 30 seconds, then she jumped in a minute.

To be rendered compatible with plural morphology or pluractional phrases, it must simply be possible to find some way of bundling the stuff that mass nouns like *mud* apply to and the activity that verbs like *move* apply to, such that they support non-arbitrary counts in the context of evaluation. This property of a given N or V in particular—whether it directly supports non-arbitrary counts—has, in other literatures, been attributed to the kinds of concepts named by N or V: object and event concepts support such counts, regardless of the context, while substance and process concepts do not (see Wellwood 2015, 2018 for

---

[8] An anonymous reviewer suggests that (6) improperly tests the telicity profiles of modified VPs, rather than those of the embedded Vs as we have suggested. However, cumulativity inferences are always made on the basis of sentences which, whether we like it or not, contain functional material with the potential to mask the lexical implications of a given V. Such inferences are informative, then, only to the extent that we can carefully control the grammatical context so that it supports just what we think the verb semantics supports. Careful comparison of (6) with (3) should reveal that the prepositional phrases in (6) are doing no more or less than the unobjectionable indefinite singular or plural morphology in (3).

recent discussion, and references). Whether located in (mental) concept or (physical) extension, the relevant asymmetries are attributed to whether the N or V has atoms in its extension, as required by plural morphology (overt -s with nouns, covert PL with verbs; see e.g. Ferreira 2005) among other grammatical devices.

When plural, of course, both count nouns and telic VPs support cumulativity inferences, (7). This reflects a shift to talk of pluralities, instead of their atomic minimal parts.

(7) a. If these₁ are toys, and those₂ are toys, then these ₁₊₂ are toys.
b. If Ann jumped for 30 seconds, and then jumped again for 30 seconds, then she jumped for a minute.

2.2 The Semantics of Comparatives

These particular ontological distinctions matter for nominal and verbal comparatives, but not for adjectival and adverbial comparatives—at least, not so far as we have seen in the literature. We now quickly sketch the formal details of the semantics for comparatives that we will assume, drawing out where and how ontology matters. The basic set-up is that gradable adjectives and adverbs (GAs) lexically specify particular measure functions for their comparative forms (in the tradition following Seuren 1973 and Cresswell 1976), while measure functions are selected by the comparative morphology in an ontology-sensitive way with NPs and VPs.

Standard assumptions about the semantics of adjectival comparatives hold that GAs lexically introduce specific measure functions. On one popular way of formalizing this, the adjective directly expresses a measure function that is taken as an argument by a comparative operator; in this case, a sentence like (8a) would be interpreted as in (8b) (e.g., Cresswell 1976, Kennedy 1999)—true just in case the temperature of the coffee is greater than δ, the degree contributed by the *than*-clause.[9,10] A simple extension of this approach to adverbial comparatives like (9a) would look as in (9b) (see Wellwood 2019: ch. 2)—true just in case the speed of Ann's running is greater than δ'.

---

9 Standard compositional assumptions would, in present terms, unpack δ in (8b) as $\mathbf{max}(\lambda d \ . \ \mathbf{hot}(s) \geq d)$, and δ' in (9b) as $\mathbf{max}(\lambda d \ . \ \exists e(\mathbf{ag}(e, b) \ \& \ \mathbf{run}(e) \ \& \ \mathbf{fast}(e) \geq d))$. See Bhatt & Pancheva 2004 for recent discussion of the syntax of the *than*-clause.

10 A prominent alternative expands on the style of interpretation in (8b) to accommodate, in particular, scope-related phenomena; see Bartsch & Vennemann 1972, Heim 2000. On such a formulation, the interpretation of (8a) would look like $max(\lambda d \ . \ \mathbf{hot}(c) \geq d) > max(\lambda d \ . \ \mathbf{hot}(s) \geq d)$, which is truth-conditionally equivalent to (8b).

(8) a. The coffee is hotter than the soup is.
 b. $\mathbf{hot}(c) > \delta$

(9) a. Ann ran faster than Betty did.
 b. $\exists e(\mathbf{ag}(e, a)\ \&\ \mathbf{run}(e)\ \&\ \underline{\mathbf{fast}(e) > \delta'})$

Generally, GA-specified measure functions are not sensitive to whether their inputs have any interesting mereological structure.[11] Nominal and verbal comparatives are different. Here, the selection of measure functions varies, both within and across predicates, but the available measure functions are restricted to those that preserve ordering relations on their inputs. As described by Wellwood, Hacquard & Pancheva (2012), building on important observations by Schwarzschild (2002, 2006) and Nakanishi (2007), comparatives targeting mass NPs and atelic VPs well demonstrate these properties: (10a) can be interpreted as a comparison by weight or volume, but not by temperature, while (11a) can involve distance or duration, but not speed. Subsequent works thus posit that part of the interpretation of *more* is a variable, call it μ, valued by the assignment function σ. Permissible values of $\sigma(\mu)$, applied to argument $\alpha \in D_p$, must be monotonic with respect to $\leqslant_p$. Informally, this just means that permissible measure functions preserve strict ordering relations.

(10) a. Ann bought more coffee than Betty did.
 b. $\exists e(\mathbf{ag}(e, a)\ \&\ \mathbf{buy}(e)\ \&\ \exists x(\mathbf{th}(e, x)\ \&\ \mathbf{coffee}(x)\ \&\ \underline{\sigma(\mu)(x) > \delta''}))$

(11) a. Ann ran more than Betty did.
 b. $\exists e(\mathbf{ag}(e, a)\ \&\ \mathbf{run}(e)\ \&\ \underline{\sigma(\mu)(e) > \delta'''})$

Relatedly, the measurand must be drawn from a domain that has such structure, non-trivially. This claim explains the oddity of count NPs (?*more toy*) and perfective telic VPs (?*die (that time) more*) in the comparative (Wellwood, Hacquard & Pancheva 2012) in terms of the independently-motivated assumption that the extensions of such predicates are simply unordered sets of atomic entities. These 'flat' structures are presupposed by plural morphology, however, and any comparative targeting a plural XP (e.g., *toy-s*, or *jump*-PL) is fine and inter-

---

[11] This is not to say that no theory of GAs or GA comparatives is sensitive to ordering relations in the mapping to degrees. However, such theories are limited to considerations of 'base orderings' between individuals as introduced by the GA, and some homomorphic relationship between the base ordering and scalar structure; see for example Bale and Schwarzschild, this volume.

TABLE 9.1 Hypothesized links between phrasal form, meaning, and dimensions for comparison. Bare occurrences of count nouns like *toy* and eventive verbs like *jump* are semantically restricted to atomic elements (**at**), which themselves are the minimal parts of pluralities.

Expression	Semantics	Dimension
toy	$\lambda x : \mathbf{at}(x) . \mathbf{toy}(x)$	-
toy-s	$\lambda X . [\forall x : X(x) \& \mathbf{at}(x)]\mathbf{toy}(x)$	number
coffee	$\lambda y . \mathbf{coffee}(y)$	volume, weight
coffee-s	$\lambda X . [\forall x : X(x) \& \mathbf{at}(x)]\exists y(x \triangleleft_m y \& \mathbf{coffee}(y))$	number
jump	$\lambda e : \mathbf{at}(e) . \mathbf{jump}(e)$	-
jump-PL	$\lambda E . [\forall e : E(e) \& \mathbf{at}(e)]\mathbf{jump}(e)$	number
move	$\lambda e' . \mathbf{move}(e')$	distance, duration
move-PL	$\lambda E . [\forall e : E(e) \& \mathbf{at}(e)]\exists e'(e \triangleleft_t e' \& \mathbf{move}(e'))$	number

preted as a comparison by number. According to Bale & Barner (2009) and Wellwood (2018), this restriction is due to the fact that plural syntax introduces formally distinct structures—a set of pluralities ordered by a plural or individual part-of relation—against which the selection of $\sigma(\mu)$ can be determined. The shift in dimensionality, for example, from *more coffee* to *more coffees* can, in turn, be explained in terms of a shift in 'what is measured'. Table 9.1 summarizes one approach to this (cf. Wellwood 2018).[12]

2.3 Theory Evaluation

The theory of comparatives just sketched captures some interesting and important facts about semantic competence. Speakers allow the dimension for comparison with both nominal and verbal *more* to vary, but not without limit: both the observed variability and constraints are correlated with, if not explained by, abstract referential properties of what is targeted for measurement and comparison. Ultimately, of course, the explanatory power of a theory like this will depend on the extent to which it can predict new observations. In the present

---

12   We use the colon in terms like $\lambda \alpha : \mathbf{at}(\alpha)$ and $\forall \alpha : A(\alpha)$ to indicate domain restriction.

case, the theory will be predictive only once we have an independent theory of 'the domain' D—that is, some independent way of verifying whether we are right about the properties we've hypothesized for different sorts of entities in D. Generally, two options are considered: either our domain is identical with the world as described by physical or metaphysical theory, or with the way we represent the world, as described by cognitive scientists. In the former case, semantics interacts with metaphysics; in the latter, it interacts with systems of perception and reasoning.

That is, assume that predicate P introduces domain, D_P, with such and such properties. The theory will then say what the semantic significance of combining bare *more* with P should be, in light of the properties of D_P. This is alright, as far as it goes. A semantic theory describes a certain relation between linguistic objects and non-linguistic objects, and so it seems appropriate that explanations in semantics should sometimes depend, in part, on properties of those relata. On the morphosyntax side, theories of morphology and syntax provide independent checks on the theory; but what about on the non-linguistic side? Put differently, how can we determine the properties of D_P? So far, the independent evidence that we've considered for those properties comes from other areas of semantic analysis (e.g., the mass/count and telicity literatures).

Armed only with linguistic evidence for the properties of the relevant non-linguistic objects, the theory cannot predict, for example, how the combination of *more* and P will be interpreted, for novel P. In such a case, there is no other linguistic data to check for the referential properties of P. We think that a semantic theory should be able to predict dimensional choices in such cases, since this is precisely the situation that young acquirers of English are plausibly regularly faced with, and, as Chomsky (1965) famously reminded us, an explanatory linguistic theory must be able to explain language acquisition.

While in many cases it may be appropriate to think about the domain in terms of what we 'talk *as if*' there is (e.g., Bach 1986), to be predictive we must go beyond this. This is what we would like to do in the remainder of this chapter: to think explicitly about how subtle features of linguistic structure might align with representations and operations in non-linguistic cognition. While features of metaphysical reality might be relevant in explaining semantic competence at some point, we directly face the question of how linguistic and non-linguistic cognition are connected: the primary data of formal semantics—judgments of sentential truth and falsity in context—is output by minds, after all (cf. Pietroski 2010).

In approaching this question from the perspective of cognitive science, there is a huge body of work in psycholinguistics, language acquisition, vision science, and conceptual development linking mass/count language (at least as applied to the concrete, or basic level categories, as we have focused on here) to the conceptual distinction between object and substance (see Rips & Hespos 2015 for a broad overview). Recently, Wellwood, Hespos & Rips (2018b) have extended this type of research into the atelic/telic distinction, characterizing the event/process distinction as conceptual in nature, and parallel to the distinction between object/substance. In particular, they discovered that the same feature which cues people towards 'atomic' concepts in the static domain—namely, non-arbitrariness of form, in this case spatial—also cues people towards 'atomic' concepts in the dynamic domain, where (non-)arbitrariness is primarily temporally determined.

The right kind of test that *more* is sensitive to ontological features, and that these features are at least worked out independently of language, has been conducted for nominal mass/count and conceptual object/substance by Barner & Snedeker (2004). These authors presented their research participants with novel stuff, the features of which were manipulated between those independently thought to influence categorization in terms of object versus substance concepts (amongst which are shape complexity, regularity, or repetition, etc.; again, see Rips & Hespos 2015). Next, they varied the sizes of the stuff/things and apportioned them in varying numbers, such that agent A had more if it by number and agent B had more of it by size. Now they could test whether ontological category influences dimensional choices, and they found that it did: participants strongly preferred to compare *more* N by number when given salient 'object' cues for N, whereas they strongly preferred area given 'substance' cues.

Such a test provides compelling evidence for the ontology-sensitivity of nominal *more* (as well as for the cognitive interpretation of that theory[13]). An appropriate test of verbal *more*, then, will have the same structure. Here, though, the independent evidence for a conceptual event/activity distinction is thinner on the ground, but this may be because it hasn't yet been sought out in earnest. Here is how we think it best to proceed to the relevant test in a series of steps, of which the present contribution is only the first.

An initial study uses known verbs, and tests the semantic theory's claims about the interpretation of verbal and adverbial comparatives. Ideally, this test uses 'ambiguous' displays which can be described in various ways, and in which it is possible to compare along multiple competing dimensions (cf. Odic, Pietroski, Hunter, Halberda & Lidz 2018). Here, different linguistic forms are

---

13 Or at least, it seems to us that the cognitive interpretation will directly support the linking hypotheses needed for Barner & Snedeker's result to count as evidence for the theory in the first place.

evaluated against identical displays, making it possible in principle to attribute observed differences in evaluation to properties of the linguistic objects themselves. The second test constructs 'unambiguous' displays like those Barner & Snedeker used, which in this case are independently thought to suggest event versus activity categorization. Now, the strong prediction of the semantic theory can be tested: described with verb v, if some action independently suggests event categorization, then v *more* should be evaluated by number; if the scene suggests activity categorization, other dimensions should be permitted if not obligatory.

And so we proceed to the first step (Experiments 1 and 2), laying some of the preliminary foundations for the second (Experiments 3 and 4). Because we are only getting part of the way to the prediction that we ultimately aim to test, we can't answer here some of the interesting theoretical questions that would arise should the dynamic test go the way of Barner & Snedeker's static test. For example: what kind of a meaning is that of *more*? If we should consider that meaning as at least related to some 'domain-general' concept (e.g., Odic 2018), what does that tell us about meaning in general, and about the cognitive power of language, specifically (cf. Spelke 2003)?

For now, we turn to the experimental work.

3   Experiments

We investigate the evaluation of comparatives with event and activity verbs against dynamic displays that make multiple competing dimensions for comparison available. Testing adverbial comparatives that explicitly indicate the dimension for comparison (*more times*, *longer*, and *higher*), we can see how well participants are able to target and compare relations along each of the available dimensions. Testing verbal comparatives with bare *more*, we can see whether participants are sensitive to a target verb's event structure in selecting the dimension for comparison. Finally, we can test variants on the visual scene to see how that impacts dimensional selection when grammar leaves multiple options open.

As described below, we found that participants were highly accurate in their evaluation of adverbial comparatives along the stated dimensions, irrespective of the verb (Experiments 1 and 2). Moreover, they were highly consistent with a number-based evaluation for *jump more* (i.e., their responses were qualitatively the same as for the evaluation of *jump more times*; Experiment 1). In contrast, given the same dynamic scenes, our participants were far less likely to evaluate comparatives with *move more* by number, instead selecting number and distance at roughly the same rate (Experiment 2). Yet, 'undoing' certain features of our dynamic displays to make them more activity-like did not substantially impact participants' choice of number versus distance for *move more* (Experiments 3 and 4).

In what follows, we first describe the methodological similarities and differences between Experiments 1–4 taken together, followed by an overview of the results of the four experiments, and, finally, a detailed presentation of the results of the individual experiments. While this order of presentation is non-standard, we believe it helps to eliminate much redundancy in the text and to ensure that the similarities and differences between the experiments can be quickly and easily grasped.

3.1   *Overview*

Our four experiments all involved asking comparative questions about two objects, A and B, where the extent to which each of their movements instantiated different dimensional values (number, height, and duration) was varied independently. In Experiments 1 and 2, these movement patterns were programmed to look, as much as possible, like jumps: the velocity of A or B's back-and-forth movement would change as the object approached the maximum point in its trajectory, and again as it made its return; and the object would pause briefly between one back-and-forth movement and the next. Experiment 1 tested the evaluation of comparatives with *jump* against these displays, where Experiment 2 used *move* and the same displays. Experiments 3 and 4 only tested the evaluation of comparatives with *move*. Experiment 3 eliminated velocity changes from the displays, and Experiment 4 further eliminated the pauses in between each back-and-forth movement.

We predicted that, presented with a comparative that explicitly states the intended dimension for comparison (i.e., *more times*, *higher*, and *longer*), participants would base their evaluation on the appropriate dimension (number, height, and duration, respectively), regardless of the verb. Presented with bare *more*, the lexical semantics of the verb should impact participants' dimensional choices: they should use number for *jump more* because *jump* is an event verb; however, because *move* is an activity verb that can be used in event VPs, participants in principle should be more flexible in their dimensional choices. Since we anticipated that any of number, height, or duration could be viable options for quantification with *move more*, our experiments were designed so that we would be able to tease out which of these dimensions participants preferred to use.

Thus, Experiments 1 and 2 were designed to establish two things. First, that the lexical semantics of the verb plays no role in dimensional selection for

TABLE 9.2　Participant information for all experiments

Experiment	Number of participants	Total observations
1	20	4800
2	20	4800
3	21	5040
4	21	5040

explicit adverbial comparatives, and second, that the lexical semantics of the verb does play a role in the evaluation of comparatives with bare *more*. Experiments 3 and 4 inquired as to whether certain low level features of the visual scene could push around participants' selection of number versus height when evaluating *move more*, while leaving responses to the adverbial comparatives unchanged. The modifications we made to the dynamic displays of Experiments 1 and 2 that define Experiments 3 and 4 might, we reasoned, reduce the salience of a 'jump'-type parse of the scene, and thus lead participants to prefer the activity VP parse of *move more*. If so, this would decrease the proportion of number-based responses.

To preview our results, we found that people interpreted *jump more* the same as *jump more times*, but they did not interpret *move more* this way. Even for identical displays, *more* latches onto a different dimension depending on the event structure of the verb, as we expected. Yet, in contrast, we did not find that independent manipulations of the visual scene predicted which dimension people would land on for *move more*, which we found uniformly supported both the resolution 'move more times' and 'move farther'.

3.2　Methodology

3.2.1　Participants

All of our participants were Northwestern University undergraduate students recruited through the Linguistics Department subject pool in accord with approved Institutional Review Board practices. Each received 1 lab credit for their participation, and each saw 240 trials. Study participation lasted 45 minutes on average. The total number of participants and observations by experiment are reported in Table 9.2.

3.2.2　Design

Participants evaluated comparative questions against scenes of a red star (object A in our shorthand) and a blue heart (object B) moving. Experiment 1 tested comparatives with *jump* and Experiments 2–4 tested comparatives with *move*. Each experiment manipulated 2 factors: COMPARATIVE and SIMULTANEITY. COMPARATIVE had 4 levels (*higher, longer, more times*, and *more*) which, combined with the verb tested in a given experiment, defined the questions that we asked participants; i.e. (12) and (13).

(12) Questions for Experiment 1:
    a. Did the red star jump HIGHER than the blue heart?
    b. Did the red star jump LONGER than the blue heart?
    c. Did the red star jump MORE TIMES than the blue heart?
    d. Did the red star jump MORE than the blue heart?

(13) Questions for Experiments 2, 3, and 4:
    a. Did the red star move HIGHER than the blue heart?
    b. Did the red star move LONGER than the blue heart?
    c. Did the red star move MORE TIMES than the blue heart?
    d. Did the red star move MORE than the blue heart?

COMPARATIVE was manipulated within subjects, in order to allow us to compare how the evaluation of bare *more* comparatives (the test conditions) compared with that of each of our adverbial comparatives (the control conditions) for each participant. The control for number was *more times*, the control for height was *higher*, and the control for duration was *longer*. Since participants responded with a simple 'yes' or 'no' to each question, we could compare responses to the test conditions by transforming these responses into each of three 'correct by' measures, e.g. a participant's 'yes' or 'no' response was coded as 1 for 'correct by number' if that response was predicted by a number-based comparison, and 0 otherwise. (See Section 3.2.3). Each set of 'correct by' measures could then be used to compare responses to test questions with *more* and the appropriate control question.

The factor SIMULTANEITY had 2 levels (sequential and simultaneous) and was manipulated within subjects. Half of the videos each participant saw showed the red star and the blue heart's movement patterns sequentially and the other half simultaneously. In sequential trials, the red star completed all of its back and forth movements before the blue star started moving, and in simultaneous trials the two started at the same time. Initial pilot studies showed that some dimensions were easier or harder to track depending on this presentation mode: duration (and sometimes height) was more difficult in the sequential presentation, whereas number was more difficult in the simultaneous presentation. By incorporating both modes, we can control for any effects

FIGURE 9.1 Screenshot of trial display for horizontal split (left) and vertical split (right)

of presentation mode on dimensional selection. In particular, we expect to see different 'correct by' measures impacted differently depending on the presentation mode, in line with our pilot observations.

3.2.3 Stimuli

The stimuli for this experiment were created in Matlab version 8.6 using Psychophysics toolbox (Brainard 1997; Pelli 1997; Kleiner, Brainard, and Pelli 2007).

First, the background against which our objects moved differed based on the verb tested in the experiment (see Figure 9.1, Table 9.4), in order to differentially make description in terms of *jump* or *move* more felicitous.

In each of our dynamic displays, our two objects moved different numbers of times, reaching different heights at differing durations. The parameters determining each object's particular movements were drawn from the set in Table 9.3. (Due to a programming error, the possible heights in Experiments 3 and 4 differed from those of Experiments 1 and 2.) Each row in Table 9.3 defines a 'parameter set', indexing values along each of our three dimensions (e.g., 2, 600, 8 describes a parameter set of 2 moves to 600 pixels high for 8 seconds). Each experimental trial was defined by assigning non-identical parameter sets to the two objects, generating 30 unique pairs of parameter sets, or trial types.[14] On any given trial, object A "won" according to one or two of the parameters, and B won on the remainder. Thus, any two dimensions would agree on the 'winner' about 33% overall in Experiments 1 and 2; due to the programming error affecting the height values in Experiments 3 and 4, the level of agreement between pairs of parameters was 66%.

---

14 There was one trial that differed from this design due to a programming error. The trial where A's parameters were the set 3, 800, 4, and B's were the set 2, 600, 8 was accidentally coded to have A's height to be 600 pixels.

TABLE 9.3 Parameter sets for dimensions of movement (including separate heights for Experiments 1 and 2 versus Experiments 3 and 4)

Number	Duration (seconds)	Height (pixels) E1, E2	Height (pixels) E3, E4
2	8	600	480
2	6	800	280
3	8	400	680
3	4	800	280
4	4	600	480
4	6	400	680

TABLE 9.4 Display and animation differences between experiments

Experiment	Sine curve	Pauses	Screen split
1	✓	✓	horizontal
2	✓	✓	vertical
3	✗	✓	vertical
4	✗	✗	vertical

The specific manner in which the objects moved was the same for Experiments 1 and 2, but differed by design for Experiments 3 and 4 (see Table 9.4). Initially, we wanted the objects' movements to look as much like real jumping as possible. In Experiments 1 and 2, the objects' back-and-forth movement pattern followed a sine curve, such that they slowed down as they moved upwards and sped up as they returned to their starting position, and they paused briefly between each movement.[15] Experiment 3 subtracted the sine curve pattern, and Experiment 4 furthermore subtracted the temporal pauses between movements.

---

15 The temporal pauses contributed to our calculation of total duration. Due to a programming error, however, the pauses between jumps were 0.10 seconds instead of the intended 0.15 seconds, which puts the actual duration off by 0.05–0.15 seconds from the round numbers presented in Table 9.3.

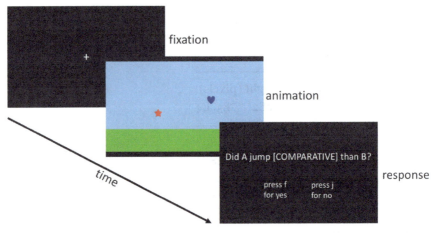

FIGURE 9.2 Trial structure from Experiment 1

3.2.4 Blocking

All of our experiments were blocked by SIMULTANEITY, with half of the participants seeing all of the sequential animations first and the other half seeing the simultaneous animations first. We made this choice in order to avoid any potential switching costs related to changes in the presentation mode from trial to trial. Within each of the two blocks, trials were furthermore divided into four sub-blocks, one for each level of the COMPARATIVE factor, also to avoid incurring any potential switching costs. The order of the sub-blocks was randomized, and each contained the full set of 30 unique trial types as discussed above. The order of these trials was randomized within each sub-block.

3.2.5 Procedure

The experiments were run on a computer using Matlab. Following the informed consent process, the participant began the study on an instructions screen, and pressed the space bar to proceed to the experiment. This began the first block, which started by telling the participant which question they would be asked for the first sub-block.[16] Pressing the space bar again advances to the first trial. For each trial, the participant saw a fixation cross, followed by the animation, and then they would see a response screen with a question and response key options (see Figure 9.2). Participants were asked to respond to each question

---

16   We hypothesized that asking the question first would guide participants' attention to their preferred dimension and thus reduce noise in the measurements. Asking the target question following the presentation of the stimulus would require participants to encode

with a key press, where F indicated 'yes' and J indicated 'no'. Pressing F or J advances to a new screen, which prompts the participant to press the space bar to advance to the next trial, or to advance to the next block or sub-block if they have completed the current sub-block.

3.2.6   Data Coding and Analyses

For all experiments, we coded our participants' raw 'yes'/'no' responses using three 'consistency measures', one for each of the dimensions number, height, and duration (cf. Section 3.2.2). For example, on a given trial A may have exceeded B along the dimensions number and height, but not duration; thus, a 'yes' response on this trial would be counted as consistent for number and for height, but not for duration; a 'no' response would register as consistent for duration, but not for number or height. In our statistical analyses, we conducted three separate sets of analyses based on each of these consistency measures: for consistency with number, the set of responses in the *more* condition was compared with those for *more times*; for consistency with height, *more* was compared with *higher*; and for duration, *more* was compared with *longer*.

To conduct these statistical analyses for Experiments 1 and 2, we constructed distinct subsets of our data that overlapped in the set of responses to the test comparative *more*, and which differed otherwise in including responses to the control comparative relevant for a given consistency measure (e.g., checking consistency by number for *more* uses the 'correct by number' measure, and those responses are compared to *more times* responses using the same measure). For each of these subsets, we conducted generalized linear mixed effects model comparisons with maximal random effects structure, including random slopes and intercepts by subject (Barr et al. 2013), and using the relevant consistency measure as the dependent variable (e.g., the responses to *more* and *more times* were compared based on the 'consistency by number' measure). In each analysis, we report model comparisons for our 2 factors, which were contrast coded: COMPARATIVE (two levels, different for each subset of the data analyzed) and SIMULTANEITY. The significance levels that we report for a given factor were calculated by comparing the relevant maximal model to a nearly identical model differing only in its exclusion of the relevant factor. All analyses were conducted using R's *lme4* package (Bates et al. 2014).

---

all relevant dimensional information; it may be interesting to know how many of these dimensions, and with what accuracy, can be faithfully recorded, but such questions are orthogonal for present concerns.

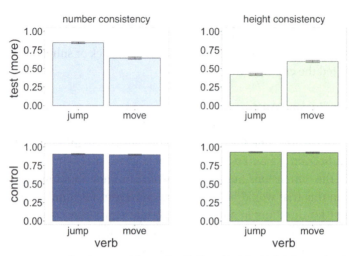

FIGURE 9.3 Consistency with number (left) and height (right) for test (top) and control (bottom) conditions for verbs *jump* (Experiment 1) and *move* (Experiment 2)

Additionally, we conducted paired two-sided t-tests in Experiments 2–4, as noted below, by comparing participant means for consistency with number and height in the *move more* condition.

3.3 Results

3.3.1 Overview of Findings

The main results of these experiments are summarized in Figure 9.3, which plots the consistency of responses based on number versus height, as a function of the verb combined with bare *more* versus the relevant control adverbial. As the figure shows, our participants were highly consistent with the expected dimension for the control conditions with adverbial comparatives, regardless of the verb, but dimensional choices differed with *more* depending on the verb. As we predicted, participants were highly consistent with number for *jump more*, much more so than for *move more*. In the latter case, participants roughly equivocated between number and height. This finding is significant in that people make crucial reference to the event structure of the verb in resolving dimensional selection with *more*.

As Figure 9.4 shows, the changes in the visual scenes did not impact participants' ability to carry out number-based comparisons of the movements (i.e., performance with *more times*), but those changes also failed to decrease participants' proportion of number-based choices with *move more*. In other words, participants persisted in choosing number and height equally often in our three *move* experiments. These findings suggest again a critical role for the linguistic

QUANTIFYING EVENTS AND ACTIVITIES   323

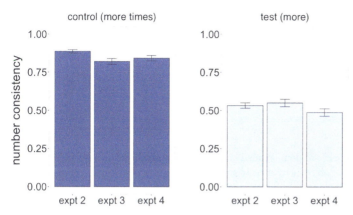

FIGURE 9.4 Consistency with number for trials that are unambiguous between number and height for Experiments 2, 3, and 4 with *move* for control condition (*more times*, left) and test condition (*more*, right)

information in fixing dimensional selection. However, before concluding that purely visual information is irrelevant in this respect, a number of additional questions must be addressed. We discuss these in more detail below.

3.3.2   Experiment 1: *jump*

In this experiment, we were interested in determining (i) the extent to which participants are able to estimate and compare number, height, and duration in simple dynamic scenes, as determined by their responses to our control comparatives, and (ii) whether they choose number as the relevant dimension for evaluating *jump more*. Our participants were asked all of the four questions that can be formed from (14) in separate blocks (once for simultaneous presentation, and again for sequential).

(14) Did the red star **jump** HIGHER/LONGER/MORE TIMES/MORE than the blue heart?

In overview, we found for (i) that participants were highly accurate at tracking each of the dimensions for comparison that we varied, roughly equally so for each dimension, and for (ii) that participants' responses to *jump more* questions were nearly as highly consistent with number as were their responses to *jump more times* questions (see Figure 9.5).

Table 9.5 shows the results of the generalized linear mixed effects model comparisons for our two factors (see Section 3.2.6). First, we found that responses to *more* were only marginally different from responses to *more times*

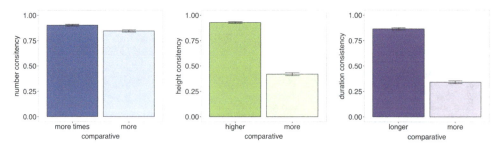

FIGURE 9.5 Experiment 1 responses coded for consistency with number (left), height (center), and duration (right). For each graph, the left bar plots the control comparative, and the right bar plots the test comparative *more*.

with respect to consistency by number ($p = 0.07$), while those responses were massively different from the relevant controls for consistency with height (*higher*) and consistency with distance (*longer*). Inspecting the means in Table 9.5, these results support the conclusion that *jump more* was judged roughly equivalently to *jump more times*, but completely differently from *jump higher* or *jump longer*.

As can also be seen in Table 9.5, we found that SIMULTANEITY had a significant effect on all three consistency measures, in the directions we expected based on our pilot studies. Consistency with number declined in the simultaneous mode relative to the sequential mode; in contrast, consistency with height and consistency with duration declined in the sequential mode relative to the simultaneous mode. These results validate our inclusion of both presentation modes to test dimensional specification with *more*. We found no interaction effects between SIMULTANEITY and COMPARATIVE with two of our consistency measures (number: $\chi^2 < 1, p = 0.35$; height: $\chi^2 < 1, p = 0.25$), but a marginal effect on the third (duration: $\chi^2 = 3.5, p = 0.06$).

These results were as expected based on the semantic theory. Our participants evaluated our dynamic scenes based on the dimension specified explicitly by the control comparatives, and based on number when bare *more* was paired with *jump*. These results thus establish a baseline for 'ceiling' performance at evaluating number, height, and duration for our displays, and a basis for comparison of the effects of lexical semantics on that evaluation. If we replace the event verb *jump* with the activity verb *move*, while keeping the visual stimuli essentially unchanged, will we see different dimensional choices with bare *more*?

TABLE 9.5 Generalized linear mixed effects model output for factors COMPARATIVE and SIMULTANEITY (Experiment 1)

Measure	Factor	Level	Mean	β	SE	χ^2	p
number	COMPARATIVE	more times / more	0.90 / 0.85	0.57	0.30	3.3	0.07
	SIMULTANEITY	seq / simul	0.90 / 0.85	0.99	0.25	14.5	<0.001 ***
height	COMPARATIVE	higher / more	0.93 / 0.42	3.12	0.23	48.4	<0.001 ***
	SIMULTANEITY	seq / simul	0.66 / 0.69	-0.30	0.13	5.3	0.02 *
duration	COMPARATIVE	longer / more	0.87 / 0.34	2.66	0.20	46.5	<0.001 ***
	SIMULTANEITY	seq / simul	0.56 / 0.62	-0.30	0.11	6.9	<0.01 ***

3.3.3 Experiment 2: *move*

In this experiment, we wanted to determine (i) the extent to which people are able to estimate and compare the three possible dimensions available in our dynamic scenes in the control conditions, and (ii) whether they are flexible in their choice of dimension for evaluating *move more*. Participants were asked all of the four questions formed from (15) in separate blocks (once for simultaneous presentation, and again for sequential).

(15) Did the red star **move** HIGHER/LONGER/MORE TIMES/MORE than the blue heart?

In overview, we found for (i) that participants were highly accurate when tracking the appropriate dimension for comparison and (ii) that participants' responses to *move more* were flexible in the chosen dimension, choosing either number or height to evaluate the comparative (see Figure 9.6).

Table 9.6 shows the results of the generalized linear mixed effects model for our two factors. For COMPARATIVE, we see a significant effect for all three con-

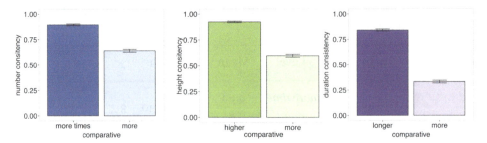

FIGURE 9.6 Experiment 2 responses coded for consistency with number (left), height (center), and duration (right). For each graph, the left bar plots the control comparative, and the right bar plots the test comparative *more*.

sistency measures. This result, combined with the mean consistency for the controls, suggest that participants were quantifying by the expected dimension for adverbial comparatives. It additionally shows that participants were not fully consistent with one potential dimension when evaluating *move more*. Instead, results show that participants were using both number- and height-based quantification at a level above what we would expect from potential overlap between the two dimensions, while they were not using duration-based quantification to evaluate *move more*.

We see in Table 9.6 that there are also significant main effects of SIMULTANEITY on both consistency with number and duration. As in Experiment 1, this result is not surprising given the relative difficulty of tracking different dimensions in different presentation modes. The results here are in line with our predictions.

While two of our consistency measures showed no interaction between COMPARATIVE and SIMULTANEITY (number: $\chi^2 < 1, p = 0.32$; height: $\chi^2 < 1, p = 0.56$), there was a significant interaction for the consistency with duration measure (β=-1.21, SE=0.32, χ^2=11.7, $p < 0.001$). This interaction is such that only the COMPARATIVE level *longer* was largely impacted by SIMULTANEITY (*longer*, sequential: 0.79; *longer*, simultaneous: 0.89; *more*, sequential: 0.34; *more*, simultaneous: 0.33). This result is easily explained by the fact that participants chose not to evaluate *move more* based on duration. Because they did evaluate *move longer* in this way, this evaluation was selectively impacted by trials where duration was harder to track.

Table 9.6 shows that number was used to evaluate *move more* 64% of the time, while height was used to evaluate *move more* 60% of the time. We found that there was no significant difference between the means (t(19)=0.75, $p = 0.46$).

Participants used both number and height to evaluate *move more*, which the semantic theory permits. It is unclear to us why our participants didn't use

TABLE 9.6 Generalized linear mixed effects model output for factors COMPARATIVE and SIMULTANEITY (Experiment 2)

Measure	Factor	Level	Mean	β	SE	χ^2	p
number	COMPARATIVE	more times / more	0.90 / 0.64	1.85	0.20	34.4	<0.001 ***
	SIMULTANEITY	seq / simul	0.79 / 0.75	0.51	0.19	6.7	<0.01 **
height	COMPARATIVE	higher / more	0.92 / 0.60	2.52	0.30	30.2	<0.001 ***
	SIMULTANEITY	seq / simul	0.74 / 0.78	-0.04	0.28	0.01	0.91
duration	COMPARATIVE	longer / more	0.84 / 0.33	2.81	0.24	43.4	<0.001 ***
	SIMULTANEITY	seq / simul	0.57 / 0.61	-0.54	0.21	6.1	0.01 *

duration, however. They were able to track this dimension, as shown by performance on *longer* (both in Experiments 1 and 2), and duration should be a viable option theoretically. It is possible that our visual stimuli made two of the available dimensions more salient than the others, masking what might otherwise be the use of duration. We speculate that, if we made the animations look less event-like, and so more activity-like, that might lead participants to decrease their consistency with number, and make greater use of the available continuous dimensions.

3.3.4 Experiments 3 and 4

We conducted two alternate versions of Experiment 2, each 'undoing' a salient feature of the visual displays that we initially included to make the animations more jump-like (and so, potentially, more liable to event-based categorization and number-based quantification). Experiment 3 undid the changes in speed from the previous experiments, instead using a constant speed, and Experiment 4 furthermore undid the pauses between individual movements. In this section, we hone in on participants' responses to *move more*, and compare those responses for their consistency with number versus their consistency with height. We consider these two measures, in particular, in order to see if participants continue to use number and height equally, as they did in Experiment 2. Because the means for consistency with duration fall within the region of overlap with another dimension in both experiments, we have no evidence that the experimental manipulations encouraged use of duration, and thus did not include this measure in detail in this analysis.

Our results suggest that these differences in the manner of movement did not lead to different preferences for the evaluation of *move more* at all. For example, Experiment 2 showed equal use of number and height, while use of duration was in the region expected by overlapping dimensions (consistency with ... number: 0.64; height: 0.60; duration: 0.33). These results are roughly equal to Experiment 3 (number: 0.81; height: 0.78; duration: 0.49), and to Experiment 4 (number: 0.78; height: 0.79; duration: 0.51).

Experiment 2 found that participants used number and height equally often to evaluate *move more*. If our present experimental manipulations decreased number-based responses, we would expect the means for consistency with number and consistency with height to be different. Yet, they appeared to be roughly equivalent both in Experiment 3 (number: 0.81, height: 0.78) and in Experiment 4 (number: 0.78, height: 0.79), and statistical analyses confirm this equivalence. We found that there was no significant difference between these means for Experiment 3 ($t(20)=1.28, p = 0.21$) or Experiment 4 ($t(20)=-0.36, p = 0.72$). This result suggests that, as in Experiment 2, participants were using number and height equally as often to evaluate *move more*, which further suggests that the experimental manipulations had no impact on their choice of dimension.

So far at least, we have no evidence that the visual scene pushes around dimensional preferences when grammar makes multiple ones available, as it does with *move more*. Future research is needed to know whether and when we might expect the visual scene to have this impact.

4 General Discussion

We showed that the semantic theory of adverbial and verbal comparatives makes good predictions when evaluated in a formal experimental setting. Comparatives with bare *more* and *jump* are evaluated by number, while those with *move* are more flexible. Furthermore, while we observed that dimensional selection was sensitive to verb semantics with *more*, the verb had little impact on that selection when the dimension to be used was specified explicitly (*more times*, *higher*, *longer*).

Experiment 1 showed that participants were able to quantify based on the expected dimensions for comparison in control conditions (i.e., those with adverbial comparatives), and that they also chose the predicted dimension of number for *jump more*. Experiment 2 confirmed that the dimensions chosen for quantification in adverbial comparatives does not differ by verb, while also showing that, even when the visual display is identical, the change in verb impacts quantification of the verbal comparative. Our participants used both number and height equally to evaluate *move more*. Perhaps surprisingly, we did not detect participants using duration for such comparisons, though their performance in the *move longer* condition suggests that this dimension was reliably available to them.

With Experiments 3 and 4, we wanted to further investigate if we could push down the proportion of number-based responses by making the visual displays intuitively less event-like. However, these changes did not lead us to observe different preferences: our participants still used number and height equivalently often. Minimally, these results suggest that the lexical semantics of the verb is more important to dimensional selection (compare Experiments 1 and 2) than is the visual scene (compare Experiments 2, 3, and 4). However, it is still possible that visual properties could impact dimensionality—we just may not have uncovered the proper visual cues to manipulate.

This, we contend, suggests the need for follow-up studies that can tell us more about how dynamic scenes are parsed, independently of language. In other words, it requires a cognitive psychology of the event/activity distinction.

References

Bach, Emmon. 1986. Natural language metaphysics. *Logic, Methodology and Philosophy of Science* 7. 573–595.

Bach, Emmon & Wynn Chao. 2012. Semantic types across languages. *Semantics. An International Handbook of Natural Language Meaning* 10. 2537–2558.

Bale, Alan & David Barner. 2009. The interpretation of functional heads: using comparatives to explore the mass/count distinction. *Journal of Semantics* 26(3). 217–252.

Barner, David & Jesse Snedeker. 2004. Mapping individuation to mass-count syntax in language acquisition. In Kenneth Forbus, Dedre Gentner & Terry Regier (eds.), *Proceedings of the Twenty-Sixth Annual Conference of the Cognitive Science Society*, 79–84. Chicago IL.

Barr, Dale J., Roger Levy, Christoph Scheepers & Harry J. Tily. 2013. Random effects structure for confirmatory hypothesis testing: Keep it maximal. *Journal of Memory and Language* 68. 255–278.

Bartsch, Renate & Theo Vennemann. 1972. *Semantic structures: A study in the relation between semantics and syntax*. Frankfurt am Main: Athenaum.

Barwise, John & Robin Cooper. 1981. Generalized quantifiers and natural language. *Linguistics and Philosophy* 4. 159–219.

Bates, Douglas, Martin Maechler, Benjamin M. Bolker & Steven Walker. 2014. *lme4: Linear mixed-effects models using Eigen and S4*. R package version 1.1–7. http://CRAN.R-project.org/package=lme4.

Bhatt, Rajesh & Roumyana Pancheva. 2004. Late merger of degree clauses. *Linguistic Inquiry* 35(1). 1–46.

Brainard, David H. 1997. The Psychophysics Toolbox. *Spatial Vision* 10. 433–436.

Chomsky, Noam. 1965. *Aspects of the theory of syntax*. Cambridge, Massachusetts: MIT Press. 251.

Cresswell, M.J. 1976. The semantics of degree. In Barbara Hall Partee (ed.), *Montague grammar*, 261–292. New York: Academic Press.

Ferreira, Marcelo. 2005. *Event quantification and plurality*. Boston MA: Massachusetts Institute of Technology dissertation.

Geurts, Bart & Rick Nouwen. 2007. 'At least' et al.: the semantics of scalar modifiers. *Language*. 533–559.

Gillon, Brendan S. 2012. Mass terms. *Philosophy Compass* 7(10). 712–730.

Heim, Irene. 2000. Degree operators and scope. In Brendan Jackson & Tanya Matthews (eds.), *Proceedings of SALT X*, 40–64. Cornell University, Ithaca, NY: CLC Publications.

Kennedy, Chris. 1999. Gradable adjectives denote measure functions, not partial functions. *Studies in the Linguistic Sciences* 29(1). 65–80.

Kleiner, Mario, David Brainard & Denis Pelli. 2007. *What's new in Psychtoolbox-3?* Perception 36 ECVP Abstract Supplement.

Koslicki, Katherin. 1997. Isolation and non-arbitrary division: Frege's two criteria for counting. *Synthese* 112(3). 403–430.

Link, Godehard. 1983. The logical analysis of plurals and mass terms: a lattice-theoretical approach. In Rainer Baeuerle, Christoph Schwarze & Arnim von Stechow (eds.), *Meaning, use and interpretation of language*, 302–323. Berlin, Germany: DeGruyter.

Moltmann, Frederike. 2017. *Natural language ontology*. Oxford Research Encyclopedia of Linguistics. 10.1093/acrefore/9780199384655.013.330.

Nakanishi, Kimiko. 2007. Measurement in the nominal and verbal domains. *Linguistics and Philosophy* 30. 235–276.

Odic, Darko. 2018. Children's intuitive sense of number develops independently of their perception of area, density, length, and time. *Developmental Science* 21(2).

Odic, Darko, Paul Pietroski, Tim Hunter, Justin Halberda & Jeffrey Lidz. 2018. Individuals and non-individuals in cognition and semantics: the mass/count distinction and quantity representation. *Glossa: a journal of general linguistics* 3(1).

Parsons, Terence. 1990. *Events in the semantics of English: a study in subatomic semantics*. Cambridge, Massachusetts: MIT Press.

Pelletier, Francis Jeffry. 2011. Descriptive metaphysics, natural language metaphysics, sapir-whorf, and all that stuff: evidence from the mass-count distinction. *Baltic International Yearbook of Cognition, Logic and Communication* 6(1). 7.

Pelli, Denis G. 1997. The VideoToolbox software for visual psychophysics: Transforming numbers into movies. *Spatial Vision* 10. 437–442.

Pietroski, Paul. 2010. Concepts, meanings, and truth: First nature, second nature, and hard work. *Mind & Language* 25(3). 247–278.

Rips, Lance J. & Susan J. Hespos. 2015. Divisions of the physical world: Concepts of objects and substances. *Psychological Bulletin* 141(4). 786–811.

Schwarzschild, Roger. 2002. The grammar of measurement. In B. Jackson (ed.), *Proceedings of SALT XII*, 225–245. Cornell University, Ithaca, NY: CLC Publications.

Schwarzschild, Roger. 2006. The role of dimensions in the syntax of noun phrases. *Syntax* 9(1). 67–110.

Seuren, Pieter A.M. 1973. The comparative. In Ferenc Kiefer & Nicolas Ruwet (eds.), *Generative Grammar in Europe*, 528–564. Dordrecht: D. Reidel Publishing Company.

Spelke, Elizabeth S. 2003. What makes us smart? Core knowledge and natural language. *Language in mind: Advances in the study of language and thought*. 277–311.

von Stechow, Arnim. 1984. Comparing semantic theories of comparison. *Journal of Semantics* 3(1). 1–77.

Wellwood, Alexis. 2015. On the semantics of comparison across categories. *Linguistics & Philosophy*, 38(1), 67–101.

Wellwood, Alexis. 2018. Structure preservation in comparatives. In Sireemas Maspong, Brynhildur Stefánsdóttir, Katherine Blake & Forrest Davis (eds.), *Semantics and Linguistic Theory (SALT) 28*, 78–99. CLC Publications.

Wellwood, Alexis. 2019. *The meaning of* more. (Studies in Semantics and Pragmatics). Oxford UK: Oxford University Press.

Wellwood, Alexis, Valentine Hacquard & Roumyana Pancheva. 2012. Measuring and comparing individuals and events. *Journal of Semantics* 29(2). 207–228.

Wellwood, Alexis, Susan J. Hespos & Lance Rips. 2018a. How similar are objects and events? *Acta Linguistica Academica* 15(2–3). 473–501.

Wellwood, Alexis, Susan J. Hespos & Lance Rips. 2018b. The *object : substance :: event : process* analogy. In Tania Lombrozo, Joshua Knobe & Shaun Nicholas (eds.), *Oxford Studies in Experimental Philosophy*, vol. II, chap. 8, 183–212. Oxford UK: Oxford University Press.

CHAPTER 10

Split Semantics for Non-monotonic Quantifiers in *Than*-Clauses

Linmin Zhang

1 Introduction

This paper aims to account for the interpretation of comparatives containing non-monotonic quantifiers in their *than*-clause (see (1)). Our intuitive interpretation for these sentences is sketched out in (2). Each of these sentences addresses a comparison between Mary's height and the height of some boys, and it also tells us about the cardinality of all those boys who are not as tall as Mary is.

(1) a. Mary is taller than **exactly two boys** are.
    b. Mary is taller than **some but not all boys** are.
    c. Mary is taller than **between 2 and 4 boys** are.
    d. Mary is taller than **an even number of boys** are.

(2) Mary is taller than some boys are, and the total cardinality of all these boys is
$$\begin{cases} \text{exactly 2} \\ \text{above zero and below the total number of all boys} \\ \text{between 2 and 4} \\ \text{an even number} \end{cases}$$

Intriguingly, though we have a clear intuition for the meaning of these sentences, a straightforward compositional account does not seem readily available.

According to the canonical 'A-not-A' approach to the semantics of comparatives (see Seuren 1973, 1984, Gajewski 2008, Schwarzschild 2008), a comparative addresses the existence of some intermediate degree between two measurements: the **matrix subject's measurement** and the **comparative standard**. As shown in (3), here the matrix subject's measurement is expressed in terms of the set of degrees that Mary's height meets or exceeds (i.e., from 0 to 6 feet), and the comparative standard (i.e., the *than*-clause) denotes the set of degrees that John's height meets or exceeds (i.e., from 0 to 5 feet 8 inches). A comparative relates these two sets of degrees with the use of an existential closure '∃' and a negation operator (i.e., a set complement operator), meaning that the difference set between these two sets is a non-empty set.

(3) (Suppose Mary is 6 feet tall, and John is 5 feet 8 inches tall.)
Mary is taller than John is.
∃d[d ∈ {d : Mary is d-tall} ∧ d ∉ {d : John is d-tall}]
(There is a degree d s.t. Mary's height meets d but John's height doesn't meet d.)

This semantic derivation for comparatives is typically implemented in a purely bottom-up (i.e., from local to global) compositional way. Namely, the semantics of the *than*-clause is already fully derived before it is further used in the derivation of sentential-level meaning. As shown in (4), the *than*-clause—*than John is (tall)*—addresses a degree question: *how tall John is* (see Zhang & Ling 2017a, which analyzes a *than*-clause as a fragment answer to its corresponding degree question).[1] In other words, it is based on the measurement of John's height that this comparison under discussion is performed.

(4) Mary is taller than John is.
⟦than John is⟧ ⤳ *how tall is John?*

However, when we try to follow the same 'A-not-A' recipe to derive the meaning for (1a), as shown in (5), the derived truth condition is too weak. Under the scenario in (5), our intuition is that (1a) is false, because Mary is in fact taller than all the five boys are. Nevertheless, any degree d between 5′2″ and 5′4″ makes (1a) true because Mary is d-tall but exactly two boys are not d-tall. Thus, what the derivation yields is the semantics of *Mary is taller than the two shortest boys are*, not the semantics of (1a) (see Schwarzschild 2008).

(5) (Suppose Mary is 6 feet tall, and the boys A, B, C, D, E measure 5′, 5′2″, 5′4″, 5′6″, and 5′8″, respectively.)
Mary is taller than exactly two boys are. (= (1a))
(There is a degree d such that Mary is d-tall but exactly two boys are not d-tall.)

---

1 Fleisher (this volume) adopts a similar (but not exactly the same) view.

A potential solution is to use a maximality operator in the main clause to limit the range of Mary's height (see (6) and the discussion in Gajewski 2008, cf. Heim 2000). (6b) indeed gives the correct truth condition for (1a). Thus, given the five boys in the scenario in (5), for (1a) to be true, Mary's height should fall into the range between $5'2''$ and $5'4''$.

(6) Max $\stackrel{def}{=} \lambda D_{dt}$. $\iota d[d \in D \land \forall d'[d' \in D \to d' \leq d]]$
   a. Mary is taller than John is.
      Max($\{d :$ Mary is d-tall$\}$) $\in \{d :$ John is not d-tall$\}$.
   b. Mary is taller than exactly two boys are.
      Max($\{d :$ Mary is d-tall$\}$) $\in \{d :$ exactly two boys are not d-tall$\}$.

However, this solution is problematic for at least two reasons. First, in terms of compositionality, it is not fully motivated. It is unclear where this maximality operator should be located in the LF, and why there is this asymmetry between the semantics of the two values undergoing comparison. Even if the first problem can be overcome (e.g., by motivating the use of two maximality operators in both the matrix sentence and the *than*-clause), an even more crucial and fundamental issue is how to generate this range of values between $5'2''$ and $5'4''$, or in other words, how to determine the semantics of comparative standard here. As illustrated in (7), when we modify comparative morpheme -*er* by using *less* or adding a numerical differential, surprisingly, the range of values serving as comparative standard co-varies. That is to say, the semantic contribution of this *than*-clause—*than exactly two boys are (tall)*—seems unfixed.

(7) (Suppose the boys A, B, C, D, E measure $5'$, $5'2''$, $5'4''$, $5'6''$, and $5'8''$, respectively.)
   a. Mary is **taller** than exactly two boys are.   (= (1a))
      (Mary's height is compared with the height of the two shortest boys.)
      ⇝ Mary's height is between $5'2''$ and $5'4''$.
   b. Mary is **less tall** than exactly two boys are.
      (Mary's height is compared with the height of the two tallest boys.)
      ⇝ Mary's height is between $5'4''$ and $5'6''$.
   c. Mary is **between 1 and 3 inches taller** than exactly two boys are.
      (Mary's height is compared with the height of A and B, or that of B and C, etc.)
      ⇝ Mary's height $\in \{5'3'', 5'5'', 5'7'', 5'9''\}$.

This observation is further supported by our intuitive judgments regarding the degree questions in (8). In contrast to felicitous degree questions (8b)–(8d),

(8a)—the one corresponding to the *than*-clause of (1a)—sounds degraded and infelicitous: it is unclear which two boys are under discussion. Notice that degree question (8d) is nevertheless felicitous. This question contains an existential quantifier, and we can give a felicitous answer by choosing any two random boys in a relevant context and addressing their height. However, for (8a), it is not the case that the height of any two random boys suffices to address this question, but somehow it is elusive to determine which two specific boys are relevant. Similarly, (9) shows that those degree questions corresponding to (1b)–(1d) all sound degraded to some extent.

(8) a. ??How tall are exactly two boys?
    b. How tall is John?
    c. How tall is every boy?
    d. How tall are two of the boys?

(9) a. ??How tall are some but not all boys?
    b. ??How tall are between 2 and 4 boys?
    c. ??How tall are an even number of boys?

By now, the challenge is clearer. For typical comparatives, their *than*-clause addresses its corresponding degree question, and its fixed meaning makes it possible to derive the sentential meaning in a purely bottom-up compositional way. That is to say, the semantics of the *than*-clause is first derived and becomes the base for the semantic derivation of the matrix sentence. However, for those comparatives containing non-monotonic quantifiers in their *than*-clause, the semantics of their *than*-clause is not yet fully determined by itself, making a purely bottom-up compositional derivation for sentential meaning impossible. In some sense, it is the rest of the sentence that restricts the actual interpretation of the *than*-clause in these cases (see (7)). Therefore, no matter what approach to the semantics of comparatives is adopted, it is necessary to implement some kind of delayed, top-down (i.e., from global to local) mechanism in the semantic derivation for sentences in (1).

It turns out that these comparatives in (1) are not unique in invoking some delayed, top-down mechanism in semantic derivation. Haddock (1987) observes that under the scenario shown in Figure 10.1, (10) is a felicitous expression to denote R2. Even though in this context, there are multiple salient, relevant hats and multiple salient, relevant rabbits, (10) means the unique rabbit of the unique rabbit-hat pair such that the former is in the latter. The uniqueness of the rabbit and the hat in (10) can only be evaluated with a delayed, top-down mechanism, based on the introduction of multiple (interweaving)

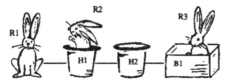

FIGURE 10.1   The rabbit in the hat

restrictions (here hat u, rabbit v, and in u v), not just based on the introduction of a single restriction (e.g., hat u).

(10) the rabbit in the hat
   $[\![(10)]\!] = v$, where v = the rabbit in u
   u = the hat that v is in

To account for Haddock's definite descriptions and related phenomena (e.g., relative readings of superlatives), Bumford (2017a,b) proposes a split analysis for definiteness. Essentially, the semantics of the definite determiner *the* comprises two parts: it first builds a set of witnesses that satisfy restrictions, and then it tests this set for uniqueness. In other words, the semantics of an expression of definiteness is decomposed into an indefinite (or existential) and a definite (or exhaustive) component. This idea appeared very early in the literature. The distinction between these two components has already been noted by Russell (1905). Crucially, Bumford (2017a,b) further argues that these two components are not necessarily in immediate succession, and the test of uniqueness can be delayed (see also Brasoveanu 2013).

In this paper, I propose a similar split, two-stage semantics for comparatives containing non-monotonic quantifiers in their *than*-clause. Specifically, I propose that the semantic contribution of both the embedded non-monotonic quantifiers and the embedding morpheme *than* is twofold. These expressions first introduce discourse referents (aka **drefs**) in the building of witness sets during the stage of bottom-up composition, and then they impose tests of maximality (and cardinality) during the stage of top-down evaluation. Overall, the semantics of these comparatives is as sketched out in (2) and consists of two parts: a comparison derived via a bottom-up compositional process, and some cardinality requirement imposed as top-down delayed (or post-supposed) evaluation.

In the following, I first introduce the core idea of Bumford (2017a,b)'s split approach to the semantics of definiteness (Section 2). Then I combine this split approach together with an interval-subtraction-based approach to comparatives (Zhang & Ling 2015, 2020) to analyze the core data shown in (1) (Section 3). Section 4 further compares the scopal behavior of comparatives and cumulative-reading sentences and addresses the implications of the current proposal for the theories of comparatives and degree semantics. Section 5 concludes.[2]

2 Bottom-Up Composition and Delayed Evaluation

The core idea underlying Bumford (2017a,b)'s split account for definiteness has two components, both originating in the development of dynamic semantics. Within dynamic semantics, meanings are considered **updates** from an 'input' discourse context (e.g., assignment function) to 'output' discourse context(s), which potentially includes newly introduced drefs.

The first component is canonical in dynamic semantics. During a bottom-up compositional derivation, indefinites introduce drefs in a **non-deterministic** way (i.e., there can be multiple salient instantiations for a variable), and predicates add restrictions on them. As illustrated in (11), this sentence makes an update such that for the set of outputs (e.g., assignment functions), there are drefs for the two variables u and v that satisfy the restrictions giraffe v, girl u, and see v u. Obviously, with this kind of step-by-step bottom-up compositional derivation, the set of outputs becomes increasingly restricted.

(11) A girl saw a giraffe.

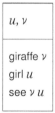

The second component is that some kind of restrictions on drefs (most notably definiteness and quantity-related restrictions like cardinality) are tests imposed in a top-down, post-supposed, potentially delayed way on outputs (e.g., assignment functions) (see also Brasoveanu 2013, Charlow to appear, Bumford

---

2   Throughout the paper, I try to keep the formalism easy to follow and sufficiently clear. A complete compositional dynamic mechanism that I use here is developed by Charlow (2014) (see also Bumford 2017a,b).

2017a,b, Zhang 2018). As a consequence, linguistic expressions carrying this kind of restrictions often give the impression that they take wide scope, though the derivational mechanism involved is distinct from QR-style operations (see Section 4 for discussion, see also Charlow 2014, Bumford 2017b).

This second component is primarily motivated by the interpretations of definiteness. In these cases, drefs that satisfy restrictions need to be unique or (mereologically) maximal so that updates become **deterministic** (i.e., there can only be one unique instantiation). The effect of delayed evaluation is most evidently observed in cases involving multiple restrictions that interleave and work together to define definiteness.

For example, as illustrated in (12), *the hat* typically denotes the unique hat in a context. Here the indefinite component of *the* (which introduces a dref to be further restricted) and the definite component of *the* (which requires the dref—the one satisfying hat x—be unique) come into force in immediate succession. Thus uniqueness is evaluated on the set of outputs (here ⟨entity, assignment-function⟩ pairs) with the single restriction hat x, leading to the absolute interpretation for the uniqueness of *the hat*.

(12) ⟦the hat⟧ = ιx . hat x
    $\lambda g. \{\langle x, g^{\nu \mapsto x}\rangle \mid x = \iota x$. hat $x\}$

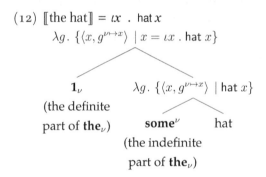

        1$_\nu$ $\lambda g. \{\langle x, g^{\nu \mapsto x}\rangle \mid$ hat $x\}$
  (the definite
  part of **the**$_\nu$)   **some**$^\nu$ hat
                (the indefinite
                part of **the**$_\nu$)

However, the example of Haddock (1987) (see (10) and Figure 10.1) suggests that the definite component of *the* can come into play at a later stage. As shown in (13), for the two instances of *the* in *the rabbit in the hat*, during bottom-up composition (see the part in the frame in (13)), their indefinite component each introduces a dref. Then it is after the introduction of all relevant restrictions (i.e., hat x, rabbit y, and in xy) that the definite component of the two instances of *the* simultaneously requires drefs x and y (which together satisfy those restrictions) be unique. Thus uniqueness tests are imposed as delayed evaluations, on a set of outputs with more restrictions. Consequently, under our given scenario shown in Figure 10.1, *the rabbit in the hat* felicitously denotes the unique rabbit of the unique rabbit-hat pair such that the former is in the latter.

(13) the rabbit in the hat

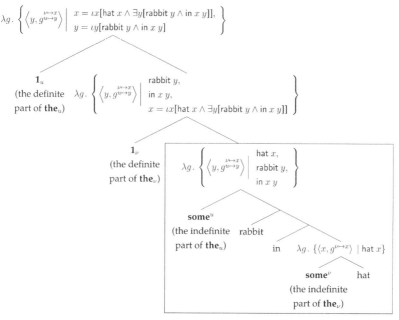

It is worth emphasizing that to derive this **relative** definiteness for *the rabbit in the hat* in (13), the uniqueness tests of *the* are applied to a set of outputs with multiple restrictions (here hat x, rabbit y, and in $x\,y$). In contrast, for the **absolute** reading of *the hat* in (12), the uniqueness test is applied to a set of outputs with a single restriction—hat x. Therefore, the derivation of an absolute versus a relative reading depends solely on the timing of applying top-down evaluations: whether it is after one or multiple restrictions have been introduced. As pointed out by Bumford (2017a,b), this immediately accounts for the relative reading of superlatives.

As shown in (14), immediately applying top-down evaluations (here 1_y and **shortest**$_v$) on a set of outputs with a single restriction paper x leads to the absolute reading (see (14a)). In contrast, applying top-down evaluations to a set of outputs with multiple restrictions (i.e., paper x, contributor y, and write $x\,y$) leads to the relative reading (see (14b)).

(14) the contributor who wrote the shortest paper
   a. The absolute reading of *the shortest paper*:
   $\lambda g. \{\langle x, g^{\nu \mapsto x}\rangle \mid x = \iota x \in G[\neg \exists z \in G. \text{shorter } x\, z]\}$,
   where $G = \{x \mid \text{paper } x\}$

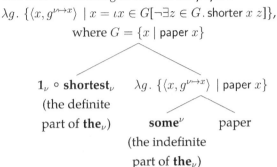

$\qquad\quad 1_\nu \circ \textbf{shortest}_\nu \qquad \lambda g. \{\langle x, g^{\nu \mapsto x}\rangle \mid \text{paper } x\}$
$\qquad\quad$ (the definite
$\qquad\quad$ part of **the**$_\nu$) $\qquad\quad$ **some**$^\nu\qquad$ paper
$\qquad\qquad\qquad\qquad\qquad$ (the indefinite
$\qquad\qquad\qquad\qquad\qquad$ part of **the**$_\nu$)

   b. The relative reading of (14):

$\lambda g. \left\{ \left\langle y, g^{\nu \mapsto x}_{u \mapsto y} \right\rangle \;\middle|\; \begin{array}{l} x = \iota x \in G[\neg \exists z \in G. \text{shorter } x\, z], \\ y = \iota y[\text{contributor } y \wedge \text{write } x\, y] \end{array} \right\}$,
where $G = \left\{ x \;\middle|\; \text{paper } x, \text{contributor } y, \text{write } x\, y \right\}$

$\quad 1_u \qquad\qquad\qquad\qquad\quad\; \left\{ \left\langle y, g^{\nu \mapsto x}_{u \mapsto y} \right\rangle \;\middle|\; \begin{array}{l} \text{contributor } y, \text{write } x\, y, \\ x = \iota x \in G[\neg \exists z \in G. \text{shorter } x\, z] \end{array} \right\}$,
(the definite $\quad \lambda g.$
part of **the**$_u$) $\qquad$ where $G = \left\{ x \;\middle|\; \text{paper } x, \text{contributor } y, \text{write } x\, y \right\}$

$\qquad\qquad\qquad\qquad 1_\nu \circ \textbf{shortest}_\nu \qquad\qquad\qquad\qquad\quad \left\{\;\;\;\;\;\;\; \text{paper } x,\;\;\;\;\;\right.$
$\qquad\qquad\qquad\qquad$ (the definite $\quad\; \lambda g. \left\{\left\langle y, g^{\nu \mapsto x}_{u \mapsto y}\right\rangle \;\middle|\; \text{contributor } y,\right.$
$\qquad\qquad\qquad\qquad$ part of **the**$_\nu$) $\qquad\qquad\qquad\qquad\qquad\quad \left.\;\;\;\;\;\;\; \text{write } x\, y\;\;\;\;\;\;\right\}$

For the interpretations in (14), for all the outputs already restricted in a certain way (e.g., outputs with drefs satisfying paper *x*, contributor *y*, and write *x y* in (14b)), the restriction with regard to length ranking (i.e., shortest *x*) first filters out those outputs in which *x*'s measurement is not ranked shortest, then the uniqueness requirement from the definite component of *the*$_y$ further imposes that this dref, which satisfies all restrictions, be unique.

Similarly, for the example in (15), modified numeral *exactly 7* brings two restrictions: the cardinality requirement is attached to the (mereological) maximality requirement of this modified numeral.[3] It is based on the maximal

---

3 See Brasoveanu (2013), Charlow (to appear), Zhang (2018)'s analysis of modified numer-

drefs satisfying the relevant restrictions (i.e., the drefs denoting the total sum of papers published by some professor) that the cardinality test can be performed.

(15) the professor who published exactly 7 papers

When there are multiple instances of *exactly*, as illustrated by the cumulative-reading sentence in (16), the cardinality requirements brought by them are applied as delayed evaluations simultaneously, on two drefs that both need *a priori* to be maximal. Therefore, (16) means that the maximal plural drefs X and Y are such that: their atomic members x and y satisfy restrictions movie y, boy x, and see $y\,x$, and the cardinality of X equals 3, while the cardinality of Y equals 5 (see also Brasoveanu 2013 for details).

(16) Exactly three boys saw exactly five movies. (Brasoveanu 2013)

To sum up, with Bumford (2017a,b)'s split, two-stage mechanism, restricting requirements of definiteness are applied as potentially delayed top-down evaluations, at a stage when outputs have got (less or more) restricted during bottom-up composition.

3 Proposal

Based on Bumford (2017a,b)'s split approach to definiteness and cardinality, here I analyze the semantics of comparatives as a relation among three definite degree-related descriptions and propose a two-stage derivation for those comparatives containing non-monotonic quantifiers in their *than*-clause.

---

als. The below contrast empirically shows that modified numerals introduce maximal drefs (see Szabolcsi 1997, de Swart 1999, Krifka 1999, Umbach 2005, Charlow 2014):
(i) a. Four babies cried. (✓ Perhaps there were other babies crying, but I was unsure.)
   b. At least four babies cried. (# Perhaps there were other babies crying, but I was unsure.)

3.1 The Semantics of Comparatives: A Relation among Three Definite Degree-Related Descriptions

First I introduce Zhang & Ling (2015, 2020)'s interval-subtraction-based framework for the semantics of comparatives. Within this framework, the semantics of comparatives is analyzed as a relation among three definite degree-related descriptions that mutually restrict each other. More specifically, the matrix subject's measurement and the comparative standard can be considered two definite positions on a certain scale, and the third definite description is the difference between them (see the illustration in (17)).

(17) 6 o'clock is 1 hour later than 5 o'clock is.

$\underbrace{\text{6 o'clock}}$	$-$	$\underbrace{\text{5 o'clock}}$	$=\underbrace{\text{1 hour}}$
matrix subject's measurement: a definite position		comparative standard: another definite position	the differential

Zhang & Ling (2015, 2020) adopt interval subtraction to formally implement the relation among these three definite degree-related descriptions in a generalized way. An interval is a convex set of degrees so that it represents a position in a not-very-precise way.[4] Thus an interval like $\{x \mid a \leq x < b\}$ means a position ranging from a to b and can also be written as $[a, b)$, with a **closed lower bound** '[' and an **open upper bound** ')'.

As shown in Figure 10.2 and (18), a comparison can be characterized in terms of interval subtraction: subtracting the interval representing the comparative standard (here $[x_1, x_2]$) from the interval representing the matrix subject's measurement (here $[y_1, y_2]$) results in a third interval—the differential (here $[y_1 - x_2, y_2 - x_1]$). Obviously, this differential denotes the largest range of possible differences between any two random points (i.e., degrees) in the two intervals representing the two positions (see (19) for two examples).

(18) Interval subtraction: (see Moore 1979)

$\underbrace{[y_1, y_2]}$	$-$	$\underbrace{[x_1, x_2]}$	$=\underbrace{[y_1 - x_2, y_2 - x_1]}$
minuend: matrix subject's measurement		subtrahend: comparative standard	difference: differential

---

4 A convex totally ordered set P is a totally ordered set such that for two random elements a and b in the set (suppose $a \leq b$), any element x such that $a \leq x \leq b$ is also in the set P. Evidently, sets such as $\{x \mid x \leq 2 \lor x > 4\}$ are not convex sets.

(19) a. Example 1: [5, 9] − [1, 4] = [1, 8] (1 and 8 are the minimum and maximum distances between the positions [5, 9] and [1, 4] respectively).
b. Example 2: (5, +∞) − [3, 4] = (1, +∞) (This operation can be generalized to intervals with open and/or unbounded ends.)

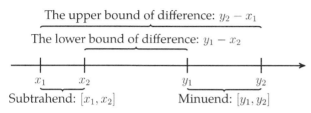

FIGURE 10.2 The subtraction between two intervals. Here $[y_1, y_2]$ is the minuend, $[x_1, x_2]$ is the subtrahend, and the difference between these two intervals is the largest range of possible differences between any two random points in these two intervals— $[y_1 − x_2, y_2 − x_1]$.

Within this framework, as illustrated in (20), gradable adjectives relate atomic individuals (of type e) to positions on a relevant scale, and positions are represented as intervals (of type $\langle dt \rangle$). (20) means that the interval representing the height of individual x falls within (i.e., is a subset of) interval I.[5] For example, when measurement uncertainty is taken into consideration, the height of a certain giraffe falls at a position close to, say the value '20 feet' on a scale, with an uncertainty estimate of 0.5 feet. Thus the height of this giraffe—height(a certain giraffe)—is $20' \pm 0.5'$, and this measurement can be considered an interval: $[20' − 0.5', 20' + 0.5']$. Of course, when measurement uncertainty is not considered, the height of a giraffe, say 20 feet, can still be represented as an interval, $[20', 20']$, which is actually a singleton set of degrees in which the lower and upper bounds are equivalent. Thus, any measurement result can be represented as an interval.

(20) $[\![\text{tall}]\!]_{\langle dt, et \rangle} \stackrel{\text{def}}{=} \lambda I_{\langle dt \rangle} . \lambda x_e . \text{height}(x) \subseteq I$

Obviously, to account for the absolute interpretation of gradable adjectives (see (21)), we only need to assume that there is a silent context-dependent interval I^C_{pos} which ranges from the lower to the upper bound of tallness for a relevant

---

5 I use '⊆' to relate an interval and the measurement of an individual (see (20)). I use '=' in interval subtraction (see (18)).

comparison class (see e.g., Bartsch & Vennemann 1972, Cresswell 1976, Stechow 1984, Kennedy 1999). Then when the interval argument of a gradable adjective is specified with numerical values, the semantics of measurement constructions can be derived (see (22)).

(21) ⟦My giraffe is tall⟧ ⇔ height(my giraffe) ⊆ I^C_{pos} Absolute interpretation

(22) ⟦My giraffe is between 19 and 20 feet tall⟧   Measurement construction
⇔ height(my giraffe) ⊆ [19′, 20′]

The comparative morpheme *more/-er* is considered the default differential in all comparative sentences. Thus, as shown in (23), it denotes the most general positive interval, which is (0, +∞).[6]

(23) ⟦more⟧$_{⟨dt⟩}$ $\stackrel{\text{def}}{=}$ (0, +∞)   most general positive interval
Presupposition of additivity: there is a value serving as base item (i.e., standard) for an increase.

Following Zhang & Ling (2017a), I analyze a *than*-clause as a fragment answer to its corresponding degree question. Thus, a *than*-clause denotes an interval that represents the standard for comparison. More specifically, as illustrated in (24), the semantic derivation of a *than*-clause involves two parts: generating a degree question (i.e., a set of intervals) via a silent lambda operator (Hausser & Zaefferer 1978) and picking out a definite interval via the use of *th(-an)* (see also Heim 1985, Beck 2010).[7]

(24) ⟦(that tree is taller) than my giraffe is (tall)⟧
  a. Generating a degree question: λI . height(my giraffe) ⊆ I
  b. Deriving its fragment answer: ιI[height(my giraffe) ⊆ I]

The semantics of *th(-an)* will be discussed in greater detail in Section 3.3. Basically, I propose that it introduces a dref that is an interval and checks its definiteness. Obviously, the interval (−∞, +∞) would be a trivial fragment answer to all degree questions. Thus, for a degree question, a felicitous fragment answer

---

[6] This differential-based view for *more/-er* is innovative and distinct from almost all existing analyses. See Zhang & Ling (2020) for empirical motivation and a thorough discussion.
[7] Perhaps it is worth noting that all English words starting with *th* (pronounced as ð) express definiteness: e.g., *the, they, that, then, there, these, thus*, etc. It should be reasonable that *than* contributes definiteness as well.

needs to be informative, and the definiteness of *th(-an)* needs to be based on informativeness. Therefore, given an individual or a group of individuals, *th(-an)* picks out the **narrowest** possible interval that all the relevant measurements fall into (see also Beck 2010). For example, for ⟦than my giraffe is (tall)⟧, *th(-an)* picks out the interval representing the measurement of my giraffe (e.g., a singleton set of degrees if the measurement is very precise); while for ⟦than every giraffe is (tall)⟧, *th(-an)* picks out the interval *I* such that the measurement of each giraffe falls into *I* (i.e., the interval ranging from the measurement of the shortest giraffe(s) to that of the tallest giraffe(s)).

I assume that *(th-)an* performs interval subtraction. As shown in (25), it takes two intervals representing the subtrahend and the difference as inputs and returns the unique interval representing the minuend. However, to facilitate reading, I will use '⊖' for this operation and write *-an* along with *th*. In the following, I use *than* to mean *th(-an)*.

(25) ⟦an/ ⊖ ⟧$_{⟨dt,⟨dt,dt⟩⟩}$ $\stackrel{\text{def}}{=} \lambda I_{\text{standard}} \cdot \lambda I_{\text{differential}} \cdot \iota I[I - I_{\text{standard}} = I_{\text{differential}}]$

Given the formula of interval subtraction in (18), the degree-related values serving as the comparative standard, the minuend's value, and the differential mutually constrain each other, so that knowing two of them is sufficient to deduce the third one.

In a typical step-by-step bottom-up semantic derivation for a comparative, as shown in (26), the value of the *than*-clause (i.e., the comparative standard) and the value of the differential are first derived (see (26a) and (26b)), and based on these two values, the minuend's value is computed (see (26c)). Finally, at the level of the matrix clause, the gradable adjective relates the minuend's value and the sentence subject (see (26d)).

(26) Mary is taller than every boy is.
　　LF: Mary is tall ⊖ [-er than every boy is (tall)]
　　a. I_{standard} : ⟦than every boy is (tall)⟧
　　　 = ⟦th-(an)⟧⟦λ*I* . every boy is *I* tall⟧
　　　 = ι*I*[∀*x*[boy(*x*) → height(*x*) ⊂ *I*]]
　　　 (Roughly, this means [height(shortest boys), height(tallest boys)]. To facilitate notations, I avoid writing endpoints of height(*x*) in this kind of cases.)
　　b. $I_{\text{differential}}$: ⟦-er⟧ = (0, +∞)
　　c. ⟦ ⊖ [-er than every boy is tall]⟧
　　　 = ι*I*′[*I*′ − I_{standard} = $I_{\text{differential}}$]
　　　 = ι*I*′[*I*′ − ι*I*[∀*x*[boy(*x*) → height(*x*) ⊆ *I*]] = (0, +∞)]

d. ⟦Mary is tall ⊖ [-er than every boy is (tall)]⟧
   ⇔ height(Mary) ⊆ $\iota'[I' - \iota[\forall x[\text{boy}(x) \to \text{height}(x) \subseteq I]] = (0, +\infty)]$
   ⇔ height(Mary) ⊆ $\iota'[I' - [\text{height}(\text{shortest boys}), \text{height}(\text{tallest boys})] = (0, +\infty)]$
   ⇔ height(Mary) ⊆ (height(tallest boys), $+\infty$) \hfill (see (18))

The last three lines of (26d) are equivalent. They all mean that on the scale of height, the difference between the position representing Mary's height and the narrowest interval that each boy's height falls into is a positive value. After simplification (see (18)), this means that Mary's height exceeds the height of the tallest boy(s), and based on the semantics of this sentence, there is no upper bound to limit her height.

3.2 The Semantics of Than-Clauses Containing Plural Individuals

To prepare for the semantic analysis presented in Section 3.3, here I address the semantics of *than*-clauses containing plural individuals and their entailment pattern.

I assume that for gradable adjectives like *tall* (see (20)), their entity argument is an atomic individual. In other words, the measurement of height is always performed on atomic individuals. Thus, when a *than*-clause contains a plural individual, I assume a silent distributivity operator Dist (see (27)) to relate the plural individual and the predicate. As shown in (28), a *than*-clause containing a plural individual X denotes, in effect, the interval ranging from the measurement of X's least-ADJ (here shortest) atomic member(s) to the measurement of X's most-ADJ (here tallest) atomic member(s).

(27) Dist $\stackrel{\text{def}}{=} \lambda X_e . \lambda P_{\langle et \rangle} . \forall x \sqsubseteq_{\text{atom}} X[P(x)]$
   i.e., for each atomic part x in the plural individual X, predicate P holds for x.

(28) ⟦than X are Dist (tall)⟧
   = ⟦th(-an)⟧⟦λI . X are Dist I tall⟧
   = $\iota[\forall x \sqsubseteq_{\text{atom}} X[\text{height}(x) \subseteq I]]$
   i.e., the most informative interval that the height of each atom of X falls into.

Suppose that X and Y are plural individuals and that Y is part of X. For example, X denotes the group consisting of all the boys, and Y denotes the group consisting of all the blond boys. Then for comparatives containing X or Y in their *than*-clause, (29) shows how the entailment relation of their hosting *than*-clauses follows from the part-whole relation between X and Y.

(29) If Y is part of X (i.e., Y ⊑ X),
then ⟦than Y are Dist ADJ⟧ ⊆ ⟦than X are Dist ADJ⟧
E.g., [h(shortest blond boys), h(tallest blond boys)] ⊆ [h(shortest boys), h(tallest boys)]

Obviously, since Y is part of X, the most informative interval that the measurement of each atomic part of X falls into is necessarily such that the measurement of each atomic part of Y also falls into. Thus the interval ⟦than Y are Dist ADJ⟧ should be a subset of the interval ⟦than X are Dist ADJ⟧, i.e., the former entails the latter (see (29)).

For the current purpose, the entailment pattern of *than*-clauses brought by this kind of part-whole relationship (as shown in (29)) dictates how the definiteness test of a *than*-clause-internal plural individual constrains, in turn, the definiteness test for its embedding *than*-clause (i.e., the interval that the measurement of each atomic part of this plural individual falls into). More specifically, for a mereologically maximal plural individual X, ⟦than X are Dist ADJ⟧ (i.e., the narrowest interval such that the measurement of atomic members of X falls into) cannot be narrower than ⟦than Y are Dist ADJ⟧ (Y ⊑ X) (i.e., the narrowest interval such that the measurement of atomic members of Y falls into). Therefore, with the restrictions interval I and $\forall x \sqsubseteq_{atom} X[\text{measurement}(x) \subseteq I]$, to guarantee that we get the largest possible cardinality of X, we need *a priori* to get the mereologically maximal X in the widest possible I. This will be crucial for the analysis presented below.

3.3 The Semantics of *Mary Is Taller Than Exactly Two Boys Are*

Following Charlow (2014) and Bumford (2017a,b), I adopt a compositional dynamic semantics, in which modified numerals (e.g., *exactly*+N) and definite determiners (e.g., *the* or *than*) interact with the dynamics in two ways. Like indefinite determiner *a*, their indefinite component non-deterministically allocates a dref to some variable of its input assignment function. Then their definite component tests the **definiteness** of this dref across its output assignment functions. For modified numerals, requirements of cardinality are attached to the tests of definiteness. Crucially, the tests of definiteness (and cardinality) can be imposed at a later stage, as delayed evaluations.

I first show how the indefinite and definite components of *the* work in deriving the semantics of definite singular and plural individuals (see (30) and (31)). The indefinite component **some**^{v} combines with the restrictor *boy*/*boys* to produce a dynamic indefinite update. Given an input assignment, it returns a set of ⟨output-denotation-corresponding-to-the-constituent, output-assignment⟩ pairs (here ⟨individual, output-assignment⟩ pairs), one for each boy or each plural individual made of boys (i.e., each sum of boys).

In (30), the set of outputs is tested for uniqueness. Obviously, since there is one output for every boy in the domain, the test $\mathbf{1}_\nu$ fails unless the domain contains only one unique salient boy. When the test does not fail, the description denotes the determinate update that assigns the unique boy to ν.

(30) The definiteness of a singular individual means it is **unique**.
The meaning of *the boy*:

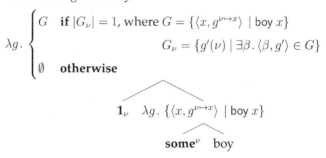

Similarly, in (31), the set of outputs is tested for maximality. The maximality operator $\mathbf{M}_\nu$ filters out the outputs in which ν is not assigned the maximal sum of boys. Thus [[the boys]] means $\lambda g\ .\ \{\langle X, g^{\nu \mapsto X}\rangle \mid X = \Sigma\ \text{boy}\}$, i.e., the determinate update in which ν is assigned the largest sum of boys.

(31) The definiteness of a plural individual means it is **mereologically maximal**.
The meaning of *the boys*:
$\mathbf{M}_\nu \stackrel{\text{def}}{=} \lambda m\ .\ \lambda g\ .\ \{\langle \alpha, h \rangle \in m(g) \mid \neg\exists \langle \beta, h'\rangle \in m(g)\ .\ h(\nu) \sqsubset h'(\nu)\}$[8]
$\lambda g\ .\ \{\langle X, g^{\nu \mapsto X}\rangle \mid \text{boys}\ X, \neg \exists Y [\text{boys}\ Y \wedge X \sqsubset Y]\}$

```
         ────────────
      M_ν    λg. {⟨X, g^{ν↦X}⟩ | boys X}
              ──────────
              some^ν  boys
```

Now with the use of this split mechanism, (32) shows the step-by-step bottom-up composition of a comparative:

---

8 The type of $\mathbf{M}_\nu$ is $(g \to \{\langle \alpha, g\rangle\}) \to (g \to \{\langle \alpha, g\rangle\})$. Here g means the type for assignment functions, and $\{\langle \alpha, g\rangle\}$ means the type for a set of $\langle \alpha$, assignment-function$\rangle$ pairs. The usual notation for types $\langle \alpha, \beta\rangle$ is written as $\alpha \to \beta$.

(32) ⟦Mary is taller than exactly two boys are⟧—bottom-up composition:

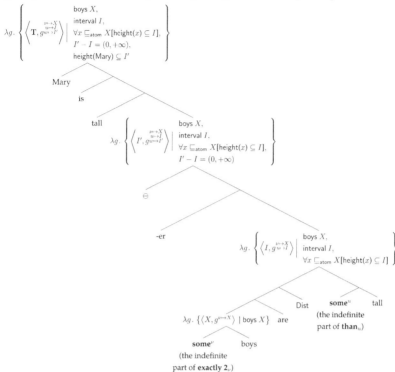

In (32), **some**^{v} combines with the restrictor *boys* to produce a dynamic indefinite update. Then within the *than*-clause, I assume that the indefinite component of *than*, **some**^{u}, also produces a dynamic indefinite update, returning a set of ⟨interval, output-assignment⟩ pairs, one for each interval. With the help of Dist, the gradable adjective *tall* relates each atomic member of plural individual v with interval u so that for the outputs, there are restrictions boys X, interval I, and $\forall x \sqsubseteq_{\text{atom}} X[\text{height}(X) \subseteq I]$. Further restrictions are introduced at the matrix level: Mary's height is a subset of interval I' such that the difference between I' and I is $(0, +\infty)$. Thus, by the end of this bottom-up compositional derivation, we obtain a set of ⟨truth value, output assignment⟩ pairs, and the sentence is true when eventually, there exist assignments satisfying all the restrictions.

(33) is the definition of a maximality operator for intervals. It filters out the outputs in which their interval variable u is not assigned the widest possible interval. Thus, the application of this **MaxI**$_u$ yields the determinate update that assigns u the widest possible interval.

(33) The maximization of an interval:
$$\mathbf{MaxI}_u \stackrel{\text{def}}{=} \lambda m \,.\, \lambda g \,.\, \{\langle \alpha, h \rangle \in m(g) \mid \neg \exists \langle \beta, h' \rangle \in m(g) \,.\, h(u) \subset h'(u)\}$$

(34) checks the cardinality of atomic members in a sum.[9]

(34) Cardinality requirement:
$$2_\nu \stackrel{\text{def}}{=} \lambda m \,.\, \lambda g \,.\, \begin{cases} G \text{ if } |\text{atoms}(\Sigma G_\nu)| = 2, \text{ where } G = m\,g \\ \qquad\qquad G_\nu = \{g'(\nu) \mid \exists \beta \,.\, \langle \beta, g' \rangle \in G\} \\ \emptyset \text{ otherwise} \end{cases}$$

In the following, I assume that height(Mary) is a singleton set of degrees, in which both the upper and lower bounds are written as precise-height(Mary). With the use of interval maximality operator $\mathbf{MaxI}_u$, (mereological) maximality operator $\mathbf{M}_\nu$, and cardinality requirement 2_ν, (35) shows how the tests of definiteness and cardinality brought by *than* and *exactly two* are applied as delayed, top-down evaluations:

(35) ⟦Mary is taller than exactly two boys are⟧—delayed top-down evaluation:

$$\lambda g \,.\, \left\{ \left\langle \mathbf{T}, g^{\nu \mapsto X}_{w \mapsto I'} \right\rangle \,\middle|\, \begin{array}{l} I' = [\text{precise-height(Mary)}, \text{precise-height(Mary)}], \\ I = \iota I[I = (-\infty, \text{precise-height(Mary)})\, \wedge \\ \exists X[\text{boys}\, X \wedge \forall x \sqsubseteq_{\text{atom}} X[\text{height}(x) \subseteq I]]], \\ X = \Sigma X \,.\, \text{boys}\, X \wedge \forall x \sqsubseteq_{\text{atom}} X[\text{height}(x) \subseteq I] \end{array} \right\}, \text{ if } |X| = 2$$

$2_\nu \circ \mathbf{M}_\nu$
(the definite part of **exactly** 2_ν) $\lambda g \,.\, \left\{ \left\langle \mathbf{T}, g^{\nu \mapsto X}_{w \mapsto I'} \right\rangle \,\middle|\, \begin{array}{l} \text{boys}\, X, \\ \forall x \sqsubseteq_{\text{atom}} X[\text{height}(x) \subseteq I], \\ I' = [\text{precise-height(Mary)}, \text{precise-height(Mary)}], \\ I = \iota I[I = (-\infty, \text{precise-height(Mary)})\, \wedge \\ \exists X[\text{boys}\, X \wedge \forall x \sqsubseteq_{\text{atom}} X[\text{height}(x) \subseteq I]]] \end{array} \right\}$

$\mathbf{MaxI}_u$
(the definite part of $\mathbf{than}_u$) $\lambda g \,.\, \left\{ \left\langle \mathbf{T}, g^{\nu \mapsto X}_{w \mapsto I'} \right\rangle \,\middle|\, \begin{array}{l} \text{boys}\, X, \\ \text{interval}\, I, \\ \forall x \sqsubseteq_{\text{atom}} X[\text{height}(x) \subseteq I], \\ I' - I = (0, +\infty), \\ \text{height(Mary)} \subseteq I' \end{array} \right\}$

---

9   I use 'o' to attach a cardinality test to a test of mereological maximality.

As discussed earlier in Section 3.2, to guarantee that the cardinality of X (which satisfies all the relevant restrictions along with I and I') is the largest possible value, we need to *a priori* obtain the mereologically maximal X in the widest possible I. Therefore, among the tests imposed by $\mathbf{MaxI}_u$, $\mathbf{M}_y$, and 2_y, the test of interval maximality $\mathbf{MaxI}_u$ first applies to outputs and rules out all those outputs in which the interval dref assigned to u is not maximally wide, thus yielding the determinate update such that w is assigned the unique interval I' that is equal to [precise-height(Mary), precise-height(Mary)], and u is assigned the unique interval I that is equal to $(-\infty, \text{precise-height(Mary)})$ (and I also needs to satisfy the restriction $\exists X[\text{boys } X \wedge \forall x \sqsubseteq_{\text{atom}} X[\text{height}(x) \subseteq I]]$).

Then the test of $\mathbf{M}_y$ filters out all those outputs in which the sum of boys is not maximal, yielding the determinate update such that v is assigned the largest sum of boys X which satisfies the restriction $\forall x \sqsubseteq_{\text{atom}} X[\text{height}(x) \subseteq (-\infty, \text{precise-height(Mary)})]$.

Finally, the cardinality restriction 2_y checks whether the cardinality of atomic members in this largest boy-sum X is equal to 2. Our intuitive interpretation for this sentences is thus derived: Mary is taller than some boys are, and the total cardinality of these boys is equal to 2 (see (2)).

In some sense, all these three tests $\mathbf{MaxI}_u$, $\mathbf{M}_y$, and 2_y are fundamentally due to the embedded modified numeral *exactly two*. The cardinality restriction cascades down so that the dref assigned to v is required to be the maximal plural individual and the dref assigned to u the widest possible interval.

Previously, in Section 3.1, the definiteness of 〚th(-an)〛 was defined on the base of informativeness. Thus, the meaning of *than these boys are* (*tall*) is the narrowest possible interval I such that the measurement of each atomic boy (of the plural individual *these boys*) falls into I. However, here, when there are no given individuals at hand, during the bottom-up composition (see (32)), a dynamic indefinite update for the interval variable u outputs many interval drefs, each of which can potentially be the narrowest possible interval for some plural individual. As shown in (35), it is with the use of $\mathbf{MaxI}_u$ that the widest interval is picked out among this set of potentially narrowest possible intervals. This is actually not counter-intuitive. Imagine an extreme case: Mary is taller than exactly two boys are, and the height of one of these two boys is just slightly below Mary's height, while the height of the other boy is a very low value. Obviously, the narrowest possible interval including their height is $(-\infty, \text{precise-height(Mary)})$,[10] i.e., the widest one among the set of

---

10   A negative value (e.g., -5 feet) for height is physically impossible, but not semantically impossible.

potentially narrowest possible intervals. It is exactly for the sake of the taller boy in this extreme case that the test of **MaxI**$_u$ is necessary. Without the use of **MaxI**$_u$ in (35), I' can be any interval including height(Mary). For example, I' can be [precise-height(Mary) − 2″, precise-height(Mary) + 2″], and then I is (−∞, precise-height(Mary) − 2″). Consequently, if a boy's height falls into [precise-height(Mary) − 2″, precise-height(Mary)), he would be overlooked during the tests of **M**$_y$ and 2$_y$, because he is not even considered shorter than Mary.

It is evident that the semantics of the other three sentences in (1) can be accounted for in the same way, with a split, two-stage derivation and the application of three tests (i.e., **MaxI**$_u$, **M**$_y$, and a specific cardinality restriction) as delayed evaluations. (36) sketches out the cardinality restrictions specific to (1b)–(1d).

(36) Sketches of cardinality requirements for (1b)–(1d):
(Here Z is the sum of all boys, and X is the largest sum of boys such that $\forall x \sqsubseteq_{atom} X[\text{height}(x) \subseteq (-\infty, \text{precise-height}(Mary))]$.)
a. **some-but-not-all**$_y$: $0 < |X| < |Z|$.
b. **between-2-and-4**$_y$: $|X| \in [2, 4]$.
c. **an-even-number**$_y$: $|X|$ modulo $2 = 0$.

Overall, for all these sentences in (1), the bottom-up derivation addresses a comparison between Mary's height and the height of some boys, while the top-down evaluation addresses the cardinality of all those boys who are not as tall as Mary is. The tests of **MaxI**$_u$, **M**$_y$, and the relevant cardinality restrictions are all delayed evaluations within this two-stage derivation. Therefore, the cardinality of non-monotonic quantifiers embedded within *than*-clauses is eventually evaluated at the matrix clause level, giving the impression that these embedded non-monotonic quantifiers take wide scope. However, delayed evaluations do not involve any QR-style operations, and thus the current account does not suffer any QR-related island issues (see also the discussion below).

3.4   *Extensions*

3.4.1   The Effects of Varying Differentials

The current analysis can be easily extended to account for all the sentences in (7), and the semantic contribution of *than exactly two boys are (tall)* stays constant across all these cases. What varies across these sentences is the value of differentials. As a consequence, the application of the interval maximality operator **MaxI**$_u$ yields different unique widest intervals.

For (7b) (repeated here as (38)), I follow Zhang & Ling (2017b, 2020) and analyze *less* as the most general negative interval that serves as the default differential in *less-than* comparatives (see (37)). Thus, as shown in (38), in this case, the widest interval I satisfying all relevant restrictions is (precise-height(Mary), $+\infty$). Then for boy-sums whose atomic member's height falls into this interval, the cardinality of the maximal boy-sum is 2. In other words, this sentence means that Mary is less tall than some boys are, and the cardinality of all those boys taller than Mary is 2.

(37) $[\![\text{less}]\!] \stackrel{\text{def}}{=} (-\infty, 0)$ \hfill (most general negative interval)
Presupposition of additivity: there is a value serving as base item (i.e., standard) for a decrease (i.e., negative increase).

(38) $[\![\text{Mary is \textbf{less tall} than exactly two boys are}]\!]$—delayed top-down evaluation:

$$\lambda g. \left\{ \left\langle T, g^{\substack{\nu \to X \\ u \to I \\ w \to I'}} \right\rangle \,\middle|\, \begin{array}{l} I' = [\text{precise-height(Mary)}, \text{precise-height(Mary)}] \\ I = \iota I[I = (\text{precise-height(Mary)}, +\infty) \wedge \\ \exists X[\text{boys } X \wedge \forall x \sqsubseteq_{\text{atom}} X[\text{height}(x) \subseteq I]]], \\ X = \Sigma X. \text{boys } X \wedge \forall x \sqsubseteq_{\text{atom}} X[\text{height}(x) \subseteq I] \end{array} \right\}, \text{if } |X| = 2$$

$2_\nu \circ \mathbf{M}_\nu$
(the definite part of **exactly 2**$_\nu$) $\lambda g.$ $\left\{ \left\langle T, g^{\substack{\nu \to X \\ u \to I \\ w \to I'}} \right\rangle \,\middle|\, \begin{array}{l} \text{boys } X, \\ \forall x \sqsubseteq_{\text{atom}} X[\text{height}(x) \subseteq I], \\ I' = [\text{precise-height(Mary)}, \text{precise-height(Mary)}], \\ I = \iota I[I = (\text{precise-height(Mary)}, +\infty) \wedge \\ \exists X[\text{boys } X \wedge \forall x \sqsubseteq_{\text{atom}} X[\text{height}(x) \subseteq I]]] \end{array} \right\}$

MaxI_u
(the definite part of **than**$_u$) $\lambda g.$ $\left\{ \left\langle T, g^{\substack{\nu \to X \\ u \to I \\ w \to I'}} \right\rangle \,\middle|\, \begin{array}{l} \text{boys } X, \\ \text{interval } I, \\ \forall x \sqsubseteq_{\text{atom}} X[\text{height}(x) \subseteq I], \\ I' - I = (-\infty, 0), \\ \text{height(Mary)} \subseteq I' \end{array} \right\}$

For (7c) (repeated here as (40)), the explicit numerical differential *between 1 and 3 inches* restricts the default differential $(0, +\infty)$ (see (39)). Thus, as shown in (40), in this case, the widest interval I satisfying all relevant restrictions is [precise-height(Mary) $- 3''$, precise-height(Mary) $- 1''$], and then for boy-sums whose atomic member's height falls into this interval, the cardinality of the maximal boy-sum is 2.

(39) $[\![\text{between 1 and 3 inches ... -er}]\!] = [1'', 3''] \cap (0, +\infty) = [1'', 3'']$

(40) ⟦Mary is **between 1 and 3″ taller** than exactly two boys are⟧—delayed evaluation:

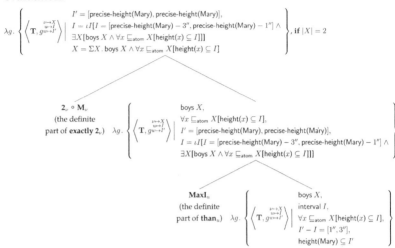

From (38), (40), and my above analysis for (1a), it should become evident that after the indefinite component of *exactly two* introduces a dref (i.e., a plural individual), this dref gets more and more restricted along the derivation. Thus, for these sentences in (7), the difference with regard to the value of differentials leads to different restrictions for interval drefs and eventually different maximal intervals (i.e., $I = (-\infty, \text{precise-height}(\text{Mary}))$, $I = (\text{precise-height}(\text{Mary}), +\infty)$, and $I = [\text{precise-height}(\text{Mary}) - 3'', \text{precise-height}(\text{Mary}) - 1'']$, respectively. Then the different maximal intervals further lead to different restrictions for plural individuals and eventually different maximal plural individuals.

Therefore, apparently, under the scenario in (7), it seems that the semantics of the comparative standard is not fixed, and for each sentence, Mary is compared with a different group of boys. In fact, the semantics of *exactly two boys* thus embedded in *than*-clauses is very similar to the semantics of *the hat* in *the rabbit in the hat*. For both *exactly two boys* and *the hat*, due to delayed evaluations, the drefs receive non-local restrictions that are beyond these DPs. Without these non-local restrictions, *the rabbit* would become uninterpretable in Haddock's scenario (see Figure 10.1, where there are multiple hats), while the actual interpretation of *exactly two boys* cannot be fixed so that the degree question corresponding to *than exactly two boys are (tall)* sounds degraded (see (8)).

3.4.2 Exactly two boys vs. few boys

It is worth noting that under the current account, as shown in (41), even though degree questions containing *exactly two boys* sound degraded (see (41a)), comparatives containing this kind of non-monotonic modified numerals in their *than*-clause are nevertheless good and natural. Overall, the cardinality restriction of *exactly two* applies to outputs with more restrictions (i.e., here not just the restriction boys X, but also other restrictions related to measurement and comparison) so that eventually, the dref is the maximal plural individual which consists of two boys not as tall as Mary is.

(41) a. #How tall are **exactly two boys**? (= (8a))
 b. Mary is taller **than exactly two boys are**.

In contrast, both degree questions and comparatives containing *no boys* or *few boys* are unacceptable (see (42) and (43)). The reason is simple. In my analysis, there is an existential requirement on the interval dref: $\exists X[\text{boys } X \wedge \forall x \sqsubseteq_{\text{atom}} X[\text{height}(x) \subseteq I]]$. While the cardinality restriction of *exactly two* can eventually guarantee the satisfaction of this requirement, *no boys* or *few boys* cannot guarantee that this requirement be satisfied.[11]

(42) a. *How tall are **no boys**?
 b. *Mary is taller **than no boys are**.

(43) a. *How tall are **few boys**?
 b. *Mary is taller **than few boys are**.

In this sense, the unacceptable comparative (43b) patterns with (44a), but not (44b). The contrast between (44a) and (44b) indicates that *few boys* is incompatible with collective predicates (here *lift the piano together*), but compatible with distributive predicates (see Solt 2007, Zhang 2018). According to Zhang (2018), a collective predicate requires its subject to be a group noun, and the very felicity of a group noun, in turn, requires that it be formed from a non-empty set of items, but expressions like *few boys* fail to guarantee this non-emptiness. Thus, the parallelism between (43b) and (44a) suggests that for plural individuals embedded within *than*-clauses (e.g., *exactly two boys*, *few*

---

11 Notice that *few boys are above 7 feet tall* is a true and felicitous sentence under the scenario that no boys are above 7 feet tall. Thus *few boys* does not guarantee that the above existential requirement be satisfied.

boys), restrictions like $\forall x \sqsubseteq_{\text{atom}} X[\text{height}(x) \subseteq I]$ (i.e., a predicate relating a plural individual with a certain interval) are similar to collective predicates. In other words, here we consider this interval I a continuous, non-dividable whole (i.e., a convex set of degrees) and relate it with a plural individual.

(44) a. *Few boys lifted the piano together.
 b. Few boys smiled.
 c. A few boys lifted the piano together.

This makes the current account different from many other approaches to the semantics of comparatives: those so-called 'entanglement' theories (see Fleisher 2016's discussion). According to a typical 'entanglement' theory—the degree-plurality-based approach (see Beck 2014, Dotlačil & Nouwen 2016), a *than*-clause denotes a sum of degree entities, and this sum of degree entities can be distributed over the matrix clause. For example, for *Mary is taller than the boys are*, the height of each of the boys is considered an atomic degree entity, and Mary's height exceeds each atomic degree entity (i.e., it is not the case that Mary's height is compared with a whole interval that each boy's height falls into). This kind of approach brings two predictions. First, the same analysis should work for both (43b) and the core sentence under discussion—*Mary is taller than exactly two boys are*. Second, (43b) should thus be judged good and pattern with acceptable sentences like (44b) (i.e., those with distributive predicates), instead of unacceptable sentences like (44a) (i.e., those with collective predicates). Neither prediction is borne out.

4 Discussion

My proposed account for the semantics of non-monotonic quantifiers embedded in *than*-clauses is crucially based on two ideas. First, comparatives express a relation among three definite degree-related descriptions that mutually constrain one another. Thus given the values of two of them, the value of the third is restricted. Second, definiteness is composed of two parts: one introduces drefs and builds sets of potential witnesses, and the other tests a set of witnesses for definiteness. Therefore, usually we use the values of the standard (i.e., the semantics of a *than*-clause) and the differential to derive the minuend's value for the semantics at the matrix clause level. However, for *Mary is taller than exactly two boys are*, we use the minuend's value and the differential to compute the value for the standard and furthermore, restrict the plural individual embedded in the *than*-clause.

In terms of scope, according to the first idea, comparatives involve no scopal interaction among the minuend's value, the standard, and the differential. Then according to the second idea, for those (quantificational) expressions that impose restrictions as delayed evaluations, they eventually have the effects of taking wide scope without causing any island-related issues resulted from QR operations (see also Larson 1988, Gajewski 2008, van Rooij 2008, Schwarzschild 2008).[12] Therefore, my analysis suggests that the only way for *than*-clause-internal quantifiers to take wide scope is exceptional scope-taking (see Charlow 2014), and universal quantifiers and distributivity operators embedded within a *than*-clause are always bounded by scope islands.

Thus clausal comparatives (see (46), cf. phrasal comparatives) are like cumulative-reading sentences (see (45)) in that there is no scope ambiguity.[13] (46) has only one reading: there exists a certain girl such that her smartness exceeds each boy's smartness. This sentence cannot mean that for each boy, there exists a certain girl such that she is smarter than him (in some way). Similarly, for the sentences in (47) and (48), only the external reading of *different* is available.[14]

---

12   To argue that *than*-clauses are scope islands and QR-style operations are not available for *than*-clause-internal quantifiers to take scope, Larson (1988) shows that covert or overt *wh*-movement is impossible in these cases (see (i)). The non-availability of *wh*-movement also rules out the possibility for antecedent-contained deletion (see (ii)).
(i) a. *[Which boy]$_i$ is Mary taller than t_i is?
    b. *I am wondering who is taller than who else is.
(ii) *Mary is taller than [[every boy]$_i$ [Lucy is taller than t_i is] is].

13   *Few boys saw exactly five movies between them* sounds degraded as a cumulative-reading sentence. This also adds to the parallelism between the semantics of *than*-clause-internal quantifiers (see (42b)) and the cumulative reading. See the discussion on *few* in Section 3.4.2 (see also Solt 2007, Zhang 2018).

14   There is some discrepancy between the judgments I report here (in (46), (47), and (48)) and those reported in Fleisher (2018). Fleisher (2018) claims that the internal reading of *different* (i.e., the '*every* > *different*' reading) is available for (i):
(i) A different boy is exactly six inches taller than every girl is.   *every* > *different* – OK
    (Fleisher 2018)
Among my informants, many of them claim that the '*every* > *different*' reading is only acceptable when the word *is* embedded in the *than*-clause is deleted, i.e., their judgments suggest that this '*every* > *different*' reading might be only available for phrasal comparatives, but not for clausal comparatives.

It is worth noting that for clausal comparatives, our intuitive judgment on the availability of an inverse scope reading might not be reliable, due to the garden-path effects (i.e., corresponding phrasal comparatives do have an inverse scope reading).

To fully settle this issue of judgments, especially with regard to whether the '*every* > *different*' reading is truly available for clausal comparatives (e.g., (i) and (47)), a rigorous

(45) Exactly three boys saw exactly five movies between them.
Cumulative-reading
⤳ The cardinality of the maximal set of boys who saw movies is exactly 3, and the cardinality of the maximal set of movies seen by boys is exactly 5.

(46) Some girl is smarter than every boy is.   Unambiguous

(47) A different girl is smarter than every boy is.   Unambiguous
    a. The **external** reading of *different* is available: it **presupposes** that there is a certain girl x such that x's smartness exceeds each boy's smartness, and it **asserts** that there is another girl y ($y \neq x$) such that y's smartness also exceeds each boy's smartness.
    b. The **internal** reading of *different* is unavailable: for each boy, there is a girl such that she is smarter than him (in some way), and there is a one-to-one mapping between boys and girls.

(48) A different girl is not smarter than every boy is.   No 6-way ambiguity
Only the external reading of *different* is available:
    a. $\exists > \neg$: There is another girl y, and y is not smarter than every boy is.
    b. $\neg > \exists$: There is no other girl s.t. she is smarter than every boy is.

This parallelism between the scopal behavior of comparatives and cumulative-reading sentences has profound implications for theories of comparatives and degree semantics.

    First, this challenges the parallel treatment of degrees and entities (of type e) with regard to (i) the quantification with the use of '$\exists$' and '$\forall$' (cf. the 'A-not-A' approach shown in (3) and Seuren 1973, 1984, Gajewski 2008, Schwarzschild 2008) and (ii) the notion of plurality (see Beck 2014, Dotlačil & Nouwen 2016 and the discussion in Section 3.4.2). Second, this also challenges the use of a negation operator '$\neg$' to characterize comparison (cf. Klein 1980, Larson 1988, Alrenga & Kennedy 2014).

    '$\exists$', '$\forall$', and '$\neg$' all lead to scope interaction and scopal ambiguity. Moreover, with the use of these treatments, the definiteness of degrees, which is similar to the definiteness of cardinalities, is overlooked. The relation among the three definite degree-related descriptions in a comparative should just be like

---

large-scale judgment elicitation or experiments with the use of an eye-tracker or EEG would be necessary, and I leave this for future research.

the relation among the three numbers in (49): the definite value '12' minus the definite value '4' is equal to the definite value '8'. After all, cardinalities are real numbers, and intervals, as shown in Section 3.1, are real numbers characterized in a generalized, not necessarily precise way.[15]

(49) 12 minus 4 is equal to 8.

This view is in line with those approaches that treat comparatives along with other cardinality-related phenomena, e.g., those 'larger-than'-based or interval-based theories (e.g., Russell 1905, Cresswell 1976, Stechow 1984, Heim 1985, Rullmann 1995, Schwarzschild & Wilkinson 2002, Heim 2006, Krasikova 2008, Beck 2010, 2011). As Beck (2010) states, 'I want to come out of the calculation of the semantics of the *than* clause holding in my hand *the* degree we will be comparing things to'. In my current account, I simply replace *the* degree with its more generalized version—*the* interval. Thus a *than*-clauses as well as the measurement at the matrix clause level and the value for the differential all denote definite descriptions of cardinality-like values. Of course, as I have argued throughout this paper, we do not always hold *the* value serving as the standard beforehand, and sometimes the exact definiteness (e.g., picking out *the* value from a set of cardinality-like values) can only come into play at a later stage.

The current account makes use of this 'degrees as numbers' view and adopts a dynamicized version of splitting the indefinite and definite contributions of definite degree-related descriptions, based on recent works by Brasoveanu (2013), Charlow (2014), Bumford (2017a,b). It is worth noting that a solution in this same spirit for sentences in (1) is also what Gajewski (2008) was after.

As shown in (50), Gajewski (2008) proposes to use a non-local exhaustive operator EXH that pragmatically strengthens the sentence meaning and rules out the weaker reading that Mary is taller than the two shortest boys are. A problem for this account is that pragmatically strengthened meanings are usually cancelable, but the exhaustiveness of modified numerals is not

(50) Mary is taller than exactly two boys are.   = (1a)
    EXH [$\exists d$[Mary is d-tall and 2 students are not d-tall]]   (Gajewski 2008)
    ⤳ Mary cannot be taller than 3 students are.

---

[15] Whether real numbers are semantically primitive or should be constructed from other more primitive items is a totally different issue that I cannot discuss here. For relevant discussion, see Bale (2011) as well as Schwarzschild (this volume) and Bale (this volume).

Thus, by analyzing degree-related values as definite intervals and drawing parallelism between intervals and cardinalities, the current account also extends the application of dynamic semantics into degree semantics. Further theoretical and empirical implications are for future research.[16]

5 Conclusion

With the use of existing, independently motivated mechanisms (i.e., Bumford 2017a,b's split approach to definiteness and Zhang & Ling 2015, 2020's interval-subtraction-based approach to the semantics of comparatives), I have accounted for the semantics of comparatives containing non-monotonic quantifiers (e.g., *exact two boys*) within their *than*-clause. Essentially, the semantic derivation for these sentences undergoes two stages. First, during bottom-up composition, drefs (i.e., plural individual and intervals) are introduced and a comparison is established. Then, during delayed top-down evaluations, the cardinality restriction of the embedded non-monotonic quantifier is applied to the maximal plural individual in the widest interval. This account explains why the semantics of *than*-clauses containing non-monotonic quantifiers seems unfixed or incomplete *per se*: due to delayed evaluations, plural individuals introduced by non-monotonic quantifiers like *exactly two boys* continue getting restricted from matrix clauses. This account brings the semantics of comparatives in line with the semantics of other definiteness-related phenomena, including cardinality and cumulative-reading sentences, and at the same time, broadens the application of dynamic semantics. Presumably, the semantics of degrees (or intervals) can be considered a more generalized development of the semantics of cardinality.

6 Acknowledgements

This research was financially supported by the Program for Eastern Young Scholar at Shanghai Institutions of Higher Learning (to L.Z.). For comments, suggestions, and discussions, I thank Dylan Bumford, Lucas Champollion, Peter Hallman, Haoze Li, Jia Ling, Mingming Liu, Roger Schwarzschild, and Anna Szabolcsi. Errors are mine.

---

16 There will be many interesting topics for further exploration: e.g., the coordination of cardinalities or degree-related values (see also Bale (this volume)).

References

Alrenga, Peter & Christopher Kennedy. 2014. *No more* shall we part: Quantifiers in English comparatives. *Natural Language Semantics* 22(1). 1–53.

Bale, Alan. 2011. Scales and comparison classes. *Natural Language Semantics* 19(2). 169–190.

Bartsch, Renate & Theo Vennemann. 1972. The grammar of relative adjectives and comparison. *Linguistische Berichte* 20. 19–32.

Beck, Sigrid. 2010. Quantifiers in *than*-clauses. *Semantics and Pragmatics* 3(1). 1–72.

Beck, Sigrid. 2011. Comparative constructions. In Claudia Maienborn, Klaus von Heusinger & Paul Portner (eds.), *Semantics: An international handbook of natural language meaning*, vol. 2, 1341–1390. de Gruyter.

Beck, Sigrid. 2014. Plural predication and quantified 'than'-clauses. In Luka Crnič & Uli Sauerland (eds.), *The art and craft of semantics: A Festschrift for Irene Heim*, vol. 1, 91–115. MIT Working Papers in Linguistics 70.

Brasoveanu, Adrian. 2013. Modified Numerals as Post-Suppositions. *Journal of Semantics* 30(2). 155–209.

Bumford, Dylan. 2017a. Split-scope definites: Relative superlatives and Haddock descriptions. *Linguistics and Philosophy* 40(6). 549–593.

Bumford, Dylan. 2017b. *Split-scope effects in definite descriptions*. New York University dissertation.

Charlow, Simon. to appear. *Post-suppositions and semantic theory*. To appear in *Journal of Semantics*.

Charlow, Simon. 2014. *On the semantics of exceptional scope*. New York University dissertation.

Cresswell, Max J. 1976. The semantics of degree. In Barbara Partee (ed.), *Montague grammar*, 261–292. New York: Academic Press.

Dotlačil, Jakub & Rick Nouwen. 2016. The comparative and degree pluralities. *Natural Language Semantics* 24(1). 45–78.

Fleisher, Nicholas. 2016. Comparing theories of quantifiers in *than* clauses: Lessons from downward-entailing differentials. *Semantics and Pragmatics* 9(4). 1–23.

Fleisher, Nicholas. 2018. *Than* clauses as embedded questions. In *28th Semantics and Linguistic Theory (SALT) 28*, 120–140.

Gajewski, Jon. 2008. More on quantifiers in comparative clauses. In *18th Semantics and Linguistic Theory (SALT) 18*, 340–357.

Haddock, Nicholas J. 1987. Incremental interpretation and combinatory categorial grammar. In *The 10th International Joint Conference on Artificial Intelligence*, vol. 2, 661–663. Morgan Kaufmann Publishers Inc.

Hausser, Roland & Dietmar Zaefferer. 1978. Questions and answers in a context-dependent Montague grammar. In *Formal Semantics and Pragmatics for Natural Languages*, 339–358. Springer.

Heim, Irene. 1985. *Notes on comparatives and related matters*. Unpublished ms., University of Texas, Austin.

Heim, Irene. 2000. Degree operators and scope. In Brendan Jackson & Tanya Matthews (eds.), *10th Semantics and Linguistic Theory (SALT)* 10, 40–64.

Heim, Irene. 2006. *Remarks on comparative clauses as generalized quantifiers*. Unpublished ms., MIT.

Kennedy, Christopher. 1999. *Projecting the adjective: The syntax and semantics of gradability and comparison*. Routledge.

Klein, Ewan. 1980. A semantics for positive and comparative adjectives. *Linguistics and Philosophy* 4(1). 1–45.

Krasikova, Sveta. 2008. Quantifiers in comparatives. In *12th Sinn und Bedeutung (SuB)* 12, 337–352. Citeseer.

Krifka, Manfred. 1999. At least some determiners aren't determiners. In Ken Turner (ed.), *The semantics/pragmatics interface from different points of view*, vol. 1, 257–291. Amsterdam: Elsevier Science B.V.

Larson, Richard K. 1988. Scope and comparatives. *Linguistics and Philosophy* 11(1). 1–26.

Moore, Ramon E. 1979. *Methods and Applications of Interval Analysis*. SIAM.

van Rooij, Robert. 2008. Comparatives and quantifiers. In Olivier Bonami & Patricia Cabredo Hofherr (eds.), *Empirical Issues in Syntax and Semantics*, vol. 7, 423–444. Citeseer.

Rullmann, Hotze. 1995. *Maximality in the semantics of wh-constructions*. University of Massachusetts at Amherst dissertation.

Russell, Bertrand. 1905. On denoting. *Mind* 14(56). 479–493.

Schwarzschild, Roger. 2008. The semantics of comparatives and other degree constructions. *Language and Linguistics Compass* 2(2). 308–331.

Schwarzschild, Roger & Karina Wilkinson. 2002. Quantifiers in comparatives: A semantics of degree based on intervals. *Natural Language Semantics* 10(1). 1–41.

Seuren, Pieter A.M. 1973. The comparative. In Ferenc Kiefer & Nicolas Ruwet (eds.), *Generative Grammar in Europe*, 528–564. Springer.

Seuren, Pieter A.M. 1984. The comparative revisited. *Journal of Semantics* 3(1). 109–141.

Solt, Stephanie. 2007. Few and fewer. *Snippets* 15. 8–9.

Stechow, Arnim von. 1984. Comparing semantic theories of comparison. *Journal of semantics* 3(1–2). 1–77.

de Swart, Henriette. 1999. Indefinites between predication and reference. In *9th Semantics and Linguistic Theory (SALT)* 9, 273–297.

Szabolcsi, Anna. 1997. Strategies for scope taking. In Anna Szabolcsi (ed.), *Ways of scope taking*, 109–154. Springer.

Umbach, Carla. 2005. Why do modified numerals resist a referential interpretation? In *15th Semantics and Linguistic Theory (SALT)* 15, 258–275.

Zhang, Linmin. 2018. Modified numerals revisited: The cases of *fewer than 4* and *between 4 and 8*. In Robert Truswell, Chris Cummins, Caroline Heycock, Brian Rabern & Hannah Rohde (eds.), *21st Sinn und Bedeutung (SuB) 21*, 1371–1388.

Zhang, Linmin & Jia Ling. 2015. Comparatives Revisited: Downward-Entailing Differentials Do Not Threaten Encapsulation Theories. In Thomas Brochhagen, Floris Roelofsen & Nadine Theiler (eds.), *20th Amsterdam Colloquium*, 478–487.

Zhang, Linmin & Jia Ling. 2017a. Ambiguous than-clauses and the mention-some reading. In *27th Semantics and Linguistic Theory (SALT) 27*, 191–211.

Zhang, Linmin & Jia Ling. 2017b. Little: not a dichotomy-based negation operator, but a trivalence-based polar opposition operator. In Aaron Kaplan, Abby Kaplan, Miranda K. McCarvel & Edward J. Rubin (eds.), *34th West Coast Conference on Formal Linguistics (WCCFL) 34*, 590–598. Cascadilla Press.

Zhang, Linmin & Jia Ling. 2020. *The semantics of comparatives: A difference-based approach*. Manuscript. https://ling.auf.net/lingbuzz/005223

CHAPTER 11

Nominal Quantifiers in *Than* Clauses and Degree Questions

Nicholas Fleisher

1 Introduction

The scopal behavior of quantifiers in comparative *than* clauses has attracted a great deal of attention in the recent literature. Such quantifiers often appear to take scope at the matrix level, despite their syntactic location within—and, consequently, their putative scopal confinement to—the subordinate finite *than* clause. This phenomenon has led to a wide variety of new proposals about the syntactic and semantic structure of *than* clauses, and these in turn have led to intriguing, if poorly understood, observations about the interactions between nominal quantification and degree operators.

One such interaction has come to be known as the Heim–Kennedy Constraint (Heim 2001, 2006, Bhatt & Pancheva 2004, Alrenga & Kennedy 2014). While specific formulations differ, the core generalization is as in (1):

(1) Heim–Kennedy Constraint (received version): A nominal quantifier is barred from taking scope between a degree quantifier and its trace.

The Heim–Kennedy Constraint restricts degree operators' scopal interactions with nominal quantifiers.[1] It does not restrict their interactions with modals. In this connection, Nouwen & Dotlačil (2017) make some novel observations about interpretive asymmetries between wide-scoping nominal quantifiers and wide-scoping modals in *than* clauses. They conclude that nominal quantifiers must take scope at an exceptionally high position within the *than* clause, and they suggest that this invites a new and more stringent version of the Heim–Kennedy Constraint:

---

[1] Here and throughout, I use the term "nominal quantifier" to mean a quantifier over individuals. As an anonymous reviewer points out, nominals can also be used to quantify over times and other types of things (e.g. *every day*). I have nothing to say about quantifiers over such types here.

(2) Heim–Kennedy Constraint (version of Nouwen & Dotlačil 2017): A nominal quantifier is barred from taking scope between a degree abstractor and the variable it binds.

Here I suggest that the high scope position occupied by nominal quantifiers in *than* clauses is the same as the one occupied by quantifiers in pair-list readings of embedded questions. Many have suggested that such quantifiers move higher than ordinary quantifier raising (QR) usually permits (Chierchia 1993, Dayal 1996, 2016, Szabolcsi 1997), and Nouwen & Dotlačil recognize that the relevant reading of the *than* clause is a pair-list reading. Rather than propose an additional layer of degree morphology in *than* clauses, as Nouwen & Dotlačil do, I take this to support the view that *than* clauses should be treated on a par with embedded questions more generally (Fleisher 2018). If the scopal behavior that we see in *than* clauses reflects this more general property of embedded questions, then it likely does not motivate the revisions to the Heim–Kennedy Constraint proposed by Nouwen & Dotlačil.

While *than* clauses and embedded questions both support pair-list readings with quantifiers (as well as single-point readings; see section 6), only the latter support functional readings. I suggest here that this is due to a selectional property of *than* itself; it thus need not trouble the claim that *than*'s clausal complement has the structure of an embedded question. Specifically, I claim that *than* needs to extract a degree from (the trace of) its complement, but the functional reading involves abstraction over functions rather than degrees, with the result that the requisite degree cannot be extracted.

The structure of the paper is as follows. In section 2, I review Nouwen & Dotlačil's observations about the extraordinarily high scope of nominal quantifiers in *than* clauses and their proposed analysis. In section 3, I discuss the parallels between *than* clauses and embedded questions (Fleisher 2018) before sketching a proposal in section 4 that treats nominal quantifiers' scope in *than* clauses on a par with that of quantifiers in pair-list readings of embedded questions. In section 5, I discuss functional readings. Section 6 concludes.

2 Nominal Scope in *Than* Clauses

Scopal phenomena within the *than* clause have led many authors to rethink traditional degree-based treatments of gradable expressions and inspired a corresponding technical ingenuity in the literature. Schwarzschild & Wilkinson (2002) were the first to propose a semantics for *than* clauses based on scalar intervals rather than degrees, and much of the subsequent literature has followed their lead.[2] Of particular note is Heim (2006), who proposed a mechanism for moving between degree-based lexical entries for gradable expressions and interval-based denotations for the larger constituents in which they are found. Heim accomplishes this by introducing a "point-to-interval" operator, Π, defined in (3). (The two arguments of Π are intervals, type ⟨d,t⟩; the *max* operator picks out the greatest degree satisfying a particular degree property.)

(3) $[\![\Pi]\!] = \lambda D \lambda D' . max(D') \in D$

A constituent consisting of Π plus its first argument (henceforth, the "Π-phrase") forms a generalized quantifier over degrees. Heim proposes that the Π-phrase is merged in the degree argument position within the *than* clause and then raises to take scope, leaving behind a degree trace. As she shows, certain ambiguities involving modals in *than* clauses can then be analyzed as scopal ambiguities arising from the interaction between the modal and the Π-phrase. This is sketched in (4) and (5).

(4) The paper is longer than it should be.
  a. *than*-clause LF: $\lambda 1 \: [\Box \: [\Pi \: t_1] \: \lambda 2 \: [\text{it is } t_2\text{-long}]]$
  b. Semantic value: $\lambda D \: . \: \Box(\lambda w.\text{its length in } w \in D)$

(5) The paper is longer than it needs to be.
  a. *than*-clause LF: $\lambda 1 \: [[\Pi \: t_1] \: \lambda 2 \: \Box \: [\text{it is } t_2\text{-long}]]$
  b. Semantic value: $\lambda D \: . \: max(\lambda d \: . \: \Box(\lambda w.\text{its length in } w \geq d)) \in D$

In (4), the *than* clause characterizes intervals D such that it is deontically necessary that the paper's length be contained in D. When composed with the matrix clause, this yields a maximum-related reading, in which we understand that the paper's actual length exceeds its length in any accessible world; in other words, the paper is too long. In (5), the *than* clause characterizes intervals D such that the greatest degree of length that the paper must achieve in all deontically accessible worlds is contained in D; this degree is the paper's minimum required length. When composed with the matrix clause, this yields a minimum-related reading, in which we understand that the paper's actual length exceeds the minimum required threshold; in other words, the paper is

---

2 In more recent work, Schwarzschild has developed a degree semantics based on scalar segments (see Schwarzschild, this volume, and references therein).

long enough and then some. (For further discussion of minimum- and maximum-related readings in *than* clauses, see Rullmann 1995, Krasikova 2011, Beck 2013, and Zhang & Ling 2017.)

Nouwen & Dotlačil's key observation is that nominal quantifiers in *than* clauses do not yield minimum- or maximum-related readings of this sort. This is something that we can see clearly only once we introduce a non-upward-entailing differential phrase into the matrix clause (Fleisher 2016). A sentence like (6), with universal *every*, cannot mean that John is exactly six inches taller than just the tallest girl (as would be the case on a maximum-related reading) or just the shortest girl (as on a minimum-related reading). Rather, it has only a pair-list reading, where for each girl *g*, John is exactly six inches taller than *g* is. This leads to an inference that the girls' heights are all the same.

(6) John is exactly six inches taller than every girl is.

Nouwen & Dotlačil conclude that the nominal quantifier *every girl* must take scope higher than the position where the universal modal takes scope in examples like (4). They introduce two operators above the projection where the *wh* degree or interval operator moves on standard analyses, and propose that the nominal quantifier takes scope between them. The higher of the two novel operators dynamically collects the values assigned to a designated variable introduced by the lower novel operator, one per degree returned by the *than* clause when the universal nominal quantifier scopes between them. The result is a degree plurality. (These novel operators compose vacuously when nothing takes scope between them, returning just a single *than*-clause degree. I refer the interested reader to Nouwen & Dotlačil 2017 for details, and to Dotlačil & Nouwen 2016 for a theory of how the degree plurality denoted by the *than* clause composes with the matrix clause.)

Nouwen & Dotlačil suggest that the range of readings in examples like (6) is limited because the Heim–Kennedy Constraint severely restricts the range of positions where the nominal quantifier may take scope within the *than* clause. There are two steps in the argument. First, they take the lack of a maximum-related reading to indicate that a nominal quantifier cannot take scope where the universal modal takes scope in examples like (4); as they note, this is a position that intervenes not between a degree quantifier and its trace, but merely between a *wh* degree or interval operator and its trace. Second, they conclude that the Heim–Kennedy Constraint bars nominal quantifiers from taking scope between any degree or interval abstractor and its trace; this is their version of the Heim–Kennedy Constraint, stated above in (2). They suggest that the higher operators they introduce provide a licit scope position for the quantifier, and that the lack of ambiguity in such *than* clauses is due to this position's being the only one where the nominal quantifier can take scope.

There are at least two considerations that might lead one to question Nouwen & Dotlačil's analysis. First, the expectation that *than* clauses with wide-scoping universal nominal quantifiers should yield maximum-related readings parallel to those with wide-scoping universal modals is based on a particular assumption about how the *than*-clause interpretation proceeds. Nouwen & Dotlačil adopt Beck's (2010) proposal that the sets of intervals yielded by the LFs in (4) and (5) are subject to a pair of operators that (i) choose the maximally informative (i.e. smallest) such interval and then (ii) select the greatest degree from that interval. With a wide-scoping universal modal as in (4), this yields the maximum permissible degree of length, i.e. the paper's length in the accessible world where it is longest. With a universal nominal quantifier as in (6), it would yield the maximum height of any girl, i.e. the height of the tallest girl. If this is the contribution of the *than* clause in each case, then it is indeed a mystery why examples with wide-scoping nominal quantifiers, like (6), lack maximum-related readings.

But Beck's selection theory is not the only way to proceed with the interpretation of the *than* clause. Heim (2006) proposes that what we see in (4) and (5) are the complete semantic values for these *than* clauses. In other words, for Heim, the *than* clause denotes a generalized quantifier over degrees, and the *than* clause itself raises to take scope. As long as the *than* clause takes scope above the matrix differential, we generate a pair-list reading for an example like (6), not a maximum-related reading. Expectations about whether a *than* clause with a wide-scoping universal nominal quantifier should generate a maximum-related reading are thus tied to the choice of implementation. And as we will see below in section 3, there are independent reasons to favor an approach that has the *than* clause denote a degree quantifier rather than a degree term. (For discussion and sample derivations within Heim's approach, see Heim 2006, Beck 2010, and Fleisher 2016, 2018.)

A second reason to question Nouwen & Dotlačil's analysis is that the high scope position they propose for nominal quantifiers in *than* clauses is structurally analogous to what has been proposed for quantifiers in pair-list readings of questions (Chierchia 1993, Dayal 1996, 2016, Szabolcsi 1997). Rather than propose novel structure in the upper periphery of the *than* clause, we might achieve a more general analysis by pursuing connections between *than* clauses and questions. In section 3, I review a broad array of arguments from Fleisher (2018) that support treating *than* clauses as embedded questions. Then in section 4, I sketch an analysis of nominal scope-taking in *than* clauses that treats it on a par with pair-list readings more generally.

Both of these considerations—the non-trivial connection between the maximum-related reading with nominal quantifiers and the style of implementation, and the strong parallel we find with questions, including non-degree questions—would appear to weaken the case for Nouwen & Dotlačil's proposed revision of the Heim–Kennedy Constraint. On the first score, it is possible to craft an analysis where a nominal quantifier takes scope immediately beneath a *wh* interval operator without erroneously generating a maximum-related reading. On the second, pair-list readings are found even in the absence of a degree operator whose scope the nominal quantifier putatively must escape.[3]

3 Parallels between *Than* Clauses and Embedded Questions

Than clauses and embedded questions show some remarkable syntactic and semantic similarities. Diagnostics from *wh*-movement, scope, binding, and quantificational variability suggest a close connection between the two constructions (Lerner & Pinkal 1991, Moltmann 1992, Moltmann & Szabolcsi 1994, Zhang & Ling 2017, Fleisher 2018). Moreover, by attending to the ways in which *than* clauses resemble embedded questions, we gain new arguments for treating *than* clauses themselves as scope takers rather than as degree terms. In this section I sketch these parallels and set the stage for the analysis of pair-list readings in the next section.

It has long been recognized that comparative *than* clauses contain a *wh* or A′ dependency involving the degree argument position (Bresnan 1973, Chomsky 1977), as evidenced by this position's variable sensitivity to different classes of islands for extraction. In this, *than* clauses mirror *wh*-questions. Examples are shown in (7).

(7) a. John is taller than Mary says he is _.
    b. ??John is taller than Mary wonders whether he is _.
    c. *John is taller than the rumor that he is _ caused a scandal.

Beyond this syntactic similarity, *than* clauses and questions behave alike with respect to a number of semantic diagnostics. The matrix-scope-like pair-list reading that we find with nominal quantifiers in *than* clauses is also found with

---

3 Nouwen & Dotlačil (2017: 16) note a further worry about their proposal, namely the fact that it "relies on the modelling of anaphoric dependencies in dynamic semantic frameworks, which is odd given that we are dealing with an essentially non-anaphoric phenomenon here."

embedded questions, as shown in (8) (Lerner & Pinkal 1991, Moltmann 1992).[4] An embedded-clause quantifier can make a matrix subject quantificationally dependent on it in both *than* clauses and embedded questions, as in (9) (Moltmann & Szabolcsi 1994).[5] Binding data point toward a syntactic scope-taking account of this inversion, as in (10), where QR of the embedded clause would move the bound pronoun outside the scope of its antecedent (Szabolcsi 1997). And *than* clauses mirror embedded questions in supporting quantificational variability effects in the presence of an appropriate quantificational adverbial, as in (11) (Fleisher 2018).

(8) a. John is taller than every girl is.
    b. John knows how tall every girl is.

(9) a. Some boy is exactly six inches taller than every girl is. OK: *every > some*
    b. Some boy knows how tall every girl is. OK: *every > some*

(10) a. Some boy$_1$ is exactly six inches taller than every girl says he$_1$ is.
        **every > some*
     b. Some boy$_1$ knows how tall every girl says he$_1$ is. **every > some*

(11) a. For the most part, John is less than a foot taller than every girl is.
        'John is less than a foot taller than most girls'
     b. For the most part, John knows how tall every girl is.
        'John knows how tall most girls are'

Examples like (9a) are of particular interest, as they help us decide among theories of *than*-clause composition. The inverse-scope reading of this sentence is true iff for every girl *g*, there is some boy who is exactly six inches taller than *g* is. Unlike in other well-known cases with a non-monotone matrix differential

---

[4] I confine my attention here to matrix predicates that select both interrogative and non-interrogative complements ("responsive" embedders, in the terminology of Lahiri 2002; predicates that select "extensional" complements, in the terminology of Groenendijk & Stokhof 1984).

[5] The inclusion of a non-upward-entailing differential is crucial for differentiating the inverse-scope reading from the surface-scope reading. Larson (1988), Nouwen & Dotlačil (2017), and Zhang (this volume) claim, on the basis of examples like *Some boy is taller than every girl is*, that such inversion is impossible. But here the inverse-scope reading ('for every girl *g*, some boy is taller than *g* is') entails the surface-scope reading (more precisely, the reading where *every girl* scopes above the degree operator but below the subject: 'some boy is taller than the tallest girl'), and vice versa.

phrase, here there is no inference that the girls are all equal in height. Theories that derive the same-height inference via the internal composition of the *than* clause (Alrenga & Kennedy 2014) or via the interaction between the *than* clause and the non-monotone differential (Beck 2010, Zhang & Ling 2015) thus have difficulty accounting for such examples.

As a general matter, scope inversion presents difficulties for theories in which the *than* clause denotes a degree or interval that saturates an argument position in the matrix clause ("encapsulation" theories, in the terminology of Fleisher 2016; for a novel analysis of non-monotonic quantifiers in *than*-clauses that falls within this class, see Zhang, this volume). In order to evaluate the truth of (9a) on the inverse-scope reading, we need to know all of the girls' heights. This is information that encapsulation theories tend to discard, retaining only the height of the tallest girl (or the heights of the tallest and shortest girls). A natural way to get the girls' heights is to quantify over the girls. This is precisely what "entanglement" theories do, typically by having the *than* clause take scope. In such a configuration, the *than*-clause-internal nominal quantifier attains widest scope when the full clause is composed (for details and discussion, see Fleisher 2016).

The empirical considerations stemming from examples like (9a) thus lead us to prefer the entanglement approach to comparatives (Fleisher 2018). This yields yet another parallel with embedded questions, where pair-list readings and related phenomena have led many to treat embedded questions as scope takers (Chierchia 1993, Szabolcsi 1997, Lahiri 2002). Alongside the syntactic and semantic parallels adduced above, this points us in a promising direction for our analysis of *than*-clause-internal quantifiers.

4 Pair-List Readings in Questions and Comparatives

The wide-scope readings that we find with nominal quantifiers in *than* clauses are remarkably similar to the pair-list readings we find with quantifiers in questions. In this section I sketch an analysis of *than* clauses that treats them as embedded degree questions. I identify the high scope position that Nouwen & Dotlačil (2017) propose for *than*-clause-internal quantifiers with the high scope position that Chierchia (1993) proposes for quantifiers in pair-list readings. The result is an analysis of quantification in *than* clauses that capitalizes on our understanding of quantification in questions, and that pushes us toward a unification of these two domains.

I begin by laying out some proposals from Fleisher (2018) about the internal and external syntax of the *than* clause. I propose that the *than* clause (or, more precisely, the clausal complement of *than*) has the structure and interpretation of a degree question. I follow Chierchia (1993) and Szabolcsi (1997) in proposing that this question constituent is in fact a lifted question, i.e. a generalized quantifier over questions. As a result, it must raise to take scope. Its trace serves as the argument of an answerhood operator, ANSDEG, introduced by *than*; ANSDEG is defined in (12) and exemplified in (13).[6] This operator returns the degree found in the maximally informative answer to the question. A sample derivation is shown in (14).

(12) $\text{ANSDEG}_w(Q) = \iota d[\text{ABST}(Q)(d) = \text{MAXINF}_w(Q)]$, where:
  a. $\text{ABST}(Q)$ is the intension of Q's abstract (in the sense of George 2011)[7]
  b. $\text{MAXINF}_w(Q)$ is the strongest true answer to Q in w (cf. Beck & Rullmann 1999)

(13) a. $\text{ABST}(\text{how tall is John?})(d) = {}^\wedge\text{tall}(\text{John}, d)$
  b. $\text{MAXINF}_w(\text{how tall is John?})$
    $= \text{MAXINF}_w(\lambda p.\exists d : p = {}^\wedge\text{tall}(\text{John}, d))$
    $= {}^\wedge\text{tall}(\text{John}, d_{J,w})$ (where $d_{J,w}$ = John's max height in w)
  c. $\text{ANSDEG}_w(\text{how tall is John?})$
    $= \iota d[\text{ABST}(\text{how tall is John?})(d) = \text{MAXINF}_w(\text{how tall is John?})]$
    $= \iota d[{}^\wedge\text{tall}(\text{John}, d) = {}^\wedge\text{tall}(\text{John}, d_{J,w})]$
    $= d_{J,w}$

(14) Mary is taller than John is.
  a. LF: [*wh* λ₁ John is t₁-tall] λ2 [Mary is taller than t₂]
  b. Semantic value: $\lambda Q \,.\, Q(\text{how tall is John?}) \,(\lambda Q.\text{Mary is taller}_w \text{ than } \text{ANSDEG}_w(Q))$
    $= 1$ iff Mary is taller$_w$ than $\text{ANSDEG}_w(\text{how tall is John?})$
    $= 1$ iff Mary is taller$_w$ than $d_{J,w}$

---

6 ANSDEG is identical to the operator I call ANS$_d$ in Fleisher (2018). I have changed its name here in order to avoid any terminological confusion with the answerhood operator of Dayal (1996), which is often called Ans$_D$ or similar. Dayal's Ans$_D$ returns a proposition; ANSDEG returns a degree.

7 A question's abstract is its syntactic and semantic skeleton, the structure that serves as the argument of an interrogative operator. As George (2011: 23) puts it, following Groenendijk & Stokhof (1984), "it is what is structurally common to a '*wh*'-question and the analogous relative clause .... [T]he intension of an abstract will be the property (or relation) that the '*wh*'-question is a question about." The intension of the abstract of the question *how tall is John* is the function $\lambda w \lambda d.\text{tall}_w(\text{John}, d)$. Strictly speaking, then, in my notation above, $\text{ABST}(Q)(d)$

In his analysis of questions, Chierchia (1993) proposes that pair-list readings arise when a subject is quantified into a lifted question, as sketched in (15).[8] Chierchia implements this via a syntactic absorption operation that moves the quantifier above the interrogative complementizer. As Dayal (2016: 112 ff.) emphasizes, the key semantic requirement is that the quantifier be interpreted outside the question nucleus, i.e. above the point at which the essential propositional variable is introduced (C, on most accounts). If *than* clauses share the basic structure and interpretation of questions, then we can analyze *than*-clause-internal quantifiers along these lines.

(15) 〚than every girl is tall〛 = 〚how tall is every girl?〛 = $\lambda \mathcal{Q} . \forall x \in girl : \mathcal{Q}$(how tall is x?)

When this lifted-question-style *than* clause raises and takes scope, the embedded quantifier ends up with widest scope, yielding a pair-list reading:

(16) John is taller than every girl is.
 a. LF: [*wh* λ_1 every girl is t_1-tall] λ_2 [John is taller than t_2]
 b. Semantic value: $\lambda \mathcal{Q} . \forall x \in girl : \mathcal{Q}$(how tall is x?) (λQ.John is taller$_w$ than ANSDEG$_w(Q)$)
  = 1 iff $\forall x \in girl$: John is taller$_w$ than ANSDEG$_w$(how tall is x?)
  = 1 iff $\forall x \in girl$: John is taller$_w$ than $d_{x,w}$

A nominal quantifier thus achieves wide scope inside a *than* clause just as it does in an embedded question; when the embedded constituent (*than* clause or question) itself takes scope, we get a pair-list reading. By treating the *than* clause as an embedded degree question, we avail ourselves of the scope-taking mechanism(s) that have been proposed for quantifiers in questions.

---

is a shorthand for $^\wedge$ABST$(Q)(w)(d)$, the result of supplying the intension of Q's abstract with world and degree arguments and taking the intension of the result.

[8] Chierchia's actual proposal involves existential quantification over minimal witness sets of the quantifier, not quantification by the quantifier itself. This is to account for the unavailability of pair-list readings with downward-entailing quantifiers, a restriction that we find in *than* clauses as well; for further discussion, see Szabolcsi (1997), Lahiri (2002), Beck (2010), Aloni & Roelofsen (2014), and Dayal (2016). For perspicacity's sake, I will use the simpler notation involving direct quantification by the quantifier, with the understanding that this should be taken as a shorthand for a treatment in terms of witness sets. Note in this connection that it is not clear how to prevent downward-entailing quantifiers from taking exceptionally high *than*-clause-internal scope in Nouwen & Dotlačil's (2017) theory.

One might object that in assimilating the analysis of *than*-clause-internal quantifiers to that of question-internal quantifiers, we are trading one set of mysteries for another. It is unclear what permits quantifiers to move to such an unusually high position in questions; the questions literature has produced no consensus on the matter. Analyses of quantifiers in questions differ both in their underlying architecture (e.g. whether they treat pair-list readings as a type of functional reading) and in their empirical coverage (e.g. whether they account for certain domain exhaustivity inferences); for a recent overview and discussion, see Dayal (2016: ch. 4). Moreover, it is unclear whether the behavior of quantifiers in *than* clauses can help us choose among the analyses that have been proposed in the questions literature.

That said, the syntactic and semantic parallels between *than* clauses and embedded questions are, I suggest, too numerous and thoroughgoing to ignore. While there are many analyses of quantifiers in questions, they largely agree on an exceptionally high scope position for quantifiers in pair-list readings, much as Nouwen & Dotlačil suggest for *than* clauses. Rather than treat quantifiers' behavior in *than* clauses as a quirk stemming from a reformulated Heim–Kennedy Constraint, we can appeal to what has been observed and proposed for quantifiers in embedded *wh*-clauses of all kinds, including those without degree abstraction. If the mysteries of *than*-clause-internal scope-taking are the same as those of question-internal scope-taking, then our stock of mysteries is reduced.

5 Functional Readings

If *than* clauses are to be analyzed as embedded questions, then all else being equal we should expect quantifiers in *than* clauses to exhibit the same range of readings as we find with quantifiers in questions. In this section I examine a case where this parallel fails: functional readings. Question-internal quantifiers, including those in degree questions, give rise to functional readings, but *than*-clause-internal quantifiers do not. Here I suggest that this is due to an independent factor in *than* clauses: the ANSDEG operator, which needs to return a degree. Functional readings of degree questions involve abstraction over functions rather than over degrees, with the result that ANSDEG cannot return a degree as required. The lack of functional readings in *than* clauses thus does not undermine the proposal to treat *than* clauses as embedded questions.

Functional readings of questions are those where the answer can be stated in the form of an abstract function (as opposed to the complete graph of a function, as on a pair-list reading). Examples with non-degree and degree questions are shown in (17).

(17) a. Q: Which book did every student₁ read?
A: The one her₁ advisor recommended.
b. Q: How tall is every girl₁?
A: Taller than her₁ mother.

One salient difference between functional readings and pair-list readings is that functional readings are available even with downward-entailing quantifiers, as shown in (18). (I turn to embedded questions here, as matrix *wh*-questions support a narrower range of quantifiers; for discussion, see Szabolcsi 1997.)

(18) a. John knows which book no student₁ read: the one her₁ advisor recommended.
b. John knows how tall no girl₁ is: as tall as her₁ father.

Where ordinary individual questions are typically analyzed as involving existential quantification over individuals, functional readings involve quantification over Skolem functions, i.e. functions from individuals to individuals (Engdahl 1986, Chierchia 1993). In the (a) examples above, the answer to the question (or the specification of John's knowledge, in the embedded question case) includes a type $\langle e,e \rangle$ function: λx.the book x's advisor recommended.

In the (b) examples, by contrast, the answers/specifications involve functions from individuals to degree quantifiers, type $\langle e, \langle dt,t \rangle \rangle$, as shown in (19).[9]

(19) a. *taller than her mother* ⤳ $\lambda x \lambda D.max(D) > max(\lambda d.\text{tall}(x\text{'s mother}, d))$
b. *as tall as her father* ⤳ $\lambda x \lambda D.max(D) \geq max(\lambda d.\text{tall}(x\text{'s father}, d))$

The (non-lifted) semantic values of an ordinary degree question and a functional degree question are shown in (20a) and (20b), respectively. When we supply the function from (19b) as the value for f in an answer to (20b), we get an appropriate answer meaning—viz. that no girl is as tall as her father is—as shown in (21).

---

9 Romero (1998: 122 ff.) proposes a similar treatment of functional readings of *how many* questions, involving functions from individuals to individual quantifiers.

(20) a. ⟦how tall John is⟧ = λp.∃d : p = ^tall(John, d)
    b. ⟦how tall no girl is⟧ = λp.∃f : p = ^no girl(λx.f(x)(λd.tall(x, d)))

(21) ^no girl(λx.⟦(19b)⟧(x)(λd.tall(x, d)))
    = ^no girl(λx.max(λd.tall(x, d)) ≥ max(λd.tall(x's father, d)))

When we turn to *than* clauses, we find that the functional readings we see in degree questions are missing. While the content of John's knowledge in (22a) can be, for example, the function named by *exactly as tall as her mother*, there is no reading of (22b) where it comes out true just in case John's height relative to his mother exceeds every girl's height relative to hers (e.g. where every girl is exactly as tall as her mother and John is taller than his mother).

(22) a. John knows how tall every girl is.
    b. John is taller than every girl is.

How can we account for this disparity? The question is particularly urgent for an analysis that treats *than* clauses as embedded degree questions, as I have proposed above. Why do quantifiers in degree questions support a reading that those in *than* clauses do not?

I suggest that the answer lies in the way that a *than* clause must be integrated into the rest of the comparative sentence. In the semantics sketched in the previous section, the *than* clause—or, more precisely, its question-type trace—must be mapped onto a degree that can serve as the standard of comparison in the main-clause degree relation. This mapping is effected by the AnsDeg operator, which takes a degree question and extracts the degree in its maximally informative true answer.

In a functional reading, the question involves existential quantification not over degrees, but over type ⟨e,⟨dt,t⟩⟩ functions, as shown in (20). The maximally informative true answer to (20b) is the one whose value for *f* yields the strongest proposition; in other words, it is the proposition ^no girl(λx.f(x)(λd.tall(x, d))) that entails ^no girl(λx.f'(x)(λd.tall(x, d))), for all f'. This is not a denotation from which AnsDeg can extract a degree. The reason is that a functional question of this sort is not a question about degrees; it is a question about relations between individuals and degree quantifiers. Unlike with ordinary degree questions, the answers to a functional degree question do not vary with respect to the value of the degree argument of the core scalar predicate, and the maximally informative true answer is not one that can be expressed via a simple scalar value (e.g. *six feet*). The mechanics of the AnsDeg operator are meant to reflect this deeper semantic property: AnsDeg cannot return a degree from a functional degree question because such questions are about something other than degrees.[10] If the work of a *than* clause is to take a question-like structure and deliver a degree that can be used in a matrix degree relation, then functional degree questions will be excluded (alongside all non-degree questions).[11]

The fact that *than* clauses fail to support functional readings while ordinary embedded degree questions allow them thus should not be taken as a strike against the theory proposed here. The absence of functional readings in *than* clauses is due to an independent fact about their external syntax and semantics, one that appears to have no bearing on the deep and abiding internal parallels between *than* clauses and degree questions.

6 Summary and Outlook

The question of how nominal quantifiers interact with degree operators is a major challenge and mystery, as the abundant literature of the last twenty years attests. Here I have suggested that insights from the questions literature may shed new light on this mystery. Comparative *than* clauses share a large number of syntactic and semantic properties with degree questions, including, crucially, properties relating to the behavior of nominal quantifiers within them.

Questions with quantifiers—including degree questions—support at least three types of readings: pair-list readings, functional readings, and what Nouwen & Dotlačil (2017) call single-point readings. Answers of these three varieties are shown in (23). The three readings correspond to the three different lifted-question meanings shown in (24); note that lifting is truth-conditionally vacuous in the functional and single-point cases (Chierchia 1993).[12]

---

10   Note in this connection that the abstract of a functional degree question will take a type $\langle e,\langle dt,t\rangle\rangle$ argument where an ordinary degree question abstract takes a type d argument. We thus cannot supply a degree argument to the intension of a functional degree question's abstract, as would be required according to the definition of ANSDEG.

11   I hasten to add that this characterization should not be misread as an endorsement of an encapsulation approach to *than* clauses (Fleisher 2016). In cases where the *than* clause contains a quantificational subject, the Chierchia/Szabolcsi-style lifted-question approach adopted here ensures that the structure that ANSDEG operates on is one that excludes the quantifier; indeed, ANSDEG falls within the scope of the quantifier, as is characteristic of entanglement theories. See (16).

12   Note that the expression in (24c) correctly captures the single-point reading only if we take the gradable predicate to have an 'exactly' semantics; elsewhere, I have been assuming that such predicates have an 'at least' semantics. Alternatively, we could stipulate an 'at least' denotation like the following: $\lambda Q . Q(\lambda p.\exists d : p = {}^\wedge \forall x \in \text{girl} : max(\lambda d' .\text{tall}(x, d'))$

(23) John knows how tall every girl₁ is:
    a. Anne is 5-foot-6, Becca is 5-foot-8, ...   PAIR-LIST
    b. as tall as her₁ mother.   FUNCTIONAL
    c. 5-foot-6.   SINGLE-POINT

(24) a. $\lambda Q \,.\, \forall x \in \text{girl} : Q(\lambda p.\exists d : p = {}^\wedge\text{tall}(x, d))$ PAIR-LIST
    b. $\lambda Q \,.\, Q(\lambda p.\exists f : p = {}^\wedge \forall x \in \text{girl} : f(x)(\lambda d.\text{tall}(x, d)))$ FUNCTIONAL
    c. $\lambda Q \,.\, Q(\lambda p.\exists d : p = {}^\wedge \forall x \in \text{girl} : \text{tall}(x, d))$ SINGLE-POINT

The single-point reading involves a presupposition that all of the girls are equal in height (Nouwen & Dotlačil 2017); an interlocutor who understood (23) on its single-point reading might reasonably object to this presupposition in an appropriate context. Importantly, *than* clauses support this reading, as well, despite its near-total absence from the discussion in the literature. For example, in response to a polar question like *Is John taller than every girl is?*, one might reasonably object that not all the girls are equally tall.

The parallels between *than* clauses and degree questions are thus quite extensive. Wide-scope readings for nominal quantifiers in *than* clauses appear to be entirely parallel to pair-list readings of quantifiers in embedded questions, as borne out by diagnostics involving scope inversion, quantificational variability effects, and unavailability with downward-entailing quantifiers. Functional readings are absent from *than* clauses due to an independent requirement of the matrix degree relation (implemented via the ANSDEG operator in the analysis here), not because of any internal structural disparity between *than* clauses and degree questions. And both constructions support single-point readings.

This leads to a set of theoretical takeaways quite different from what we started with. In particular, the analysis of *than* clauses as degree questions suggests a very different outlook on the Heim–Kennedy Constraint. As seen in (24), both functional readings and single-point readings involve a nominal quantifier taking scope above a degree variable but below the operator that binds it. These are configurations that the Heim–Kennedy Constraint rules out, apparently erroneously, on either its typical formulation or the reformulation proposed by Nouwen & Dotlačil (2017).[13]

    $= d$). It remains mysterious why, when a quantificational subject scopes low in a degree question or *than* clause, we are bound to find a single-point reading and never a minimum-related reading, which we would get on an 'at least' semantics for (24c). I leave a fuller investigation of the single-point reading to future work.

13   In the case of the functional reading in (24b), the variable in question is f, which is strictly speaking not a degree variable but a variable of type $\langle e, \langle dt, t \rangle \rangle$, mapping individ-

The pair-list reading that we find with nominal quantifiers in *than* clauses appears, then, to result from how the quantifier interacts with the interrogative complementizer—however incompletely understood these interactions may remain—not from any (even more poorly understood) constraint on scopal interactions between nominal quantifiers and degree expressions. I hope that the present approach may afford new insights on the interactions between quantifiers and degrees, and that it may help us achieve an explanation or elimination of the Heim–Kennedy Constraint.

References

Aloni, Maria & Floris Roelofsen. 2014. Indefinites in comparatives. *Natural Language Semantics* 22. 145–167. https://doi.org/10.1007/s11050-013-9103-z.

Alrenga, Peter & Christopher Kennedy. 2014. *No more* shall we part: quantifiers in English comparatives. *Natural Language Semantics* 22. 1–53. https://doi.org/10.1007/s11050-013-9099-4.

Beck, Sigrid. 2010. Quantifiers in *than*-clauses. *Semantics and Pragmatics* 3(1). 1–72. https://doi.org/10.3765/sp.3.1.

Beck, Sigrid. 2013. Lucinda driving too fast again—the scalar properties of ambiguous *Than*-clauses. *Journal of Semantics* 30. 1–63. https://doi.org/10.1093/jos/ffr011.

Beck, Sigrid & Hotze Rullmann. 1999. A flexible approach to exhaustivity in questions. *Natural Language Semantics* 7. 249–298. https://doi.org/10.1023/A:1008373224343.

Bhatt, Rajesh & Roumyana Pancheva. 2004. Late merger of degree clauses. *Linguistic Inquiry* 35. 1–45. https://doi.org/10.1162/002438904322793338.

Bresnan, Joan W. 1973. Syntax of the comparative clause construction in English. *Linguistic Inquiry* 4. 275–343.

Chierchia, Gennaro. 1993. Questions with quantifiers. *Natural Language Semantics* 1. 181–234. https://doi.org/10.1007/BF00372562.

---

uals to degree quantifiers. It is therefore not entirely clear whether we should expect the Heim–Kennedy Constraint to bar the nominal quantifier from scoping between it and the existential operator that binds it. The syntactic element whose denotation is f (or $f(x)$, if we adopt a Chierchia-style double-indexing approach) originates in the degree argument position within the *than* clause and takes scope via QR. Its scope relative to the nominal quantifier appears to obey the Heim–Kennedy Constraint; there is no available variant of (24b) with a reading where the degree quantifier $f(x)$ outscopes *every girl*. On the present analysis, however, we need not appeal to the Heim–Kennedy Constraint to explain this; $f(x)$ must scope below the nominal quantifier because it needs the nominal quantifier to bind its internal argument, x.

Chomsky, Noam. 1977. On *wh*-movement. In Peter W. Culicover, Thomas Wasow & Adrian Akmajian (eds.), *Formal syntax*, 71–132. New York: Academic Press.

Dayal, Veneeta. 1996. *Locality in WH quantification: questions and relative clauses in Hindi*. Dordrecht: Kluwer.

Dayal, Veneeta. 2016. *Questions*. Oxford: Oxford University Press.

Dotlačil, Jakub & Rick Nouwen. 2016. The comparative and degree pluralities. *Natural Language Semantics* 24. 45–78. https://doi.org/10.1007/s11050-015-9119-7.

Engdahl, Elisabet. 1986. *Constituent questions*. Dordrecht: Kluwer. https://doi.org/10.1007/978-94-009-5323-9.

Fleisher, Nicholas. 2016. Comparing theories of quantifiers in *than* clauses: lessons from downward-entailing differentials. *Semantics and Pragmatics* 9(4). 1–23. https://doi.org/10.3765/sp.9.4.

Fleisher, Nicholas. 2018. *Than* clauses as embedded questions. In Sireemas Maspong et al. (eds.), *Proceedings of Semantics and Linguistic Theory 28*, 120–140. Washington, D.C.: Linguistic Society of America. https://doi.org/10.3765/salt.v28i0.4402.

George, B.R. 2011. *Question embedding and the semantics of answers*. Los Angeles: UCLA Ph.D. dissertation. https://semanticsarchive.net/Archive/DZiMDlmZ/.

Groenendijk, Jeroen & Martin Stokhof. 1984. *Studies on the semantics of questions and the pragmatics of answers*. Amsterdam: University of Amsterdam Ph.D. dissertation.

Heim, Irene. 2001. Degree operators and scope. In Caroline Féry & Wolfgang Sternefeld (eds.), *Audiatur vox sapientiae: a festschrift for Arnim von Stechow*, 214–239. Berlin: Akademie-Verlag.

Heim, Irene. 2006. Remarks on comparative clauses as generalized quantifiers. Ms., MIT. https://semanticsarchive.net/Archive/mJiMDBlN/.

Krasikova, Svetlana. 2011. *Modals in comparatives*. Tübingen: Universität Tübingen Ph.D. dissertation.

Lahiri, Utpal. 2002. *Questions and answers in embedded contexts*. Oxford: Oxford University Press.

Larson, Richard K. 1988. Scope and comparatives. *Linguistics and Philosophy* 11. 1–26. https://doi.org/10.1007/BF00635755.

Lerner, Jean-Yves & Manfred Pinkal. 1991. Comparatives and nested quantification. In P.J.E. Dekker & M.J.B. Stokhof (eds.), *Proceedings of the Eighth Amsterdam Colloquium*, 329–347. Amsterdam: ILLC.

Moltmann, Friederike. 1992. *Coordination and comparatives*. MIT Ph.D. dissertation. https://dspace.mit.edu/handle/1721.1/12896.

Moltmann, Friederike & Anna Szabolcsi. 1994. Scope interactions with pair-list readings. In *Proceedings of NELS 24*. Amherst: GLSA.

Nouwen, Rick & Jakub Dotlačil. 2017. The scope of nominal quantifiers in comparative clauses. *Semantics and Pragmatics* 10(15). https://doi.org/10.3765/sp.10.15.

Romero, Maribel. 1998. *Focus and reconstruction effects in* wh-*phrases*. Amherst: University of Massachusetts Ph.D. dissertation.

Rullmann, Hotze. 1995. *Maximality in the semantics of WH-constructions*. Amherst: University of Massachusetts Ph.D. dissertation.

Schwarzschild, Roger & Karina Wilkinson. 2002. Quantifiers in comparatives: a semantics of degree based on intervals. *Natural Language Semantics* 10. 1–41. https://doi.org/10.1023/A:1015545424775.

Szabolcsi, Anna. 1997. Quantifiers in pair-list readings. In Anna Szabolcsi (ed.), *Ways of scope taking*, 311–347. Dordrecht: Kluwer.

Zhang, Linmin & Jia Ling. 2015. Comparatives revisited: downward-entailing differentials do not threaten encapsulation theories. In Thomas Brochhagen, Floris Roelofsen & Nadine Theiler (eds.), *Proceedings of the 20th Amsterdam Colloquium*, 478–487. http://semanticsarchive.net/Archive/mVkOTk2N/AC2015-proceedings.pdf. Amsterdam: ILLC.

Zhang, Linmin & Jia Ling. 2017. Ambiguous *than*-clauses and the mention-some reading. In *Proceedings of SALT 27*, 191–211. Washington: Linguistic Society of America. https://doi.org/10.3765/salt.v27i0.4144.

Index

absorption   373
activity   305, 313–314, 316, 324–327
adjective
   absolute   171, 244
   gradable, *see* predicate, gradable
   positive   169, 181
   quantity   145, 272, 277–280, 284, *see also* quantity word
   relative   171, 181
adverb   15–16, 133
agreement   92, 96, 124, 210–211, 290–292
alternative   46, 59–60, 65–66, 68–70, 72–75, 84, 93, 106, 112, 114
alternative semantics   59, 66
antecedent contained deletion   86
anti-singleton   64–66, 68
approximation   44, 47
assignment function   337–338, 347–349
atomicity   305–307, 313
attitude verb   72–73, 232–233, 252, 257–258, 294

blocking   57–59, 68, 107, 109, 116
bound
   lower   35, 45–49, 67, 342, 350
   upper   45–49, 66–67, 70–71, 342, 350
Bulgarian   108–109, 112–113, 115

cardinality   1, 16–18, 23–28, 55, 271, 281–283, 286, 299, 332, 341, 347, 350, 352–355, 358–359
cataphora   194
choice function   148
cliticization   287–288
cognition   121, 312
cognitive science   304, 312
commensurability   30, 205, 208, 243–244
comparative   1, 123, 164, 166, 221–222, 231, 239, 282, 332–334, 342–360
   adjectival   271–273, 276, 277–277, 289, *see also* comparative, quality
   adverbial   310–311, 314–316
   clausal   10, 81–82, 121–122, 128–129, 133–137, 144, 252–263, 294
   conjoined   168, 205–213, 220–222

exceed   168
explicit   169–173, 179, 181–182
implicit   169–173, 179, 181–182
nominal   271, 273–301, *see also* comparative, quantity
particle   166–167
phrasal   9, 81–82, 122, 130, 132–137, 144, 231
quality   17–18, *see also* comparative, adjectival
quantity   17–18, *see also* comparative, nominal
comparative marker, *see* parameter marker
comparison class, *see* set, comparison
conjunction   177, 205, 217–222, 225–226, 260, 268
conservativity   6–7, 14–16
correlatives
   degree   193–194
countability   306
count/mass distinction   22–23, 305–307, 312
cumulativity   306–309, 341, 358

de-dicto   232
definiteness   20, 80, 83n6, 87, 101–103, 106–109, 138–141, 146, 194, 336–341, 344–351, 356, 358–359
degree   1, 205, 221, 242
   derived   216, 231, 233–234, 242, 250
   reference to   23–29, 233–234, 249
   unspecified   297, 300
degree additivity   48–49, 233
degree quantifier, *see* quantifier
degree question, *see* question
degree selection   304
degreeless treatment   172, 189–192, 293
degree-to-stuff conversion   295
delayed evaluation   335–339, 347, 350–354, 357
differential   223–224, 232, 238, 245–248, 255–260, 271–301, 342, 344–345, 353–354, 356–357, 359, 367
dimension   124, 146, 152, 282, 286, 296–297, 304–305, 311, 313–316, 322–329
discourse context   337

discourse referent   336, 344, 347, 351, 354–356
disjunction   224–226
distributed morphology   65, 233, 236n
distributivity   306, 346, 355–357
domain widening   64
dynamic semantics   347

ellipsis   10, 81, 86, 121, 128, 131, 209–213, 225, 258–260, 295
encapsulation   371
entailment   5–6, 50, 307, 346–347
  downward   5–6, 8, 12, 14, 142, 252, 375
  upward   5–6, 13
entanglement   356, 371
equative   14–15, 27, 126, 137, 153, 164–166, 174–199, 238, 260n
  conjoined   177
  demonstrative   163, 176, 185, 188–189, 193–198
  explicit   179, 181–183, 185–189, 193–196
  generic   190–192
  implicit   179, 181–185, 189–192
  predicate   176–177, 181–184
  relative   174, 186, 189
equivalence class   215–216, 223
evaluativity   169–170, 173, 181–188, 190–192, 195
event   231, 235–237, 304–305, 314–316, 322, 327, 329
event identification   237, 374
exhaustivity   359
existential closure   60, 65, 70, 72, 191–192, 333
experiment   314–329

first order   2, 18, 29, 155–156, 194
focus   28, 59, 79, 84–85, 87, 101, 104–115
French   271–302
functional reading   374–378

gapping   209–213, 224

Heim-Kennedy Constraint   1, 64, 364–365, 369, 374, 378–379
Hindi-Urdu   81, 132–135

implicature
  Gricean   66–67, 165, 195

ignorance   46, 50–51, 59, 66, 72–74
quantity   66, 69–70, 195
indefinite, see definiteness
  epistemic   46, 49–52
intersection, see conjunction
interval semantics   14, 47, 342–360
interval subtraction   342
iota operator   148–149
language acquisition   312
less   126, 238, 352–353

Mandarin   293–294
manner   190–192
mass/count distinction, see count/mass distinction
Maxim of Quantity   66
maximality   19, 100, 129, 194, 260, 334, 347–355, 368
measure function   24–25, 55, 124, 144–146, 149–151, 206–207, 234, 245, 249, 259, 295–297, 304, 309–310
measure phrase   24–29, 49, 95–98, 106, 127, 145, 150, 163n, 172, 238–239, 248–249, 254, 259, 262, 272–273, 276, 280–281, 283–284, 296, 299–300
measurement   244–248, 304, 344
measurement operator   145–146, 154
measurement system   244–249
measurement unit   246–247, 283
metaphysics   23–24, 305, 311–312
minimality   257–259, 260
modality   252, 257–258, 260–263, 294, 366–368
modifier
  degree   16–17, 163
  factor   182, 184–188, 195–196
monotonicity, see entailment and quantifier, non-monotonic
movement
  across the board   259
  copy theory of   16

Navajo   87, 122–128, 130, 135–156, 238
negative polarity item   6, 13, 142–143, 252, 263
noun
  count, see count/mass distinction
  mass   300–301, 305, 310
nuclear scope   3

INDEX

numeral   23, 45, 98–99, 274
  additive   45, 55–57
  bare   24, 277, 284–285
  complex   24n
  indeterminate   28, 44, 47, 52–54, 59, 63–64, 68, 72, 74
  modified   25, 45, 47, 347
  multiplicative   49, 53

ontology   234, 239, 306–309, 313

pair-list reading   13, 365, 367–368, 371–375, 377–379
parameter marker   166, 174–175, 177–179, 182–184, 188–190, 232, 251
partial order   219–220, 243
permutation invariance   4–5, 9, 12, 23, 26–28
pied piping   63
pluractionality   308
plural   17–18, 309, 341
plural individual   17–18, 22–28, 61, 98, 296, 346–349, 351, 354–356
pointwise function application   60–62, 65, 69, 74, 101, 225
Polish   85, 88–89, 91–97, 100, 108, 115
positive polarity item   142–143
possible individual   231, 240–250, 261
predicate
  collective   355–356
  gradable   79–80, 124, 163–164, 169, 214–217, 231, 239–240, 245–246, 309, 343, 349
presupposition   50, 65, 82, 98–99, 105, 110, 378
pronoun
  reciprocal   137
  reflexive   133
property
  gradable, see predicate, gradable

Q'eqchi'   235
quantificational variability effects   370
quantifier
  degree   1, 7–29, 63, 122, 155, 163–164, 185, 190, 253, 260–262, 366, 368
  generalized   1, 2–7, 28–29, 63, 122, 155–156, 372
  individual   1, 2–7, 12, 163, 165, 257, 332

non-monotonic   6, 332, 352, 356, 367, 370–371
quantifier raising   3–4, 11, 16, 63, 80, 99n, 110, 129, 135, 142–143, 253, 260–262, 282, 293–295, 352
quantifier scope   13–14, 134, 143, 153–154, 294, 357–358, 364–370
quantity word   272–277, 297
question
  degree   90–96, 100, 106, 174, 271, 333, 335, 344, 355, 369, 371–373
  embedded   365, 369–370, 373–374
question under discussion   194–195
quotient structure   214–216, 221

relation
  degree   8, 18, 20, 206–207, 376, 378
relative clause   127, 148, 150n31, 190, 192–194
  amount   86, 174n7
relativization   288–289
restriction
  quantifier   3, 4n, 10, 16, 114, 302
  selectional   242, 245n13

scale   8, 124, 144, 166, 171, 205–206, 231, 250, 304
  derived   214–220, 223–227
scope, see quantifier
segment   14, 231–250, 255–258
segment identification   237, 255
set   2, 10, 215
  comparison   82, 86–87, 97, 99, 110–115
  minimal, see minimalization
  witness   257–260, 336, 356, 373n
similative   174, 176, 190–192
single-point reading   377–378
Skolem function   375
small clause   131, 147
sortal   1, 8, 12, 280, 299
Spanish   291n
standard marker   126, 130, 166–167, 174–175, 177–178, 189–190, 251
standard of comparison   10, 11, 122–123, 128, 134–136, 141–142, 144, 166, 194, 221, 235, 239, 252–256, 332, 344–347, 349, 354, 356, 359, 364, 368–369, 371–374
  scope of   152, 263, 371
subcomparatives   127, 136, 148–150
sub-extraction   287–290

sufficientive   185, 188, 195–196, 199
superlative   1, 18–19, 123
   absolute   19, 21–22, 82, 84–85, 104, 339–340
   modal   86–87, 97
   quality   19–20
   quantity   20–22
   movement of   20, 83n5, 84–85, 109–111, 114
   relative   20–21, 82, 84, 104, 107, 110, 114, 339–340

telicity   308, 310, 313, 315, 324–325
than, *see* standard of comparison
Turkish   85, 88–90, 92, 94, 98, 102–103, 115
type shift   25–28, 55, 63, 190, 192, 194

uniqueness   100, 335–336, 338–340, 348

valency reduction   140–141
vector   233
vision   312

Printed in the United States
By Bookmasters